G000080514

BREXIT: A POLITICAL CRISIS FOR EUROPE

Impact Assessment and Lessons Learnt for the European Union

Thomas Levermann
Guido Reinke

London – Brussels – New York
GOLD RUSH Publishing 2017

Brexit: A Political Crisis for Europe. Impact Assessment and Lessons Learnt for the European Union
Copyright © 2017 GOLD RUSH Publishing®
All rights reserved.

ISBN-10: 1908585099
ISBN-13: 9781908585097

For further information or if you wish to submit any comments or ideas for future publications, please email to the email address below.

GOLD RUSH Publishing® books may be purchased for educational, business, or sales promotional use. We are an independent publishing house promoting innovative publications.
For information please email: info@GoldRushPublishing.org.

© Thomas Levermann, Guido Reinke, 2017
Brexit: A Political Crisis for Europe. Impact Assessment and Lessons Learnt for the European Union
Includes text, diagrams and tables. First Printing, December 2017
978-1-9085850-9-7 (ISBN 13) *paperback*
Available for sale in bookshops, online at Amazon.com, and other channels worldwide.

GOLD
RUSH
Publishing

Hard as it is to say now,
I look forward to a United States of Europe, in which the barriers
between the nations will be greatly minimised and unrestricted
travel will be possible.

Winston Churchill, British statesman and Prime Minister of the
United Kingdom (1874-1965)

Europe will not be made all at once, or according to a single plan.
It will be built through concrete achievements which first create a
de facto solidarity.

Robert Schuman, Luxembourg-born German-French statesman
(1886-1963)

We are the reformers. Reform ends if we leave, not just for us but also
our friends in Europe who want our voice heard in Europe.

David Cameron, Prime Minister of the UK from 2010 to 2016

PREFACE

This book rose like a Phoenix from the ashes the United Kingdom's 23 June 2016 EU Referendum. The result came as a shock, especially as the polls leading up to polling day predicted a very different result. Yet in the final weeks the gap between the *remain* and *leave* camps had closed dramatically. Brexit surprised and divided the people of the United Kingdom, and sent shockwaves far beyond London and even Brussels. Both EU officialdom and the chanceries of the Member States were not only stunned by what happened, but also left wondering how it could have happened. What had been built over 43 years was gone with the wind in just one day.

The political and constitutional crisis that has followed is unprecedented. Many questions have been asked, but few answers given. Only time will tell if this referendum will spell the beginning of the end of the United Kingdom as we have known it since the Union with Scotland in 1707, or not. But it could equally well lead to the crumbling of the European Union. In the mist of this chaos, and lacking any precedents, the idea occurred to the authors to document, analyse, and draw some hard lessons from *Brexit*. The intention of this book is to provide the people, even those who voted for Brexit, an audit-like account of the benefits and shortcomings of the EU, the implications of Brexit and the future, from the viewpoint of two citizens who love the UK and want nothing more than a win-win-win outcome. This book takes an independent stance that delves much more deeply into the facts than the one-sided arguments of the Remain and Leave campaigns, which were so polarising and ignored so many key facts. What was missing from the debate is in this book.

Has the European Union entered a new era? After decades of enlargements, has the EU reached a point where citizens and Member States would rather *leave* than *remain*? That is the question on everybody's mind after the shock of Brexit. Since the European Economic Community (EEC) was founded by the Treaty of Rome in 1957, "Europe" has undergone five enlargements, the latest when Bulgaria and Romania joined on 1 January 2007 and Croatia on 1 July 2013. The six founding members promoted economic integration, but the current 28 members are following a path of a political integration as well that has been 60 years in the making. Now, after 23 June 2016, and for the first time in EU history, a well-established Member State, the UK, has voted to leave the club, not join it. The impact of this event will be that the EU will have to question its political agenda for the first time, asking some searching questions in hopes of righting the balance between centralisation and subsidiarity, enlargement and consolidation, regulation and de-regulation.

This book was written to analyse hard facts, to outline for business and for citizens the immediate past and the likely future of the UK, and to summarise the key lessons to be learned by the European Union's supranational institutions, and Member States too. It will explore possible Brexit scenarios and what they may mean for both the UK and the EU. The authors' motivation for writing this book is to catalyse business transformation, economic reform and civil society engagement on all levels of governance. Simply objecting to a thing requires no skill; it is generating innovative ideas and workable plans that will really tax the imagination and commitment of all citizens. In the Queen's own words, in her Christmas Broadcast of 1957, "It has always been easy to hate and destroy. To build and to cherish is much more difficult."

One may learn from the epic "Gone with the Wind", where Scarlett O'Hara (the UK), a strong-willed but ruined Georgia plantation owner's daughter marries the wealthy Rhett Butler (the EU). It was not a romantic relationship from the beginning; Scarlett married Rhett for his money and business influence, not for love. The limits of their marriage are exposed when Rhett bursts out, "No, I don't think I will kiss you, although you need kissing badly." Yet when Rhett, fed up with her ever greater detachment, he finally decides to leave her – (not she him, the one difference with the comparison) – it precipitates a crisis in Scarlett's life that she never expected. Then comes the famous exchange of words: as Rhett is fixing to leave Scarlett for good, she says to him, "Rhett, Rhett… if you go, where shall I go? What shall I do?" and Rhett answers coldly, "Frankly, my dear, I don't give a damn." The drama ends with Scarlett bursting out: "Tara! Home. I'll go home. And I'll think of some way to get him back. After all … tomorrow is another day." Its assertion of independence is rooted in legitimate grievances, but in the end the UK does need Europe. Even if the UK never loved or bonded with the EU, it needs it for economic reasons and for influence in the world.

If the European project is ever to succeed, the European Union must find a way to inspire a unity that will "win the hearts of its people and give them something *fresh* that they have not seen before". This applies equally to politicians in the Member States, who could have done so much more to articulate European policies in a more unifying way. If national politicians are going to criticise "Europe" for years on end, while Eurocrats refuse to listen and to transform, nobody can expect citizens to give their minds let alone their hearts to Europe. People forget easily. For too many people in Europe living in peace and freedom, prosperity and stability, is taken for granted. What is taken too little for granted is that it takes more effort to keep it that way than to walk away from what has been built up over the last 60 years.

ACKNOWLEDGEMENTS

The authors are grateful to everybody who has ever inspired them to the writing of this book: the politicians who proved that truth is secondary so long as you are a great showman; the others who exhibited how it has become accepted to mislead the public to achieve political goals; electorates who voted against all odds and so many warnings of economic hardship; a deeply polarised and traumatised populace that is adrift and without political leaders they trust; one honourable Prime Minister who kept his word and resigned; the peoples of Scotland and Northern Ireland who are being dragged into something that they did not want; and a new government that is now faced with planning some way out of this chaos.

We would like to extend our gratitude to those few professionals and journalists who first analysed the situation before reporting it. But we owe even more gratitude to the vast number of opinion leaders and media outlets that misinformed their audiences, spread fake news (especially of omission), and thus failed to contribute in any constructive way to the Remain campaign. They proved how ill-informed even our "opinion leaders" are.

We would like to thank Jerry W. Bains, whose legal background in particular gave us intellectual stimulation and helped us to understand the multi-dimensional complexity of the legal landscape. His sharp pen also saved us from embarrassing typographical and grammatical errors.

Above all, we are thankful to all our friends and family, who have given us so much support and encouragement, particularly when we were floundering in the welter of information and fast-moving developments. This book is dedicated to all of them, and to all who have supported us in our efforts to understand the reasons, analyse the impact, and summarise the lessons of these troubled times, but more importantly, who have shown us their enthusiasm.

Thomas Levermann and Guido Reinke

TABLE OF CONTENTS

LIST OF FIGURES

Success is not final,
failure is not fatal:
it is the courage to continue that counts.

Winston Churchill (1874-1965)

EXECUTIVE SUMMARY: HARD FACTS ABOUT BREXIT

Brexit has divided the United Kingdom. The EU Referendum campaign and the aftermath of the vote have been riddled by false claims, populism and misinformation. People in the Remain as well as the Leave camps have long felt betrayed and disillusioned that UK politics has not delivered on its promises. For many it seems that the main goal for most politicians is to get elected to pursue their personal or partisan objectives and their own agenda, while ignoring the manifesto and previous promises made.

Brexit was a wake-up call for the European Union as well. Some Member States are genuinely worried about the disconnect between politicians and electorates. The toxic combination of the desire for a peaceful revolution, the replacement of "established" parties and an ill-informed population enables minority but articulate opinion leaders to steal the thunder from the political establishment. Social media and new communication technologies, sometimes even traditional media, provide platforms that can be taken over to promote unbalanced, often populistic, and ineffectively challenged views. Fake news, lies by omission, and winning votes with emotional and simplistic nationalistic slogans (such as "let's get back control" or "make the country great again") are the tried and true methods of winning contentious campaigns over hot-button issues. It's a perfect storm, with serious consequences not only for the United Kingdom, but for all of Europe.

Unlike many publications on Brexit, this book is all about providing a balanced view of the facts. The authors of this book have worked, lived and experienced life in Brussels, London and various cities on the continent first-hand. They have been exposed to European and UK politics, rubbed shoulders with people on the receiving end of political decisions, and observed how the media has been portraying reality on a daily basis.

The following checklist presents an overview of the hard facts about Brexit contained in this book. The Sections in brackets provide further details, explain statistics and calculations, and put some of the facts into context.

1. Historical facts: The United Kingdom before Brexit

    1.1 *The European Coal and Steel Community was formalised in the Treaty of Paris of 18 April 1951.* This was the forerunner, first of the European Economic Community, and finally of the European Union. (Ref: Section 1.1)

    1.2 *The European Economic Community was created by the Treaty of Rome of 1957.* It aims to bring economic integration among its members.

    1.3 *The European Union Customs Union (EUCU) is a principal component of the European Economic Community consisting of all EU Member States plus Monaco and some territories of the UK outside the EU (viz. Guernsey, Jersey, the Isle of Man, and Akrotiri and Dhakalia), Andorra, San Marino and Turkey.* Customs duties on goods crossing borders were abolished. Integral to the Customs Union is that the EU negotiates on behalf of the Union as a whole in international trade deals, while the Member States agree not to negotiate separately.

    1.4 *The UK's first EU membership application under PM Harold Macmillan was blocked by French President Charles De Gaulle on 15 January 1963* over concerns that UK membership could open the door to direct American influence and lead to a European Community dominated by the United States. (Ref: Section 1.1)

    1.5 *The UK has been an EU Member State for 45 years.* The UK ultimately did join the European Economic Community (EEC), now called European Union, on 1 January 1971. (Ref: Section 1.1)

    1.6 *In 1984 Margaret Thatcher won a permanent rebate on the UK's contribution to the EU budget.* This was negotiable because around 70% of the EU budget is spent on the Common Agricultural Policy, which the UK benefits little from. (Ref: Section 1.1)

    1.7 *The UK never signed the Schengen Agreement, which abolished internal border checks after 1985.* This agreement covers 400 million people in 26 countries, including four non-EU countries (Norway, Iceland, Switzerland, and Liechtenstein). (Ref: Section 1.1)

    1.8 *The Single European Act (effective as of 1 July 1987) began to abolish trade barriers inside the EEC.* It mandated that the Single Market should be completed by 31 December 1992. The Single Market goes beyond the Customs Union by abolishing all impediments whatsoever (not merely the pecuniary exaction of customs duties) to the freedom of movement of goods, services, capital and labour (Ref. Section 1.1).

    1.9 *The single currency (euro) was introduced on 1 January 2002.* It is now legal tender in 19 Member States and is used daily by 337 million Europeans (status 1 January 2018). (Ref: Section 1.1)

    1.10 *In the Scottish Independence referendum of 18 September 2014 55.3% (of an 84.6% turnout) voted against independence.* A Yes vote could have ended a

307-year-old Union formalised in 1707 with the Act of Union. (Ref: Section 1.1)

1.11 *On 20 February 2016 David Cameron secured a deal which gave the UK "special status" in the EU.* The media ignored this amazing agreement, which covered migration and new rules about benefits, exclusion from bail-outs in the Eurozone, veto power over EU legislation by a qualified majority (55%) of national parliaments, exemption from EU case law for deportations on security grounds. (Ref: Section 1.2)

2. Brexit: The basic facts

2.1 *Brexit Definition: The word "Brexit" is an amalgamation of the words 'British' and 'exit',* used to describe Britain's exit from the European Union.

2.2 *Since 1972 there have been 48 referenda about the European Community across the whole of Europe.* The UK was the only country that held an in-out referendum, if one does not count Greenland, which gained independence from Denmark after being entailed in Denmark's accession. (Ref: Section 1.1)

2.3 *In the UK's first in-out referendum in 1975, called the United Kingdom European Communities membership referendum, a majority of 67.2% (of a 64% turnout) voted to stay in the European Communities (EC).* Opposition leader Margaret Thatcher argued passionately in favour of Britain remaining in Europe. (Ref: Section 1.1)

2.4 *The Brexit referendum was "advisory" only and not legally binding.* The legal status of a referendum is bespoke by Parliament singly – in the Brexit case by the European Union Referendum Act 2015; as also affirmed by the High Court. (Ref: Section 1.3.3)

2.5 *Before the referendum, about 34% of UK residents gave the BBC as their chief information source,* followed by newspapers (20%), family members (18%), and social media (16%). Social media was preferred by about 33% of the 18 to 24-year-olds as a major information source compared to just 8% of over-65s. (Ref: Section 4.5)

2.6 *Article 50 of the Treaty of Lisbon gives any EU member the right to quit the EU unilaterally.* The process allows the leaving country two years to negotiate an exit deal, and once it is set in motion, it cannot be stopped except by unanimous consent of all Member States. (Ref: Section 1.3.3)

2.7 *At the end of February 2017, three former UK Prime Ministers raised their concerns about (a hard) Brexit and recommended a power-sharing arrangement.* This included former Deputy Prime Minister Nick Clegg as well as John Major, Gordon Brown and Tony Blair. (Ref: Section 1.3.3)

2.8 *The majority of MPs in the Commons, a total of 480 out of 650, campaigned for Britain to stay in the European Union at the last election.* Of the 30 Cabinet ministers in office when Theresa May was appointed PM in July 2016, 24 were for Remain and six for Leave. (Ref: Section 1.3.4 and 4.3)

2.9 *Net immigration into the UK fell from 2015 to 2016.* Net immigration from the EU was 133,000 (250,000 arriving and 117,000 leaving) in 2016, down 51,000 or 28% on 2015. Non-EU net immigration was estimated to be 175,000 (264,000 arriving and 88,000 leaving) last year, a fall of 14,000 or 8% (at most) compared to the previous year. The net emigration of British citizens was 60,000 (74,000 returning and 134,000 leaving). (Ref: Section 1.3.2, 25 May 2017)

2.10 *Total immigration of non-British was 308,000 in 2016, making a net immigration total of 248,000 after deducting the net emigration of the British. Leaving the EU will not bring the total under the government's target of 100,000, as only 43.2% are EU immigrants; the other 56.8% are non-EU immigrants.* As there is a labour shortage in various sectors and future trade agreements will also require offering more visas to other (non-EU) countries, Brexit will have less impact on immigration than is often claimed (at least implied). (Ref: Section 1.3.2)

2.11 *Net immigration to the UK has not been below 100,000 since 1997.* Theresa May promised to bring net immigration below 100,000 a year before the general elections; however, after the election this pledge was omitted from the Queen's speech (which sets out the new Government's agenda). (Ref: Section 1.3.2)

2.12 *The EU administration is smaller than it is perceived to be, comprising a total of 47,600 fonctionnaires.* In 2016 33,000 personnel worked for the European Commission, 6,000 for the European Parliament and around 3,500 for the European Council. In comparison, the UK has 418 Councils (principal authorities) employing 21,050 councillors, around 1 million full-time "public servants" (in England alone), with Country Councils such as Derbyshire employing 36,000 personnel alone, and Birmingham Council 20,000. In the US, the State of California employed more than 883,000 public servants in 2014, which works out to 2,205 public servants per 100,000 citizens, compared to just 9 per 100,000 for the EU. (Ref: Section 4.2)

3. The EU Referendum: Facts about the results
   3.1 *The electorate in the EU Referendum included besides UK citizens Commonwealth citizens from 52 countries (an estimated one million)* who were resident in the UK, as well as resident citizens of Ireland (around 382,000), of Gibraltar (16,500), of Malta (27,000), and of Cyprus 59,000). (Ref: Section 2.6.5)
   3.2 Not eligible in the EU Referendum were British citizens resident outside the UK for more than 15 years (1.2 million British resided in the EU of which likely more than half were believed to be affected); EU citizens resident in the UK

(3.3 million), with exception of EU citizens from Ireland, Malta and Cyprus; persons aged 16 or 17 (of which in the UK in 2014 1,534,192 citizens were in this age group). (Ref: Section 2.6.5)

3.3 *The polls forecasting the outcome were wrong.* On the eve of the vote, the polls predicted a narrow victory for the Remain campaign – 51% to 49%. By D-Day the result seemed too close to call, though slightly in favour of Remain by 52%. (Ref: Section 2.1)

3.4 *The EU Referendum took place on the 23 June 2016. Those voting Leave totalled 51.9% (17,410,742 votes) and those voting Remain totalled 48.1% (16,141,241 votes).* The turnout of 33,551,983 represented 71.8% of the electorate. (Ref: Section 1.3.2 for all election results, Section 2.1 for the analysis)

3.5 *Of the UK population of 64,354,195* (Ref: Section 2.2), *the 17,410,742 Leave voters comprised 27.04%* and the 16,141,241 *Remain voters comprised 25.08%.* (Ref: Section 1.3.5).

3.6 *England voted to leave the EU*: 53.4% Leave, 46.6% Remain (Turnout 73.0%).

3.7 *Wales voted to leave the EU*: 52.5% Leave, 47.5% Remain (Turnout 71.7%).

3.8 *Scotland voted to remain in the EU*: 38.0% Leave, 62.0% Remain (Turnout 67.2%).

3.9 *Northern Ireland voted to remain in the EU*: 44.2% Leave, 55.8% Remain (Turnout 62.7%).

3.10 *Gibraltar voted to remain in the EU*: 4.09% Leave, 95.9% Remain (Turnout 83.6%).

3.11 *London voted to remain in the EU*: 40.1% Leave, 59.9% Remain.

4. The EU Referendum: The aftermath

4.1 *The criteria of eligibility helped Leave win the EU Referendum.* If the same rules had applied to the EU Referendum as to the last referendum held in the UK, for Scottish Independence in 2014, Remain would have won: 3.3 million EU citizens and 1.534 million 16- and 17-year-olds would have been eligible to vote. Many of the 5.5 million British expatriates were not allowed to vote either. (Ref: Section 2.2)

4.2 *On 5 September 2016 a petition was discussed in the House of Commons requesting that, as the votes on neither side numbered more than 60%, on a turnout less than 75% (thus less than an absolute majority of eligible voters), another referendum should be held.* The petition was launched on 15 May, before the Referendum day, and attracted 4.15 million signatures afterwards, but it was rejected by the Government on the grounds that The European Union Referendum Act had not set a threshold for either an absolute majority or a minimum turnout. (Ref: Section 1.3.1)

4.3   *Two days after the Referendum, the Leave camp admitted that their claim that Brexit would free up £350 million a week for the NHS "was a mistake", and that many of their claims needed rethinking.* (Ref: Section 1.3.2)

4.4   *Due to withdrawal from the EU, the UK will not participate in the next European Parliament elections in May or June 2019.* The UK would have elected 73 Members out of 751 of the European Parliament (MEP). (Section 1.3.2)

5.   The Brexit process: The preparation of the UK and EU governments

5.1   *On 11 July 2016 Theresa May was elected leader of the Conservative Party* after David Cameron's resignation over the defeat of Remain. (Ref: Section 1.3.2)

5.2   *On 24 September 2016 Jeremy Corbyn, the Labour opposition leader, was re-elected* with 51.8% of the votes. (Ref: Section 1.3.2)

5.3   *The Great Repeal Bill* (announced on 2 October 2016) would enshrine all existing EU law into British law. (Ref: Section 1.3.2)

5.4   *On 3 November 2016 the High Court ruled that PM May must submit the execution of Article 50 of the Lisbon Treaty (formally starting the process of seceding from the EU) to a specific vote of the Commons, and might not use the Prerogative Power pursuant to Section 2 of the 1972 European Communities Act.* The Government contested this judgement (rather than ignoring it), but it was affirmed by the Supreme Court on 24 January 2017. (Ref: Section 1.3.2, 1.3.3)

5.5   *The Government reached out to prospective trading partners, including India, the Philippines, Malaysia, the Gulf States, Jordan, Saudi Arabia, and the United States.* During discussions with Indian Prime Minister Modi, he told May that any post-Brexit trade deal must include an increase in the number of skilled Indian workers and students allowed to migrate the UK. (Ref: Section 1.3.2) In fairness, it should be pointed out that the news was not all gloomy. With the election of Trump, the UK has been told that it will be put at the head of the queue (in contrast to Obama's threat to relegate it to the back of the queue) of the countries with which the US intends to conclude bilateral trade deals.

5.6   *On 17 January 2017 Theresa May announced that the UK will leave the Single Market.* Chancellor Philip Hammond and Brexit secretary David Davis caused surprise by expressing a willingness to pay to retain Single Market access. (Ref: Section 1.3.2)

5.7   *On 18 January 2017 the Government laid out 12 negotiating objectives, categorised under five rubrics: (1) certainty and clarity, (2) a stronger Britain, (3) a fairer Britain, (4) a truly global Britain, and (5) a phased approach.* No detailed impact analyses or plans for industrial sectors were included. (NOTE: these are the Government's "red lines") (Ref: Section 1.3.6, 1.3.7)

5.8 *On 13 March the EU Withdrawal Bill passed the House of Commons unamended.* This vote took place six days after the House of Lords endorsed calls to guarantee the rights of EU citizens living in the UK within three months of Article 50 being triggered by a "meaningful" Parliamentary vote on the final terms of withdrawal. (Ref: Section 1.3.2)

5.9 *On 15 March 2017 Brexit Secretary David Davis admitted that the government has done no impact assessment to calculate the costs of a No Deal or other hard Brexit.* The Withdrawal Bill received Royal Assent on the following day. (Ref: Section 1.3.2)

5.10 *PM May admitted that net immigration is not expected to fall under 100,000 per year.* This is also Exiting Secretary David Davis's expectation. (Ref: Section 1.3.2)

5.11 *On 30 March the UK formally triggered Article 50 of the Lisbon Treaty to leave the EU.* Britain's EU ambassador, Sir Tim Barrow, handed a six-page letter signed by Theresa May to European Council President Donald Tusk. (Ref: Section 1.3.2, 1.3.5)

5.12 *On 29 April 2017 the European Parliament enacted guidelines for the EU's negotiators, ahead of the Brexit talks.* The resolution authorised "phased negotiations" and provided that the UK's rights and obligations in regards to EU citizens and financial obligations had to be negotiated first before discussions of the future relationship, including trade arrangements, could start. (NOTE: These are the EU's red lines) (Ref: Section 1.3.2, 1.3.6, 1.3.7)

5.13 *On 28 June 2017 the snap early election (surprise-announced on 18 April) produced a hung parliament after the Conservatives lost 13 seats, Labour won 32 seats, and the Liberal Democrats won 3 seats.* UKIP, which had forced the referendum, won no seats. On 4 September of the previous year Theresa May had affirmed, "I'm not going to be calling a snap election." (Ref: Section 1.3.2)

6. The actual Brexit process: The negotiations

6.1 *On 29 April 2017, without the UK's input, the remaining EU-27 leaders agreed negotiating guidance for Brexit talks.* (Section 1.3.2)

6.2 *The UK is expected to leave the EU on 30 March 2019.* The two-year timeframe set out in Article 50 TEU will end on 29 March 2019.

6.3 *Phase One of Brexit focusses on (1) rights of EU citizens resident in the UK, (2) the financial settlement agreement, and (3) other separation issues such as the Northern Irish border.* The 5-rounds of negotiations started on 19 June 2017 and finished on 9 October with a deadlock.

6.4 *On 20 October, the European Council decided that insufficient progress had been made and Phase Two would be delayed.* It was expected that Phase Two will start in January 2018.

6.5   *Phase Two will negotiate the future relationship with the EU.* This Phase includes trade deals, the transition deal, and ongoing participation in European programmes (such as R&D and Erasmus) and agencies (such as Euratom).

7.   The costs of EU membership

7.1   *The Leave campaign had wrongly claimed that the UK was contributing £350 million per week to the EU budget.* The average net contribution 2010-2014 was £170 million per week. (Ref: Section 2.4.3)

7.2   *The gross contribution of the UK to the EU budget (*after rebate*) was £14.698 billion in 2014, while the net budget contribution was £9.872 billion.* This means that UK residents have received payments of around £4.819 billion. The figures for funding received by the UK from the EU compiled by the UK's Office for National Statistics (ONS) excludes an estimated £1.4 billion allocated directly to UK recipients, as under the R&D Framework Programmes, by EU institutions. (Ref: Section 2.4.3)

7.3   The net contribution of each UK resident to the EU budget between 2010 to 2014 was £2.65 to £2.94 per week (38 to 42 pence per day) on average. Thus, the average net contribution per person was £137.60 to £152.82 per year.

7.4   *The average EU net contribution* per capita *in the UK was £130.03 per year in 2014*, or £2.5 per week, or 36 pence a day – after taking into account the £1.4 billion Framework Programme funding to UK recipients, by which the UK's net contribution was lessened to £8.472 billion. (Ref: Section 2.4.3)

7.5   *The UK contribution to the EU by income brackets varied.* Taxpayers earning £30,000 per year or less pay £55 per year or 15.45 pence per day, while earners of £50,000 per year or more pay £137.79 per year or 38.71 pence per day. See Section 2.4.4., Figure 12 for details.

8.   The benefits of EU membership

8.1   *EU citizenship creates a level playing field for all Europeans, who have the same rights and obligations.* The concept of EU citizenship was introduced by the Maastricht Treaty (1993), which established rights of residence in other EU countries; employment mobility in the Single Market (no need to need to apply for working permits or visas); employer access to the Single Market (free movement of goods, services and capital); political rights (to vote and stand for office in local elections); mutual diplomatic protection for consular authorities of any Member State; unemployment compensation and other protections of the "social agenda"; other rights such as access to health care, education and research funding; and legal equality, including of pension benefits. (Ref: Section 2.5)

9. The UK's future relationship to the EU

    9.1   *Brexit will lead to a loss of political influence by the UK.* It is widely assumed that the UK will lose political influence by withdrawing from the EU. Existing relationships such as to the Commonwealth, the UN, and other international organisations may not be impaired; however, the UK will have no influence any more over EU affairs. (Even the most committed Euro-phobes have to admit that there is some truth to the saying "Keep your friends close and your enemies closer".)

10. Brexit repercussions

    10.1   *The* acquis Communautaire *(or just the* acquis*), the corpus of European Community law, encompasses all of the accumulated legislation, regulatory acts, and judicial decisions ever made by the EU supranational organs.* It covers 35 policy sectors, namely, the four freedoms of: (1) goods, (2) people, (3) services, and (4) capital; (5) public procurement procedures; (6) company law; (7) intellectual property law; (8) competition law; (9) financial services; (10) Information Society and Media; (11) agriculture; (12) food safety; (13) fisheries; (14) transport; (15) energy; (16) taxation; (17) economic and monetary policy; (18) statistics; (19) social and employment policy; (20) industrial policy; (21) Trans-European Networks; (22) regional policy and its instruments; (23) judiciary and fundamental rights; (24) justice, freedom and security; (25) science and research; (26) education and culture; (27) environment; (28) consumer and health protection; (29) Customs Union; (30) external relations; (31) foreign, security and defence policy; (32) financial controls; (33) financial and budgetary provisions; (34) institutions; and (35) other topics. Chapter 3 provides a Policy Impact Assessment of Brexit across all 35 Policy domains. (Ref: Figure 14 Summary)

    10.2   *Brexiteers often refer to Iceland, Liechtenstein, Norway and Switzerland as models of the UK's future relationship with the EU. Even though these EFTA countries are not EU Member States, they have signed up to the Schengen Agreement (offering unrestricted access to EU labour market); have a higher immigration level than the UK; and have access to the Single Market. They contribute to the EU budget and adopt most EU regulations.* They are willing to make these sacrifices to get access to the Single Market. (Ref: Section 5.5)

    10.3   *In January 2017 the Government announced that an "immigration skill levy" of up to £1,000 per year for EU skilled workers could be introduced after Brexit.* This fee would be paid by employers. (Ref: Section 1.3.2)

    10.4   *Academia and the impact of Brexit*: 32,000 non-British EU academics, representing 17% of UK university teaching and research staff, currently work in the UK. (Ref: Section 1.3.2)

10.5 *Without a trade deal, WTO tariffs would apply by default to UK-EU trade, which would cause a significant inflation in prices for consumers.* WTO rules allow tariffs on cotton and wool fabrics of up to 8%, sugar confectionary up to 13.4%, consumer electronics up to 14%, dairy products up to 17.3%, edible fruits and nuts up to 20.8%, meat up to 26%, spirits up to 32% and tobacco up to 74.9%. (Ref: Section 1.3.10)

10.6 *Financial institutions domiciled in the UK announced that they plan to move staff to Member States, which afford them access to the Single Market through "passporting" (bypassing financial services registration in each Member State other than the home country).* Included were Lloyd's of London, Goldman Sachs, AIG, HASPC, JP Morgan, USB, Standard Chartered, and others. (Ref: Section 1.3.2)

10.7 *In 2015 UK exports to the EU accounted for 44% of total UK exports of £240 billion, of which 47% were goods and 39% were services.* At the same time, in 2016 53% of imports into the UK came from other Member States. (Ref: Section 2.4)

10.8 *A new, proposed "settled status" would grant EU nationals and their families who have resided continually in the UK for five years or more the same rights as British citizens, after Brexit.* The Government announced this at the June Brexit negotiations. (Ref: Section 1.3.2)

INTRODUCTION

Brexit will have far-reaching repercussions for multiple stakeholders. Its ultimate outcomes are uncertain in the extreme. Although all parties involved in the Brexit negotiations and the parties affected by Brexit try to take a positive, proactive approach, it is impossible to predict timelines and the final deal.

The objective of this book is to provide European citizens, industry, advisors, politicians, and UK and EU institutions convenient compendium of insights into the complexity of Brexit. The structure and content of the information herein may also serve as a template for Member States that in future may form the intention to leave the EU. The authors took care that the general content of this book and its specific impact assessments should be relevant not only to the UK, but also to the wider European context. In particular, the authors were concerned for –

1. *European citizens* to understand implications of Brexit for jobs, inflation, and the quality of life.
2. *Industry and entrepreneurs* to assess risks accurately and be able to construct an approach to how to deal with a situation with a very uncertain outcome.
3. *Advisors* to get an overview of key EU domains that are impacted, key challenges and priorities for identify solutions.
4. *Politicians* (on the EU and its Member States' part) to manage stakeholders more effectively and structure their negotiating strategy more realistically (under the "European Council (Art. 50) guidelines for Brexit negotiations"), the better to achieve the best possible outcome for their country and its citizens.
5. *EU institutions* to support the development of a structured, transparent process that leads to the best outcome for all parties, in particular for citizens of the Member State intending to leave the EU (Article 50 of the Lisbon treaty permits Member States to leave the EU unilaterally; however, no clear process for this had ever been defined before Brexit).

This book is divided into three Parts. The first Part (*What really happened: Background, Reasons and Analysis*) sets the scene and provides an overview of key events and background information. Chapter One provides a chronological summary of events, from the lead-up to the UK's joining the EU, to preparing the 2016 in-out referendum, and the turbulent events since the Brexit-vote. Chapter Two presents relevant statistical information about the voters and about the economic implications forecast by independent institutes and governmental organs. It also presents a thought-provoking summary of the benefits of EU citizenship. This Chapter analyses why the Leave campaign won and inquires in detail into the motives.

Part Two (*What are the implications of Brexit: An impact assessment*) provides a structured approach to the 35 policy domains affected by Brexit defined in the *Community acquis*, based on the classification drawn up to facilitate negotiations with accession countries. The authors have used it to assemble a systematic structure for policy domains relevant to secession negotiations as well. Each section provides a clear definition of the policy domain, and outlines the implications of it for UK citizens and industry and for EU organs. All of these analyses are summarized methodically in an assessment table. Although the authors have analysed the policy domains comprehensively, their focus has been on organising the main themes and providing a structure for such a complex topic.

Part Three (*Lessons learned for the European Union and United Kingdom*) sums up the key lessons to be learned from referenda and political debate. Chapter Four analyses the importance that the facts made salient by the media can play in influencing referendum outcomes. It shows how democratic processes can be undermined by populist views, and how social media can influence public opinion. Chapter Five concludes by bringing together all the results of the authors' analysis and experience, and draws from them the master lessons.

PART I

What really happened: Background, Reasons and Analysis

The most effective way to destroy people is to deny and obliterate their own understanding of their history.

George Orwell (1903-1950)

CHAPTER 1

A BRIEF HISTORY OF BREXIT: FORTY-FIVE YEARS OF EU MEMBERSHIP

Those who have published books on Brexit to date have positioned themselves either in the Leave or in the Remain camp. In taking sides, it is all too easy to become enmeshed (not all that consciously) in defending one's own "team", losing sight of the facts. Political controversy about a topic with significant and possibly grave implications for millions of British citizens, for international business, and for the future of the United Kingdom, is of course salutary; however, even political debates, to be fruitful, need to be based on facts, not just emotion, blame games, and a monomaniacal reiteration of the same talking points as if that could make truth of falsehood, or as if by dint of sheer repetition hearts and minds could be won.

This book strives to be different: it offers an objective, comprehensive impact assessment presenting both the positive and negative implications of Brexit, within the limits of what at present is foreseeable. At the moment it is impossible to forecast where the negotiations between the UK government and the EU will end up. They may lead to a "hard Brexit", *i.e.* leaving the Single Market as such, with the legal consequence of nullifying UK liability in the EU courts for observing the four basic principles of European economic integration: free movement of goods, services, capital *and people*; or it could lead to a "soft Brexit" in which the UK continues to adhere to some these principles. The impact assessment herein shall assume a hard Brexit, as it is more consequential, and as it reflects most clearly the question posed in the referendum of 23 June 2016: "Should the United Kingdom remain a member of the European Union or leave the European Union?" The question after all did not imply the impossible, a new form of EU membership: "Should the United Kingdom renegotiate its membership of the European Union?" In these uncertain and risky times in UK and EU politics, what is needed above all is a realistic and methodical approach that features a cost-benefit analysis of interest to business as well as the rest of society. The "worst case" of a hard Brexit is therefore highly relevant. The impact assessment format is probably the best way to reach this objective, as it delivers black-and-white results about the material consequences of opting between membership and non-membership of the EU. Our assessment is based on economic and business methods – in contrast to political debate, which is far less disciplined and the conclusions of which are the outcome of acrimonious debate. The net result is not necessarily based on facts, but on personality and who is more persuasive and skilful at influencing people.

Before presenting any impact assessment, it will be useful to glean some historical insight into what actually has happened; hence this Chapter begins with an historical overview of the course of the UK's membership of the European Union. Though not every potentially significant event in 45 years of membership can be included, such an overview can at least touch on why the UK joined in the first place, against a background of the milestones in the creation of the EU. Also examined is why and how the EU Referendum was called, and what events followed on 23 June 2016. The timeline is presented in a table, to allow readers of different backgrounds, and from outside the UK, to arrive at a common understanding of the political crisis at national and European level which the referendum has precipitated.

1.1 JOINING THE CLUB

With resolutions like Winston Churchill's 1946 call for a United States of Europe reaching a crescendo in 1949, directly after the most devastating war in human history, several European states at the instigation of the United Kingdom set up the Council of Europe, the first intentionally pan-European organisation as such. On 9 May 1950 French Foreign Minister Robert Schuman proposed an Economic Community that would integrate the coal and steel industrial sectors of Western Europe – the two elements necessary to make weapons of war (Schuman declaration). The idea was formalised as a European Coal and Steel Community (ECSC) in the Treaty of Paris of 18 April 1951.

Since then, Europe has undergone a number of political crises. Konrad Adenauer, Robert Schuman and Jean Monnet – the founding fathers of the ECSC, which later evolved into the European Economic Community (EEC)[1] – were avowed Europeanists and integrationists.

---

1   The European Communities (EC) – (colloquially referred to as the European Community) – comprise three communities which variously existed separately from 1952 until 1993: the 1952 European Coal and Steel Community (ECSC), the 1958 European Atomic Energy Community (EAEC), also known as Euratom, and the 1958 European Economic Community (EEC), which is the customs union that became the Single Market. The 1993 Maastricht Treaty created the European Union (EU), which amalgamated the Communities, introduced European citizenship, and raised the three Pillars of cooperation: (1) the Single Market, (2) the Common Foreign and Security Policy (CFSP), and (3) Justice and Home Affairs (JHI). The 1999 Treaty of Amsterdam reduced JHI to Police and Judicial Cooperation in Criminal Matters. The ECSC ceased to exist in 2002 when its founding treaty expired, and was merged into the EU by the 2003 Treaty of Nice, which also made changes to accommodate Eastern Enlargement (the incorporation of the former Warsaw Pact countries *inter alia*). The 2009 Treaty of Lisbon dissolved all Communities and Pillars into one, integrated Union, which became the legal successor to the previous Community/Union. Euratom remained an entity distinct from the EU but governed by the same institutions.

However, many pre-eminent European statesmen and leaders who participated in the ECSC decidedly departed from their vision. Charles de Gaulle, for example, was first and foremost a French nationalist. He floated the idea of a Council of heads of state with its Secretariat in Paris. In 1960 he proposed a nine-point plan titled "A Note on the Subject of the Organization of Europe", and submitted it to German Chancellor Konrad Adenauer. De Gaulle's scheme aimed to achieve a political pact to shut out not only American but also British influence in post-War Europe. De Gaulle pushed for an intergovernmental, not an integrated Europe. The resulting political upheaval over competing views of Europe's future led to the Empty Chair Crisis in July 1965, when De Gaulle boycotted EEC institutions to protest the decided trend toward integrationism (sometimes called supranationalism) in lieu of the intergovernmental arrangement he preferred, which would have conserved national sovereignty. The crisis was resolved by way of the Luxembourg Compromise, which gave a *de facto* veto to every state on all topics of legislation, and thus over the process of integration (which was noticeably retarded thereafter).

A further agreement on integration was reached on 1 July 1967, when the Merger Treaty (or Brussels Treaty) created a single set of European institutions combining the executive bodies of the European Coal and Steel Community (ECSC), European Atomic Energy Community (Euratom), and the European Economic Community (EEC). From then on, this single institutional structure would be referred to as the European Communities (EC). The EC has undergone a significant evolution since those early days, as witness the following Treaties:

- *The Single European Act* (1 July 1987): This was the first major revision of the 1957 Treaty of Rome and aimed to establish a Single Market (or Common Market) by 31 December 1992. It adopted a more collaborative legislative process (Cooperation Procedure) which gave the European Parliament some say in legislation and introduced qualified majority voting in the Council of Ministers, in lieu of the unanimity customary since the Luxembourg Compromise.
- *Schengen Treaty* (14 June 1985) and Convention (1990): This created Europe's Schengen Area, within which borders internal to the EU are largely abolished. The Schengen Treaty abolished systematic national border controls and set up instead a common visa policy. It is currently acceded-to by 26 European countries, including several non-EU countries: Norway (2001), Iceland (2001), Switzerland (2009), and Liechtenstein (2011). It covers a population of over 400 million people.
- *Maastricht Treaty or Treaty of the European Union* (1 November 1992): This treaty expressly aims at European integration. It created the Three Pillars structure of the European Union: (1) the European Communities, handling economic, social and environmental policies, (2) the Common Foreign and Security Policy (CFSP), taking care of foreign policy and military matters, and (3) Justice and

Home Affairs (JHI), bringing together co-operation in the fight against crime. It also prepared the introduction of the single European currency, the euro.

- *Amsterdam Treaty* (1 May 1999): This Treaty made substantial changes to the Treaty of Maastricht, for example, reducing JHI to Police and Judicial Co-operation in Criminal Matters (PJCCM). Member States agreed to devolve powers to the European Parliament across diverse policy domains from civil and criminal laws, and to make institutional changes to accommodate expansion as new member nations joined the EU.
- *Nice Treaty* (1 February 2003): This Treaty further reformed the institutional structure of the EU to accommodate eastern expansion.
- *Lisbon Treaty* (1 December 2009): This Treaty aimed to enhance the efficiency and democratic legitimacy of the EU. Amendments introduced qualified majority voting to the Council of Ministers in at least 45 policy domains, further empowered the European Parliament, consolidated the EU's legal personality and created a multi-year President of the European Council and a High Representative of the Union for Foreign Affairs and Security Policy. The Treaty gave member states for the first time an express legal right to leave the EU and a procedure for doing so.

Britain's membership of the European Union was never straightforward. Its first membership application by PM Macmillan (Tory) in 1961 was rejected because French President De Gaulle worried that it might lead to an Atlantic Community dominated by the United States. The second application was successful, and the UK joined the EEC together with Ireland and Denmark on 1 January 1973.

However, two years later the UK was already holding an in-out referendum under PM Harold Wilson (Labour) one year after he won the 1974 general election. A majority of 67.2% voted to stay in the EC, or Common Market (of a 64% turnout).

Holding national referenda or plebiscites on changes to the EU is not uncommon. Since 1972, a total of 48 referenda have been held by EU Member States and accession candidates. Most referenda have posed the question whether an accession candidate should join the EU, although this is not a requirement of the accession treaty ratification process. Other referenda concerned the adoption of the euro, participation in EU-related policies, and immigration (Wikipedia, 2017). Over the years, a number of countries have held more significant referenda to give citizens the opportunity to ratify (or veto) issues and changes which may fairly be called "constitutional" in scope and nature, even in cases where the effect is merely to exert pressure on the EU or on Member States to implement policy changes. Countries that have held treaty referenda in the last fifty years include the UK (1975, 2016), Greenland (1982), Italy (1989), Denmark (1992, 1993), Italy (1989), Ireland (2001, 2002, 2008, 2009), France (1992, 2005), the Netherlands (2005), Luxembourg (2005), and Greece (2015).

The only country to have left the EU before Brexit was Greenland, an autonomous territory of Denmark. Greenland joined the EEC as part of Denmark in 1973; however, after home rule was established and the eurosceptic party Siumut won the 1979 Greenland parliamentary election, an in-out referendum was agreed. In 1982 Greenlanders voted to leave the EC by a 53% majority. This resulted in the Greenland Treaty on the terms of its separation from the EU, which occurred in 1985.

Three referenda were held on the Maastricht Treaty. In 1989 an Italian referendum resulted in 88.1% approving (of an 81.0% turnout), while the Danish referendum rejected the Maastricht Treaty by a 50.7% vote (of an 83.1% turnout). To induce Denmark's ratification, the country was conceded four opt-outs from provisions of the Treaty, covering Economic and Monetary Union, Citizenship, Justice and Home Affairs, and Common Defence. A second referendum in 1993 then approved the Treaty with opt-outs by a 56.7% majority (of an 86.5% turnout). The French Maastricht Treaty referendum in 1992 resulted in a knife-edge victory of 51.0% in favour (of a 69.7% turnout).

In 1994 Norway held a referendum on whether to join the European Union. After a protracted and heated debate, 52.2% voted No (of an 88.6% turnout). Norwegians had previously rejected membership of what had been the EEC in a 1972 referendum, and before that a Norwegian application to join the EU had been blocked by a French veto in 1962. The reasons for rejecting EU membership were mainly concerning fundamental differences in economic structure between Norway and the EU. In contrast to the EU's more industrial economy, Norway's is based heavily on natural resources, especially oil and fish.

In 1998, two referenda were held over the Treaty of Amsterdam. Ireland approved the new Treaty by 61.7% (of a 56.2% turnout) and Denmark voted 55.1% in favour (of a 76.2% turnout).

In 2001 Ireland again held a referendum, on the Nice Treaty, which the Irish rejected by a 53.9% majority (of a 34.8% turnout). In the following year, after numerous reassurances that the Treaty would not obligate Ireland to submit to any Common Defence jurisdiction, the Treaty was approved in a referendum in 2002 (the so-called "Nice II referendum") with a 62.9% majority (of a 49.5% turnout).

The 2004 Eastern Enlargement of the European Union consisted of the accession of ten candidates. Eight countries from Central and Eastern Europe and the Mediterranean islands Malta and Cyprus joined. Previous to that in 2003, referenda on joining the EU were held in all these states except Cyprus, with the following results: Malta 53.6% in favour (of a 90.9% turnout), Slovenia 89.6% in favour (of a 60.2% turnout), Hungary 83.3% in favour (of a 45.6% turnout), Lithuania 91.9% in favour (of a 63.4% turnout), Slovakia 93.7% in favour (of a 52.1% turnout), Poland 77.5% in favour (of a 58.9% turnout), the Czech Republic 77.3% in favour (of a 55.2% turnout), Estonia 66.8% in favour (of a 71.5% turnout), and Latvia 67.5% in favour (of a 71.5 % turnout). All ten candidate countries were admitted as members of the EU on 1 May 2004.

In 2005 Spain and Luxembourg held referenda on the Treaty establishing a Constitution for Europe (TCE), also known as the European Constitution, the aim of which was to replace the existing European Union treaties with a single text. The citizens of both of those countries endorsed it; however, it failed in referenda in France and the Netherlands. This terminated the ratification process. The aim was to replace the existing European Union treaties with a single text. The Lisbon Treaty, a mere revision of the TCE, was then substituted.

In 2008 Ireland caused an uproar when it became the only country to hold a referendum on the Lisbon Treaty. The voters rejected it by a majority of 53%. As all EU Member States must ratify a treaty before it can become law, Lisbon was effectively killed by the Irish. Irish and EU politicians jolted it back to life by insisting that the people "rethink" their decision, and a second referendum was imposed in 2009, when 67% approved it (of a of 59% turnout).

In July 2015 the Greek people voted by 61% (of a 62.5% turnout) to reject the harsh austerity regime demanded by the EU and other global financial institutions as the price of a multi-billion-euro bailout of the country's external debt. However, shortly afterwards, the left-wing government, worried that the country's financial system would collapse, acceded to a bailout with even harsher conditions than the ones rejected by the voters.

Another referendum with similarities to the Brexit referendum was the Hungarian migrant quota referendum on 2 October 2016. As in the UK, the people and government wanted to regain control of their borders. The referendum aimed to decide whether or not Hungary should accept migrant quotas imposed by the EU without the National Assembly's approval. Despite 98.4% voting against a quota, the turnout of 44.0% was too low to validate the result.

The key lessons learned from all these referenda covering membership, treaties, immigration and specific topics like the euro, are that:

(1) Besides the UK's EU Referenda in 1975 and 2016, none of the other 46 referenda was an in-out vote of an existing Member State, Greenland's exit in 1982 being exceptional as it had been entailed (willy-nilly) by Denmark's accession. All other Member State referenda were on topical issues rather than membership.

(2) Member States that have held referenda have managed them by conditioning their validity on a minimum turnout and absolute-majority thresholds. Public opinion changes over time along with events like the euro, immigration, and economic crisis, which also change over time. Statesmen have avoided staking membership of the EU on a paper-thin majority produced in the heat of debate.

(3) Although peoples have voted against EU treaties on a number of occasions, after further negotiations and amendments, second referenda were held or the government accepted the amendments in behalf of its people.

The two EU Referenda in the UK were very different and, as we are now learning by the 2016 referendum, have had far-reaching consequences. In 1975 Harold Wilson's Labour government referred to the British public the question whether the UK should quit or remain in the EEC. The actual query on the ballot paper in this first EU Referendum was, "Do you think the UK should stay in the European Community (Common Market)?" Just two years earlier, in 1973, the government of Tory Prime Minister Edward Heath had made the decision to join the EEC; however, Labour's 1974 electoral manifesto promised a referendum on continued membership.

Britons were polarised into Yes and No camps, a divide that cut across political parties. Opposition leader Margaret Thatcher argued passionately in favour of Britain remaining in Europe. In a television interview she told viewers, "I think it's absolutely vital that everyone should turn out in this referendum and vote yes, so that the question is over once and for all; we are really in Europe, and ready to go ahead" (BBC, 1975). *The Guardian* quoted her as advocating Britain's membership: the EEC is "the largest trading and aiding unit in the world", and "[it] is a very great advantage for this country to be part of that very much larger trading block". Many Commonwealth countries also supported UK membership (*The Guardian*, 1975:8).

The Tories had their share of Eurosceptics, but the Labour Party was much more rancorously split over the issue. As with the 2016 referendum, collective responsibility was suspended, allowing senior Cabinet ministers, not just backbenchers, to campaign against the Government position. Tony Benn was a leading figure in the No camp, and widely demonised in the press because, unlike the Brexit referendum, most daily newspapers back then supported the Yes side.

Key arguments of the Yes camp stressed economic considerations; the UK's voice in international affairs; collective defence; and the EEC as guarantor of a peaceful and prosperous future for Europe and the UK. Further points raised by the Yes camp included closer cooperation on matters of trade, employment, and social issues. The majority voted Yes - 17,378,581 people (67.2%) - to remain in Europe (BBC, 22 February 2017).

Interestingly, the UK was the driving force behind the Single Market, which revived the flagging common market in the 1980s, when the economy of the EEC began to fall behind the rest of the developed world. Having just brought the UK economy back from the brink of its 1970s crisis, Margaret Thatcher appointed Baron Arthur Cockfield European Commissioner for Internal Market, Tax Law and Customs in 1984. Cockfield became a driving force in reviving the common market. Only a few months after arriving in Brussels, he produced a White Paper (*Completing the Internal Market*, June 1985) for the Delors Commission which encompassed hundreds of institutional changes to reform the Customs Union structures. These barriers to trade were targeted with a timetable for their abolition by the Single European Act, a treaty which reformed the decision-making mechanisms of the EEC and set a deadline of 31 December 1992 for the completion of what became known as the Single Market. It came into force on 1 January 1993.

All of these referenda carry no legal obligation but are merely advisory. In the Westminster system of parliamentary supremacy, Parliament makes the final decision; indeed, the opinion of some lawyers is that Parliament must enact a repeal of the European Communities Act 1972 that ushered the UK into the EEC if Brexit is to happen. On the other hand, Teresa May's government might well have concluded the opposite, that the Government are entitled by that very Act to execute any article of any treaty with the EU, including Article 50 of the Lisbon Treaty, using the prerogative power according to Section 2 of the Act, without submitting it to a Parliamentary vote. And they probably would have faced no revolt from even the Labour opposition. This case is outlined below in detail. Regardless whether submitted to a Parliamentary vote or not, the political consequences of ignoring the people would be considerable. The dilemma is complicated by a weakening economy, and some polls suggest Brexiteers feel betrayed by the Leave campaign's broken promises made with no preparations to carry them out (Kuper, 2017). It is highly speculative what will happen in the next three years, and this book makes no predictions about political outcomes going forward. The only conclusion that has any certitude is that, whatever happens next, the challenges ahead will be painful due to the risky economic and financial situation of Europe and a highly polarised domestic public opinion in the UK.

The table below provides an overview of key developments and milestones of what is today known as the European Union, the better to understand the context of *"the club"* which the UK was joining. The European Union did not pop up from nowhere, it emerged over the last 60 years and had to overcome many challenges. The table shows that it has never been set in stone, but adapts to reality and continues to evolve.

1.2   P.M. CAMERON AND THE PLANNING OF THE 2016

British politicians and public have always been critical of Europe; however, economic and security motives convinced Britain to become part of the European project. Britain's role in the forefront of the industrial revolution and its history as an imperial powerhouse (ending in the Commonwealth) are closer to many British hearts than the European Union. For Westminster politicians, these familiar institutions were more manageable than the Byzantine dynamics of the intergovernmental European Union with its strong partners driving constant reform. While the Commonwealth can be seen as holding onto traditions and values, the European Union is a encroaching process of ever closer collaboration and integration.

The 1975 UK referendum was about membership of the European Single Market. Margaret Thatcher as PM in 1984 negotiated a rebate for the UK, which secured for the UK a perpetual special relationship to the EU. Tory and Labour politicans continued to be highly critical all the same. This was especially visible in the European Parliament, where Britain's Conservative MEPs joined with 26 Tory MEPs the 55-seat-strong "anti-federalist" party grouping, fulfilling David Cameron's controversial pledge to form a new bloc large enough to qualify for full recognition in Strasbourg. The grouping was the fourth largest bloc in the new European parliament (Mulholland, 2009).

Figure 1: Timeline – Milestones of the EU

Date/ Event	Details
18 Apr 1951: Treaty of Paris, creating the European Coal and Steel Community (ECSC)	The founding members of the Treaty were France, West Germany, Italy, Belgium, the Netherlands, and Luxembourg. The aim of the ECSC was to reconstruct the economies on the European continent and ensure lasting peace by placing the basis of armaments production in common hands. It came into force in 1952.
1954: No to European Defence Community	A majority of French parliamentarians rejected the European Defence Community.
1957: Treaty of Rome, the founding agreement of the European Economic Community (EEC)	The Treaty created the European Economic Community (EEC), which was a Customs Union, and the European Atomic Energy Community (Euratom) It came into force on 1 January 1958.
1961: Britain applies to join the EEC	On 1 August 1961 Britain, under Tory PM Macmillan applied to join the EEC. On 15 January 1963 French President Charles De Gaulle rejected this application on the grounds that it might lead to an Atlantic Community dominated by the United States.
1966: Luxembourg Compromise following the Empty Chair Crisis	General de Gaulle withdrew the French representative from the Council of Ministers to prevent France being outvoted.
1967: Merger Treaty creates the European Communities (EC)	All three "communities" (ECSC, EEC and Euratom) become known collectively as the European Communities (EC), although the communities remained in themselves legally distinct.
1973: Treaty of Accession (signed in Brussels)	On 1 January 1973 the United Kingdom, Ireland and Denmark joined the EC.
1975: UK referendum	On 6 June 1975 the UK held an in-out referendum on belonging to the European Economic Community (ECC)/Common Market; in which a majority voted to remain by a majority of 67.2% or 25,903,194 people (of a 64.0% turnout).
1979: European Parliament	The first direct elections to the European Parliament took place.
1981: One new member	Greece joined the EC.
1984: Thatcher secures budget rebate for the UK	Margaret Thatcher negotiated at the EU Summit a UK permanent rebate on the EU budget. This was possible because around 70% of the EU budget was spent on the Common Agricultural Policy (CAP) but the UK benefitted little from this money as distributed.
1985: Schengen Agreement	Schengen led to the removal of internal borders within the EC. It currently comprises 26 European countries (but not the UK) covering a population of over 400 million people.
1986: Two new members	Spain and Portugal joined the EC on 1 January 1986.
1986: The Single European Act (SEA, signed in Luxembourg)	The Act set the European Community an objective of establishing a Single Market by 31 December 1992. SEA reformed the legislative process by introducing the Cooperation Procedure and by extending qualified majority voting.
1992: The Maastricht Treaty	This Treaty formally renamed the EEC the European Union (EU) and paved the way for the single currency, the euro.
1992: 1st Danish referendum	Denmark rejected Maastricht in a referendum (50.5% voted No of a turnout of 83.1%).

Date/ Event	Details
1993: 2nd Danish referendum	The Danes voted in favour of the Maastricht Treaty in a second referendum.
1995: Three new members	Sweden, Austria and Finland joined the EU.
1997: The Amsterdam Treaty	This Treaty increased the powers of the European Parliament, including legislating on immigration, adopting civil and criminal laws, and enacting foreign and security policy (CFSP). It entered into force in 1999.
1998: European Central Bank (ECB)	The ECB was founded.
1999: Euro creation	The euro was created and national currencies were fixed to it at an agreed rate unalterably (without leaving the Eurozone).
2001: Nice Treaty	This Treaty reformed the institutional structure of the European Union and abolished many national vetoes in order to sustain eastward expansion.
2002: Euronotes and coins	Euronotes and coins were introduced into circulation; old national currencies were phased out. The euro zone (officially called euro area), is a monetary union that has adopted the euro (€) as their common currency and sole legal tender. 19 out of the 28 EU member states have joined the Eurozone.
2003: Constitutional convention	A constitutional convention was established, tasked with drawing up a constitution for the EU. It was presided over by ex-French President Valéry Giscard d'Estaing. The ratification process was brought to an end in June 2005after the French and Dutch voters rejected the document.
2004: Ten new members (1st Eastern enlargement)	Poland, Hungary, Slovakia, Slovenia, the Czech Republic, Cyprus, Malta, Estonia, Lithuania and Latvia all joined the EU.
2005: Spain, Luxembourg, French and Dutch referendum	Spain (76.7% to 17.24% in favour, 42.32% participation) and Luxembourg (56.52% to 43.48% in favour, 87.77% participation) endorsed the European Constitution. The Constitutional Treaty was rejected in referenda by the French (54.68% against to 45.32% for, of a 69.34% turnout) and by the Dutch (61.54% against to 38.46% for, of a 63.30% turnout).
2007: Lisbon Treaty	The Treaty abolished national vetoes, created a European Constitution and a European diplomatic corps. Changes included the move from unanimity to qualified majority voting in at least 45 policy areas in the Council of Ministers and a more powerful European Parliament. The Treaty for the first time gave member states the explicit legal right to leave the EU or rejoin it and procedures to do so.
2007: Two new members (2nd Eastern Enlargement)	Romania and Bulgaria joined the EU.
2008: 1st Irish referendum	Ireland rejected the Lisbon Treaty in a referendum (53.4% rejection).
2009: 2nd Irish referendum	The Irish voted again and this time in favour of the Lisbon Treaty.
2009: Lisbon Treaty (in force)	Lisbon Treaty entered into force.
2009: Eurozone crisis begins	PASOK government in Greece announced that its budget deficit was much higher than previously thought.
2010: Bail-out of Greece	Greece received its first bail-out from the EU and the International Monetary Fund (IMF).
2010:	Ireland accepted a bail-out deal with the EU and IMF.

Date/ Event	Details
Bail-out of Ireland	
2011: Bail-out of Portugal	Portugal received its first bail-out from the EU and the IMF.
2011: Schengen Agreement partly suspended	The Schengen Agreement was suspended on the border between France and Italy. This was due to the arrival of migrants fleeing political turmoil in North Africa.
2013: One new member (3rd Eastern Enlargement)	Croatia joined the EU.
2015: Migration crisis and Schengen Agreement partly suspended	A migration crisis engulfed the EU, with around one million "refugees" arriving in Germany by the end of the year; some EU member states decided to close their borders to migrants.
2016: Dutch referendum	On 6 April 2016 the Dutch held a referendum on the EU's Association Agreement with Ukraine, which had been enacted on 1 July 2015; in which 61% of a 32.28% turnout voted No to the Approval Act.
2016: UK referendum	On 23 June 2016, the UK holds a referendum on EU membership (details below).
2016: Hungarian referendum	On 2 October 2016, Hungary held a referendum on EU quota allocation for refugees. While an overwhelming majority of voters rejected the EU's migrant quotas turnout was too low (98.36% of votes were against the quota allocation, with a turnout of 44.04%).

Almost 4.3 million people voted in the Scottish Independence referendum on 18 Sept 2014. Both countries – the Kingdom of Scotland and the Kingdom of England – had entered the Union in 1707. This Union, which has lasted nearly seven times longer than membership of the European Union, was at stake. The causes of this referendum were the devolution that had started with "home rule for Scotland" in the 1920s, and the increasing power of the Scottish National Party (SNP). In 1997 a Scottish devolution referendum had been held, in which a majority of 74.29% (of a 60.4% turnout) approved the creation of a Scottish Parliament with devolved powers, including tax-varying powers. The 2014 referendum question, which voters answered with "Yes" or "No", was: "Should Scotland be an independent country?" The No side won with 2,001,926 (55.3%) as against 1,617,989 (44.7%) voting Yes. The 84.6% turnout was the highest ever recorded for an election or referendum in the United Kingdom since the introduction of universal suffrage.

The in-out Scottish Independence referendum may have got a debate about an in-out EU Referendum started. Unlike in other European countries, however, the British people are widely considered ill-informed about European politics (*The Guardian*, 27 November 2015). Recent research carried out by the Electoral Commission found that the "majority" of people they spoke to "stated that their personal understanding of how the EU worked was low" and that they felt "under-informed about the EU as an institution, as well as about the arguments for and against the UK remaining a member" (Electoral Commission, October 2013). At the beginning of the debate and referendum campaign, the media (such as the BBC) started educating the populace about the basic set-up of European institutions instead of analysing the implications of leaving the EU. Nigel Farage's UK Independence Party (UKIP) had been lobbying for years to "get the UK out of Europe". When Conservative constituents started defecting *en masse* to vote UKIP, David Cameron and the Tory leadership took fright and made a promise in their own Party electoral manifesto to call a referendum.

The EU Referendum Act received Royal Assent in December 2015, after being exhaustively debated in Parliament during its passage and agreed by both the House of Commons and the House of Lords. It laid out the terms under which the referendum would take place, setting the date, defining the franchise and the question to appear on the ballot paper. The Act set no threshold for validity or minimum turnout, which some observers identified as a fatal mistake.

Prime Minister Cameron had secured a deal in Brussels in February 2016, which he claimed would give the country "special status" in the EU. On reflection, considering that Cameron had to negotiate with 27 EU leaders within a short period of time, everybody who understands the often lengthy decision-making processes in EU politics would have to admit that Cameron did right well for the UK. A censorious media widely misrepresented Cameron's success in negotiating such a deal, some of which, surprisingly, applied not only to the UK but to all Member States. Across the policy domains the deal would:

- *Migration and benefits*: "limit the access of [European] Union workers newly entering its labour market to in-work benefits for a total period of up to four years from the commencement of employment" if the UK, or any other member state, can show that EU migrants are "putting an excessive pressure on the proper functioning of its public services".
- *Eurozone safeguards*: exempt the UK from budgetary responsibility for future bail-outs of Eurozone states and concede "reimbursement" if a Eurozone state rescue-measure calls on general EU funds.
- *Budgets and EU waste*: contain a pledge by the European Commission to continue its ongoing effort to cut red tape by applying the 2015 Better Regulation Agenda.
- *Child benefit*: put EU migrant children onto the new rates who were receiving child benefits in their home countries.
- *Red card for national parliaments*: commit the Council Presidency, in case 55% of national EU parliaments object to an EU legislative proposal, "within 12 weeks" to hold a "comprehensive discussion" on the objections raised and "discontinue the consideration of the draft legislation".
- *Ever closer union*: insert into the EU treaties, when they are next opened, a new reference to make it clear that the words "ever closer union do not apply to the United Kingdom".

- *Security*: specifically permit the UK to take "necessary restrictive measures" against individuals deemed to represent "a genuine and serious threat" to public safety, notwithstanding ECJ case law to the contrary. (The case law of the European Court of Human Rights has also been considered an impediment to national security, but that is a separate jurisdiction over which the EU has no power, and ought *not* to be confused with it.)
- *Multi-currency union*: stipulate that, while the Union's objective is to establish "an economic and monetary union whose currency is the euro", it is simultaneously stipulated that "not all member states have the euro as their currency".

However, Cameron could not win any changes to the *Working Time Directive* after Labour and the trades unions made clear that they would not support renegotiation on these points. He was not able to repatriate EU social and employment law, generally either, which he had committed himself to in the 2010 Conservative Party manifesto.
(Foster and Kikrup, 24 February 2017)

The table below lays out milestones on the way to the referendum. It starts with the Scottish referendum, which was the first and one of three referenda under the Cameron Government, the Alternative Vote referendum (2011) and the EU Referendum (2016) being the other two. The EU Referendum was the only one that received a *yes* vote. The other two were rejected; nevertheless, any of them might have led to significant constitutional changes. Manifestly, compared to previous PMs, Cameron was unusually liberal in submitting important decisions to *the people*, which ought to be seen as positive, by default; however, as the EU Referendum teaches, the outcome can lead to unexpected complications if the referendum result forces changes the country is not really ready for. Scotland, which rejected Brexit, is now having ongoing debates about another Scottish Referendum as a direct result of the Brexit vote.

Figure 2: Timeline – Events in the build-up of the EU Referendum

Date/ Event	Details
21 Mar 2013: Referendum (Scotland) Bill Committee	MSP Nicola Sturgeon of the Scottish National Party, destined to become First Minister by the time of Brexit, was the one who introduced the Scottish Independence Act in the Scottish Parliament. The Scottish National Party, as the ruling party in Scotland, and led then by the then First Minister of Scotland Alex Salmond, saw to it ensured that the bill was passed.
14 Nov 2013: Scottish Independence Referendum (Franchise) Act 2013	The Act made the arrangements for this referendum. It came into force on 18 December. This followed an agreement between the Scottish and UK governments to make exception to the Scottish devolution scheme, which ordinarily reserves constitutional matters to Westminster.
12 Jan 2014: 95 Tory MPs call for EU law veto	95 Conservative MPs in a letter to David Cameron demanded that power is vested in Parliament to veto every aspect of EU law, proposing that the Commons should get back its authority to block new EU legislation, as if it were traditional international law, and repeal existing EU law that threatens Britain's "national interests".
18 Sept 2014: Scottish independence referendum	The Scottish independence referendum question, to be which voters answered with Yes or No, was, "Should Scotland be an independent country?" The "No" side won, with 2,001,926 (55.3%) voting against independence and 1,617,989 (44.7%) voting in favour. The turnout of 84.6% was the highest ever recorded for an election or referendum in the UK since the introduction of universal suffrage.
17 Dec 2015: European Union Referendum Act 2015	An Act to make provision for the holding of a referendum in the United Kingdom and Gibraltar on whether the United Kingdom should remain a member of the European Union.
20 Feb 2016: Cameron finalises with 27 other European leaders a special deal for Britain.	The special deal featured migrations and benefits, exclusion of the UK from bail-outs of Eurozone states; an EU commitment by the EU to cut red tape; a reduction in child benefits for EU children living in the UK; the right of 55% of Member State parliaments to move reconsideration of EU legislation; detachment of the UK from any "ever closer union"; freedom to take security measures against dangerous persons; and recognition of a multi-currency Union.
20 February 2016: EU Referendum date set for 23 June	After briefing his Cabinet, PM Cameron made an. historic announcement in Downing Street describing the vote as one of the biggest decisions "in our lifetimes".
15 Apr 2016: Referendum campaign kicks off	The official campaign period kicked off with campaign events and rallies across the country.
5 May 2016: Devolved elections across Britain	Elections were held for the devolved governments: the Welsh Assembly, Scottish Parliament, and Northern Ireland Assembly. The nearness of the referendum could not have failed to impact the election results.
27 May 2016: Purdah starts	In the final four weeks before the EU Referendum, civil servants were forbidden by law to make any announcements about controversial initiatives or campaign that might have swayed the public and influenced their vote.
2 and 3 June 2016: Question and answer session on Sky News.	PM Cameron (for Remain) and Justice Secretary Michael Gove (for Leave) took part in a live face-to-face debate and an audience question-and-answer session on Sky News.
3 June 2016: *The Express* Debate	EU Referendum campaigns clashed during the *Express* Debate at *Express* HQ. UKIP leader Nigel Farage, Conservative MP Jacob Rees-Mogg and Labour MP Kate Hoey made the case for Brexit. Labour MPs Chuka Umunna and Siobhain McDonagh and Innocent Smoothies co-founder Richard Reed pushed for Britain to remain in the EU.
7 June 2016: ITV Programme debate	PM Cameron and UKIP leader Nigel Farage faced separate 30-minute question-and-answer sessions during an ITV programme.
21 June 2016: BBC Debate at Wembley Arena	PM Cameron refused to take part in the debate because he did not want to go head-to-head with Tory Eurosceptics.

1.3 DAY ZERO AND THE AFTERMATH OF THE REFERENDUM

On Thursday, 23 June 2016 people were asked whether the United Kingdom should remain a member of the European Union or leave the European Union (for detailed statistical information, refer to Chapter Two). Schools, libraries, church halls, and sports centres were turned into polling stations and opened from 7 am in the morning to 10 pm in the evening. 41,000 polling stations opened at 382 local counting areas. The ballot paper that voters were asked to complete is presented in the figure below.

Figure 3: The referendum ballot paper for voters

Referendum on the United Kingdom's membership of the European Union
Vote only once by putting a cross **✗** in the box next to your choice
Should the United Kingdom remain a member of the European Union or leave the European Union?
Remain a member of the European Union ☐
Leave the European Union ☐

Early results arrived around midnight and by around 3.30 am, when results in around 200 counting areas were known, the overall picture became clear. By 6 am the last counts had arrived, and the result could be "called" by broadcasters and news agencies. The country was able to watch the referendum results unfold over breakfast. The UK, Europe, and the whole world were stunned to learn that Leave had won. All polls and forecasts had indicated that the Remain camp would win, although it was widely acknowledged that the race would be tight.

1.3.1 Day One: Political chaos and a divided society

Day One after the EU Referendum was pure chaos: politically, economically, and for British society. The United Kingdom was suddenly less united than before. Both the Conservative and Labour Parties were plunged into deep leadership crises; after David Cameron announced his resignation as Prime Minister, the country found itself without leadership; Scotland began to consider a second referendum for independence, given its preference for remaining in the EU; stock markets were in free-fall, and the pound sterling lost more than 10% of its value in a few hours; and the people were deeply divided by region, age and social class.

The day started with the announcement by Prime Minister David Cameron outside 10 Downing Street at 08:15 BST that he would resign, saying:

> I was absolutely clear about my belief that Britain is stronger, safer and better off inside the European Union, and I made clear the referendum was about this and this alone – not the future of any single politician, including myself.
>
> But the British people have made a very clear decision to take a different path, and as such I think the country requires fresh leadership to take it in this direction.
>
> I will do everything I can as Prime Minister to steady the ship over the coming weeks and months, but I do not think it would be right for me to try to be the captain that steers our country to its next destination.
>
> This is not a decision I have taken lightly, but I do believe it is in the national interest to have a period of stability and then the new leadership required.
>
> (Cameron, 24 June 2016)

Boris Johnson, the ex-Mayor of London and the public face of Vote Leave, said that there was "no need for haste" about severing the UK's ties. He added that voters had "searched in their hearts" and the UK now has a "glorious opportunity" to pass its own laws, set its own taxes, and control its own borders. Nicola Sturgeon, now the Scottish First Minister held a Cabinet meeting at Holyrood, stating that after Scotland – like London and Northern Ireland – voted overwhelmingly to remain in the EU, a second independence vote was now "on the table".

German chancellor Angela Merkel expressed "great regret" at the outcome, but stated that the EU was strong enough to find the "right answers" to Britain's vote to leave. Ireland's Taoiseach (i.e., Prime Minister) Enda Kenny met with his Cabinet to consider the "very significant implications" for Ireland, Britain and the EU. The Irish government, which remained neutral during the Scottish independence referendum, actively encouraged Irish citizens in the UK to vote Remain. Dublin's concerns were what the vote meant for the border with Northern Ireland, and what effect a weaker pound sterling might have on trade (estimated at over €1 billion between both countries every week). Sinn Fein called for a vote on whether North Ireland should remain part of the UK or should reunite with Ireland, something that is not a priority for the Irish government due to lack of support.

Gibraltar, where the Rock's British residents emphatically (96%) voted to remain in the EU, woke up to the news of an announcement by Spain's acting Foreign Minister, Jose Manuel Garcia-Margallo, that the decision to leave opened up "new possibilities" over Gibraltar's status and the prospects of the Spanish flag flying on the Rock.

Far-right National Front leader Marie Le Pen was among the first to respond with a cry of "victory for freedom!", expressing hopes for a referendum in France and elsewhere in the EU.

The European Council President Donald Tusk said in his first announcement that it was not the time for hysterical overreaction and that the EU was "determined to keep our unity at 27" member states. Martin Schulz, President of the European Parliament, said that Brexit would not precipitate a domino effect across Europe.

Volatility in the pound sterling and plummeting stock market values dominated the economic news. The Athens stock exchange fell 15% immediately after opening, with bank shares plummeting 30%. In Spain, Prime Minister Mariano Rajoy called for calm. The country is home to an estimated one million British residents, who worried about what the decision meant for their right to live and work in the EU and get free healthcare.

On 25 July 2016, First Minister Sturgeon put forth the key Scottish interests that must be protected, which she summarised as follows:

- *Democratic interests* – "the need to make sure Scotland's voice is heard and our wishes respected"
- *Economic interests* – "safeguarding free movement of labour, access to a single market of 500 million people and the funding that our farmers and universities depend on"
- *Social protection* – "ensuring the continued protection of workers' and wider human rights"
- *Solidarity* – "the ability of independent nations to come together for the common good of all our citizens, to tackle crime and terrorism and deal with global challenges like climate change"
- *Having influence* – "making sure that we don't just have to abide by the rules of the single market but also have a say in shaping them".
(BBC, 25 July 2016a)

BBC Radio 5 live released on 5 September 2016 the results of a ComRes poll about the post-Brexit mood of the nation. Six in ten UK adults (62%) surveyed said they were positive about Britain's future after the Leave vote; however, a quarter (26%) said they have now thought about leaving Britain and living abroad following the referendum. For those aged between 18 and 34 this figure was more than two in five (43%). (BBC, 5 September 2016b).

Brexit Secretary Davis stated on 4 September, "It is about seizing the huge and exciting opportunities that will flow from a new place for Britain in the world. There will be new freedoms, new opportunities, new horizons for this great country" (*Financial Times*, 4 September 2016). On the same day Japanese Prime Minister Shinzo Abe presented Theresa May a 15-page report setting out its Brexit demands at the G20 summit in Hangzhou, China. (This quasi-ultimatum echoed the pre-referendum warning of US President Barack Obama in April that if the UK voted to leave, it would find itself at the "back of queue" for trade talks with the US.) The Japanese business community has close ties with the UK and Abe's letter publicly announced the existence of parameters for what is acceptable for Japanese companies with offices in the UK. The letter demanded also more transparency, stressing that "[w]hat Japanese businesses in Europe most wish to avoid is the situation in which they are unable to discern clearly the way the negotiations are going, only grasping the whole picture at the last minute. It was imperative that the outcome is free of unpleasant surprises and reducing the risks emanating from uncertainty." Companies like Nomura Bank, Hitatchi, Honda, Nissan, and Toyota employ about 140,000 people in the UK and need certainty for future investment decisions. Like many international firms, Japanese multinationals see Britain as a base from which to export products and services to the Single Market. The threat to relocate certain financial institutions could not have been clearer: "If Japanese financial institutions are unable to maintain the single passport obtained in the UK, they would face difficulties in their business operations in the EU and might have to acquire corporate status within the EU anew and obtain the passport again, or to relocate their operations from the UK to existing establishments in the EU" (Wintour, 4 September 2016).

The House of Commons Petitions Committee at Westminster Hall debated a petition that attracted 4.15 million signatures, more than any other in the past five years, demanding a 2nd referendum (House of Commons, 5 September 2016). The petition stated, "We the undersigned call upon HM Government to implement a rule that if the remain or leave vote is less than 60% based a turnout less than 75% there should be another referendum." Ironically, William Oliver Healey who originally submitted the petition on May 25, a month before the vote, was hoping it might save Brexit if a second referendum were triggered in the case that Remain won the referendum by a narrow margin. But the petition gained momentum only on Friday morning the day after the referendum, when so many thousands were signing it online that it crashed the UK Parliament and the Government Digital Service website. The petition advocates stressed that the terms of Brexit were and still are unclear, and that the sovereign right of the Scottish and Northern Irish vote (and sovereignty) to remain in the EU was undermined. The Liberal Democrats, Scottish National Party, and some Labour MPs called for the UK's eventual settlement with the EU to be put to the British people in the form of a second referendum. The Tory government, however, ruled this out. The formal government response was that "[t]he European Union Referendum Act received Royal Assent in December 2015, receiving overwhelming support from Parliament. The Act did not set a threshold for the result or for minimum turnout" (UK Parliament, 5 September 2016).

The Brexit debate involved not only Scotland, the regions and Westminster, but also the metropole. London voted Remain. Because of the economic importance of London for the country, and the need to attract *talent* (i.e. skilled labour) and access to the Single Market, the Mayor of London, Sadiq Khan demanded a seat at the negotiating table. He was also floating the idea to issue "London only" work permits to attract talent to the city. The Mayor also demanded the Government agree a devolution deal for London, granting him more control over skills and training services, tax raising powers, national rail services, criminal justice, and health services. (Khan, Sadiq, 22 September 2016). He said London must "take back control", and a petition calling for London to declare independence attracted more than 180,000 votes by the end of October (Change.org, 2016) James O'Malley, who started this petition, argues that London is an international city and should remain at the heart of Europe. A study by the Centre for Cities revealed that London in particular has seen its share of the urban tax take increase considerably. In 2004/05 London generated as much economy tax as the next 24 biggest cities, while in 2014/15 London increase its share as much as the next 37 cities (McGough and Piazza, 2016). A report by the Centre for Economics and Business Research (CEBR) revealed that "[o]ne pound in every five earned by Londoners is used to fund the rest of the country … Northern Ireland pays tax worth just 27.7%t of GDP generated by Northern Ireland. This compares to London, which pays tax equivalent to 45.2% of GDP created in the capital … Overall, London provides a net subsidy of 20.3% of GDP. Northern Ireland receives a net subsidy of 29.4%, while Wales receives a subsidy of 26.0 per cent and the North East 22.2 per cent" (CEBR, 13 February 2012). The Office of National Statistics (ONS) calculated that the median UK salary is currently £27,531, while the City of London is the highest-earning region, boasting an average salary of £48,023 (Office of National Statistics, 2015). Based on data from the ONS and CEBR, Londoners are contributing in average £9,605 a year in transfer payments to the rest of the UK, which compares to £131.03 a year net contribution to the EU budget. This means that Londoners contribute to the rest of the UK 73 times more than to the EU budget. Following the argument used by the Leave campaign to "take back control", this would be a strong argument to convert London into a city state. London could become an economic powerhouse like Singapore or Hong Kong. Nothing seemed impossible anymore.

1.3.2 A chronological timeline from the day of the referendum

The following table lists key events since the EU Referendum on 23 June 2016. It is a list of facts, persons and expressions of views, of political players' announcements of steps to be taken, in brief, how the Brexit tale unfolded after abstracting from all the fuss. The authors have endeavoured to remain as un-biassed as possible, leaving readers to form their own opinion on events and acts.

Figure 4: Timeline – Events after the EU Referendum

Date/ Event	Details
23 June 2016: EU Referendum	UK public voted 51.9% to 48.1% to leave the European Union. The referendum turnout was 71.8%. ▪ England: 53.4% Leave, 46.6% Remain (Turnout 73.0%) ▪ Wales: 52.5% Leave, 47.5% Remain (Turnout 71.7%) ▪ Scotland 38.0% Leave, 62.0% Remain (Turnout 67.2%) ▪ Northern Ireland: 44.2% Leave, 55.8% Remain (Turnout 62.7%) ▪ Gibraltar: 4.09% Leave, 95.9% Remain (Turnout 83.6%)
24 June 2016: National declaration of the referendum result and resignation of David Cameron as Prime Minister.	The official announcement that Brexit was victorious, followed by the resignation of David Cameron. In his resignation speech, Mr Cameron said, "I do not think I can be the captain to take the country to its next destination." The FTSE 100 dropped by 8.3%.
25 June 2016: Leave camp rolled back its pledge on NHS spending, immigration, and the timeframe for leaving the EU.	Conservative Former Defence Minister Liam Fox said, "A lot of things were said in advance of this referendum that we might want to think about again." Nigel Farage told Good Morning Britain that the claim written on the side of the Vote Leave Battle Bus – that leaving the EU would release £350m a week that could be spent on the NHS – "was a mistake", adding that "[i]t wasn't one of my adverts".
26 Jun 2016: Wave of resignations in Labour Party.	Jeremy Corbyn sacks Hilary Benn as Shadow Foreign Secretary, triggering a wave of resignations from Shadow Cabinet members in protest at Jeremy Corbyn's leadership and "lacklustre" referendum campaign.
26 June 2016: George Osborne urged to resign.	George Osborne was urged to resign by Eurosceptic ministers.
26 June 2016: Poll shows surge in support for independence in Scotland.	Nearly 60% of Scots support Scottish independence after Britain voted to leave the EU according to an opinion poll by the *Sunday Post*.
27 June 2016: UK credit rating downgrade post-Brexit.	Standard & Poor's (S&P) and Fitch Ratings downgraded the United Kingdom's credit rating from an AAA to an AA. S&P said, "In our opinion, this outcome is a seminal event, and will lead to a less predictable, stable, and effective policy framework in the U.K.."
28 June 2016: EU Brexit summit.	French and German politicians urged the UK to invoke Article 50, the withdrawal procedure.
28 June 2016: Labour Party in crisis	Labour MPs overwhelmingly support a vote of no confidence in Jeremy Corbyn.
30 June 2016: Boris Johnson withdraws from leadership contest.	Michael Gove said, "I have come, reluctantly, to the conclusion that Boris cannot provide the leadership or build the team for the task ahead. I have therefore decided to put my name forward for the leadership."
30 June 2016: Conservative leadership bid for PM.	The race narrows to five candidates: Michael Gove, Theresa May, Stephen Crabb, Liam Fox, and Andrea Leadsom. Boris Johnson withdraws from leadership contest
4 July 2016: Nigel Farage resigns as UKIP leader.	Nigel Farage quits as leader of UKIP, saying, "I want my life back."
11 July 2016: Theresa May elected as Tory leader. Next general election is postponed until 2020.	Theresa May is elected leader of the Conservative Party. She drops a hint that she will wait until 2020 before calling the next general election.
11 July 2016:	Theresa May of the Conservative Party becomes the new PM: "Together we will build

Date/ Event	Details
Theresa May confirmed as new Prime Minister.	a better Britain."
11 July 2016: "All options must be on the table" for Scotland.	Scotland's First Minister Nicola Sturgeon stressed "I expect early engagement with the incoming Prime Minister on that subject as we look to maintain Scotland's EU status, in line with the democratic wishes of the people of Scotland."
11 July 2016: May quotes: "Brexit means Brexit" and "Best deal for Britain in leaving the EU".	Theresa May famously says, "Brexit means Brexit and we're going to make a success of it." She committed herself to "negotiate the best deal for Britain in leaving the EU and forge a new role for ourselves in the world".
12 July 2016: Debate on second referendum.	The petition for a second EU Referendum must be debated in Parliament in the near future now that more than 4.1 million people have signed it.
13 July 2016: Handover of the PM office from David Cameron to Theresa May.	Following Prime Minister's Questions, Cameron went to Buckingham Palace to offer his resignation to the Queen. Theresa May arrived at the Palace for her private audience with the Queen. She became the Queen's 13th Prime Minister after accepting the monarch's offer to form a new government.
13 July 2016: May announces new Cabinet.	New ministers with key Brexit responsibilities are: • Philip Hammond, Chancellor of the Exchequer • Boris Johns, Foreign Secretary • David Davis, Secretary of State for Exiting the EU • Liam Fox, the new International Trade Secretary Of May's 22 cabinet ministers 15 supported Remain and 7 Leave.
14 July 2016: Bank of England monetary policy decision for financial stimulus.	The Bank of England's Monetary Policy Committee (MPC) maintained the Bank Rate at 0.5% and the stock of purchased assets financed by the issuance of central bank reserves at £375 billion.
15 July 2016: May meets with Sturgeon at Edinburgh.	Theresa May told First Minister Nicola Sturgeon she was ""willing to listen to options"" on Scotland"s future relationship with the EU, but unwilling to consider a second referendum on Scottish independence.
16 July 2016: May's first Cabinet meeting.	May signalled that she could delay formal notification to Brussels of Britain's exit *per* Article 50 of the Lisbon Treaty.
17 July 2016: "Scotland is in a strong position to block Brexit."	Scotland's First Minister bluffs that she will not allow the UK to take Scotland out of the EU against its wishes.
20 July 2016: May meets Chancellor Angela Merkel in Berlin.	A joint UK-Germany statement is released stressing the two countries' economic partnership. Germany is the UK's second-largest trading partner worldwide and the second-most important source of foreign direct investment into Britain. In Germany 1,300 British companies employ more than 220,000 people.
21 July 2016: May meets François Hollande in Paris.	The French President urged the UK to start Brexit negotiations as soon as possible. He stressed, "Being in the single market means accepting freedom of movement."
24 July 2016: New attempt to negotiate "special deal for Britain" EU considers migration "emergency brake" for UK for up to seven years.	Diplomats worked on a deal to give the UK an "emergency brake" for up to seven years. The deal is to give PM May more concessions than won by PM Cameron, despite French doubts. This would involve contributing to the EU budget, though probably at a lower rate, and the UK would lose its seat at the negotiating table for rules on the Single Market.
11 Aug 2016: Channel Islands may get AIFMD passport.	Jersey and Guernsey may be viewed as more attractive, especially on the back of a European Securities and Markets Authority recommendation to the European Parliament, Council and Commission that both islands should be counted amongst the "third countries" granted an AIFMD (Alternative Investment Fund Management

Date/ Event	Details
	Directive) *passporting* (see Section 5.1).
13 Aug 2016: EU funding for farms, science, and other projects will be replaced by the UK Treasury by 2020.	Chancellor of the Exchequer Philip Hammond announced that the Treasury would guarantee EU-funded projects, which could cost up to £6 billion a year, as well as subsidies and other payments under the Common Agricultural Policy (CAP) for up to £3 billion a year.
22 Aug 2016: EU leadership meeting.	The leaders of Germany, France and Italy meet to discuss the future of the EU in a post-Brexit world.
25 Aug 2016: The First Minister of Scotland warns of Brexit costs.	Mrs Sturgeon published an analysis of possible Brexit consequences, saying the Scottish economy could be losing between £1.7 billion and £11.2 billion a year by 2030.
27 Aug 2016: No parliamentary vote before opening negotiations.	Theresa May did not plan to hold a parliamentary vote in the Commons before executing Article 50.
31 Aug 2016: Theresa May holds first Cabinet meeting after summer break.	May told Cabinet the UK would not stay in the EU "by the back door" but will "push ahead" to trigger Brexit without Parliamentary approval at her countryside residence Chequers.
1 Sept 2016: Services and manufacturing recovers after Brexit vote.	August saw solid rebounds in the trends in UK manufacturing output and incoming new orders. Companies reported solid inflows of new work from both domestic and export sources, the latter aided by the sterling exchange rate. Employment rose for the first time in the year-to-date. At 53.3 in August, the seasonally adjusted Markit Economics/CIPS Purchasing Managers' Index (PMI) recovered sharply from the 41-month low of 48.3 (which was the lowest level since April 2009) posted in July following the EU Referendum (below 50% means contraction). This drop and rebound likely indicates a market consolidation after reaction to the Brexit shock, due to economic stimulation through a post-referendum devaluation of the pound sterling.
1 Sept 2016: Calls for second Scottish independence referendum.	Nicola Sturgeon said there was a "democratic deficit" at the heart of the Westminster system and launched a "new conversation" on independence as she urged Scotland to "control its own destiny".
2 Sept 2016: Green Party calls for second EU Referendum.	Green MP Caroline Lucas argues that the slogan "Brexit means Brexit" means "nothing until we know what the terms of any Brexit deal will be" and "once the principles of any new deal have been set out, we want them to put it to a second referendum".
4 Sept 2016: Japanese government warns of the consequences of the UK leaving the common market.	At the G20 summit in China Japanese Prime Minister Shinzo Abe presented a document entitled "Japan's Message to the UK and EU". It warns of dire consequences for "the interests of the world" if an open Europe cannot be maintained.
4 Sept 2016: May rules out snap election.	Speaking on the BBC's Andrew Marr show, PM May said she does not want to call a snap election before 2020 because she believes the UK needs stability. She stated, "I'm not going to be calling a snap election. I've been very clear that I think we need that period of time, that stability to be able to deal with the issues that the country is facing and have that election in 2020."
5 Sept 2016: No point-based system for EU nationals and no more money for the NHS.	Theresa May has rejected an Australian-style point system for controlling EU migration, one of the key promises of Leave campaigners during the referendum. May also refused to commit to increasing the health care budget by £100 million a week.
5 Sept 2016: Debate of petition 131215 relating to EU Referendum rules.	The petition attracted 4.14 million signatures and was debated in the House of Commons. It called for a 2nd referendum petition.
5 Sept 2016: Control of UK borders is "not	In his first statement to the Commons about Brexit, Secretary David Davis said, "If a requirement of membership is giving up control of our borders, I think that makes it

Date/ Event	Details
negotiable".	very improbable."
7 Sept 2016: "Britain will become a global leader in free trade."	Returning from the G20 summit, Theresa May told the House of Commons that Britain would seek to become a global leader in free trade and would not retreat to protectionism.
7 Sept 2016: No running commentary on Brexit negotiations.	The PM told MPs that the government would not "reveal our hand prematurely" or comment on "every twist and turn". She refused to say whether she wanted the UK to stay in the European Single Market.
9 Sept 2016: Brexit threatens the delivery of public services unless spending is increased.	The First Division Association, a Union for Senior Managers and Professionals in Public Service, says Brexit will mean a cut in public spending unless funding is increased. Dave Penman, General Secretary of the FDA, warned that the funding settlement cutting ministry budgets over a decade should be reconsidered in the light of the Brexit vote.
12 Sept 2016: David Cameron quits as Conservative Member of Parliament.	Cameron stood down as MP for Witney and left the House of Commons because he did not want to be a "distraction" for the new PM.
14 Sept 2016: Jean-Claude Juncker speech at Europe House in London.	In his annual State of the Union address to the European Parliament, the President of the European Commission, Jean-Claude Juncker, took stock of the EU's achievements, the challenges that lie ahead, and set the political direction for the coming year. Mr Juncker said Britain "could not have à la carte access" to the Single Market and leave the free movement of people and goods off the "menu".
14 Sept 2016: EU sets up an Article 50 taskforce.	The EU Article 50 taskforce is led by chief negotiator and former French Foreign Minister, Michel Barnier, and Sabine Weyand, a German trade official. The taskforce would "prepare and conduct negotiations with the UK, taking into account of the framework for its future relationship with the European Union".
15 Sept 2016: 15% of UK university staff are at risk.	The German academic exchange service DAAD estimated that many academic staff will leave universities. 32,000 non-British EU academics (17% of UK university teaching and research staff) work currently in the UK.
16 Sept 2016: Special EU summit in Bratislava without UK.	The special EU summit met without the UK in an attempt to steer a new course following the Brexit vote. Tusk called on EU leaders to take a "brutally honest" look at the EU's problems.
17 Sept 2016: The Visegrad or V4 Group defends free movement of workers.	Slovakia, Hungary, Poland and the Czech Republic said they were ready to take steps to protect rights of citizens to live and work in the UK.
22 Sept 2016: London wants say in Brexit negotiations.	The Mayor of London, Sadiq Khan, meet the President of the European Parliament, Martin Schulz, at City Hall to stress London's openness and the importance of the capital's having a seat at the negotiating table.
23 Sept 2016: London must "take back control".	A petition calling for London to declare independence gathered 175,175 signatures. (After 100,000 signatures a petition must be put to debate in Parliament.)
24 Sept 2016: Labour Party leadership crisis.	Jeremy Corbyn was re-elected as Labour leader with 51.8% of the vote after defeating his challenger Owen Smith who had called for a second referendum.
25 Sept 2016: BBC defends Brexit bias accusations.	BBC's head of news James Harding defended himself against claims by the Leave camp that post-referendum coverage has been "gloomy or hysterical"; while Remainers accused it of being too impartial.
28 Sept 2016: UK car industry sends a strong warning to the UK government.	The UK car industry launched a pro-EU Single Market campaign in Paris, insisting that only continued membership of the Single Market can guarantee the success of the UK car industry.
29 Sept 2016: The UK has "a golden opportunity to forge a new role for ourselves in	International Trade Secretary Liam Fox said, "The UK's trade with the European Union will be 'at least as free' after Brexit as it is now" and hailed the "golden opportunity" to forge new links.

Date/ Event	Details
the world".	
29 Sept 2016: Labour plans to back pro-immigration policy.	Jeremy Corbyn sparked anger amongst his opponents by suggesting that Labour would continue to back an Open Door policy on immigration.
30 Sept 2016: "London passports" are an option.	Sadiq Khan, Mayor of London, revealed his plans to unilaterally issue a "London only" work permit.
2 Oct 2016: Announcement to start negotiations in March 2017, and Great Repeal Bill which would end primacy of EU law in UK.	The UK would begin the formal Brexit negotiation process by the end of March 2017. The timing of triggering Article 50 of the Lisbon Treaty meant the UK would leave the EU by summer 2019. PM May said that voters had given their verdict "with emphatic clarity". She also gave details of a Great Repeal Bill, which would remove the European Communities Act 1972 from the statute book and enshrine all existing EU law into British law. May told delegates at the conservative conference in Birmingham, "We are going to be a fully independent, sovereign country – a country that is no longer part of a political union with supranational institutions that can override national parliaments and courts."
5 Oct 2016: Hard Brexit could cost financial sector £20 billion and 35,000 jobs.	An Oliver Wyman conducted a report with the *TheCity UK*'s Senior Brexit Steering Committee and with major sectoral trade associations. This report concluded that loss of access to the Single Market, if it causes loss of production scale inside the UK, could undermine the UK's trade with countries outside the EU. Thus, a very hard Brexit scenario could cause a GDP decline of £20 billion, putting up to 35,000 jobs at risk. The knock-on effect on the production ecosystem could make the government lose up to £18 billion in tax revenue. (Oliver Wyman, 2017). The report says that "Severe restrictions could be placed on the EU-related business that can be transacted by UK-based firms. In this lowest access scenario, where the UK's relationship with the EU rests largely on World Trade Organisation (WTO) obligations, 40-50% of EU-related activity (approximately £18-20 billion in revenue) and up to an estimated 31-35,000 jobs could be at risk, along with approximately £3-5 billion of tax revenues per annum." (Oliver Wyman, 2017).
5 Oct 2016: UKIP leadership crisis.	Diane James quits as leader of UKIP after only 18 days in the post.
10 Oct 2016: Retailers warn of Brexit price rises.	The British Retail Consortium warned that failure to strike a good Brexit deal and reverting to WTO rules could bring tariffs on clothing of up to 16% and on meat up to 27%. The UK retail industry employs up to 200,000 EU nationals.
10 Oct 2016: EU Summit in Brussels.	PM May expressed interest in a "strong EU" as a partner. Donald Tusk, President if the European Council said, "There will be no negotiations until Article 50 is triggered by the U.K." He also said, "The basic principles and rules, namely the single market and the indivisibility of the four freedoms, will remain our firm stance." French President Hollande said, "If Theresa May wants a hard Brexit, then the negotiation will be hard."
12 Oct 2016: Brexit is no mandate for pulling out of the Common Market.	Kenneth Clarke, Conservative grandee and former Chancellor of the Exchequer, stated, "I don't think there's a mandate for pulling out of the completely open access that we have at the moment ... and we feel perfectly free to go on a voyage of discovery to see how much we can retain." Stephen Gethins said he joined the SNP because he believed in "a Scotland that was equal in the family of nations throughout the European Union".
18 Oct 2016: PM May blocks Boris appointing a long-standing aide to his staff.	Foreign Secretary Boris Johnson was disallowed to hire Will Walden, his former advisor and Director of Communications at London City Hall and his media advisor during the EU Referendum campaign. Downing Street questioned his proposed remuneration and he withdrew his application.
20 Oct 2016:	The Brussels summit, attended by the leaders of EU member states, did not focus on

Date/ Event	Details
May attends EU summit in Brussels.	the UK's exit. European Council President Donald Tusk insisted that no formal talks between the UK and the EU can begin until Article 50 is triggered. The official agenda was instead dominated by migration, trade and Russia. PM May promised that until the UK does leave the EU, it will be a "responsible, active, engaged member".
20 Oct 2016: Limited transparency for UK Parliament during Brexit negotiations.	Brexit Secretary David Davis said he wanted Parliament to be "involved throughout" the process, but added, "There will be a balance to be struck between transparency and good negotiating practice, and I am confident we can strike that balance."
22 Oct 2016: House of Lords EU committee requests vote on the Government's negotiation strategy.	The House of Lords EU Committee said Parliament should vote on the Government's negotiation strategy before Article 50, and predicted the talks would be "unprecedented in their complexity and their impact upon domestic policy" (UK Parliament, 2016).
23 Oct 2016: British Bankers' Assoc. warns major lenders are poised to hit relocate button.	Anthony Brown, head of the British Bankers' Association warned that Britain's biggest banks are preparing to relocate out of the UK in the first few months of 2017, while smaller banks are making plans to get out before Christmas. The Government's stated intention to take control of freedom of movement into the UK and the possible loss of *passporting* rights (exclusively for members of the Single Market) are given as the main reasons.
23 Oct 2016: Scottish Parliament claimed to have legal right to block Article 50.	First Minister Sturgeon and her Government in Edinburgh claimed that Section 2 of the Scotland Act of 2016 gives them legal power to block the UK from triggering Article 50.
25 Oct 2016: Tesco expects that prices will rise following the Brexit slump in the pound.	Tesco's Non-executive Chairman John Alan said he expected costs to rise and warned against an immigration clampdown. Tesco expects a 3% price hike for supermarket customers. Earlier the same month, Unilever demanded a 10% increase in prices due to the weak pound.
26 Oct 2016: Top lawyer calls for "clarity" on EU residency post-Brexit.	QC Marina Wheeler, wife of Foreign Secretary Boris Johnson, told the Joint Committee on Human Rights that, in the interests of EU nationals living in the UK and British citizens living abroad, and "on an ethical basis", clarity is needed "as soon as possible" on their post-Brexit situation. She told the Committee she didn't think EU nationals already living in the UK had recourse to Article 8 of the European Convention on Human Rights, which guarantees the right to a private and family life.
26 Oct 2016: Minister says promises made in the referendum campaign are not binding on Government.	Wales Office Minister Guto Bebb during a parliamentary debate said, "To claim that promises made in a referendum campaign are binding on government is in effect a nonsense."
27 Oct 2016: Nissan will build new models in UK.	Nissan announced that, after receiving "support" and assurances from the Government, the new Qashqai vehicles and the latest X-Trail models will be built in Sunderland, which is manufacturing over 600,000 cars a year.
2 Nov 2016: Irish government hosts Brexit forum.	Ireland's Taoiseach (Prime Minister) Enda Kenny said it was time to "intensify our engagement" and that Brexit presents the "most significant economic and social challenge of the last 50 years". Irish government held an all-island forum to examine the implications of Brexit. The question of what will happen to the Irish border in the wake of Brexit has been the subject of much debate and is identified as one of the priority areas by both the EU and UK.
3 Nov 2016: High Court rules that need Parliamentary must enact Article 50 trigger.	The High Court ruled that British MPs have the right to invoke Article 50 (or choose not to) instead of the PM through the Royal Prerogative. The Executive alone cannot remove or limit rights protected in domestic law. The Referendum Act 2015 only made provision for an advisory referendum. It gave no statutory authority to trigger Article 50. Ms Gina Miller, the businesswoman and philanthropist who brought the case against

Date/ Event	Details
	the Government, argued that because Article 50 would revoke the legislation (the European Communities Act 1972) which took Britain into Europe, it would require an Act of Parliament to leave the EU. The legal fees were crowd-funded by Miller and Remain supporters. Nigel Farage feared "a betrayal may now be near at hand" and warned of "public anger". PM May vowed to fight the High Court judgment in the Supreme Court, arguing she could execute Article 50 by Royal Prerogative and offering MPs a vote on the results of the negotiations only.
3 Nov 2016: Brexit touted as a titanic success.	Foreign Secretary Boris Johnson said he believed Europe was coming to terms with the UK's departure. He added that Britain will make a "titanic success of Brexit" and that "we are taking the machete of freedom to the brambles of EU regulation".
7 Nov 2016: Visas offer to Indian nationals made bargaining chip in trade relations with India after Brexit.	PM May was urged by Indian Prime Minister Narendra Modi during a state visit to India to accept more skilled Indian workers and students. UK business leaders pressurised the PM concede to the demand "to boost the UK economy" and help secure a post-Brexit trade deal. The EU27 without the UK has an estimated population of 450 million, while India's population is 1,310 million (hence is far more of an immigration threat).
8 Nov 2016: US Presidential election: pro-Brexit Republican Trump Wins.	Donald J. Trump won the Electoral College with 304 votes (62,985,106 votes from the people, 45.9%) compared to 227 votes (65,853,625 votes from the people, 48.0%) for Hillary Clinton. During the Presidential campaign Trump had called himself "Mr Brexit" to predict his would be a shock underdog victory (suggesting his strong approval of Leave) (Langfitt, 8 November 2016).
21Nov 2016: Britain to have lowest corporation tax of world's top 20 economies.	PM May promised in a speech to business leaders ahead of the Autumn Statement that Britain's corporation tax would be cut to 17%. by 2020 (or even earlier).
23 Nov 2016: Autumn statement reveals massive borrowing.	Chancellor of the Exchequer Philip Hammond told the Commons that Britain will borrow £233 billion over the next six years, which is £130 billion more than forecast in March. Government borrowing will be £68.2 billion this year and £59 billion next year, with an adjusted growth from 2.1% to 1.4% next year.
24 Nov 2016: Autumn Statement.	PM May committed Britain to the lowest corporation tax of the world's 20 biggest economies.
24 Nov 2016: IFS outlook for wages is "dreadful".	The Institute for Fiscal Studies (IFS) said workers would earn less in real wages in 2021 than they did in 2008, thanks to immigration.
1 Dec 2016: UK could pay EU for access to Single Market. United Government front on Brexit is questioned.	Chancellor of the Exchequer Philip Hammond and Brexit Secretary David Davis surprised observers by expressing willingness to pay to retain lucrative access to the Single Market. They reassure business that the Government present a united front on Brexit.
2 Dec 2016: Liberal Democrats win by-election in Richmond Park as Non-Brexit party.	Liberal Democrat leader Tim Farron claimed his party is "back in the big time" after it fought on the issue of Brexit and ousted ex-Conservative MP Zac Goldsmith in the Richmond Park by-election.
4 Dec 2016: Austrian general election.	During the second round re-run of the Presidential election, Alexander van der Bellen, the environmentalist and former Green Party leader who had the backing of Austria's political establishment, won by a narrow margin (53.8%). Norbert Hofer on the Austrian right remained defiant as the Freedom Party (FPÖ) candidate (46.2%).
10 Dec 2016: Supreme Court on Article 50: 7-4 decision for Remain.	The Supreme Court affirmed the High Court, meaning the Government must pass a law to execute Article 50. This will actually make it harder for the SNP and Liberal Democrats to amend any legislation and attempt to delay it.
11 Dec 2016:	Two claimants from pressure group British Influence claim that quitting the EU does not mean leaving the European Economic Area and the PM has "no mandate" for

Date/ Event	Details
Judicial review case in the High Court in a bid to keep Britain in the Single Market.	withdrawal from the Single Market as that question did not appear on the referendum ballot paper, nor was it in the Tories' 2015 general election manifesto. If the claimants win, MPs would be able to vote to stop the Prime Minister's expressed wish to make a clear and clean break with Brussels, as Parliament would have the final say on Britain's membership of the EEA.
31 Dec 2017: The Consumer Prices Index jumps 1.6%.	Inflation leaped to its highest in two and a half years. The weakening pound continued to drive prices higher: the Consumer Price Index of 1.6% was higher than the government expected.
3 Jan 2017: Ivan Rogers, Britain's EU ambassador attacks "muddled" Brexit thinking in resignation letter.	Rogers called on his staff to challenge "ill-founded arguments" and said that "serious multilateral negotiating experience is in short supply in Whitehall".
11 Jan 2017: UK employers are proposed to have to pay a £1,000-a-year fee per EU skilled worker.	Immigration minister Robert Goodwill said that the Brexit result showed voters believe that companies are relying too heavily on migrants. Under plans being considered by the government, employers would have to pay a £1,000-a-year fee for every EU skilled worker they bring in after Brexit. Goodwill suggested that the new "immigration skills charge" that would apply to non-EEC nationals should be also applied to EU citizens. The charge would be £364 for SMEs or charitable sponsors and £1,000 for medium or large sponsors per year. (Gov.uk, 2017; *Merrick*, 11 January 2017).
17 Jan 2017: Theresa May announces that UK is to leave the Single Market at a speech at Lancaster House.	Theresa May said in a speech to announce her priorities for Brexit that the UK "cannot possibly" remain within the European Single Market, as staying in it would mean "not leaving the EU at all". At the same time, Britain is maintaining the common travel area between the UK and Irish Republic and "control" of migration between the UK and the EU.
17 Jan 2017: Theresa May insists that leaving the EU with "no deal for Britain is better than a bad deal".	The PM outlined at her speech at Lancaster House the 12 priorities for Brexit negations warned European leaders that the UK is prepared to crash out of the EU if she cannot negotiate a reasonable exit deal. This would be defaulting onto the higher tariffs of World Trade Organisation rules.
17 Jan 2017: May announces a "phased process" for the financial sector.	May promised to avoid a "disruptive cliff-edge" Brexit through "a phased process of implementation". This was to address concerns in the City and financial sector, as existing *passporting* would be maintained.
17 Jan 2017: Guy Verhofstadt welcomes PM May's "clarity", adding that "the days of UK cherry-picking and Europe a la carte are over".	Guy Verhofstadt, the European Parliament's lead negotiator on Brexit, said, "Britain has chosen a hard Brexit. May's clarity was welcome – but the days of UK's cherry-picking Europe *a la carte* are over. [...] Threatening to turn the UK into a deregulated tax heaven will not only hurt British people – it is a counter-productive negotiating tactic." He also warned that the UK cannot access the Single Market, which allows the free movement of goods, services *and* workers between its members, while restricting the free movement of people.
18 Jan 2017: Brexit Secretary want to set timetable to leave the EU by 2021.	On BBC Radio 4 Brexit Secretary David Davis stated that the transition period "won't be a long time [...] a year or two". The government was under pressure from the Tory right to complete Brexit as quickly as possible.
18 Jan 2017: London's mayor warns that London businesses will struggle to survive without EU access.	At a keynote speech at the Global Economic Summit in Davos, Sadiq Khan attacked PM May's plans for a hard Brexit, warning that her tough stance could "rip Britain apart".
19 Jan 2017: PM Theresa May at the World Economic Forum in Davos.	May told leaders at the WEF that the UK will be a "world leader" on trade and promised a "bold, confident, open Britain" after Brexit. European Commissioner for Economic Affairs Pierre Moscovici said Brexit would be bad for the UK and the EU.
20 Jan 2017:	Trump was inaugurated the 45th US President. A few days before, he said that

Date/ Event	Details
Inauguration of Trump; he offers UK future trade deal.	Britain was right to vote Brexit, and that he will offer it a "quick" trade deal. He stressed his fondness for the UK and suggested that other Member States could follow its lead in leaving the EU.
20 Jan 2017: IMF warns of a bumpy Brexit ride.	International Monetary Fund Chief Christina Lagarde warned at the World Economic Forum in Davos that the Brexit deal that the UK strikes with Brussels is unlikely to be as good as the current arrangement. She also hailed the "extraordinary" response by the Bank of England, which helped the UK's economy to defy gloomy forecasts.
24 Jan 2017: Judgement of the Supreme Court on Article 50.	The Supreme Court delivered its ruling on the Government's appeal of the High Court ruling that the Royal Prerogative should not be used to trigger Brexit without a Parliamentary vote. This is seen as one of the most significant constitutional decisions in a generation. The ruling states that PM May has not the power to trigger Article 50 using a royal prerogative, but needs an authorising Act of Parliament.
24 Jan 2017: David Davis promises free trade agreement and a comprehensive customs agreement will deliver the exact same benefits as Single Market.	David Davis announced in the House of Commons, "This Government are determined to deliver on the decision taken by the people of the UK in the referendum granted to them by this House to leave the EU, so we will move swiftly to do just that." He promised "a comprehensive free trade agreement and a comprehensive customs agreement that will deliver the exact same benefits as we have" in the EU.
26 Jan 2017: First reading of the Brexit Bill in the House of Commons.	MPs started to debate the European Union (Notification of Withdrawal) Act 2017, which will start the formal process of Britain's exit from the EU by triggering Article 50 of the Lisbon Treaty.
26 Jan 2017: Davis resists EU pressure to organise the UK's exit before talks on Britain's future relations with Brussels begin.	David Davis, UK's Brexit Secretary, revealed that the Government told Brussels that a "clear idea" of Britain's future trading relationship with the EU must be sorted out before practical divorce terms can be agreed.
28 Jan 2017: PM May met President Trump at the White House.	Trump boosted May's confidence by telling her "Brexit is going to be wonderful thing for your country" as the two leaders held a joint press conference. Future economic cooperation and trade was one important discussion point, as UK-US trade is worth £150 billion per year and the US is the UK's single biggest source of foreign direct investment.
17 Feb 2017: Tony Blair calls on Brits to "rise up" against Brexit.	Tony Blair, the former Labour PM, said it was his "mission" to inspire Britons to "rise up" and change one another's minds on Brexit. He claimed that people voted in the referendum "without knowledge of the true terms of Brexit". He urged "a way out from the present rush over the cliff's edge".
28 Feb 2017: John Major attacks "unreal" Brexit vision.	John Major, former Tory PM said Britons were being offered an "unreal and over-optimistic" vision of what Brexit will look like. He called for "more charm and a lot less cheap rhetoric" from the Government toward the EU. He claimed there is "little chance" that the advantages of being part of the EU Single Market could be replicated once the UK leaves.
2 Mar 2017: House of Lords urges Tories to back Brexit Bill amendment on EU citizens.	The Lords by 358 votes to 256 called on the Government to guarantee the rights of EU citizens living in the UK within three months of Article 50 being triggered.
7 Mar 2017: Government suffers its second defeat in the Lords, who demanded a "meaningful" Brexit Bill amendment vote in the Commons.	The House of Lords by 366 votes to 268 called on the Government to hold a "meaningful" vote in Parliament on the final terms of withdrawal. The turnout in the Lords for the vote on this resolution was the largest since 1831, according to Parliament's website (House of Lords, 16 March 2017).
7 Mar 2017: House of Lords votes against 2nd referendum.	The Liberal Democrat proposed amendment to the EU (Notification of Withdrawal) Bill calling for a second referendum was easily defeated by 336 votes to 131 (majority of 205) in the House of Lords.

Date/ Event	Details
	The Archbishop of Canterbury, Justin Welby, said that a second Brexit referendum would only cause more division.
7 Mar 2017: Lord Heseltine gets sacked by the PM.	The former Conservative Deputy Prime Minister led the rebellion in the House of Lords that gave the Government its second defeat on Brexit. He said he deeply regretted the outcome of last year's EU Referendum and that "the fightback starts here". The same evening, PM May sacked him from his role advising the Government in a number of areas; e.g., its industrial strategy.
8 Mar 2017: UK Budget 2017 includes £60 billion for Brexit.	Philip Hammond presented the Budget Statement 2017. He announced that a economy performing better than expected meant more money would be set aside for Brexit, but not spent on the NHS just yet. The £60 billion reserve will help to deal with Brexit-related uncertainty.
8 Mar 2017: London Mayor Khan got greater control over skills and infrastructure.	Philip Hammond promised special powers for the London metropolitan government to prepare for "a global future" outside the EU and provides new powers in the Chancellor's Budget for London.
13 Mar 2017: UK Parliament passes the Brexit Bill.	The EU Withdrawal Bill was passed unamended by the Commons. MPs rejected amendments protecting the status of EU nationals within three months of the start of Brexit talks by 335 votes (319 Tories, 8 DUP, 6 Labour, 1 UKIP, and one independent MP) to 287 (210 Labour, 54 SNP, 9 LibDems, 3 SDLP, 3 Plaid Cymru, 2 UUP, 3 independent MPs, 1 Green, and 2 Tory rebels). It voted by 331 to 286 votes against amendments mandating Parliament to enact any Brexit deal. The House of Lords voted (274 to 118) not to challenge the Commons again over the issue of Parliament mandating an opportunity to veto the terms of exit and by 273 to 135 not to reinsert guarantees of the status of EU residents in the UK into the bill. After 70 hours of debate the 137-word Bill triggering Article 50 was approved unamended by both Houses of Parliament.
15 Mar 2017: Davis admits that the Government has not calculated the costs of a hard or no-deal Brexit.	Brexit Secretary David Davis admitted that leaving the EU without a deal would trigger new tariffs and trade barriers, and that Britain could lose financial *passporting*. He also admitted that the costs of no deal are unknown.
16 Mar 2017: The Queen gave Royal Assent to the Brexit law.	Both the Commons and the Lords agreed the text of the European Union (Notification of Withdrawal) Bill. It received Royal Assent on 16 March 2017. PM May was free to push the button on withdrawal talks.
16 Mar 2017: Scottish independence referendum "will be rejected".	The UK government rejected calls for another Scottish Independence referendum before Brexit. Theresa May said "now is not the time". Such a referendum would risk the break-up of a 300-year-old Union of nations. (On 22 July 1706, the Treaty of Union was agreed between the Scots and English Parliaments, and in the following year twin Acts of Union were passed by both Parliaments to create the United Kingdom of Great Britain with effect from 1 May 1707.)
16 Mar 2017: Dutch general election: European heave sighs of relief after pro-European parties win.	Prime Minister Mark Rutte's centre-right VVD won by a small margin, while the anti-immigration party of Geert Wilders fell short of becoming the largest in Parliament. Significant success was achieved by the pro-EU Green-Left and D66. Results were: ▪ Mark Rutte: People's Party for Freedom and Democracy, VVD: 21.3% or 33 seats (-8) ▪ Geert Wilders: Party for Freedom, PVV: 13.1% or 20 seats (+5) ▪ Sybrand van Haersma Buma: Christian Democratic Appeal, CDA: 12.4% 19 seats (+6) ▪ Alexander Pechtold: Democrats 66, D66: 12.2% or 19 seats (+7)
17 Mar 2017: Tony Blair launched the Institute for Global Change to fight populism.	Tony Blair, former Prime Minister, intervened in current politics to launch a "non-profit" organisation to create new policy ideas and fight populism. In his view, "an indifference to liberal democracy is starting to form in parts of Europe".

Date/ Event	Details
18 Mar 2017: Gordon Brown wants Scotland to gain Brexit powers.	Gordon Brown, the former Labour Prime Minister, set out a "third option" for Scotland's future based on powers being transferred after Brexit. Scotland should get, for example, power to set VAT rates and sign international treaties.
27 Mar 2017: Labour's Shadow Brexit Secretary Keir Starmer propounds "six tests".	Labour opposes any Brexit deal if it fails any of the following six tests: 1. Does it deliver the "exact same benefits" as the UK currently has as a member of the Single Market and Customs Union? 2. Does it ensure a strong and collaborative future relationship with the EU? 3. Does it ensure the fair management of migration "in the interests of the economy and communities"? 4. Does it defend rights and protections and "prevent a race to the bottom"? 5. Does it protect national security and the UK's capacity to tackle cross-border crime? 6. Does it deliver for all regions and nations of the UK? (Bean, 27 March 2017).
27 Mar 2017: Brexit Secretary Davis admits net immigration will not always fall.	Migration was a central concern to many people's vote for Brexit. Brexit Secretary David Davis said during a BBC Question Time Special that immigrant numbers will go up "from time to time" according to supply and demand. Pressed on whether the net immigration target of below 100,000 would hold, said, "I think we will get there, but the simple truth is that we have to manage this properly. You have got industries dependent on migrants, you have got social welfare, the NHS, you have to make sure they can do the work." (Rawlinson, 27 March 2017).
28 Mar 2017: Scottish Parliament votes for another Independence referendum.	The Scottish Parliament voted by 69 to 59 for seeking permission for another referendum. They formally requested of the Government powers to put a fresh Independence vote at around the time Britain leaves the EU, in spring 2019.
29 Mar 2017: Brexit Day: PM May triggers Article 50.	Britain's EU ambassador, Tim Barrow, formally executed the two-year exit process by handing a six-page letter to EU Council President Donald Tusk.
29 Mar 2017: EU expressly rejects using existing security arrangements as a bargaining chip.	Guy Verhofstadt, the European Parliament's chief Brexit negotiator, said he would not accept any attempt to "bargain" over trade if a deal is made conditional on security arrangements. One of the EU's red lines is not to negotiate over security, as this is strikes too close to the common interest. Hence, exchange of information arrangements must continue regardless of the trade negotiating outcome.
30 Mar 2017: UK lays out plans to replace all EU laws.	Brexit Secretary Davis announced the Great Repeal Bill to transpose thousands of Executive acts directly implementing EU laws into UK statutes. This would allow the UK Parliament and Welsh, Scottish and Northern Ireland administrations to scrap, amend and improve EU laws (Department for Exiting the European Union, 2017).
30 Mar 2017: Lloyd's Council announce Brussels to host Lloyds of London's European hub.	Lloyd's of London, the 329-year-old organisation and the world's largest insurance market, decided on Brussels for its new EU subsidiary. Inga Beale, Lloyd's Chief Executive, said the move will ensure business can carry on without interruption when the UK leaves EU, allowing it to continue underwriting insurance from all 27 EU and three EEA states.
30 Mar 2017: Financial institutions halt expansions in UK.	Goldman Sachs signalled it was accelerating plans to create more jobs on the Continent, with its London-based operations halting expansion. Similar announcements were made by AIG, HSBC, JP Morgan, UBS and other financial institutions.
30 Mar 2017: Davis no longer promises a Brexit deal with "exact same benefits".	Brexit Secretary David Davis admits that a Brexit deal with "exact same benefits" is not a promise, and he does not apologise for being ambitious.
31 Mar 2017: EU guidelines for Brexit published.	Draft guidelines on Brexit (XT 21001/17) were presented by European Council President Tusk for approval by the 27 Member States. The white paper recommended a phased approach and trade negotiations only after the "divorce negotiations" are finalised.

Date/ Event	Details
31 Mar 2017: A formal letter from Sturgeon is sent to Downing Street.	Scotland's First Minister delivered a letter formally asking for powers to hold another Scottish Independence referendum. Constitutional matters were reserved to Westminster, so Holyrood must ask for permission to hold such a vote to be granted under a Section 30 order.
1 Apr 2017: Spain stakes a claim over Gibraltar in the Brexit negotiations.	The draft EU Brexit negotiating guidelines contained a clause suggesting that Spain will be able to veto any future trade deal between the EU and the UK. Gibraltar's Chief Minister Fabian Picardo stressed that the territory "is not going to be a political pawn in Brexit".
4 Apr 2017: Chancellor of the Exchequer Hammond, Bank of England Governor Mark Carney, and Trade Secretary Liam Fox lead an Easter "trade offensive".	Philip Hammond arrived in New Delhi with Mark Carney hoping to open up export markets for British fintech companies. Trade Secretary Liam Fox was promoting post-Brexit opportunities on a tour of fast-growing markets: Indonesia, the Philippines, Malaysia, and the Gulf States. PM May embarked on a two-day visit to Jordan and Saudi Arabia, where trade and security dominated the talks.
5 Apr 2017: MEPs approve guidelines for the EU negotiators ahead of the Brexit talks.	Members of European Parliament approved by 516 to 133, with 50 abstentions, a resolution laying out Parliament's red lines in the coming talks, easily exceeding the two-thirds qualified majority needed. The resolution mandated "phased negotiations" and a prohibition on exit talks on things like settlement with the EU of the UK's financial liabilities and the rights of EU citizens happening in parallel with talks on a future trade arrangement. Parliament left open the possibility that UK citizens might individually apply to keep the rights they currently enjoy. The resolution also mandated that any transition arrangements for the UK after 2019, such as tariff-free access to the Single Market, can only last a maximum of three years after the UK departs. The EU believes that the UK Treasury will need to pay about €60 billion (£51 billion) to cover unpaid budget commitments, pension liabilities, loan guarantees, and spending on UK-based projects.
5 Apr 2017: Gibraltar to enjoy "the exact same benefits" as the UK in the future.	Brexit Secretary Davis told the Chief Minister of Gibraltar, Fabian Picardo, that the UK will not do any deal on a future relationship with the EU that excludes Gibraltar.
18 Apr 2017: PM May announces snap general elections on 8 June 2017.	In a surprise announcement, PM Theresa May announced, "I have just chaired a meeting of the Cabinet, where we agreed that the Government should call a general election, to be held on 8 June. […] We have also delivered on the mandate that we were handed by the referendum result. Britain is leaving the European Union and there can be no turning back." Explaining the unplanned move, May said, "I have concluded the only way to guarantee certainty and security for years ahead is to hold this election."
19 Apr 2017: The Commons approve May's plan for a general election on June 8.	To approve the snap election the PM needed two-thirds of MPs to vote in favour, to bring forward the scheduled date in 2020. The MPs approved it by 522 votes to 13.
19 Apr 2017: UK election campaign starts.	PM May set out her case for the early election, telling MPs it was right to "put our fate in the hands of the people".
24 Apr 2017: Lib Dem membership tops 100,000 after snap election call.	LibDem Leader Tim Farron said that they were the only party opposing May's "hard Brexit agenda". The party signed up 12,500 new members in one week and claimed it would reach its highest total in history "within days" (the peak of 101,768 members was reached in 1994).
24 Apr 2017: Tony Blair expresses his desire to return to frontline politics, as Britain is being "hijacked" by Brexit backers.	The former Prime Minister told BBC Radio 4 that Theresa May is not being reasonable when it comes to Britain's departure from the EU. Blair said, "I just feel we're allowing ourselves to be hijacked by what is actually quite a small group of people with a very strong ideology." He "almost feels motivated to go right back into it [politics]".

Date/ Event	Details
25 Apr 2017: Home Office urges EU nationals not to apply for permanent residence in UK.	After receiving more than 92,000 applications in 2016, the Home Office discouraged EU nationals from applying for permanent residency.
26 Apr 2017: Theresa May met with European Commission President Jean-Claude Juncker.	While the UK government described the meeting as "constructive", a very different account emerged in the *Frankfurter Allgemeine Zeitung*. According to that newspaper, May had unrealistic expectations about the length and process of negotiations. Juncker told May that the EU was "not a golf club". If the UK did not pay the "divorce" bill of about £50 billion, there would be no trade deal. He commented, "I leave Downing Street 10 times more sceptical than I was before."
26 Apr 2017: Campaigner Gina Miller launches "Best for Britain" tactical voting campaign.	Miller's "Best for Britain" campaign backed election candidates pushing for "a real final vote on Brexit, including rejecting any deal that leaves Britain worse off". She stated, "Only tactical voting in this election can ensure that parliament plays its full role in the future of this country." (Best for Britain, 2017).
27 Apr 2017: Angela Merkel tells German MPs that the UK cannot maintain the rights it has as an EU member.	The German chancellor said it was "a waste of time" to delude oneself that exit negotiations and a new trading relationship can be negotiated simultaneously. She also told the *Bundestag*, Germany's lower house of parliament that "a third country - which is what the UK will be - cannot and will not have the same rights as an EU member stat" and that "all 27 EU countries and the EU institutions agree about that."
27 Apr 2017: EU Commission expresses scepticism about a successful outcome of the Brexit negotiations.	The *Frankfurter Allgemeine Zeitung* reported that Juncker told Merkel that May was "deluding herself" and "living in another galaxy" when it came to the issue of Brexit talks (FAZ, 2 May 2017).
27 Apr 2017: EU Trade Commissioner said bloc will do post-Brexit free trade deal with UK "for sure".	Cecilia Malmstrom, the EU Commissioner for Trade, told a conference in Copenhagen that the bloc will strike a free trade deal with the United Kingdom after Brexit "for sure".
29 Apr 2017: President Tusk called a European Council on Brexit in an EU27 format (without the UK).	European Union leaders (excluding the UK) meet in Brussels and have unanimously approved guidelines following the United Kingdom's notification under Article 50TEU.
29 Apr 2017: Brexit summit: EU accepted United Ireland declaration.	The negotiation guidelines committed the EU to protecting Ireland's interests and guaranteed that Northern Ireland could automatically rejoin the EU as part of a united Ireland. This statement resulted from Irish Taoiseach Enda Kenny, Minister for Foreign Affairs Charlie Flanagan and Europe Minister Dara Murphy's political offensive making the rounds of Europe's capitals.
30 Apr 2017: Theresa May and Tim Farron position their parties on the BBC. May refuses to rule out income tax and NI increases, and signals end of pension "triple-lock".	Theresa May repeated the mantra of "strong and stable leadership" and stressed that "this is the most important election the country has faced in my lifetime". She also affirmed her viewpoint that no deal was better than a bad deal. May indicated that the Conservatives' pledge against raising taxes does not include certain taxes nor the "triple-lock" formula by which the state pension increases each year (the basic state pension rises by either 2.5%, the rate of inflation, or average earnings growth, whichever is largest). According to leader Tim Farron the Liberal Democrats can become the main party of opposition as Labour is "locked in a death spiral".
1 May 2017: Ex-PM Blair announces comeback to fight Brexit.	Former British Prime Minister Tony Blair announced a return to domestic politics to fight Brexit and help shape the debate as Britain prepares to enter negotiations on leaving the EU.
2 May 2017: Parliament is dissolved ahead of the 8 June poll.	May informed the Queen at Buckingham Palace that the parliament has been dissolved for the 8 June election.

Date/ Event	Details
2 May 2017: Tensions mount between Downing Street and Brussels as election campaign started. May accuses EU politicians of disrupting the elections.	European leaders continued to criticise May of not understanding the complexity of the Brexit negotiations. EP Chief Negotiator Guy Verhofstadt tweeted, "Any Brexit deal requires a strong and stable understanding of the complex issues involved. The clock is ticking – it's time to get real." While the UK's approach has been to discuss Brexit behind closed doors, Europe is much more transparent. Clear messages that obtaining a free trade without free movement have been dismissed as a fairy tale by European politicians. The PM gave a speech outside No 10, urging voters to "give me your backing to fight for Britain". She claims that European politicians and officials are behind "deliberately times" threat aimed at influencing election results.
3 May 2017: The EU prepares for Brexit negotiations: clarification, European citizenship and financial settlement.	Guy Verhofstadt, Parliament's coordinator for Brexit negotiations, stated before the European Parliament's Constitutional Affairs Committee's session on Brexit that the uncertainty surrounding citizenship needs to be settled as early as possible, as it is "destroying lives". He added that the two sides should aim to agree on "sound accounting principles" for a final financial settlement and that the European Parliament has to ratify any final UK-EU deal.
3 May 2017: European citizenship for British expats living in Europe and territories that voted for Remain actually remaining separately from UK England is debated.	Prof. Miguel Poiares Maduro of the European University Institute proposed that the 1.2 million British who live in the EU are given EU citizenship. He also suggested that British citizens living in the EU but not eligible to vote in the EU Referendum could potentially challenge the Brexit decision as they will lose their European citizenship. Prof. Maduro said, "There is another possibility – that is to have that some UK citizens maintain citizenship of the European Union and others won't." He concluded, "In principle nothing would prevent the territories, for example, of Northern Ireland and Scotland to stay in the European Union and for the rest of the territory of the United Kingdom no longer to be part of the European Union."
4 May 2017: Local elections in the UK are held.	The Conservative Party made major gains in local elections across the UK, fuelled by a collapse in the UKIP vote and poor results for Labour and LibDems. A total of 4,851 seats were up for grabs in 88 councils – all 32 in Scotland, 22 in Wales and 34 country councils and unitary authorities in England. Nationwide results were: ▪ Conservatives: 28 Councils (+11) and 1,899 Seats (+563) ▪ Labour: 9 Councils (-7) and 1,152 Seats (-382) ▪ Plaid Cymru: 1 Council (no change) and 202 Seats (+33) ▪ Lib Dems: 0 Councils (no change) and 441 Seats (-42) ▪ SNP: 0 Councils (-1) and 431 Seats (-7) ▪ Green: 0 Councils (no change) and 40 Seats (+6) ▪ UKIP: 0 Councils (no change) and 1 Seat (-145)
4 May 2017: Standard Chartered and JP Morgan steps up Brexit plans.	Jose Vinals, Chairman of Standard Chartered, revealed that the bank has chosen Frankfurt to become the base of its European operations. US giant JP Morgan, which employs about 16,000 people in Britain, announced that it was already planning to move hundreds of bankers from London to Frankfurt, Luxembourg and Dublin.
5 May 2017: EU State of the Union Conference is held in Florence.	Commission President Jean-Claude Juncker outlined the achievements of the EU and that growth is twice as much as in the US. He stressed that Britain could not expect any favours in negotiations and that "[t]here should be no doubt whatsoever that it is not the EU which is abandoning the UK, it is the opposite [...] they are abandoning the EU". Ex-Cabinet minister Ian Duncan Smith accused EU politicians of "dripping poison into the ears of European leaders and the Defence Secretary Sir Michael Fallon asked that the European Commission officials should keep their views to themselves".
7 May 2017: In the French general election	During the first round on 24 April 2017 of the French presidential election, the break-down was:

Date/ Event	Details
(second and final round), the pro-European Union Emmanuel Macron wins to become the next French President.	<ul><li>Emmanuel Macron (Independent): 24.01%</li><li>Marine Le Pen (Front National): 21.3%</li><li>François Fillon (Les Republicans): 19.01%</li><li>Jean-Luc Mélenchon (La France Insoumise, Unbowed France): 19.58%</li><li>Benoît Hamon (Socialists): 6.36%</li><li>Dupont-Aignan: 4.7%</li></ul>Only the top two progressed to the second round. French voters chose pro-EU Emmanuel Macron over Rightist Front National Marine Le Pen as their next President. Le Pen wanted to negotiate with the EU for return of "full sovereignty" to France, hold a referendum on "Frexit", and possibly stop using the euro as the national currency. Results were:<ul><li>Emmanuel Macron: 66.1%</li><li>Marie Le Pen:: 36.9%</li></ul>
7 May 2017: CBI warns that EU immigrants are vital to UK economy.	The Confederation of British Industry (CBI) said that British businesses send workers to and fro across the Channel and must have access to EU workers post-Brexit. Carolyn Fairbairn, the business group's Director General, said that Britain should have an immigration system "based on need" rather than an arbitrary 100,000 target.
8 May 2017: British universities could suffer damage if there are tougher curbs on immigration.	A YouGov poll reveals that more than two-thirds are against tighter restrictions on the number of young people allowed to study at British universities. These findings clash with Theresa May's plans to impose tougher controls on international students. It is estimated that international students bring in a net £2.3 billion to London universities alone.
11 May 2017: Michel Barnier and other EU negotiators visit Dublin.	Michel Barnier spoke in both houses, the Dáil Éireann (the lower house) and Seanad Éireann (upper house), about the unique position of Ireland in the EU. He set out the Commission's approach to the negotiations and assure the Oireachtas of the priority that will be afforded to Irish interests in the process, in particular avoiding a hard border.
14 May 2017: Emmanuel Macron inauguration as French president.	France's new president promises to rebuild the nation's self-confidence and "rejuvenate and relaunch" the European Union. With 39 years he becomes the youngest leader since Napoleon.
17 May 2017: Liberal Democrat Party publishes its Manifesto.	Tim Farron, LibDems leader, launches the 2017 manifesto (100 pages, 8 pages on Brexit) with the title "Change Britain's future".
18 May 2017: Conservative Party publishes its Manifesto.	Theresa May, Conservative leader and PM, launches the 2017 manifesto (88 pages, 3 pages on Brexit) with the title "Forward, Together: Our Plan for a Stronger Britain and a Prosperous Future".
19 May 2017: Net migration of 200,000 is said to be needed for economic growth.	A report from the think tank Global Future said 200,000 immigrants a year are needed to sustain growth, maintain public finances, cope with an aging population and avert "severe staff shortages" in the NHS and important industries. It that "the Government should refrain from setting artificial targets for net migration" and argues that failure to ensure net migration at a level of 200,000 could result in "catastrophic consequences for the economy" (Global Future, May 2017).
19 May 2017: Labour Party publishes its Manifesto.	Jeremy Corby, Labour Party leader, launches the 2017 manifesto (128 pages, 9 pages on Brexit) with the title "For the many, not the few".
22 May 2017: Green Party publishes its Manifesto.	Co-leaders Caroline Lucas and Jonathan Bartley published the 2017 "Green Guarantee" (26 pages long, of which 2½ pages were on Brexit) with the title "For a confident and caring Britain".
22 May 2017: European Council appoints Michel Barnier EU negotiator for Brexit	The EU-27 European Council of Foreign Affairs Ministers formally appointed Michel Barnier EU negotiator for the Brexit talks and adopted detailed negotiating directives with almost no dissent.

Date/ Event	Details
talks.	Barnier was to be the sole point of contact for the UK's negotiation team. The European Commission's chief negotiator will have an "exclusive" mandate to thrash out with Downing Street the terms of the UK's exit.
25 May 2017: Net migration falls below 250,000 annually.	The ONS released its figures on net migration, which was estimated to be 248,000 in 2016. This was a "statistically significant" fall of 84,000 compared to the 2015 statistics, the ONS said, caused by an exodus of European workers following the Brexit referendum. Net immigration from the whole of the EU was 133,000 (250,000 arriving and 117,000 leaving) in 2016, down 51,000 or 28% on 2015. Non-EU net immigration was estimated to be 175,000 (264,000 arriving and 88,000 leaving) last year, a fall of 14,000 or 8% (at most) over the previous year. The net emigration of British citizens was 60,000 (74,000 returning and 134,000 leaving) (Migration Watch website).
25 May 2017: Business leaders warn of a skills shortage.	Business leaders warned that they faced skills shortages in the housing and construction industry (bricklayers, carpenters, etc., with a vacancy of around 60,000); in health sector (social care, nursing, etc.); in farming and food processing; in hospitality and tourism; and in the railways. Sean McKee, head of policy at London Chamber of Commerce and Industry, warned that "an arbitrary gap" on immigration would slow the economy.
25 May 2017: UK Independent Party (UKIP) publishes its Manifesto.	Paul Nuttall, UKIP leader, published the 2017 manifesto (64 pages long, of which 8 pages were on Brexit) with the title "Britain Together".
29 May 2017: SNP declares it "would pursue progressive alliance".	Nicola Sturgeon announced the SNP would seek to form a coalition to pursue "progressive policies" if the general election resulted in a hung Parliament.
30 May 2017: Scottish National Party (SNP) publishes its Manifesto.	Nicola Sturgeon, SNP leader and First Minister of Scotland, published the 2017 manifesto (48 pages long, of which 4 pages were on Brexit) with the title "Stronger for Scotland".
31 May 2017: Brexit may threaten world-class research and higher education.	Top universities in London said that safeguarding the rights of 61,000 existing students and 24,800 staff from EU countries must be a priority. Agreements to continue research funding and collaboration are necessary to keep UK universities atop the international league table.
8 June 2017: UK general parliamentary election is held. The result is a hung Parliament as the Tories lose their majority.	UK parliamentary election was held and the following results were recorded (a total of 650 seats in the UK parliament and 326 seats are required for a majority; turnout was 68.73%): • Conservatives: 318 seats (-13), 13,667,231 votes/ 42.45% (+5.52%) • Labour: 262 seats (+32), 12,874,284 votes/ 39.99% (+9.54) • SNP: 35 seats (-19), 977,569 votes/ 3.04% (-1.7%) • Liberal Democrats: 12 seats (+3), 2,371,762 votes/ 7.37% (-0.5%) • DUP (NI): 10 seats, (+2), 292,316 votes, 0.91% (+0.315) • Sinn Féin: 7 seats (+3), 238,915 votes/ 0.74% (+0.17%) • Plaid Cymru: 4 seats (+1), 164,466 votes/ 0.51% (-0.08%) • Greens: 1 seat (+0), 525,371 votes/ 1.63% (-2.14%) • Independent: 1 seat (-4), 145,375 votes/ 0.45% (+0.13%) • UKIP: 0 seats (+0), 593,852 votes/ 1.84% (-10.8%)
9 June 2017: EU is ready to start Brexit negotiations after UK.	"I do strongly hope that Britain will stay ready to open negotiations. As far as the Commission is concerned, we can open negotiations tomorrow morning", said President Jean-Claude Juncker, commenting on the UK General Election results and their implications for Brexit. Theresa May formed a new government.
12 June 2017: NHS is said to be going to face a major crisis in two decades after	Experts warned that nurses from the EU joining the NHS have dropped by 96% since the EU Referendum, and hospitals are 40,000 nurses short. In April 2017 only 46 nurses arrived from the EU compared to 1,304 EU nurses that joined the NHS in July 2016. There were currently around 21,000 EU nurses working in the NHS, making up

Date/ Event	Details
Brexit.	about 7% of the total. The overall shortage of nurses was around 30,000.
19 June 2017: Macron wins a decisive majority in the parliamentary elections.	French President Emmanuel Macron won a solid majority in French parliamentary elections. His party *La République en Marche* and its centrist ally *Modem* won 350 of the 577 seats in the National Assembly. The outgoing Socialist Government and its allies were crushed, holding onto only 44 of their former 284 seats.
19 June 2017: Brexit negotiations begin (one week of negotiations).	The formal commencement of the Brexit negotiations between the UK and EU negotiating teams in Brussels (to last one week) took place. The formal process of negotiating the terms and conditions under which the UK leaves the EU begin with Phase One, with a focus on: 1. EU citizenship rights 2. the Financial settlement agreement, including issues related to the European Investment Bank (EIB), the European Development Fund (EDF) and the European Central Bank (ECB), and 3. other separation issues, such as the Northern Irish border and the goal of peace and reconciliation enshrined in the Good Friday Agreement. Phase Two, the framework for the UK's future relationship with the EU, will not commence until the European Council decides that sufficient progress has been made in Phase One toward reaching a satisfactory conclusion on the arrangements for an orderly exit (European Council, 29 April 2017; Lords Select Committee, July 2017).
20 June 2017: Terms of negotiations are agreed.	EU Chief Negotiator Michel Barnier presented the EU's Terms of Reference for the Article 50 TEU negotiations.
21 June 2017: In the Queen's Speech (the state opening of the new Parliament), Brexit bills dominate the Government agenda.	The queen attended an austere ceremony for the State Opening of the new Parliament and in her nine-minute-long speech set out the Government's legislative plans. Eight bills out of 27 related to Brexit and its impact on key industries, including a Repeal Bill to convert EU rules into UK law, and measures on customs, trade, immigration, fisheries, agriculture, nuclear power, and sanctions.
21 June 2017: Government omits to set immigration target.	The pledge to reduce immigration below 100,000 was notably left out of the Queen's Speech. Previously it had been promised to bring net immigration below 100,000 a year if Conservatives had won the general election, embracing the contentious target that the Conservatives (when Teresa May was Home secretary had missed in their last seven years of government. On 8 May PM May said, "It will be clear that we do believe that net migration should be at sustainable levels, and sustainable levels does mean the tens of thousands." Net migration to the UK has not been below 100,000 since 1997. After eight eastern European countries joined the EU in 2004, numbers rose significantly; however, most immigrants to the UK continue to come from outside the EU.
22 June 2017: The new Government promises EU citizens the right to stay in the UK under a new "settled status" scheme.	The prime minister PM May promisesaid that those who had ""made their lives and homes in the UK will be able to stay and we will guarantee their rights"". The Government envisaged giving all EU citizens the right to stay after Brexit and granting those resident for at least five years the same rights to welfare, pensions, and education as UK citizens. No cut-off date for the package has been specified.
23 June 2017: EU response to UK offer to EU nationals after Brexit is "below expectations".	European Council President Donald Tusk said the plan was "below expectations", while German Chancellor Angela Merkel said there had been "no breakthrough". The EU proposed that EU citizens in the UK and the estimated 1.2 million Britons living in EU countries continued enjoying the same rights, enforceable by the European Court of Justice (ECJ). (European Commission, 12 June 2017).
26 June 2017 May reports to the House of Commons on the start of Brexit negotiations, and clarifies "settled status" for EU citizens.	EU citizens were offered new "UK settled status" if they have resided at least five years in the UK, with equal rights as British citizenship on healthcare, education, benefits and pensions. This was not to be available automatically and anyone who qualified would have to apply for residence status, paying the fees. A cut-off date has not been set. Irish citizens residing in the UK will not need to apply for settled status to protect their entitlements (HM Government, June 2017).
26 June 2017:	Brexit Secretary David Davis made these remark at an event for business leaders

Date/ Event	Details
David Davis says Brexit is "as complicated as moon landing", and that the UK will leave the Customs Union in two years.	hosted by the Times, suggesting the UK would no longer be part of the EU Customs Union and Single Market in the interim after the UK leaves and before any trade deal (like the one between the EU and Canada) has been negotiated. He also hinted that a "new international body" would arbitrate new trade deals.
26 June 2017: Conservatives agree pact with DUP to support May Government.	A three-page Confidence and Supply agreement was reached between the Conservatives and the 10 Democratic Unionist Party (DPU) MPs to give Theresa May's minority Government a voting majority in Parliament. In exchange, an additional £1 billion would be added to the £0.5 billion allocated to Northern Ireland over the next two years, and it was promised that no Irish border poll would be held without the "consent of the people" (UK Government, 26 June 2017). DUP leader Arlene Foster said the "wide-ranging" pact was "good for Northern Ireland and the UK". Labour leader Jeremy Corbyn slammed the deal as "clearly not in the national interest". Sinn Fein's Gerry Adams claimed it enabled a "Tory Brexit which threatens the Good Friday Agreement".
29 June 2017: Labour backs vote to not stay in the Single Market, and an amendment to the Queen's Speech proposed by Chuka Umunna was rejected.	Jeremy Corbyn, the Labour opposition leader, dismissed three Labour frontbenchers for backing a vote in Parliament for the UK to stay in the Single Market after Brexit. The proposed amendment to the Queen's speech attracted the support of 101 MPs across party lines, including 49 Labour politicians who defied the leadership. It called for the government not to leave the EU without a deal; to take a parliamentary vote on the final outcome of Brexit negotiations; to set in place transitional arrangements; and to "set out proposals to remain within the Customs Union and single market".
1 July 2017: UK household savings rate falls to a 50-year low.	According to the ONS, 1.7% of income was left unspent in the first quarter of 2017, the lowest savings rate since comparable records began in 1963 due to a squeeze on incomes from rising inflation and taxes, and falling wages. Consumers continued to spend after the Brexit vote, but some say it is unsustainable.
1 July 2017: EU prepares to relocate the agencies responsible for medicines and banking regulation out of London.	EU officially launched a competition between Member States to host two London-based EU agencies, the European Medicine Agency (EMA), employing 890 staff in 2015, and the European Banking Authority (EBA), employing 189 staff. The EMA received 36,000 visitors in 2015, who booked 30,000 hotel nights, the European Council noted. The decision will be taken in November, and the EU has demanded that the UK pays the relocation bill, as Brexit was a UK decision.
6 July 2017: EU and Japan reach free trade deal.	The EU announced that a trade deal with the world's fourth-largest economy had been signed. It is scheduled to come into effect in early 2019, just when Britain is due to leave the EU trading bloc.
6 July 2017: Michel Barnier says a free trade deal is "impossible" and that Britain is deluded over trade links after Brexit.	In a fiery address, the European Commission's chief negotiator accused Westminster of selling British voters a vision of life outside the EU bloc which is "not possible" and said the UK has much more to lose from the process. Barnier said, "[The red lines] were made clear by the EU Council and the Parliament but I am not sure whether they have been fully understood across the Channel. I've heard some people in the UK argue that one can leave the Single Market and keep all of its benefits. That is not possible. [...] I've heard some people in the UK argue that one can leave the Single Market and build the Customs Unions to achieve frictionless trade. That is not possible." "We want to be ready for all eventualities, including 'no deal', a possibility that has been mentioned again recently by several British ministers," Barnier said at a meeting of employers, trade unions, and NGOs. [...] In practice, 'no deal' would worsen the 'lose-lose' situation which is bound to result from Brexit. And the UK would have more to lose than its partners."
07 July 2017: CBI urged UK to stay in the Single Market and Customs Union until a final Brexit deal is in force.	Chamber of British Industry (CBI) head Carolyn Fairbairn said that to minimise disruption, UK businesses need a "bridge" instead of a "cliff edge" to get over the Brexit deal. Representing UK businesses that employ nearly 7 million people, she said that it was "common sense" to stay in the Single Market and Customs Union until a trade deal with the EU could be put in place. A CBI survey found that 40% of its members had scaled back their investment plans due to the sheer uncertainty

Date/ Event	Details
	surrounding Brexit.
07 July 2017: King's College London plans to open a campus in Dresden.	King's has been collaborating with Technische Universität Dresden on a research initiative, known as Transcampus, since 2015, and is planning to open a campus at Dresden. It would become the first British university to open a European campus since the referendum.
07 July 2017: Free trade deals are said to have limited benefits for the UK after Brexit.	Chancellor of the Exchequer Philip Hammond suggested that the global trade deals promised by Theresa May after Brexit would have only a modest impact on the British economy, as "much of our trade with the world is service trade, where free trade agreements won't make any particular difference". With around 40% of Britain's exports being services and 60% being goods, the UK has an unusually higher proportion of services than most other exporting countries.
7 – 8 July 2017: G-20 Hamburg summit takes place.	The G-20 countries, including the EU, met in Hamburg, Germany. In a meeting with Theresa May, Donald Trump said he expected a trade deal with the UK could be done "very quickly".
8 July 2017: Government conference includes business leaders from sectors across the UK. Ministers clarify that Britain cannot retain quasi-EU membership after 2019.	Business leaders and CEOs from Lloyds of London, Rolls-Royce, easyJet, Centrica, BMW, Whitbread, HSBC, Tesco, Shell UK, BT, GSK and 25 others met with CBI, the Federation of Small Businesses, the Institute of Directors, Brexit Secretary David Davis, Business, Energy and Industrial Strategy Secretary Greg Clark and City Minister Stephen Barcleys at Chevening House in Kent to discuss Brexit strategy. During this "private" consultation with business leaders the government tried to reset relations (but they were told by Mr Davis not to talk to the press).
9 July 2017: Vince Cable says Brexit "may never happen".	Vince Cable of the Liberal Democrat Party said that he is "beginning to think Brexit may never happen". The former minister in the Coalition Tory-LibDem government said the Lib Dems' policy of having a second referendum on the final exit deal – with the choice of staying in the EU after all on the ballot paper – was "designed to give a way out when it becomes clear that Brexit is potentially disastrous". European leaders have said Britain is welcome to change its mind on Brexit. European Parliament lead Brexit negotiator Guy Verhofstadt said the UK could stay, but only on poorer terms, but French President Emmanuel Macron said the "door remains open" until negotiations end.
13 July 2017: The Head of the National Audit Office (NAO) warns Brexit could "fall apart like a chocolate orange at the first tap". Brexit is seen as the biggest-ever peacetime challenge to UK government.	Amyas Morse accused ministers of failing to deliver a united front on successfully leaving the EU and raised the alarm over the "vagueness" Government exit plans. He said it would be a "horror show" if officials of the new Customs Declaration Service (CDS), which is supposed to be in place by January 2019, were forced to manually process imports and exports. Key issues identified in the NAO report were: Revenue & Customs (HMRC) estimates that the number of annual customs declarations will rise, after March 2019, from 55 million per year to 255 million, with an estimated 180,000 traders making customs declarations for the first time. - The NAO said that the ageing system to be replaced can cope with only 100 million declarations annually. - Border taxes currently worth £34 billion may not be properly collectible. - Business confidence may suffer if traders struggle with the new system. - The £700 billion annual flow of goods between the UK and the EU may be burdened and in the worst case disrupted. - Because of the foregoing, the UK's international reputation could suffer. Amyas "expressed interest" to Brexit Secretary David Davis and officials at the Department for Exiting the European Union (Dexeu) in seeing a report on the overall preparedness across government, but the response was "vague".
14 July 2017: The Brexit Bill may lead to a constitutional contretemps – Wales and Scotland don't support the current bill, as powers are returned	Welsh First Minister Carwyn Jones called the Repeal Bill a "naked power grab" which he could not support. He warned of an "immense constitutional crisis" if the Government goes ahead without the consent of the devolved governments. The Scottish government of Nicola Sturgeon seconded Wales; in a joint statement the two governments said they could not support the bill as is, arguing that it would return powers solely to the UK Parliament and "impose new restrictions" on the Scottish

Date/ Event	Details
solely to the UK government.	Parliament and Welsh Assembly.
	Labour leader Jeremy Corbyn also demande4d concessions in six areas, including guarantees that workers' rights would be protected and the European Charter of Fundamental Rights incorporated into British law.
	The Bill must have been passed by the time the UK leaves the EU, i.e. before March 2019.
17 July 2017: Second round of Brexit negotiations takes place (one week of negotiations).	Michel Barnier asserted that no graduation to trade negotiations can take place so long as the UK was not quits as to the financial settlement issue (*aka* the "exit bill"), EU citizens' rights were not final-appealable to the European Court of Justice, and the Irish border was not settled.
	The UK did not publish a position paper on any of these issues; but some position papers were published on the website of the European Atomic Energy Community (Euratom) and the European Court of Justice as well as the so-called Repeal Bill that transfers the EU law Britain wishes to keep onto q UK statute.
	The second round of talks failed to produce a breakthrough on any of these three key issues. 113 days after Article 50 was triggered, worries about a hard Brexit were being raised by UK politicians.
17 July 2017: David Davis calls for the negotiating teams to "get down to business", and left Brussels after less than an hour of Brexit talks.	On the first day of substantive negotiations, Brexit Secretary David Davis took part in less than an hour of deliberations with Michel Barnier, the EU's chief negotiator. After a meet and greet with Barnier and wishes to the negotiating teams to "get down to business", he returned to Westminster to partake in two parliamentary votes, prompting speculation that the Government's weakness was impeding the talks and that the Conservatives' lack of a majority could hinder progress.
	At the 45-minute meeting, photographers captured an unfortunate image of the EU negotiating team with documents piled up in front of them opposite a British team with nothing, prompting mockery on social media at the UK's presumed lack of preparedness.
	The 98-strong UK negotiating team of civil servants met with their counterparts in the Commission to work on the details. Barnier said, "We will now delve into the heart of the matter. We need to examine and compare our respective positions in order to make good progress." (Boffey and Rankin, 17 July 2017).
17 July 2017: easyJet sets up a new EU hub in Austria to cope with Brexit.	The company confirmed in a statement to the markets on Friday morning that it will create the hub to "enable easyJet to continue to operate flights both across Europe and domestically within European countries after the UK has left the EU (regardless of the outcome of talks on a future UK-EU aviation agreement)."
28 Aug 2017: Third round of Brexit negotiations take place (one week of negotiations).	More than 100 UK officials partook in the third round of talks regarding citizens' rights, a financial settlement, the Ireland-Northern Ireland border, Euratom, tariff rate quotas, and other issues. During negotiations an exit bill of €75bn was claimed by EU officials.
	David Davis, the UK chief negotiator, claimed agreement on Ireland and citizens' rights. He urged the EU to be more "flexible and imaginative" in its approach to negotiations.
	Barnier insisted that, except for fruitful early stage talks on the Northern Irish border, no significant progress had been made. He stressed the need for clear UK position papers before constructive negotiations could be entered into.
	The two parties remained deadlocked on the major issues.
3 Sept 2017: UK productivity gap widens.	Chancellor of the Exchequer Philip Hammond's plan for boosting productivity in the north of England is "at the very heart" of the Government's economic ambitions as it gets ready for Brexit. In 2015 workers in London produced 63% more output per hour than workers in Wales, the least productive part of the UK. British cities make up 11 of the 50 lowest-skilled cities in Europe (Terlow, 3 September 2017).
11 Sep 2017: Debate about a referendum on a 2nd referendum.	The Petition Committee was debating a petition "Hold a referendum on the final Brexit deal" in Westminster Hall, which is the second debating chamber of the House of Commons.

Date/ Event	Details
17 Sept 2017: Foreign Secretary Boris Johnson is accused of undermining PM May in a 4,000-word article about Brexit.	Boris Johnson published an article in *The Telegraph* in which he claimed, "Once we have settled our accounts, we will take back control of roughly £350 million per week. [..] It would be a fine thing, as many of us have pointed out, if a lot of that money went on the NHS." He also stressed that he opposed paying the EU to secure temporary access to the Single Market during the transitional phase. Sir David Norgrove said he was "disappointed" the Foreign Secretary had revived Vote Leave's pledge of £350 million a week extra for the NHS. Home Secretary Amber Rudd accused Mr Johnson of being a Brexit "back-seat driver" (Johnson, 15 September 2017).
18 Sept 2017: Oliver Robbins quits after one year in the job.	Oliver Robbins, top official at the Department for Exiting the European Union (DExEU) and Theresa May's leading Brexit advisor, moved from Permanent Secretary to a co-ordinator role at Downing Street after several reported rows with Brexit Secretary David Davis.
22 Sept 2017: PM May gives speech in Florence requesting a transition period of "about" two years after Brexit, during which current trade terms would continue to apply.	The speech before politicians and the press aimed at breaking the impasse in Brexit talks, May: ▪ proposed a transition period of two years *after* UK leaves EU. ▪ announced that UK would pay its "fair share" into EU budget and "honour commitments" made while it had been a member to avoid creating "uncertainty for the remaining member states". ▪ promised the UK will be the "strongest friend and partner" of the EU. ▪ proposed a "bold new security agreement". ▪ presaged that "people will continue to be able to come and live and work in the UK, but there will be a registration system - an essential preparation for the new regime". ▪ promised that the UK and EU would continue working together on projects promoting long-term economic development and that the UK would want to "make an ongoing contribution to cover our fair share of the costs involved". ▪ aspired that there would be "no need to impose tariffs where there are none now", and that the two sides could do "so much better" than to adopt existing models. She did not clarify if the UK would be prepared to pay into the EU for two years after it leaves in March 2019, but the "bill" has been estimated to be at least €20 billion (about £18 billion). EU chief Brexit negotiator Michel Barnier called the speech "constructive" and praised the PM for her "willingness to move forward".
24 Sept 2017: German parliamentary elections take place.	Angela Merkel won a fourth term in the German parliamentary election; however, her authority has been disminished. ▪ Conservatives (CDU/CSU): 32.9.% (−8.6%), 246 seats ▪ Social democrats (SPD): 20.5% (−5.2%), 153 seats ▪ Populist right (AfD) 12.6% (+7.9%), 94 seats ▪ Liberal Democrats (FDP): 10.7% (+5.9%), 80 seats ▪ Radical left (Linke): 9.2% (+0.6%), 69 seats ▪ Greens (Grüne): 8.9% (+0.5%), 67 seats
25 Sep 2017: The fourth round of Brexit negotiations begins on 25 September after a one-week delay (one week of negotiations).	Theresa May's speech in Florence, which promised a two-year transition deal extending current EU membership until 2021, injected energy into the Brexit negotiation. The PM also promised contribution to the EU budget and financial obligations, but without citing detailed figures. Some progress was made on securing legal certainty for citizens and businesses, settling financial obligations, and agreement in principle on Northern Ireland and Ireland and their citizens' rights.
4 Oct 2017: Bank of England calls for Brexit transition deal by Christmas.	Deputy Governor Sam Woods, who heads the Prudential Regulatory Authority overseeing large lenders in the UK, said that UK and EU must agree a Brexit transition deal by Christmas or risk banks triggering their contingency plans. If no deal is reached, banks will begin a potentially disorderly shift of operations overseas.

Date/ Event	Details
5 Oct 2017: Ex-Sainsburys CEO warns that No Deal could push up food prices.	CEO Justin King said Brexit will lead to "higher prices, less choice, and poorer quality" at supermarkets.
7 Oct 2017: EU prepares for collapse of Brexit talks.	The Conservatives became embroiled in turmoil and infighting, with a leadership challenge seen as likely in the near future. German officials admitted that they had been spending as much energy on how to handle a hard Brexit as on preparing for a negotiated solution. The BDI industry federation warned its firms that they would be "naive" not to prepare for "a very hard Brexit".
9 Oct 2017: Fifth round of Brexit negotiations takes place (three days of negotiations).	Technical working groups continued discussing the three key issues. No significant progress was made, and the EU and the UK were trapped in a deadlock, especially over Britain's financial contribution. Without UK's clear definition of its financial commitments to the EU, progress toward trade negotiations was stymied.
9 Oct 2017: Theresa May sets out Brexit options including "no deal".	The No Deal scenario has begun to appear more likely, even if it neither side in the talks wanted it.
11 Oct 2017: Farm profits "may halve" after Brexit.	A report by the Agriculture & Horticulture Development Board (AHDB) suggests that average UK farm profits could fall by as much as half after Brexit; this would mean from £38,000 a year to just £15,000. The loss of £3.1 billion in EU subsidies under the Common Agricultural Policy (CAP) will also be a contributing factor. Significant exporters like cereal growers and sheep farmers might suffer the most due to increasing costs of exporting to the EU. Food prices are expected to rise overall.
14 Oct 2017: Hillary Clinton warns that No Deal would be a "very big disadvantage".	On BBC Clinton warned Britain against leaving the EU without a deal in place. She claimed Brexit had won with a "big lie". She attacked the press especially: "The big lie is a very potent tool, and we've somewhat kept it at bay in Western democracies, partly because of the freedom of the press." Asked about the UK's trading future with America, Hagzilla said, "Well, yes, but you're making a trade deal with someone [President Trump] who says he doesn't believe in trade." His predecessor Barack Obama took a different view as he explained that Britain would go to the back of the queue for trade deals with the US if it chose Brexit, as the US focus was on a trade deal with the European Union. He said this just before the referendum.
15 Oct 2017: Hillary Clinton warns that No Deal would be a "very big disadvantage".	On the Andrew Marr show on BBC, Clinton warned Britain against leaving the EU without a deal in place. She claimed Brexit had been won with a "big lie". She attacked the press especially, saying, "The big lie is a very potent tool, and we've somewhat kept it at bay in Western democracies, partly because of the freedom of the press." Asked about the UK's trading future with America, Mrs Clinton said, "Well, yes, but you're making a trade deal with someone [President Trump] who doesn't believe in trade."
15 Oct 2017: Elections in Austria: Conservatives take the victory.	The People's Party (Conservatives), led by Sebastian Kurz, at 31 the world's youngest political head (Chancellor of Austria), won the election just barely ahead of the the right-wing Freedom Party, which came-in second in the snap election. The latter was poised to enter a coalition government as the minor partner.
19 Oct 2017: Phase One of negotiations is supposed to finish.	EU leaders met to decide if enough progress had been made to begin talking about the post-Brexit relationship. Phase One of the negotiations (the separation agreement) was timetabled for completion and the agreement between the EU and UK scheduled to be drafted by 19 October 2017. In brief, negotiating a "new partnership" covering trade, foreign policy, and other issues was supposed to have started, but had not done.
19 Oct 2017: May publishes an open letter to EU citizens.	PM May published an open letter to EU citizens before she joined the EU-27 summit in Brussels, which stated: "I have been clear throughout this process that citizens' rights are my first priority. And I know my fellow leaders have the same objective: to safeguard the rights of EU nationals living in the UK and UK nationals living in the EU."
20 Oct 2017:	EU President Jean-Claude Juncker was quoted saying, "I hate the no deal scenario. I

Date/ Event	Details
Juncker says, "The no deal scenario is not an option for us" at the European Council Brexit meeting.	want a fair deal", following EU leaders' discussions. More progress was needed on citizens' rights, Ireland and Northern Ireland, and the financial settlement. Given no results, the EU leaders were not willing to move on to Phase Two, but decided to review their judgement at the European Council December summit. EU leaders were planning not only to press ahead with Brexit but also with the "Future Of Europe" roadmap in November; the Social Summit in Gothenburg; and the Eurozone Summit in Estonia in December.
22 Oct 2017: The Spanish government pledges that British expats will not have their lives "disrupted".	Spain's Foreign Minister, Alfonso Dastis, sought to reassure to Britons living in Spain, saying, "I do hope that there will be a deal". "If there is no deal [however] we will make sure that the lives of ordinary people who are in Spain, the UK people, is not disrupted". Over 17 million Brits visit Spain every year and many of them live or retire in Spain.
31 Oct 2017: Hard Brexit can result in losses of up to 75,000 financial services jobs.	The Bank of England estimated that 75,000 jobs in the financial sector could be lost if Brexit resulted in No Deal. This number chimes with the report of the Centre of London think tank, which predicted 70,000 jobs would be lost if the UK lost access to the Single Market. In April the Bank of England ordered financial firms to draw up contingency plans for the several Brexit outcomes. Impacts on the UK economy must be mitigated.
31 Oct 2017: UK economic growth is topped again by Eurozone growth in third quarter in 2017.	The Eurozone's GDP grew by 0.6% in Q3 versus 0.4% of UK's GDP. In Q2 Eurozone GDP grew by 0.7% compared to 0.3% in the UK (which was the weakest of the G7). In 2017 GDP grew by 2.5% for the Eurozone compared to 1.5% in the UK. After the financial crisis the Eurozone is experiencing a cyclical recovery, while the UK was hit by a rise of inflation due to the post-Brexit sterling drop. Business investment was also weak due to uncertainty about trade arrangements after March 2019. On the other hand, the UK unemployment rate of 4.3% was lower than EU's (declining) unemployment rate of 8.9%. Eurozone inflation in October felt back to 1.4%, whilst UK inflation climbed to 3% in September, a five-year high. The economy of the Eurozone and the UK were drifting apart as both parties approach 2019.
1 Nov 2017: Brexit talks are resumed on 9 November.	Both the EU and the UK were interested in accelerating negotiations and planned three more rounds. David Davis aimed to achieve a transition deal for the UK by early next year.
2 Nov 2017: Bank of England raises UK interest rates for first time since 2007.	Brexit was considered the biggest factor in the next move on interest rates – either up or down – by the Bank of England. In the event, the Bank raised its rate from 0.25% to 0.50% for the first time in a decade. As a result sterling dropped more than 1% to $1.30 and the euro climbed by a cent to nearly €1.12. Inflation was expected to stay at its 2% target given modest wage rises yet rising prices in the shops. A devalued pound should boost exports, offsetting weaker consumer spending. Interest rates were expected to increase to 2% by the middle of 2021.
07 Nov 2017: John Bercow demands that the Government must publish secret reports about the economic impact of Brexit.	Speaker of the House John Bercow demanded that David Davis's Brexit Department publishes the 58 secret assessment reports about how Brexit will impact different sectors representing nearly 88% of the economy of the UK, ranging from tourism to pharmaceuticals. Activists threatened the Government with legal action if these reports were not made public. David Davis denied the existence of 58 separate sector reports. Minsters argued their publication would undermine the UK negotiation position. Davis asked for more time before handing over the secret report(s) to the House of Commons. Other reports should be available, too, about Brexit's impact on the UK regions.
9-10 Nov 2017: Brexit negotiations continue (two days of negotiations).	Negotiators meet on 9 and 10 November 2017 to break the deadlock. Barnier said the UK had provided "useful clarifications" on guaranteeing rights, although more work needed to be done on some points, including the rights of families and exporting welfare payments. One European Commission paper proposed that Northern Ireland remains a member of the Single Market (following most EU

Date/ Event	Details
	rules) to forestall a hard border.
9 Nov 2017: PM May made plans to set into law the UK's exit date and time.	Theresa May said the EU Withdrawal Bill would be articulated formally to commit the UK to Brexit at 23:00 GMT on Friday, 29 March 2019. She said, "Let no one doubt our determination or question our resolve, Brexit is happening". She added, "We will not tolerate attempts from any quarter to use the process of amendments to this Bill as a mechanism to try to block the democratic wishes of the British people by attempting to slow down or stop our departure from the European Union." MPs had previously been told that there had been 300 amendments and 54 new clauses proposed (*The Telegraph*, 9 November 2017).
10 Nov 2017: The UK is given two weeks to clarify key issues.	Barnier bespoke the deadline after meeting David Davis for talks about citizens' rights, the Irish border, and the UK's "divorce bill". On 10 November the UK reached the halfway point of the exit process.
10 Nov 2017: Lord Kerr says Article 50 can still be revoked.	The architect of Article 50 of the Lisbon Treaty 2009, former diplomat and now UK Supreme Court Justice Lord Kerr, confirmed that sending an Article 50 letter is not an irreversible act and that the Brexit process might be still halted. He warned that the "disastrous consequences" are "becoming ever clearer", and urged a pause to rethink.
4 December 2017: Brexit deadlock between PM May and President Juncker.	The May-Juncker meeting that was to conclude Phase One of the Brexit negotiations was disrupted by May's coalition partner, the DUP, which dissented from "alignment" of Northern Ireland with EU laws. May had to leave unfinished business in Brussels.
6 December 2017: Impact assessments non-existent.	Brexit Secretary David Davis told MPs that the Government has done essentially no impact assessments of Brexit on the UK economy.
8 December 2017: The UK and EU announce "agreement in principle" on Phase One of Brexit negotiations.	PM May and President Junker jointly announced that an agreement was reached on which Junker will recommend EU-27 leaders to move to Phase Two. The agreement committed the UK to "full alignment" with EU customs rules in Northern Ireland and to "no new regulatory barriers" between Northern Ireland and the rest of the UK. The agreement also included protection of the rights of EU citizens in the UK and *vice versa* after Brexit, and the terms of the UK's financial settlement with the EU.
13 December 2017: Parliament enacts a "meaningful vote" for itself on any Brexit deal.	Parliament gave itself the legal guarantee of a vote on any final Brexit deal struck with Brussels, after 11 conservative "rebels" voted for an amendment to this effect, resulting in a 309 to 305 vote. One rebel, Dominic Grieve, received a death threat.
15 Dec 2017: The EU-27 agreed that sufficient progress has been made to advance the talks to Phase Two.	At the European Council Summit the EU-27 leaders decided that "sufficient progress" had been made to move Brexit to Phase Two. This will cover the completion of the "divorce bill" (*ca.* €45 billion), and the terms of a transitional period and the future relationship. A formal trade agreement can only be finalised once the UK has left the EU on 29 March 2019 and become a "third country".
Autumn 2018 Completion of Brexit negotiations.	The Commission intends for negotiations to be complete by autumn 2018, to allow sufficient time for EU approval before the UK's planned exit date of 29 March 2019.
2019: Approval of the "final deal".	The Brexit deal must be approved by the national parliaments of each EU Member State, as well as by both the EU Council and the European Parliament by March 2019.
29 Mar 2019: All negotiations come to an end.	The two-year timeframe set out in Article 50 TEU is to end on 29 March 2019. On 30 March 2019 the UK is expected to have left the EU, including the Single Market.
30 Mar 2019 ongoing: Transitional arrangements may be made to provide a framework for a future EU-UK relationship.	Transitional arrangements will have to be clearly defined, time-limited, and subject to effective enforcement mechanisms. In the case of a time-limited prolongation of the validity in British law of the EU *acquis*, "this would require existing Union regulatory, budgetary, supervisory, judiciary and enforcement instruments and structures to apply" (European Council, 29 March 2017).
May or June 2019: European Parliament elections are timetabled to be held.	The UK was to elect 73 out of 751 Members of the European Parliament (MEPs), but due to its exit from the EU, the UK will not participate. After joining the European Communities on 1 January 1973, the UK has participated in 8 European Parliamentary elections.

1.3.3 Legal challenges to trigger Article 50

The EU Referendum result was "advisory" only and not legally binding, according to the European Union Referendum Act 2015, which merely provided that the referendum should be held, not whether or how the outcome should be enforced. A UK referendum is only enforceable if the Act of Parliament mandating it says so. In practical terms this would have meant that the Act would have provided some mechanism, such as suing the government in court, if it did not obey the will of the people. On 3 November 2016 the High Court stated that "a referendum on any topic can only be advisory for the lawmakers in Parliament", – taking into account that Parliament could repeal its own Act notwithstanding that it had previously made the result binding. Nigel Farage accepted that the referendum result was technically advisory only, but said, "I would now wish to see constitutional change to make referendums binding" (Marr, 6 November 2016).

Article 50 of the Treaty of Lisbon gives any Member State the right to exit unilaterally, and outlines a process for doing so. Before this Treaty came into force in 2009 there was no orderly way to leave the EU. The process provides the leaving Member State two years to negotiate an exit deal, and once that timetable is set in motion, it cannot be stopped except by unanimous consent of all other Member States. The final deal must be approved by a qualified majority of Member States and may be vetoed by the European Parliament.

A private plaintiff brought a legal challenge before the High Court in October 2016 to clarify the UK constitutional requirements for exit from the European Union. "The People's Challenge" was a coalition of convenience who had crowdfunded £175,000 to challenge the Brexit process in court. The lead complainants were Gina Miller, an investment manager, and Mr Deir Dos Santos, a hairdresser, both UK citizens resident in the UK. Their suit was supported by the so-called "People's Challenge" in the name of Graeme Pigney and other UK citizens resident in different parts of the UK and in other EU states. They argued that individual members of the Cabinet have no legal power to trigger Article 50 of the Lisbon Treaty because it would nullify existing rights of persons like themselves under the European Communities Act 1972 (and later ratification acts) and leave the European Union without the prior authorisation of Parliament and MPs. An argument put for the "expat" Interveners at the hearing was that Parliament had conferred a legislative competence on the EU institutions by the 1972 Act, and thus had changed the constitutional settlement in the UK.

At the hearing on 13 October, the three judges sitting as a divisional court in the High Court (the Lord Chief Justice, the Master of the Rolls and Lord Justice Sales) concluded that where an exercise of the Royal Prerogative[2] would remove legal rights, derived

---

2　　The Royal Prerogative refers to the original sources of all legal authority in the UK, and is accepted by the courts as a legal basis over and above Acts of Parliament on which Ministers of the Crown may act. Over time, the Crown's Prerogatives have been limited by courts or by Acts of Parliament which provide the alternative basis for ministers to act on, but the power to make treaties with foreign powers still falls within the Royal Prerogative.

from EU law but made available in domestic law by Parliament through the European Communities Act, only Parliament can legislate for such rights to be removed. The High Court in Belfast dismissed related claims that the Prime Minister's use of Prerogative to execute Article 50 was limited by the terms of the Northern Ireland Act 1998 and the Belfast Good Friday Agreement. Following the High Court ruling, Parliament must have a vote on authorising the Prime Minister to execute Article 50.

Requiring the Prime Minister to obtain legislative authorisation from Parliament was contested by the Government on the basis that the electorate had given the Government a clear instruction to leave the EU in the referendum held on 23 June 2016. The Government wanted to avoid the legislative authorisation from Parliament to be quick and wholly procedural. However, some MPs and Lords saw this is a chance to try and get the Government to reveal more of its Brexit negotiating position and the Parliamentarians could push their demands. Others considered it as a constitutional crisis for Parliament to refuse to authorise notification and to ignore the result of the referendum.

The court in *R. (Miller) v. Secretary of State for Exiting the European Union [2016] EWHC 2768 (Admin)* had to decide on the constitutionally correct procedure for formally notifying the President of the European Council that the UK intends to exit the EU pursuant to Article 50 of the Treaty on European Union. The case was unprecedented, so judges took it upon themselves to address the complaint's issues on the basis of first principles, even though they had the 1972 Act in front of them. Basing their reasoning on first principles gave them room to decide at their own pleasure what the first principles would be, and what weight each would have as against the others in the particular circumstances of the case. The key arguments of claimants were that:

- Ministers can't use prerogative (executive power) to frustrate legislation.
- The referendum act gave ministers no right to use the Prerogative to execute Article 50 (it was not mentioned at all).
- Ministerial prerogative is used to enter into treaties (such as EU membership) but cannot be used to change the constitution.
- The Government must demonstrate that Parliament expressly handed over powers to ministers to supersede legislation.
- Parliament did not intend the 1972 Act to create ministerial prerogative power to sweep away EU membership.
- None of the European Union-related acts created over 40 odd years gave ministers power to execute Article 50.
- Only an Act of Parliament can take away the rights linked to the EU that have been created since 1972 membership.

The Government, dissatisfied with the judgment of the High Court, appealed the case to the Supreme Court. On 24 January the Supreme Court ruled that the execution of Article 50 of the Lisbon Treaty affects the rights of British and therefore the Royal

Prerogative may not be invoked. Lord Neuberger said, "By a majority of eight to three, the Supreme Court today rules that the government cannot trigger Article 50 without an act of Parliament authorising it to do so. [...] Withdrawal effects a fundamental change by cutting off the source of EU law, as well as changing legal rights. The UK's constitutional arrangements require such changes to be clearly authorised by Parliament." (Watts and Fenton, 24 January 2017).

Because Scotland opposed Brexit, the Scottish Government tried to claim that Article 50 could not be triggered without the Scottish Parliament's separate consent, on the grounds that the Scotland Act 2016 prohibits the PM to interfere with devolved matters reserved to the Scottish parliament. Yet the Supreme Court rejected this claim (because it is not a devolved matter after all), as well as the similar claim on behalf of the Welsh Assembly that it has a legal right to be consulted by UK ministers over triggering Brexit. First Minister Sturgeon pledged to hold a Holyrood vote on the matter regardless of the ruling. The Welsh Government's chief legal officer Mick Antoniw called the ruling "a victory" in upholding the sovereignty of Parliament.

In a response to the judgement, Mr Davis told MPs that he was "determined" Brexit should go ahead as planned. MPs immediately began debating the European Union (Notification of Withdrawal) Act 2017 in the House of Commons. Labour tabled a series of amendments, one seeking to guarantee that Parliament gets to vote on any final deal with the EU. The final bill, containing just two clauses only 137 words long, was allotted five days for debate in the Commons.

At the end of February, three former Prime Ministers – John Major, Gordon Brown and Tony Blair – raised concerns about hard Brexit and called for power-sharing with the devolved Governments, Blair even advocated a redo for a chance to change the public's mind on Brexit, arguing that people were misinformed when they voted for Brexit. He stated, "The people voted without knowledge of the true terms of Brexit. As these terms become clear, it is their right to change their mind." These interventions by former PMs clearly showed that Brexit is just too important to leave it to the government alone to make the decisions. Downing Street said it was "absolutely committed" to seeing Brexit through and Iain Duncan Smith, former Tory leader responded that Blair's comments were arrogant. Nigel Farage said Blair was "yesterdays man". Nick Clegg, former Deputy Prime Minister for the Liberal Democrats said he "agreed with every word".

1.3.4 The UK government's Brexit plan

By the end of 2016 the Government still had provided no information on the negotiation strategy or plan for Brexit. Even Britain's Ambassador to the European Union, Ivan Rogers, had no details. When he resigned on 3 January 2017, he remarked that Government leaders have no understanding of how the EU operates, by what mechanisms and rules (exactly the focus of Chapter Three below). Sir Ivan had been expected to stay in his post until at least the end of 2017; however, clear tensions with Downing Street were laid bare in mid-December when it was reported that he had warned the Government it could take 10 years to complete a post-Brexit trade deal with the EU. Sir Ivan Rogers sent the following email to his staff, expressing his dismay that the Government lacked an in-depth understanding of how to conduct the negotiations:

Dear All,

[...] As most of you will know, I started here in November 2013. My four-year tour is therefore due to end in October – although in practice if we had been doing the Presidency my time here would have been extended by a few months.

[...] I have therefore decided to step down now, having done everything that I could in the last six months to contribute my experience, expertise and address book to get the new team at political and official level under way.

[...] My own view remains as it has always been. We do not yet know what the government will set as negotiating objectives for the UK's relationship with the EU after exit.

[...] Serious multilateral negotiating experience is in short supply in Whitehall, and that is not the case in the Commission or in the Council.

The government will only achieve the best for the country if it harnesses the best experience we have – a large proportion of which is concentrated in UKREP – and negotiates resolutely. Senior ministers, who will decide on our positions, issue by issue, also need from you detailed, unvarnished – even where this is uncomfortable – and nuanced understanding of the views, interests and incentives of the other 27.

The structure of the UK's negotiating team, and the allocation of roles and responsibilities to support that team, needs rapid resolution. The working methods which enable the team in London and Brussels to function seamlessly need also to be strengthened.

On a personal level, leaving UKREP will be a tremendous wrench. I have had the great good fortune, and the immense privilege, in my civil service career, to have held some really interesting and challenging roles: to have served four successive UK prime ministers very closely; to have been EU, G20 and G8 Sherpa; to have chaired a G8 Presidency and to have taken part in some of the most fraught, and fascinating, EU negotiations of the last 25 years – in areas from tax, to the MFF to the renegotiation.

[...] I hope you will continue to challenge ill-founded arguments and muddled thinking and that you will never be afraid to speak the truth to those in power. I hope that you will support each other in those difficult moments where you have to deliver messages that are disagreeable to those who need to hear them.

I hope that you will always provide the best advice and counsel you can to the politicians that our people have elected, and be proud of the essential role we play in the service of a great democracy.
(BBC, 4 January 2017)

There seems to be a lack of governance and collective responsibility for negotiating an exit. This is evident from the conflicting messages and "ideas" from government officials. Early in October 2016 at the Conservative conference in Birmingham, PM May announced that she would execute Article 50 and formally start Britain's withdrawal from the European Union at the end of March 2017. The previous August, May had stated that no parliamentary vote invoking Article 50 and opening Brexit negotiations was needed. The majority of MPs in the Commons, a total of around 480 (out of 650), campaigned for Britain to stay in the European Union at the last election (Swinford, 27 August 2016), hence, a democratic parliamentary vote could be risky and possibly bring the process to a halt. The PM considered the Supreme Court decision binding and submitted the Brexit Bill to the Commons.

1.3.5 The process of triggering Article 50 and beyond

Ironically, it was the diplomat Lord Kerr of Kinlochard who drafted the text that lays out the procedure for leaving the European Union. He had done this as part of an effort to draw up an EU constitution in the early 2000s, and it ended up in the Lisbon Treaty that came into force in 2009. Article 50, in just 264 words in five paragraphs, spells out how a Member State can voluntarily exit the EU. It specifies that a leaver should notify the European Council of its intention, negotiate a deal on its withdrawal, and establish a legal basis for future relations with the EU. Greenland was the only other country ever to vote to leave the EU, but that was from the EEC, the precursor to the EU, long before Article 50 had been drafted.

Article 50 of Treaty of Lisbon states:

1. Any Member State may decide to withdraw from the Union in accordance with its own constitutional requirements.
2. A Member State which decides to withdraw shall notify the European Council of its intention. In the light of the guidelines provided by the European Council, the Union shall negotiate and conclude an agreement with that State, setting out the arrangements for its withdrawal, taking account of the framework for its future relationship with the Union. That agreement shall be negotiated in accordance with Article 218(3) of the Treaty on the Functioning of the European Union. It shall be concluded on behalf of the Union by the Council, acting by a qualified majority, after obtaining the consent of the European Parliament.

3. The Treaties shall cease to apply to the State in question from the date of entry into force of the withdrawal agreement or, failing that, two years after the notification referred to in paragraph 2, unless the European Council, in agreement with the Member State concerned, unanimously decides to extend this period.
4. For the purposes of paragraphs 2 and 3, the member of the European Council or of the Council representing the withdrawing Member State shall not participate in the discussions of the European Council or Council or in decisions concerning it. A qualified majority shall be defined in accordance with Article 238(3)(b) of the Treaty on the Functioning of the European Union.
5. If a State which has withdrawn from the Union asks to rejoin, its request shall be subject to the procedure referred to in Article 49.

On 29 March 2017 PM May executed the two-year exit process of Article 50. Britain's new Ambassador to the EU, Sir Tim Barrow, formally notified EU Council President Donald Tusk in a six-page letter. In a statement in the Commons, the PM said, "Today the government acts on the democratic will of the British people and it acts too on the clear and convincing position of this House." She added, "The Article 50 process is now under way and in accordance with the wishes of the British people the United Kingdom is leaving the European Union. [...] This is an historic moment from which there can be no turning back." Mrs May said it was a "moment of celebration for some, disappointment for others" and promised to "represent every person in the whole United Kingdom" during the negotiations – including EU nationals, whose status after Brexit has yet to be settled. She added that while the UK would remain a "best friend and neighbour" to its EU partners, it would also look beyond the borders of Europe, saying the country can "look forward with optimism and hope and to believe in the enduring power of the British spirit" (Department for Exiting the European Union, 30 March 2017).

Shortly after Article 50 was triggered, many global banks and insurance companies announced subsidiaries in EU countries and/or staff moves in order to continue to have access to the European Common Market. For example, US insurance company AIG announced a subsidiary in Luxembourg, where currently it has only a branch. Goldman Sachs, which employs 6,000 staff in London, claimed it plans to move hundreds of bankers to Frankfurt and Paris. HSBC planned to move 1,000 investment banking jobs from London to Paris. Swiss bank UBS indicated that 1,000 of its 5,000 staff could shift, possibly to Frankfurt or Madrid. US bank JP Morgan announced that 4,000 UK jobs are at risk. Lloyds Banking Group has chosen to convert its Berlin branch into a subsidiary. Xavier Rolet, chief executive of the London Stock Exchange, has warned that 230,000 finance jobs could disappear. On the other hand, Mark Carney, the Governor of the Bank of England, has played down the risks. The concern is not only the loss of skilled workers, but also a significant reduction of tax revenue.

1.3.6 Setting the rules: UK negotiating objectives *vs.* EU negotiating guidelines

PM May set out the government's 12 negotiating objectives for leaving the European Union at a speech at Lancaster House on 18 January 2017. The overarching aim was to "get the right deal abroad while ensuring a better deal for ordinary working people". To reach these objectives, the Government would seek a new and equal partnership between the UK and EU. The following five goals were set for the negotiations to achieve: (1) certainty and clarity, (2) a stronger Britain, (3) a fairer Britain, and (4) a truly global Britain, and (5) a phased approach to support the 12 negotiation objectives. These were summarised by the PM in her speech, as follows:

1. *Certainty and clarity*: Whenever we can, we will provide it. And we can confirm today that the Government will put the final deal that is agreed between the UK and EU to a vote in both Houses of Parliament.
2. *Control of our own laws*: We will bring an end to the jurisdiction of the European Court of Justice in Britain. Because we will not have truly left the European Union if we are not in control of our own laws.
3. *Strengthen the Union*: We must strengthen the precious Union between the four nations of the United Kingdom. We will work very carefully to ensure that – as powers are repatriated back to Britain – the right powers are returned to Westminster and the right powers are passed to the devolved administrations. We will make sure that no new barriers to living and doing business within our Union are created.
4. *Maintain the Common Travel Area with Ireland*: We will work to deliver a practical solution that allows the maintenance of the Common Travel Area with the Republic of Ireland, while protecting the integrity of the United Kingdom's immigration system.
5. *Control of immigration*: The message from the public before and during the referendum campaign was clear: Brexit must mean control of the number of people who come to Britain from Europe. We will continue to attract the brightest and the best to work or study in Britain but there must be control.
6. *Rights for EU nationals in Britain, and British nationals in the EU*: We want to guarantee these rights as early as we can. We have told other EU leaders that we can offer EU nationals here this certainty, as long as this is reciprocated for British citizens in EU countries.
7. *Protect workers' rights*: As we translate the body of European law into our domestic regulations, we will ensure that workers' rights are fully protected and maintained.
8. *Free trade with European markets*: As a priority, we will pursue a bold and ambitious Free Trade Agreement with the European Union. This agreement should

allow for the freest possible trade in goods and services between Britain and EU member states. It cannot mean membership of the EU's Single Market. That would mean complying with European Court of Justice rulings, free movement and other EU rules and regulations without having a vote on what those rules and regulations are. And because we will no longer be members of the Single Market, we will not be required to contribute huge sums to the EU budget. If we contribute to some specific EU programmes that we wish to participate in, it will be for us to decide.

9. *New trade agreements with other countries*: It is time for Britain to become a global trading nation, striking trade agreements around the world. Through the Common Commercial Policy and the Common External Tariff, full Customs Union membership prevents us from doing this – but we do want to have a customs agreement with the EU and have an open mind on how we achieve this end.

10. *The best place for science and innovation*: We will continue to collaborate with our European partners on major science, research and technology initiatives.

11. *Cooperation in the fight against crime and terrorism*: We want our future relationship with the EU to include practical arrangements on matters of law enforcement and intelligence.

12. *A smooth, orderly Brexit*: We want to have reached an agreement about our future partnership by the time the two year Article 50 process has concluded. From that point onwards, we expect a phased process of implementation. We will work to avoid a disruptive cliff-edge.

(Department for Exiting the European Union, 2 February 2017)

Initially the British government did not wish to publicise their negotiation strategy or position at all. To many people, including politicians, it was even unclear if there was any plan by the government to address the Brexit negotiations. The lack of understanding of the basic rules of how the EU works (such as the four principles) and the illusion that the UK could negotiate, behind closed doors, a better deal by leaving the Union than by being part of it, was either a deliberate ploy to unite the Remain and Leave camp behind the Prime Minister, or it was sheer incompetence on the part of those advising the Government. There were even discussions if the Parliament should have a final say on the outcome of the Brexit negotiations, but a "meaningful vote", as recommended by the House of Lords, was rejected by the House of Commons.

The secrecy, vagueness, and divided views on the UK side were in stark contrast with the EU and its 27 remaining Member States. Only two days after the UK triggered Article 50, on the 31st March 2017, the European Council President Donald Tusk presented Brexit negotiations draft rules, which were approved by the Member States on 29 April 2017. The document clearly stated, "a non-member of the Union, that does not live up to the same obligations as a member, cannot have the same rights and enjoy the same benefits as a member. In this context, the European Council welcomed the recognition by the British Government that the four freedoms of the Single Market are indivisible and that there can be no 'cherry picking'." The document lays out a phased approach:

1. Disentanglement of the UK from the EU and all of its rights and obligations. This should provide clarity and legal certainty to citizens, businesses, stakeholders, and international partners.
2. Agreements on a future relationship between the EU and UK can only start once the UK has become a third country. Trade negotiations can only start once "sufficient progress has been made in the first phase towards reaching a satisfactory agreement on the arrangements for an orderly withdrawal."
3. Transitional arrangements may be made to provide a framework for the future relationship. These need to be clearly defined, limited in time, and subject to effective enforcement mechanisms. In case of a time-limited prolongation of Union *acquis*, "this would require that existing Union regulatory, budgetary, supervisory and enforcement instruments and structures to apply".

The document states that the two-year timeframe set out in Article 50 will end on 29 March 2019. It also highlights the priority of negotiations on guarantees for EU citizens living in the UK, for EU businesses, a single financial settlement that respects the obligations on both sides, recognition of the Good Friday Agreement, and a partnership on security and defence (European Council, 31 March 2017).

Gibraltar, where 96% of the population voted to remain, was specifically mentioned in Point 22 of the draft Brexit negotiation rules, which states, "After the United Kingdom leaves the Union, no agreement between the EU and the United Kingdom may apply to the territory of Gibraltar without the agreement between the Kingdom of Spain and the United Kingdom." PM May's 2200-word Art 50 notification letter to the EU did not mention Gibraltar; however, British politicians strongly reject Gibraltar becoming a bargaining chip.

The 32,000 Gibraltarians in the 2002 Gibraltar sovereignty referendum voted by 98.5% to remain part of the UK. This might be explained by its special status as a tax haven, which has attracted 8,464 registered offshore companies and the opportunity to passport an EU licence in financial services such as insurance and re-insurance, EU-wide pensions and banking and administration. As one might expect, an offshore tax haven on their doorsteps is a constant irritant to the Spanish government.

1.3.7 General elections, party positions, and red lines

Despite having rejected elections before May 2020, Prime Minister Theresa May announced a snap general election at 11am on 18 April 2017. To justify this surprising decision, she argued, "At this moment of enormous national significance there should be unity here in

Westminster, but instead there is division. The country is coming together but Westminster is not. [...] If we do not hold a General Election now, their political game-playing will continue and the negotiations with the European Union will reach their most difficult stage in the run-up to the next scheduled election. Division in Westminster will risk our ability to make a success of Brexit and it will cause damaging uncertainty and instability to the country."

European Commission President Jean-Claude Juncker, accompanied by Martin Selmayr, his Cabinet head, visited PM May at Downing Street on 26 April. After the meeting he said, "I'm leaving Downing Street ten times more sceptical than I was before." In a conversation between Juncker and Chancellor Angela Merkel following what the FAZ described as a disastrous meeting, Mrs Merkel said that Mrs May is "living in another galaxy". Downing Street was calling the "revelations" of the (internal) meeting between Theresa May and Mr Juncker published in the European press "gossip"; however, considering that it took the UK government until 17 January to grasp that they cannot re-negotiate the four principles on which Europe is build, the government seemed ill-advised about what can and cannot be achieved in negotiations (FAZ, 1 May 2017).

The "red lines" laid down before the negotiations started may be summarized as follows.
The UK government's red lines (see also 12 priorities for negotiations with the EU 27, above):

- Take back control of borders: record levels of migration had "put pressure on public services"
- No longer be under the jurisdiction of the European court of justice: "We will not have truly left the European Union if we are not in control of our own laws"
- "Explicitly rule out membership of the EU's single market" because it is incompatible with migration controls
- Leave the Customs Union, but try to strike a separate deal as an "associate member" to make trading as "frictionless as possible"
- Get exempt from having to "contribute huge sums to the EU budget", but simply pay towards specific programmes
- Seek a "new, comprehensive, bold and ambitious free trade agreement" with the EU; build trading relationships with countries beyond Europe as part of a "global Britain" strategy
  (*The Guardian*, 17 January 2017).

The European Union's red lines (based on the negotiation guidelines of 29 April 2017):
The EU has set out negotiation guidelines which include the need for a phased approach to negotiations. This requires progress on the terms of Britain's withdrawal, including settling financial commitments, before talks on a future trading relationship can start. The EU insist that negotiations should be transparent and open at all times, which

contrasts with PM May's approach: to negotiate behind closed doors and do not even brief the UK Parliament on a regular basis. The Eus red lines are:

- UK citizens in the EU and EU citizens in Britain should receive "reciprocal" treatment
- UK should pay toward costs to the EU that "arise directly from its withdrawal"
- Transitional arrangements should be time-limited to three years and be enforced by the EU's Court of Justice
- A final deal should not include a "trade-off" between trade and security co-operation
- UK should adhere to EU environmental and anti-tax evasion standards if it wants close trade ties
- European Banking Authority and European Medicines Agency should be moved out of London

Between the 17 May and 30 May, the UK parties launched their general election manifestos. Brexit was an important topic for all parties, yet interestingly, except for the Single Market and economic implications of a hard Brexit, little information was provided in most manifestos about the wider implications of Brexit for other policy sectors. The key pledges in regards to Brexit are summarized below.

Liberal Democrats (LibDems) manifesto: "Change Britain's future"

- The cornerstone is an open, tolerant and united society.
- Brexit is at the heart of the manifesto. Tim Farron stated, "We voted for departure but not the destination". The LibDems promise a deal with access to the Single Market and to give the people a final say (*i.e.* 2nd referendum) on whether to accept this deal or reject it and remain in Europe.
- The LibDems want to be a strong opposition to the Tories (and Labour) when the Brexit negotiations start.
  (LibDems manifesto website: http://www.libdems.org.uk/manifesto)
  The party leader then was Tim Farron, who has since been replaced by Vince Cable after the 2017 elections.

Conservatives manifesto: "Forward, Together: Our Plan for a Stronger Britain and a Prosperous Future"

- Build a stronger, fairer, more prosperous Britain. This implies "strong and stable leadership" to deal with economy, Brexit, social division, an ageing society, fast-changing technology and meritocracy.
- "The best possible deal for Britain as we leave the EU delivered by a smooth, orderly Brexit."

- Strike own trade agreements once the UK has left the EU. Control our own laws, immigration and secure the entitlements of EU nationals in Britain and British nationals in the EU.
- Britain will be no longer member of the Single Market or Customs Union, but we will seek a deep and special partnership, including a comprehensive free trade and customs agreement.
- The Great Repeal Bill will repatriate EU law to the UK.
- "A strong and stable Union, with no divisive Scottish referendum at this time." (Conservative Party website: https://www.conservatives.com/manifesto) The party leader and Prime Minister is still Theresa May.

Labour Party manifesto: "For the many, not the few"

- Key points are creating economy that works for all, negotiating Brexit, a national education service, a fair deal at work, social security, housing, healthcare, safer communities, infrastructure, strengthening the UK and beyond.
- "Labour accepts the referendum result and a Labour government will put the national interest first. We will prioritise jobs and living standards, build a close new relationship with the EU, protect workers' rights and environmental standards, provide certainty to EU nationals and give a meaningful role to Parliament throughout negotiations."
- Labour will immediately grant existing rights for all EU nationals living in Britain and secure reciprocal rights for UK citizens who live in the EU.
- Retain the benefits of the Single Market and Customs Union, which are essential for maintaining industries, jobs and businesses.
- "Leaving the EU with 'no deal' is the worst possible deal."
- Participate in leading EU research programmes, remain part of the Erasmus scheme, and seek to maintain membership of organisations such as Euratom and the European Medicines Agency.
- Introduce an EU Rights and Protections Bill to ensure workers' rights, equality law, consumer rights, and environmental protection. (Labour Party manifesto website: http://www.labour.org.uk/index.php/manifesto2017) The party leader is still Jeremy Corbyn.

Green Party manifesto: "For a confident and caring Britain"

- Give people the right to vote on the final terms of Brexit deal (*i.e.* a second referendum), including an option to stay in the EU.
- The Greens do not accept that either "hard" Brexit or an exit from the EU without a deal that is in the interest of the British people.

- Key objectives are to protect freedom of movement; press for remaining within the Single Market; and safeguard vital rights for people and the environment.
- Immediately guarantee the rights of EU citizens to remain in the UK and urgently seek reciprocal arrangements for UK citizens in the EU.
- Guarantee the rights of young people to study, work, live, and travel in the EU, including through schemes like Erasmus.
  (Green Party manifesto website: https://www.greenparty.org.uk/assets/files/gp2017/greenguaranteepdf.pdf)
  The party leaders are still Caroline Lucas and Jonathan Bartley.

Independent Party manifesto: "Britain Together"

UKIP sees itself as the guard dog of Brexit. In its manifesto it is stated, "UKIP have fought for Brexit all our political lives and we want to ensure that the people get the kind of Brexit they voted for on 23rd June last year." The pledge continues, "This does not mean we just control immigration and reduce the numbers of people coming to our country. It means we are not saddled with a huge divorce bill, we reclaim our waters, and we become a free independent nation once again."

(UKIP manifesto website: http://www.ukip.org/manifesto2017)

The party leader was Paul Nuttall (who resigned after the election).

Scottish National Party (SNP): "Stronger for Scotland"

- SNP aims to strengthen Scotland's influence in the Brexit negotiations. The SNP Government published a compromise proposal that would keep Scotland in the Single Market (which was rejected by the UK government).
- Scotland's economy is heavily dependent on the European Single Market and therefore needs access. As per the SNP manifesto, "80,000 Scottish jobs could be lost, wages face a £2,000 per head cut and our economy faces a hit of up to £11 billion a year by 2030. Our public finances are also threatened by the loss of EU funding for research and development, and support for our rural communities."
- As an alternative, "The SNP believes that if Scotland chooses to become independent, we should be a member state of the EU."
- Besides the oil and gas industry, the manifesto highlights the importance of alternative energies that are one of the focus areas of EU programmes: "Europe's energy markets and funding programmes – ensuring continued funding and cooperation with the EU for Scotland's renewable energy sector. The European Union is set to establish a €320 million investment fund to support wave and tidal power, in which Scotland is a world leader."
  (Scottish National Party manifesto website: https://www.snp.org/manifesto)
  The party leader is still Nicola Sturgeon.

The elections on 8 June did not result in the landslide victory and clear mandate that Theresa May was expecting and had hoped for (see timetable above). Instead of stability and leadership (her slogan during the campaign), the election resulted in a hung Parliament where the Tories won 318 seats (326 are required for a majority) and Labour won 262 seats. The outcome caused political fallout, with Theresa May's co-chiefs of staff resigning, former Tory minister Nicky Morgan predicting a leadership contest by the summer and former chancellor George Osborn telling Andrew Marr (BBC Sunday's politics show) that May is "a dead woman walking". At the same time, Jean-Claude Juncker commenting on the UK General election results said, "I do strongly hope that Britain will stay ready to open negotiations. As far as the Commission is concerned, we can open negotiations tomorrow morning."

To overcome the challenges caused by the hung parliament, Theresa May agreed a pact on 26 June with the ten Democratic Unionist Party (DUP) MPs from Northern Ireland, which was summarised on just three pages. To make the deal possible, the government committed an additional £1 billion extra to the £0.5 billion allocated for Northern Ireland over the next two years, and that there will be no Irish border poll without the "consent of the people". The "Confidence and supply agreement in the Parliament" with the DUP was controversial, as the Northern Ireland peace agreement (Good Friday Agreement) requires the UK government to be independent and favour none of the Northern Ireland political parties. The Conservative Party committed themselves in the agreement with the DUP that to respect the commitments made in the Belfast Agreement and its successors, and the DUP leader Arlene Foster vowed to bring stability to the UK with the Conservatives.

1.3.8 The negotiation teams

The Brexit negotiations finally started on 19 June 2017, one year after the referendum took place. The key persons who will be involved in the negotiations and their roles are listed below.

European Union negotiators

- **Michel Barnier**: European Commission *Chief Brexit negotiator*. He leads the Commission's Taskforce for the Preparation and Conduct of the negotiations with the UK. Former French Foreign Minister and Minister for European Affairs, and Commission Vice-President, he has been European Commissioner for regional policy and the internal market and services, overseeing reform of the financial sector. He was also elected to the European Parliament.
- **Sabine Weyand**: European Commission *Deputy chief negotiator*. She has spent more than two decades working in the European Commission, including in the industry and trade department. She served as an adviser to the previous Commission President, Jose Barroso.

- **Donald Tusk**: *EU Council President*. He was Prime Minister of Poland for two terms.
- **Didier Seeuws**: *Council Special Taskforce Chief negotiator*. Belgian diplomat and former advisor and later Chief of Staff to previous Council President Herman Van Rompuy. He is the person for the broad political questions arising from Brexit.
- **Guy Verhofstadt**: *European Parliament chief negotiator on Brexit*. He served three times as Belgian Prime Minister, President of the Alliance of Liberals and Democrats for Europe party group in the European Parliament, and MEP. Verhofstadt will lead the Constitutional Affairs Committee which will take the lead on behalf of the Parliament, and it is expected that a special task force on Brexit will be set up.
- **Jean-Claude Junker**: *President of the European Commission*. Former Prime Minister of Luxembourg, from 1989 to 2009 he was their Minister for Finances. He has been also involved in introducing the Treaty of Lisbon and handling the European financial and sovereign debt crisis.
- **Martin Selmayr**: *Chief of staff to EU Commission President* Jean-Claude Juncker. Heads a Brexit task force at the Commission.
- **Cecilia Malmström**: *EU's Trade Commissioner*. She was a Swedish politician who negotiated the latter stages of the Comprehensive Economic and Trade Agreement with Canada. She is negotiating the future trade relationship with the UK.

EU Member State key stakeholders

- **Angela Merkel (Germany)**: *Germany's Chancellor* and Europe's longest serving leader (since 2005), Conservative Party.
- **Emmanuel Macron (France)**: *President of France* since June 2017. Previously he was appointed Minister of Economy, Industry and Digital Affairs (2014) and Deputy Secretary General of the Élysée, a senior role in President François Hollande's staff (2012). He has been an investment banker at Rothschild & Cie Banque.
- **Enda Kenny (Republic of Ireland)**: *Irish Prime Minister* since March 2011. He was Minister for Defence, two-term Vice-President of the European People's Party and Ireland's Minister for Tourism and Trade. Ireland trades over £1 billion a week with Britain, shares a land border, and thousands of its citizens travel to the UK every day.

United Kingdom Government

- **David Davis**: *Secretary of State for Exiting the European Union* (DfEEU). Former Shadow Home Secretary, he emphasised the need for an export-led growth strategy and expressed his belief that Brexit would enable the UK to "take back control of trade".

- **Sarah Healey**: *Director General at the DfEEU* (second-in-command of the civil service machine tasked with delivering Brexit). Former Director for both Private Pensions in the Department for Work and Pensions, and Strategy and Education Funding in the Department for Education; and Director General for the Department for Culture, Media and Sport. She will manage a team of six directors focussing on a range of factors in the Brexit Process.

- **Sir Tim Borrow**: *UK permanent representative (UKRep) to the EU*. He replaced Sir Ivan Rogers and hand-delivered the Article 50 letter to Donald Tusk on 29 March 2017. Former civil servant in the Foreign and Commonwealth Office (FCO) since 1986, he has rendered diplomatic services for the UK in London, Kiev, Moscow, Brussels and the Ukraine.

- **Oliver Robbins CBE**: *Permanent Secretary at the DfEEU*. Former Deputy National Security Adviser to Prime Minister David Cameron, he was responsible for supporting EU negotiations and establishing the relationship between the UK and the EU.

- **Theresa May**: *UK prime minister* and Member of Parliament for Maidenhead since 1997, Home Secretary since 2010, and Conservative Party leader and Prime Minister since 13 July 2016.

- **Robin Walker**: *Parliamentary Under Secretary of State at DfEEU*. Formerly he worked in financial public relations in the City of London; then appointed as Permanent Parliamentary Secretary at the Department for Environment, Food and Rural Affairs He will be part of a ministerial team trying to achieve the best possible deal for the UK out of negotiations with the other 27 Member States.

- **Antony Phillipson**: *Director of Trade and Partnerships at DfEEU*. He was the former Prime Minister's Private Secretary for Foreign Affairs; and latterly EU External Director in the Global Issues Secretariat Cabinet Office.

- **Catherine Webb**: *Director of Market Access and Budget DfEEU* Former Director of EU Internal Issues in the Cabinet Office and a former trade and economic policy expert in the Foreign Office, she is partly responsible for managing the outcome of the negotiations regarding Britain's access to the European Market and forming a coherent exit plan.

- **Liam Fox**: *Secretary of State for international trade*. He may be tasked with producing frameworks for trade deals, which the PM will sign off.

- **Boris Johnson**: *Secretary of State for Foreign and Commonwealth Affairs*. Previously he has been MP for Henley (2001 to 2008) and Mayor of London (2008 to 2016).

1.3.9 Phase One: Positions and the start of Brexit negotiations

Nearly one year after the EU Referendum, on Monday 19 June 2017, the Brexit negotiations formally started in Brussels. To negotiate is defined by the Merriam-Webster Dictionary as "to arrange for or bring about through conference, discussion, and compromise". As the UK's position for specific policy areas has not been defined, negotiations may be considered challenging.

Opening Brexit negotiations (19 June 2017)

The EU's chief negotiator, Michel Barnier, said there would be "substantial" consequences from Brexit after the first round of talks with the UK. Barnier said he was "not in the frame of mind to make concessions or ask for concessions". Mr Barnier said the UK had decided to leave the EU – not the other way around, and each side had to "assume our responsibility and the consequences of our decisions". He summarised the negotiations, saying, "Basically, we are implementing the decision taken by the United Kingdom to leave the European Union, and unravel 43 years of patiently-built relations." As part of the opening, the EU presented the Terms of Reference for the Article 50 negotiations. As these are significant for at least the first phase of negotiations, the complete text is as follows:

> The United Kingdom and the European Commission, representing the EU, share the understanding that the following elements will guide the negotiations under Article 50 of the Treaty of the European Union (TEU):
> Negotiation Structure
> 1. The negotiating rounds will consist of plenary sessions and negotiating group meetings.
> 2. Plenary negotiating sessions should be co-chaired by the Principals and/or Coordinators who have the overall responsibility for managing the negotiating process and provide necessary guidance, as appropriate.
> 3. The following initial negotiating groups have been established:
>   - Citizens' rights;
>   - Financial Settlement;
>   - Other Separation issues.
>   In addition, a dialogue on Ireland / Northern Ireland has been launched under the authority of the Coordinators.
> 4. The Principals may decide to establish additional working groups, sub-groups or organise breakout sessions.
> 5. Each round of negotiations should comprise public officials of both sides only.
> Negotiating texts and other negotiating documents
> 6. Negotiation texts that are intended for discussion at any negotiating round should be shared at least one week in advance wherever possible.

Frequency of Negotiating Rounds

7. Negotiation rounds will be organised once every 4 weeks in principle, unless otherwise decided by mutual consent. Negotiators may meet intersessional to prepare negotiations, as required.

8. Indicative dates for first sessions have been agreed as per paragraph 9 below. Each round will include discussion of each of the issues set out in Paragraph 3.

9. Indicative dates are:
    - Opening: 19th June
    - Second round: w/c 17th July
    - Third round: w/c 28th August
    - Fourth round: w/c 18th September
    - Fifth round: w/c 9th October

Language

10. English and French will be used, as working languages, during negotiations and in working documents. Interpretation will be provided by the European Commission.

Transparency

11. For both parties the default is transparency.

12. It is for the Party providing the information to state what, if any, restrictions should apply to their further distribution.

13. Any disclosure by either the United Kingdom or the European Commission of documents originating from the other Party will be subject to prior consultation of the originating party.

14. Both Parties will handle negotiating documents in accordance with their respective legislation.

    Where possible, both Parties will seek to agree public statements relating to negotiating rounds.

    (European Commission, 19 June 2017)

Two days after the Brexit negotiations began in Brussels, on 21 June 2017 the Queen of England laid out her Government's plans in Westminster. Of 27 bills total proposed for the year, eight bills in the *Queen's Speech* related to Brexit. These were:

1. **Repeal Bill**: It will repeal the 1972 European Communities Act and convert EU law into UK law. Once the matter is devolved, the UK Parliament and the Scottish Parliament will be free to make any future changes to its laws.

2. **Customs Bill**: This will ensure that the UK has a standalone UK customs regime on exit. It will also accommodate future trade agreements with the EU and others; changes to the UK's VAT and excise tax regimes, aiming to allow the government to collect payments of customs duties, administer the customs

regime and deal with tax evasion; and control over the import and export of goods.

3. **Trade Bill**: This will establish a legal framework to allow Britain to strike free trade deals with countries around the world. It will also allow the government to set rules for unfair trading practices and for protecting domestic businesses.

4. **Immigration Bill**: This will return to the UK government the right to control immigration, ending the free movement of EU nationals into the UK. EU nationals and their families will be "subject to relevant UK law", but at the same time the UK will still allow the country to attract "the brightest and the best".

5. **Fisheries Bill**: This will allow the UK to control access to its waters and set UK fishing quotas.

6. **Agriculture Bill**: Its aim is to put in place the appropriate support for farmers and protect the natural environment after the UK leaves the Common Agricultural Policy.

7. **Nuclear Safeguards Bill**: As the UK leaves Euratom, this will establish a UK nuclear safeguards regime. It aims to ensure that the UK continues to meet its international obligations for nuclear safeguards through the International Atomic Energy Agency. It will also support international nuclear non-proliferation and protect UK electricity supplied by nuclear power.

8. **International Sanctions Bill**: As a permanent member of the UN Security Council, this Bill aims to ensure that the UK continues to play a central role in negotiating global sanctions to counter threats of terrorism, conflict and the proliferation of nuclear weapons.

(BBC, 21 June 2017a; BBC, 21 June 2017b)

The European Council also issued a procedure to plan for the withdrawal of two European agencies that are based in London, at Canary Wharf, at the moment (European Council, 22 June 2017). These are the European Banking Authority (EBA) and the European Medicine Agency (EMA). EBA's key responsibilities are:

- to ensure effective and consistent prudential regulation and supervision across the European banking sector and to harmonise European banking rules and supervisory practices;
- to assess risks and vulnerabilities in the EU banking sector through regular risk assessment reports and EU-wide stress tests; and
- to mediate in cross-border disputes between financial authorities.

The agency will have to be relocated as a consequence of Brexit. Eight offers to host EBA were received as of 1 August 2017: Brussels, Dublin, Frankfurt, Luxembourg, Paris, Prague, Vienna and Warsaw (Council of the European Union, 22 June 2017a).

While EBA was preparing for this move, it provided guidance to financial services authorities and institutions on Brexit relocations (European Banking Authority (12 October 2017a). The "Opinion of the European Banking Authority on issues related to the departure of the United Kingdom from the European Union" of 12 October 2017 (EBA/Op/2017/12) tried to establish greater certainty for UK financial services firms that seek to expand their EU-27 presence in order to retain access to the EU Single Market.[3] EBA addressed a number of relevant policy issues relating to authorisations, internal models, internal governance, outsourcing, risk transfers via back-to-back and intragroup operations, resolution and deposit guarantee scheme issues, and the prudential regulation and supervision of investment firms. This advice was addressed to credit institutions, investment firms, payment institutions and electronic money institutions. EBA also committed itself to monitoring developments so as to adjust if necessary its policy and risk analyses relating to the challenges posed by Brexit (European Banking Authority, 12 October 2017b).

The second European agency which must move out of London is EMA, which has the following responsibilities:

- to monitor, scientifically evaluate and supervise the safety and quality of medicines EU-wide and to issue scientific advice;
- to provide a single pathway for evaluating medicines, avoiding duplication by member states; and
- to foment innovation by collaborating with medicine manufacturers.

Nineteen offers to host EMA had been submitted to the Council of Ministers as at 1 August 2017 from cities all over Europe: Amsterdam, Athens, Barcelona, Bonn, Bratislava, Brussels, Bucharest, Copenhagen, Dublin, Helsinki, Lille, Valletta (Malta), Milan, Porto, Sofia, Stockholm, Vienna, Warsaw and Zagreb (Council of the European Union, 12 October 2017).

Most crucial is that this agency licenses all new medical products for use in the EU Member States. In case of No Deal, Britain is very likely to continue to accept the rulings of the EMA on drugs produced in the EU. However, difficulties arise for pharmaceutical companies based in the UK, who would may not have their products licensed for use elsewhere in the EU. The UK industry hopes that continued validity of the EU Medicinal Products Directive and Regulation in the UK in exchange for EU recognition of decisions by Britain's Medicines and Healthcare Products Regulatory Agency (MHRA) will provide UK pharmaceuticals access to the European Market.

---

3   Despite ongoing discussions between the UK government and the domestic opposition, EBA is very clear in its Opinion that the UK's decision has been to withdraw from the EU, which includes the UK leaving the European Single Market. (see HM Government, "The United Kingdom's exit from and new partnership with the European Union", February 2017).

EU27 ministers voted on the relocation of the UK-based EU agencies in the margins of the General Affairs Council (Art. 50) meeting on 20 November 2017. The selected location of the EMA is Amsterdam, the Netherlands and the EBA is Paris, France.

Extension of Phase One negotiations (October to December 2017)

The October 2017 deadline passed, and the Phase One negotiations (the so-called "divorce settlement" remained in deadlock. The Council of Ministers summit in Brussels on 19 October 2017 concluded that insufficient progress had been made, and that to move on to Phase Two to discuss the future relationship (including trade) would be premature; nevertheless, they were optimistic that the progress to be made by December would enable Phase Two to commence in January 2018.

It had been widely anticipated that a lunch meeting between PM May and the European Commission President Juncker on 4 December 2017 would conclude Phase One of the Brexit negotiations ahead of the EU summit. The agreement had had the support of Irish Prime Minister Leo Varadkar. Leaked proposals had suggested that May was planning to agree that Northern Ireland would submit to a "continued regulatory alignment" with EU laws in the future to avoid a hard border, following an agreement with the Irish Republic. Within minutes of the agreement being made public, Arlene Foster, the leader of the DUP, announced both publicly and in a telephone call to May that they dissented from it. On top of that, Scotland, Wales and London united in demanding the same alignment as Northern Ireland. At a press conference following the lunch, Juncker conceded that despite their best efforts, "it was not possible to reach a complete agreement today". May added that the main issues – the Irish border and the role of the European Court of Justice – remain unresolved. Leo Varadkar, Ireland's Prime Minister, was "surprised and disappointed" that the UK government was not in a position "to conclude what was agreed". In the ensuing days, the Government were forced into hectic bargaining between the Tories, the DUP, the Republic of Ireland, and the European Commission. The outcome was a compromise that committed the UK to support North-South Irish cooperation, an all-island economy, and the 1998 peace agreement, but without holding Northern Ireland to alignment with the whole of the Single Market *acquis*. The DUP exacted that the UK should have the initiative in finding solutions to achieve the commitments and that only in default of UK solutions should alignment be maintained with the rules of the Customs Union and Single Market– and only *to the extent necessary* to support the said commitments (European Union TF50 (2017) 19 "Joint report from the negotiators of the European Union and the United Kingdom Government", point 4 on page 8).

Finally, in the early hours of 8 December, May and Juncker announced a joint EU-UK agreement, TF50(2017)19 and TF50(2017)20. Juncker affirmed that he would certify to the EU-27 leaders that "sufficient progress" has been made and recommend moving to Phase Two of the Brexit negotiations. The agreement included:

- *Financial Settlement*: Britain will likely end up paying between £35 billion and £39 billion. At all events, a methodology for the calculation was agreed; however, the official figure will not be determined until Phase Two. Under the plan, the UK is expected to pay somewhere between €17 and €18 billion into the 2019 "multi-annual financial framework" (MFF), which is effectively the EU's budget round. It will also pay between €21 and €23 billion into a so-called RAL (*reste à liquider*) outstanding at the end of 2020, effectively a credit facility for the EU. Officials also expect the UK to pay between €2 and €4 billion for actual liabilities Britain owes the EU, such as future pensions of European civil servants. However, the EU also owes Britain its share of European Investment Bank capital, which is between €40 and €45 billion, which it will pay back to the UK over the long term (Stone, 8 December 2017).
- *Protection of citizens' rights*: The ECJ will be given power to guarantee EU citizens' rights in the UK for 8 years.
- *Addressing the unique circumstances of Northern Ireland (Irish border)*: The UK is supposed to have committed itself to maintaining "full alignment" with relevant EU internal market and customs rules in Northern Ireland "in the absence of agreed solutions". At the same time, it is also committed to a promise that "no new regulatory barriers develop" between Northern Ireland and the rest of the UK, conserving Northern Ireland's integration into the UK's domestic market. Furthermore, the Northern Irish shall have right to choose Irish/ EU or else British citizenship.
- *Role of the European Court of Justice (ECJ)*: The agreement also confirmed the status of the ECJ as the "ultimate arbiter of the interpretation of Union law". The UK courts will be under the ECJ's jurisdiction no longer, after Brexit, but will be required to "have due regard to relevant decisions" where these relate to the application or interpretation of rights granted under EU law.
- *Transition period*: A period of about two years was agreed; however, the details will be part of Phase Two of the negotiations together with the future relationship with the EU.

Heeding the caveat that "nothing is agreed until everything is agreed", the commitments in TF50(2017)19 and TF50(2017)20 are to be reflected in detail in the Withdrawal Agreement. Michel Barnier, the European Commission's chief negotiator, said that there had been "real, genuine progress" in each of the three priority negotiation areas. "By agreeing on these issues, and settling the past, we can now move forward and discuss our future relationship on the basis of trust and confidence", he said.

At the European Council Summit on 15 December the EU-27 leaders agreed to advance the Brexit talks to Phase Two. Donald Tusk, the President of the European Council, who broke the news, demanded that the UK gets "more clarity in their vision". He stressed that the next phase would be "more challenging and more demanding". Negotiations will commence in March 2018. The European Council adopted a three-page guideline (BXT 69 CO EUR 27, CONCL 8) that stated:

- the agreements on the Irish border, the so-called "divorce bill", and the rights of EU and UK citizens, must be "respected in full and translated faithfully into legal terms as quickly as possible".
- During the two-year transition period of around two years the UK will –
    (a) remain under the jurisdiction of the European Court of Justice;
    (b) be obligated to permit freedom of movement under EU rules; and
    (c) ensure a level playing field based on the same rules as other EU Member States and stay in the Customs Union and Single Market (with all four freedoms). This means that the UK must apply "the acquis adopted by EU institutions, bodies, offices and agencies [and a]ll existing Union regulatory, budgetary, supervisory, judiciary and enforcement instruments and structures will also apply, including the competence of the Court of Justice of the European Union." Interestingly, the guideline proposes "to negotiate a transition period covering the whole of the EU *acquis* while the United Kingdom, as a third country, will no longer participate in or nominate or elect members of the EU institutions, nor participate in the decision-making of the Union bodies, offices and agencies". (The *acquis* is presented and analysed in detail in Chapter Three of this book.)
- the EU is willing to begin engaging in "preliminary and preparatory discussions" on trade as part of building a "close partnership" after the UK's departure; however, any formal trade agreement "can only be finalised and concluded once the UK has become a third country" after 29 March 2019. "During the transition, the UK will have to continue to comply with EU trade policy, to apply EU customs tariff and collect EU customs duties, and to ensure all EU checks are being performed on the border *vis-à-vis* other third countries."

The guideline "calls on the UK to provide further clarity on its position on the framework for the future relationship". Chief negotiator Barnier will "continue internal preparatory discussions" on future relations, and additional guidelines may be published up until Phase Two starts in March 2018.

In Phase Two, the parties will draft the UK withdrawal agreement and begin discussing possible transitional arrangements as well as the terms of the UK's future relationship with the EU. However, the European Commission was clear that a trade agreement may be only finalised once the UK has left the EU and becomes a third country and on condition of compliance with Phase Two agreements. The Government plan to fix legally the exit date on 29 March 2019, but with the option to change this date in case Brexit negotiations with the EU last longer than anticipated.

1.3.10 PHASE TWO: THE FUTURE OF THE EU-UK RELATIONSHIP

The prospects for Phase Two are still open; everything seems possible for a special agreement that provides access to the Customs Union, especially for an EEA-type of relationship (*i.e.*, *de facto* EU membership without a vote in the legislative process, yet compliance with most EU norms). It is also true that a No Deal scenario is quite possible, depending ultimately on the UK's domestic political scene. Considering that many Westminster politicians couldn't tell the difference between the Customs Union and the Single Market, it should surprise no one that in the weeks and months after the referendum they had been aiming unrealistically at negotiating away the four freedoms at the foundation of the European Union. Finally they have understood what they failed to grasp before, that exit will be much more complex than initially thought, because membership of the European Union is deeper than Westminster comprehended. The Government's plan to charm influential Member States, negotiate in secret, and minimise the involvement of "outsiders" to the PM's inner circle had been exposed as a pipe dream.

As this book has shown in the policy impact assessment of Chapter Three, EU policy is complex and touches all aspects of life. To achieve the best possible outcome now that reality has kicked in, it is of the utmost importance that the UK government engages political stakeholders both public and private, the regional and national levels, civil society and industry. The essential usefulness of industry as a partner on governance is chronically undervalued. There is an urgency that this changes if a transition agreement and a future relationship is to be as fruitful as possible.

What is needed now, as a matter of urgency, is for ministers and politicians to actually sit down with and listen, perhaps for the first time in their careers, to the fisherman sailing territorialised waters, the farmer wresting a livelihood for thousands from stubborn soil, the researcher exacting himself in the laboratory, the banker staving off insolvency, the manufacturer cutting costs till it bleeds, the entrepreneur risking his all, the public servant facing budget reductions, the boards of large corporations collecting their bonuses, the employees and consumers who are feeling the impact of Brexit on their daily life. They know better than career politicians what they need, and what success, failure or complete disaster out of Brexit would look like. This implies the overdueness of regular public consultations to align policy with real public opinion, and the *power* of transparency to unite warring factions. Both civil society and industry need to have their say, not just for their own benefit, but for the benefit of clueless ministers. Industry, especially, must be allowed play a pro-active role in a new consultative regulatory governance for Brexit, as they have society's biggest fund of competences.[4] In recent years, "industry governance" has emerged because of a new, more cooperative approach by regulators to the intractable problems of governance. If expanded appropriately to bring in all walks of life, this is a promising model for governance generally, and one that may be inevitable at all events.

1.3.11 WHY "NO DEAL" WOULD BE THE WORST OUTCOME

Except for the 12 negotiation objectives that Theresa May announced in her speech at Lancaster House, no policy-specific objectives had been set (or at least not made publicly available) when the talks began. In this context, negotiations usually require that specific positions and objectives are defined when starting up negotiations – which was not the case when the UK started the process. To many it was clear that the worst possible outcome would be "no deal", as this would have serious implications for:

- **Travel arrangements between the UK and EU**: On the day after a no-deal Brexit, UK travellers to the EU would lose emergency health coverage that is manifested on their European Health Insurance Cards (EHIC). UK and EU residents would need to apply for working and possibly even for holiday visas.
- **Cooperation in the fight against crime and terrorism**: Also it is highly unlikely that the UK and EU would stop sharing intelligence, disruption might be possible in the short term.
- **Trade agreements**: As laid out by the EU, there will be a phased approach, consisting of an exit phase and a phase defining the new relationship. An early exit from the negotiations would mean no access to the Single Market and WTO tariffs. This would also lead to additional red tape when trading with the EU.
- *Passporting* **(financial services)**: *Passporting* allows financial services to be sold across the Single Market, with serious implications for the financial sector if the privilege is lost. British companies would need to obtain costly licences in each individual country.
- **Court litigation**: Outstanding payments could lead to possible court litigation of financial liabilities. It is estimated that the outstanding amount of loans granted by the EU was about €56 billion, pre-financing for financial commitments (€45.2

---

4   In the narrow context of European IT regulation, *industry governance* has been defined as "the pro-active role of industry in the new consultative governance of the regulatory regime, resulting in industry's predominating influence in shaping public policies, regulations and standards, in order to achieve the business objectives of enhanced innovation, competitiveness and consumer satisfaction." (Reinke, 2012). Even in the much broader arena of international relations, and given partnership with a wider array of private stakeholders, this is a thought-provoking governing template for consultative, responsive (and *therefore* responsible) leadership.

billion), receivables and recoverables as part of budget contributions (€10.3 billion, all figures apply by the end of 2015) (Bruegel, 2017).

- **Access to EU research and development programmes**: Over the period 2007-2013 the UK was given €8.8 billion out of a total expenditure by the EU of €107 billion on research, development and innovation in EU Member States, associated and third countries. This represents the fourth largest share in the EU. In terms of funding awarded on a competitive basis in the period 2007-2013 under Framework Programme 7, the UK was the second largest recipient after Germany, securing €6.9 billion out of a total of €55.4 billion (Bruegel, 2017).
- **A transitional agreement**: If an extension beyond two years is needed, all member countries need to agree and the negotiations need to continue. This also applies to a phased process of implementation and transitional agreements. Major changes would kick-in immediately.
- **The Irish border**: Frictions with Ireland could arise if a hard border and customs checks are re-introduced. Farmers could face tariffs of 30%-40% on meat and dairy produce, which would make their goods uncompetitive. This would be also a breach of the 1998 Good Friday Agreement. The Irish economy accounts for €1.2 billion a week in trade and 400,000 jobs on both sides of the border.

A hard Brexit or No Deal could weaken the pound sterling significantly. As outlined in Chapter Three, the economic implications would be very damaging and could leave the pound vulnerable to a self-reinforcing depreciation spiral. In October 2017 a risk assessment of financial institutions in Germany (retail and consumer banks, saving banks, credit unions and mortgage lenders) revealed that 99.9% of the 1,960 financial institutes in Germany believed that the pound sterling could fall by another 20% (or more). Their risk departments have set the volatility risk of the pound as extremely high and restrict sterling-based financial products available to investors from the UK in Germany, particularly consumer lending. EU Regulation (2014/17/EU) on "credit agreements for consumers relating to residential immovable property and amending Directives 2008/48/EC and 2013/36/EU and Regulation (EU) No 1093/2010" (especially Article 11(2) and Article 23 (1)b, (3), (4) and (6)), protects consumers who borrow in a foreign currency (*i.e.*, not in euros) if the exchange rate between the currency of lender (in this case euros) and the currency of the borrower (in this case pounds sterling) varies by more than 20%, by allowing the borrower to swap the dearer for the cheaper currency. Because of this new regulation and its consequent risks, German financial institutions have stopped offering credit agreements to consumers resident in the UK.

Comprising 28 Member States with a total population of over 500 million and a GDP of €13.0 trillion in 2012, the European Union (EU) is the world's largest single market, foreign investor and trader. A no-deal could mean that current WTO rules would become applicable.[5] The WTO tariffs database contains more than 19,500 products across 97 product categories (for HS12). Some examples are:

- Meat and edible meat offal (maximum of 15.4% duty)
- Fish and crustaceans, molluscs and other aquatic invertebrates (26% duty)
- Dairy produce, bird eggs, natural honey (17.3% duty)
- Edible fruit and nuts, peel of citrus fruit and melons (20.8% duty)
- Cereals (12.8% duty)
- Products of the milling industry, malt, starches, inulin, wheat gluten (19.2% duty)
- Preparations of meat, of fish or of crustaceans, molluscs and other aquatic invertebrates (26% duty)
- Sugars and sugar confectionery (13.4% duty)
- Preparations of vegetables, fruit, nuts or other parts of plants (33.6% duty)
- Beverages, spirits and vinegar (32% duty)
- Tobacco and manufactured tobacco substitutes (74.9% duty)
- Photographic or cinematographic goods (6.5% duty)
- Plastics and articles thereof (6.5% duty)
- Silk (7.5% duty)
- Wool, fine or coarse animal hair, horsehair yarn and woven fabric (8% duty)
- Cotton (8% duty)
- Carpets and other textile floor coverings (8% duty)
- Articles of apparel and clothing accessories, knitted or crochetes (12% duty)
- Ceramic products (12% duty)
- Glass and glassware (11% duty)
- Iron and steel (7% duty)
- Electrical machinery and equipment and parts thereof, sound recorders and reproducers, television image and sound recorders and reproducers, and parts and accessories of such articles (14% duty)

---

5   World Trade Organisation (WTO) tariffs information can be downloaded from the following websites:

(a) European Union agreements with WTO from Pre-Uruguay Round Schedule, Annexe to the Marrakesh Protocol (MP_, or t a Protocol of Accession (PA), Transposition of Schedules due to HS amendments, Ratifications/ Modifications to Schedules and Renegotiations under GATT Article XXVII. Details are available on the "Current Situation of Schedules of WTO Members" at https://www.wto.org/english/tratop_e/schedules_e/goods_schedules_table_e.htm (accessed June 2017).

(b) Detailed tariff data for goods and services can be downloaded at http://tariffdata.wto.org/ReportersAndProducts.aspx (accessed June 2017). Instructions on how to download WTO tariffs are available at http://tariffdata.wto.org/UserGuide/USERGUIDE_EN.htm (accessed June 2017).

- Aircraft, spacecraft, and parts of thereof (7.7% duty)
- Clocks and watches and parts thereof (6% duty)

If readers are interested in finding out import duties and taxes that EU member states (including the UK) have to pay on exports to specific countries, the EU's Market Access Database provides transparent information. It calculates a landed cost for a product by entering its specific standard Harmonized System code.[6]

The UK's ambition to make better trade deals than the EU-27 without anything in return is questionable. During PM May's first vital overseas trade mission, she offered concessions to Indian premier Narendra Modi on immigration. On 7 November 2016, she announced that the UK would introduce a fast-track visa procedure to make travel to the UK "smoother and faster" for businessmen and their families. Mr Modi stressed the importance of the freedom of travel, work and study for young people and skilled professionals. This shows that a two-way relationship brings demands from both sides. A free trade agreement with India would be huge, but also very tough. The fact is that India sounds like the EU concerning free movement of its citizens to countries who trade with the UK. The free flow of goods, (financial) services, expertise and people needs to go both ways, according to all those who believe in globalism. Mrs May, who reduced student visas from 68,000 to 12,000 in her five years as Home Secretary, may have to rethink this policy if she wants to enter into trade negotiations with India.

The May Government is under pressure to deliver at least some of the promises made by the Leave campaign during the referendum, though many promises are already falling by the wayside. The promised £350 million weekly boost to the National Health Service has been exposed as bogus: even Leave admitted within a week after the referendum that this will not happen. Brexit Secretary David Davis conceded that levels of immigration might even rise "from time to time" after Brexit. The idea of Britain striking trade deals once it leaves the EU's common commercial policy is often touted by the Prime Minister as a big opportunity. However, even this promise seems questionable. For example, the most recent trade deal that the EU has struck is the Comprehensive Economic and Trade Agreement (CETA) with Canada, which was passed by the European Parliament on 15 February 2017. It took 8 years to finalise. If enacted by Canada, it will eliminate 98% of the tariffs between Canada and the EU. It is questionable whether the UK with its 64 million people (potential customers)

---

6   European Commission Market Access Database:

     - "Exporting from the EU - what you need to know" website at http://madb.europa.eu/madb/indexPubli.htm

     - Tariffs database (Duties & taxes on imports of products into specific countries) website http://madb.europa.eu/madb/datasetPreviewFormATpubli.htm?datacat_id=AT&from=publi

has the commercial weight to negotiate better deals than the EU-27 with 450 million customers (excluding the UK). CETA is more than 1,500 pages long, and certain parts are not made public, thus it would be difficult to come to a final conclusion on which trade agreement is better, Britain's own or the EU's, but common sense would suggest that the bigger market is in the stronger negotiating position (*e.g.* Tesco can negotiate better deals with farmers than your corner shop). As the initial talks with India have shown, there is no such thing as a free lunch: the trade partner will demand something in return, which could mean cheaper or better quality products flooding the UK market, or easier access to the UK labour markets. Apparently, the number of Indian students attending British universities has fallen by 10% over the last year in the wake of concerns about immigration. The Indian PM demanded more visas for students and skilled workers.

PM May, Mr Fox, Mr Hammond, and Mark Carney, the Governor of the Bank of England, visited East Asian countries in April 2017, hoping to sell Britain abroad and sign trade deals when it leaves the EU. No deal can be signed until the UK has left the EU. Currently, just 1.7% of British exports go to India, which is a fraction of the 44% that go to the EU. Whitehall have jokingly dubbed the May plan an "Empire 2.0" strategy to rekindle old trading links; however, New Delhi is less inclined to view the colonial era in a positive light.

1.4 WHAT ELSE HAS BEEN ON THE EU'S AGENDA SINCE THE BREXIT REFERENDUM?

Anyone who has followed the news in the UK feels like the EU has come to a complete standstill since Brexit. The UK media gives people the impression that Europe is mourning and will do everything to sweeten Britain's exit to maintain full access for EU products and services to the UK. And Westminster politicians and the Brexiteers stress their strong negotiation position because everybody is supposed to be desperate to access the UK market. However, reading the European press and following the speeches of EU and Member State politicians shows a different reality. Europeans watched the chaos unfolding after the referendum in the UK, and they saw the political and economic consequences. In that time frame, European leaders have been making decisions for further integration, and new EU trade agreements have been signed with Canada and Japan.

So what does the EU and its leaders think of Brexit? Most countries seem to have got used to the fact that the UK is leaving the EU. For example, French President Macron is more concerned about driving the European agenda forward and Brexit is not on the forefront of his mind. He thinks first and foremost about European integration and France's links with Germany and the need to reform the Eurozone. As an ex-Rothschild banker, he clearly sees the opportunity to attract financial services away from the City.

Most European leaders are more concerned with the migration crisis across Europe and maintaining Europe's counter-terrorism effort. German Chancellor Angela Merkel is rejecting any special treatment for the UK in the Brexit negotiations. She was very clear that Brexit negations "will not consume the EU" at the two-day summit in Brussels in June. Merkel insisted that her priority was not the Brexit talks, but steering the EU to more European integration. After the first round of discussing EU citizens rights in the UK, in a symbolic joint press conference with the French President, Merkel said: "That was a good beginning, but – and I'm trying to word this very carefully – it was not a breakthrough. [...] We have said we want to pursue this matter in good cooperation, but what has come out yesterday was also that we still have a long way to go yet. And the 27 [other EU countries], especially Germany and France, will be well prepared. We will not allow ourselves to be divided."

The results of the recent elections in France have given the European project new momentum and confidence, especially after watching the past year of political malaise in the UK. Although it might not be obvious to many in the UK, the EU-27 leaders are convinced that the UK will lose influence and power on the world stage. Like hyenas roaming large territories in packs, influential politicians and mayors from European cities are on the hunt. They smell the opportunities in attracting European agencies (EBA and EMA) and UK businesses that desire access to the Single Market. They want their chance to get a good bite. And UK businesses need certainty and business opportunities, not politically charged debates and populism. They will be happy to accept "better deals" from Continental Europe, if the UK government does not offer them what their businesses need to prosper.

The following list provides a brief overview of some European achievements since the referendum, and is clear evidence that Brexit has – after an initial shock – not stalled the European machine.

- 8 July 2017: The *EU-Japan Free Trade Agreement (FTA) has been signed* between President Juncker, President Tusk and Prime Minister Abe (negotiations started on 25 March 2013 and it took 18 rounds to complete the negotiations). It provides easy access to the 4th richest economy in the word (by GDP) with a population of 127 million. Japan is the EU's 6th largest export market with EU exports of goods and services are worth over €80 billion every year and more than 600,000 jobs in the EU are tied to exports to Japan. *A Strategic Partnership Agreement between the EU and Japan* is being negotiated as well. (European Commission, 8 July 2017).
- 22-23 June 2017: European leaders met to discuss EU defence and security – online radicalisation, violent extremism, terrorist financing, information sharing, – but above all, an inclusive, ambitious, Permanently Structured Cooperation (PESCO) to consolidate Europe's security and defence.

- 22-23 June 2017: The heads of state / government of the Member States reaffirmed their commitment to swift and full implementation of the Paris Agreement on climate change, including its climate finance goals, and to lead the global transition to clean energy. Thus, Brexit has hardly brought the Europeanisation process to a standstill.
- 10 May 2017: The European Commission released its mid-term review of its Digital Single Market strategy, advancing integration and ever closer union. It covered the Data Economy, online platforms and cybersecurity.
- 8 March 2017: EU Trade Commissioner Cecilia Malmström announced that the EU-Singapore FTA would stipulate that tariffs on Singapore's exports to the EU will be removed in full (in the first year for 84% of the products, and in the fifth year for 100%). The FTA with Singapore signed two years ago had already caused goods trade to increase by 8% and services and investment stocks to rise by 15%. 11,000 European businesses are based in Singapore, which has become a top 10 partner of Europe in foreign direct investment. (European Commission, 29 June 2015)
- 15 February 2017: The Comprehensive Economic and Trade Agreement (CETA) with Canada was approved by the European Parliament (negotiations having started on 6 May 2009). It will remove 98% of tariffs between Canada and the EU, in everything from industry to agriculture. It also vindicates legal enforcement if IP rights. As an integrated bloc, the EU is Canada's second largest trading partner in goods and services. (European Commission, 17 February).

CHAPTER 2

REPORTS AND STATISTICS

Reports and surveys published by independent institutes are often presented by politicians as incontrovertible truth. But how reliable are they, really? Can they be trusted? Even statistical reports by the most prestigious institutes can manipulatively misinterpreted. At a minimum, politicians can just ignore the ones that do not support their argument, selectively citing the results. A humorous story illustrates how statistics alone never provide the answers electorates are seeking when deciding which way to vote. A mathematician, a physicist and a statistician went hunting for deer. When they chanced upon a buck lounging about, the mathematician fired first, missing the buck's nose by a few inches. The physicist then tried his hand, and missed the tail by a wee bit. The statistician started jumping up and down saying, "We got him! We got him!"

- The statistical reports presented in this Chapter are the same ones that business organisations rely on to make informed decisions, and may therefore be presumed to lie on the more reliable side of the spectrum. In this Chapter, we resorted to independent research in finding answers to the following questions:
  - (a) What did the polls predict months before the referendum and how did the public mood swing over time?
  - (b) In which regions and cities did the Remain camp and the Leave camp win?
  - (c) How many people where eligible electorates to vote, what percentage of the population registered, and how many actually voted?
  - (d) How did the vote differ by age?
  - (e) What are the economic forecasts of the implications of Brexit?
- In the last section of this Chapter we try find an answer to the ultimate question:
  - (f) Why did the Leave campaign win? In a time of prosperity in the UK and Europe compared to many regions of the world, and after more than a generation of peace, how was it possible for a majority of the voters to take a "leap into the dark" (David Cameron at BBC, 22 February 2016), or to file for "divorce" after 43 years of "marriage"?

The economic rational would have been to stay with the biggest trading bloc in the world. The agricultural sector, the information and communication technologies sector, the transport sector, the energy sector, the financial services sector, the academic and research and development sectors have all benefited from the Common Market, and many companies would not even exist today without European market liberalisation. Employees enjoy new rights to job security, workplace health and safety, and a working-hours maximum. Consumers have more rights in on-line shopping, personal data protection, and sector-specific regulations like no mobile phone roaming charges in other EU Member States.

2.1 THE POLLS BEFORE THE REFERENDUM

Many polls were taken leading up to the referendum, but, as with the 2015 general election polls, the predictions were wrong, as all the world knows. Nearly all polls showed the Remain campaign with a lead that only began to shrink for the first time at the beginning of May 2016 in the heat of the contest. Media spectacles and entertaining performances from the boisterous leaders of the Leave team clearly impacted on public opinion. Following a brief lead by the Leave campaign, the margin closed up again after the tragic death of Labour MP Jo Cox and the controversial UKIP migration poster. On the eve of the vote, the polls predicted a narrow victory for Remain – 51% to 49%. By D-Day the result seemed too close to call, though slightly in favour of Remain (Dunford and Kirk, 2016).

The most comprehensive polling analysis was provided by What UK Thinks, which produced an "EU Poll of Polls" based on the average of the six most recent polls of voting intentions. Their field work, which began on 3 September 2015 and concluded on 22 June 2016, comprised 168 polls. The aggregate data came from numerous polls, including online polls by TNS, phone polls by ComRes, online polls by Opinium, online polls by YouGov, phone polls by Ipsos MORI, online polls by Populus, and others (What UK Thinks, July 2017). All of these polls asked respondents how at the referendum they intended to answer the exact question that was to appear on the ballot paper.

The line graph below shows how the Poll of Polls has changed since polling (based on the question that appeared on the ballot paper) began in September 2015. The dates at the bottom of the graph tell when interviewing for the most recent poll in a set of six was concluded. Note the series includes both polls only conducted in Great Britain and those conducted across the whole United Kingdom.

Figure 5: Referendum: Vote Intention Poll of Polls

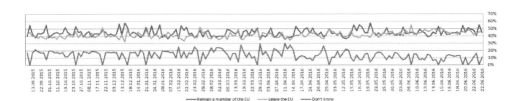

Does the referendum result mean that the electorates did make their decision? The fraction of those who showed up at the polling stations on the 23 June 2016 out of those made eligible to vote by law (see Section 2.2 below) were the ones who decided. In other referenda such as the Scottish Independence referendum other people were made eligible to vote. A strong case can be made that the electorates in national elections and in referenda should at least be self-consistent (referenda with referenda) if not also cross-consistent (referenda with elections); otherwise, the Government is empowered to influence outcomes by cherry-picking constituents deemed (on statistical grounds) to lean toward the result the Government prefer. Manifestly, this did not happen in the case of Brexit. If, however, the Scottish First Minister should press for another Scottish Independence referendum, for example, and has evidence that EU expatriates residing in Scotland have been more supportive of independence compared to Commonwealth citizens, then the holders of the referendum may influence the result by making EU citizens but not Commonwealth citizens eligible. As the diagram above shows, voter intentions and public opinion were in constant flux up to the referendum date. Interestingly, various surveys indicate that support for Remain has been increasing ever since the referendum, and if the economic or political situation were to worsen, the voices for calling Brexit off might swell to a crescendo. Also interestingly, a year after Brexit a Survation poll showed 54% of Britons would now prefer to stay in Europe (The Independent, 3 July 2017). Of course, it's just another survey and nobody knows what would happen if there would be a second referendum tomorrow. There is another poll giving the opposite result to the Survation one (YouGov UK, 29 March2017).

2.2 HOW THE COUNTRY VOTED: THE SOCIO-DEMOGRAPHIC DATA

To get a better understanding what happened at the day of the referendum, the following Section analysis the socio-demographic data. This analysis will increase our knowledge who the typical leave and remain voters were. This profiling is important as it can provide a roaster for potential future referenda in other EU Member States.

Britain voted by a small margin to leave the European Union. Of the 46,500,001 registered voters 72.2% turned out. Of these 33,551,983 voters, 16,141,241 (or 48.1%) voted to Remain and 17,410,742 (or 51.9%) to Leave[7]. Except for the Scottish Independence Referendum in September 2014, this was the highest turnout since the 1992 UK Parliamentary general election (Electoral Commission, 24 June 2016). The picture that emerged was of a heavily polarised country, with the big cities divided against the countryside and the younger generation against the older (Electoral Commission, 2016b).

---

7   There were 25,359 rejected ballot papers. More than 8.5m postal votes were issues, which represented 18.4% of the UK electorate, the highest proportion since the introduction of postal vote in on demand in Great Britain in 2001. As in previous years, turnout was higher among postal voters than in-person voters, which counted 87.6% compared to 69.2%.

Firstly, we will analyse the Remain and Leave distribution across the UK. The Remain campaign triumphed in London (2,263,519 voters of 3,776,751 votes cast were for Remain, which is 59.9% for Remain), Scotland (1,661,191 votes of 2,679,513 votes cast were for remain, which is 62% for Remain with a turnout of 67.2%)[8], and Northern Ireland (440,707 votes of 789,879, which is 55.8% for Remain with a turnout of 62.7%)[9]. Gibraltar voted for Remain by 95.9%. London scored seven of the 10 areas with the highest share of Remain votes, which included Lambeth (78.8%), Hackney (78.5%), Foley (78.3%) and Haringey (75.6%). Bigger cities that voted for Remain included Liverpool (58.2%) and Manchester (60.4%). Edinburgh polled over 74% for the Remain campaign while Belfast West polled 74.1%.

The Leave campaign won right across England (15,188,406 votes out of 28,455,402, which is 53.4% for Leave with a turnout of 73%) and Wales (854,572 votes out of 1,626,919, which is 52.5% for Leave with a turnout of 71.7%), except for the largest city Cardiff, which voted to remain by 60%. It triumphed in large northern cities, including Birmingham (50.4%), Sheffield (51.0), the Midlands, and the south and east of England. In nine areas voters polled with 70% to leave, with a high concentration on eastern England including Boston (75.6%), South Holland (73.6%), Thurrock (72.3%) and Great Yarmouth (71.5%) (Electoral Commission, 2016b).

Figure 6: Voter registration – Per area and population

Region	Eligible electorate: UKPGE May 2015	Eligible electorate:EU Referendum	ONS 2014 Population estimate	Percentage of population registered	Total number of votes cast	Turnout on voting day
England	38,736,146	38,956,824	54,316,600	71.72%	28,455,402	73.0%
Gibraltar	n/a	24,117	29,185	82.63%	20,145	84.0%
Northern Ireland	1,236,765	1,260,955	1,840,500	68.51%	789,879	62.7%
Scotland	4,099,532	3,988,492	5,347,600	74.58%	2,679,513	67.2%
Wales	2,281,754	2,270,743	3,092,000	73.44%	1,626,919	71.7%
Total	46,354,197	46,499,537	64,625,885	71.95%	33,571,858	N/A

Reference: Electoral Commission, July 2016b[10]

---

8   BBC Scotland politics website at http://www.bbc.com/news/uk-scotland-scotland-politics-36614284 (accessed at August 2016).

9   BBC EU referendum website at http://www.bbc.com/news/uk-northern-ireland-36616830 (accessed at August 2016).

10   The results presented in this chapter have been obtained from the Electoral Commission. For Referendum results detailed by region, please see website https://www.electoralcommission.org.uk/find-information-by-subject/elections-and-referendums/past-elections-and-referendums/eu-referendum/electorate-and-count-information (accessed July 2017).

The Remain and Leave distribution across the UK is illustrate in the following diagram. It clearly shows a polarised country.

Figure 7: Remain and Leave vote distribution across the UK

grey = Remain vote; black = Leave vote
Reference BBC, 24 June 2016

Leave polled the most strongly in 270 counting areas, with Remain coming first in 129. The Leave campaign triumphed right across England and Wales, winning in large northern cities including Sheffield, the Welsh valleys, across the Midlands including Birmingham, and the south and east of England. Nine areas voted by over 70% to leave, many of them in eastern England including Boston, South Holland and Great Yarmouth.

The Remain campaign, in contrast, dominated in London, Scotland and Northern Ireland. The highest share of the vote achieved by the Remain camp was in Gibraltar, which is not shown on the map above. Seven of the 10 areas with the highest share of the vote for Remain were in London, including Lambeth, Hackney and Haringey, all of which polled over 75% to stay in the European Union. Edinburgh polled over 74% for Remain and Belfast West polled 74.1%.

Figure 8: Remain and Leave vote distribution by largest regions

Votes	Leave	Remain
South East: 4,959,683	51,8%	48,2%
London: 3,776,751	40,1%	59,9%
North West: 3,665,945	53,7%	46,3%
East: 3,328,983	56,5%	43,5%
South West: 3,172,730	52,6%	47,4%
West Midlands: 2,962,862	59,3%	40,7%
Yorkshire and The Humber: 2,739,235	57,7%	42,3%
Scotland: 2,679,513	38,0%	62,0%
East Midlands: 2,508,515	58,8%	41,2%
Wales: 1,626,919	52,5%	47,5%
North East: 1,340,698	58,0%	42,0%
Northern Ireland: 790,149	44,2%	55,8%

■ Leave   ■ Remain

Depth of bars in proportional to votes cast largest areas shown above.
Reference: Electoral Commission, July 2016b

The following diagram shows the Remain-Leave distribution across age group. There is a significant correlation between age and vote, showing younger age groups more likely voting for Remain than older age groups. But many analysts were quick to note that the younger generation's overwhelming preference for staying in the EU did not translate into a result, because a majority of them simply did not turn out to vote. Because of the secret ballot, it is actually not known how many did or did not vote. A YouGov poll estimates that only 36% of 18- to 24-year-olds cast their vote in the referendum. For the following age groups the turn out was as follows:

- 25- to 34-year-olds 58%
- 35 to 44-year-olds 72%
- 45 to 54-year olds 75%
- 55 to 64-year-olds 81%
- 65+ year-olds 83%
  (Sky Data tweet, 2016).

And there is another important point that needs to be mentioned. Turnout is measured as a proportion of "voting eligible" individuals – which means people who are on the electoral register. But available registration data indicates that almost 20% of the youngest age group had not even registered in the first place, which makes matters worse in reflecting young voters preference in the EU Referendum. This means voter apathy among young people is even worse than the polling data would have us believe.

Another interesting fact is that turnout tended to be lower in areas with a higher proportion of younger residents. A clear message for everybody is that every vote counts, and as David Cameron said "The EU membership is most important decision UK voters will have to make in lifetime". Some did not take the opportunity to get their voices heard, and many of the younger generation regret this now.

Figure 9: How different age groups voted

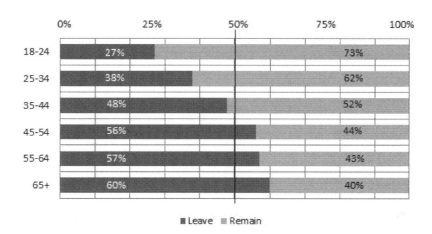

Reference BBC EU Referendum, website June 2016
(BBC, 24 July 2016a and 24 July 2016b)

2.3 WHO WAS ELIGIBLE TO VOTE, AND WHO ACTUALLY DID VOTE?

The country voted to leave the European Union. Really? According to the Electoral Commission, to vote in a EU Referendum (and in UK general election) a person must be registered to vote and also

- 18 or over [this excludes 16 and 17 year olds which are 1,534,192 in total. See section 1.2 for further details.]
- be a British citizen, a qualifying Commonwealth citizen or a citizen of the Republic of Ireland
- not be subject to any legal incapacity to vote
  (Electoral Commissions, 2017)

UK citizens were not eligible to vote if they had been living outside the UK for more than 15 years prior to 23 June 2016. Two expatriate Britons who challenged this restriction, Harry Shindler and Jacquelyn MacLennan, lost their legal battle before the Supreme Court. They argued that the 15-year rule acted to penalise them for having exercised their right of free movement, an infringement of their common law right to vote. It is estimated that more than two million British expats were affected by the decision, which marks the end of the legal battle for an expat's right to vote. These expats feared that a vote to leave the EU will lead to them being deprived of EU citizenship and the rights that go with it. An estimated 5.5m British people live permanently abroad, almost one in 11 of the UK population. Out of these 5.5m it is estimated that around 1.2m live in EU countries. The main destinations include Australia (1,300,000 resident Britons), Spain (761,000), United States (678,000), Canada (603,000), Ireland (291,000), New Zealand (215,000), South Africa (212,000) and France (200,000)[11].

On the other hand, around 960,000 Commonwealth citizens, including Cypriots and Maltese, who were EU citizens as well, were eligible to vote in the referendum. They enjoy this privilege because, while they may now be part of the EU, they once had an older allegiance to a much greater union: the British Empire. The sun set on the Empire long ago, but its legacy lives on. All of these exceptions, when aggregated, make little sense.

According to the Electoral Commission, the following electorates were excluded from voting in the EU Referendum:

- members of the House of Lords (although they can vote at elections to local authorities, devolved legislatures and the European Parliament)
- EU citizens resident in the UK (although they can vote at elections to local authorities, devolved legislatures and the European Parliament) (this includes 3.3 million people in total. See Section 1.2 for further details.)
- anyone other than British, Irish and qualifying Commonwealth citizens
- convicted persons detained in pursuance of their sentences (though remand prisoners, unconvicted prisoners and civil prisoners can vote if they are on the electoral register)
- anyone found guilty within the previous five years of corrupt or illegal practices in connection with an election
  (Electoral Commissions, 2016)

---

11   See BBC Brits Abroad website: at http://news.bbc.co.uk/1/shared/spl/hi/in_depth/brits_abroad/ html/default.stm (accessed May 2017).

2.4 WHAT IS THE ECONOMIC IMPACT

Prior to and after the EU Referendum, a large number of reports have came out predicting the post-Brexit economic growth of the UK as well as the global economy as a whole. These reports were published by international organisations, and include the *World Economic Outlook* of the International Monetary Fund (IMF), the *Annual Report* of the Institute for Fiscal Studies (IFS), and the *Economic Outlook* of the Organisation for Economic Co-operation and Development (OECD). Reports produced by European and national organisations include *The Economic Outlook after the UK Referendum* of the European Commission, the *Growth Forecast* of the Bank or England, the *Economic Review* of the National Institute of Economic and Social Research (NIESR), the *Economic and fiscal outlook* of the UK government's Office for Budget Responsibility, not to mention a large number of reports from private organisations. As the eventual Brexit deal is not yet known, all these reports are based on assumptions; however, an overall picture is emerging. Brexit is uncharted territory fraught with significant changes, but their intensity is risky and uncertain.

It is important to stress the difference between the remote implications of Brexit and its immediate after-effects. The shock of the outcome made stock markets tumble and the pound sterling immediately depreciated on the foreign exchange markets. It has also led to an influx of bargain-hunting tourists and to more UK products being sold abroad. The politicians who celebrated these short-term advantages as affirming Brexit's positive effect on the economy are naïve short-sighted. The fact is that the UK still has full access to the Single Market; nothing yet has changed. However, a hard Brexit that yielded tariffs of up to 46% on exports to the EU would seriously impact the UK economy. WTO tariffs on exports to the EU range from 32% on wine to 4.1% on liquefied gas; 9.8% for cars and 12.8% for wheat products. According to John Springford, an economist of the Centre for European Reform, the total impact of these tariffs could cost anywhere from a 2.2% of GDP (£40 billion) to 9% (Foster and Kirkup, 2017).

The following table summarises some of the findings of the key reports. Caution is advisable in interpreting these forecasts, as the future relationship between the UK and EU has yet to take shape. Nevertheless, the consistent message of them all is that Brexit will cause economic dislocation that cannot be resolved for some time, with consequences unknown and difficult to quantify.

Figure 10: Overview of economic reports and growth figures

Report	Release date	2016 and 2017 UK economic/ GDP growth prediction (percentage)		2016 and 2017 Global economic/ GDP growth prediction (percentage)	
		Before 23rd June	After 23rd June	Before 23 June	After 23rd June
IMF, *World Economic Outlook*	19 July 2016	2.2%	1.3%	3.5% global 1.6% euro area	3.4% global 1.4% euro area
European Commission, *The Economic Outlook after the UK Referendum*	July 2016	1.9%	−0.3%-1.1%	1.7% euro area	1.3%-1.5% euro area
EY, *ITEM Club Quarterly UK Forecast*	July 2016	2.6%	0.4%	n/a	n/a
Bank of England, *Growth Forecast*	30 July 2016	2%	0%	n/a	n/a
NIESR, *Economic Review*	Aug 2016	1.7%	1.0%	3.0%	3.3%
IFS, *Annual Report*	Nov 2016	2.2%	1.4%	n/a	n/a
IMF, *World Economic Outlook* (adjustment)	Jan 2017	See above	1.5%	3.5% global 1.6% euro area	3.4% global
Bank of England, *Growth Forecast* (adjusted)	Feb 2017	2%	2%	n/a	n/a
IFS, *Annual Report* (adjustment)	Feb 2017	2.0%	1.6%	n/a	n/a
PwC, *UK Economic Outlook*	Mar 2017	2.0%	1.6%	n/a	n/a
Office for Budget Responsibility, *Economic and fiscal outlook*	Mar 2017	1.4%	2.0%	n/a	n/a
OECD, *Interim Economic Outlook*	Mar 2017	1.8%	1.6%	3.0% 1.7% Euro area	3.3% 1.6% Euro area
JP Morgan, *UK Growth Forecast*	Apr 2017	1.7%	1.9%	n/a	n/a
EY, *ITEM Club Spring forecast*	Apr 2017	2.6%	1.8%	n/a	n/a
European Commission, *Spring 2017 Economic Forecast*	May 2017	1.8%	1.8%	3.2% global 1.6% euro area	3.7% global 1.7% euro area
OECD, *UK – Economic forecast summary*	June 2017	1.8%	1.6%	n/a	n/a
PwC, *UK Economic Outlook*	July 2017	1.8%	1.5%	n/a	n/a
IMF, *World Economic Outlook Update*	July 2017	See above	1.7%	3.2% global 1.8% euro area	3.5% global 1.9% euro area
Bank of England, *Quarterly inflation report*	Aug 2017	1.9%	1.7%	n/a	n/a
NIESR, *Economic Review*	Aug 2017	1.8%	1.7%	3.1%	3.6%

* ITEM stands for Independent Treasury Economic Model. The EY ITEM Club is an economic forecasting group run by Ernst & Young and based in the City of London.

It is acknowledged that the UK, European and global economies are interlocked and influence each other. The deterioration in the global economic outlook recorded above is not necessarily (probably is not) due to Brexit alone. An exogenous global economic decline would also impact the UK economy over and above Brexit. The unprecedented case of a Member State leaving the EU is a challenge to think tanks struggling to assess and predict the short- to medium-term impact on the UK economy. According to (some of) the above studies, the following was predicted for the UK in the wake of Brexit:

- The uncertainty of Brexit's impact will cause investment to be deferred, resulting in a slowdown of growth for the UK economy in the next three years, and entailing adjustments to GDP growth of between 0.3% and 1.6% in 2016.
- The heightened risks will dampen consumer spending due to a weaker jobs market and higher inflation, which is expected to rise to 3% in 2017.
- Changes to the legal and regulatory setting will increase economic, political and administrative uncertainty for businesses.
- Difficulty in quantifying the potential repercussions of Brexit on the UK economy introduces substantial risks to the economic outlook.
- Extra uncertainty may cause financial market shocks.
- Services exports which the UK currently exports to the EU will undergo shrinkage also because of new "red tape" trade barriers.

In 2015 exports to the EU accounted for 44.0% of total UK exports (£240 billion out of £550 billion total). As per ONS statistics, the proportion of exports to the EU has fallen by more than 10% over the last 15 years to 47% of goods and 39% of services in 2015, and one could argue that trade with the EU has been gradually becoming less important for the UK (Office for National Statistics, July 2016). At the same time, 53% of imports into the UK came from other countries in the EU in 2016, which means that the UK has a trade deficit with the EU (Full Fact UK, 3 April 2017).. This shows a high level of economic dependency between the UK and EU, and any factors that would impact this, such as exiting the Customs Union, could have huge consequences for the UK. The UK deficit in trade in goods and services was estimated at £4.5 billion in July 2016. Any delay in trade deals with countries outside the EU could intensify the impact of the UK's trade balance even more. (Office for National Statistics, July 2016)

It is believed that Brexit will hit the financial services industry, which generates 8% of the UK's economic output, especially hard. The loss of financial services "*passporting*" rights, which allows the citizens of one EU Member State to sell financial services directly in all other Member States without being licenced in each and every one of them separately, will lead UK financial institutions to relocate to EU countries.

Taking into account the one year of economic experience since Brexit so far, the IMF has revised its growth forecast for the UK for 2017 downwards by –0.3 to –1.7% due to weaker than expected activity in the first quarter (IMF, July 2017). More recent economic forecasts have been more moderate and projected a growth rate of 1.5% to 1.7% in 2017 and 1.4% in 2018. Although UK economic growth held up better than expected in the first six months after the referendum, in the six months following, inflation rose to squeeze household spending power. Risks to growth are still posed by Brexit and its associated uncertainties. The housing market is forecast to be subdued for the next few years as demand outstrips supply, and property prices will continue to rise in the long term. Even worse, the UK's slowing growth and increasing inflation rate (projected to reach 3%) in 2018 will confront the Bank of England with an interest rate trap. As a result, there may well be an interest rate increase in the next 12 to 18 months (PwC, July 2017).

In its inflation report of 2 August 2017, the Bank of England announced its intention of leaving interest rates at their current record low of 0.25% due to sluggish economy growth, higher borrowing costs, and increasing inflation. GDP growth was revised downwards to 1.7% from 1.9% in 2017 and to 1.6% from 1.7% in 2018. Governor Carney has blamed the current uncertainty over the Brexit negotiation outcome for the weakening investment outlook as well as for bearish collective bargaining effects for employees. Overall, the Bank of England has expressed concerns over Brexit's likely negative impact on real incomes in the foreseeable future (BoE, 2017). The UK is already afflicted by high household indebtedness and weak productivity growth, which together will impede growth. Although public sector borrowing of £46.6 billion or 2.4% of GDP in the year ending March 2017 is £25.6 billion lower than in the previous financial year, the slow economic growth, the EU exit bill of about €60 billion as well as higher borrowing costs leaves the Government little leeway to end austerity (Inman and Monaghan, 2017). The Bank of England maintains its Bank Rate at the record low rate of 0.25% to stimulate lending and hence economic growth. But at the same time, it is buying up the stock of sterling-denominated non-investment-grade corporate bonds while purchasing £60 billion worth of UK government bonds, each of which is financed by the issuance of central bank reserves, for a total of £435 billion. Ever since the EU Referendum in June 2016, sterling has been stuck at 15%-20% below its most recent peak in November 2015 of 1.54 GBP/USD. By the end of August 2017 the sterling had fallen to an 8-year low of 1.29 GBP/USD. It is expected that sterling will not significantly recover in the next three years (BoE, 2017).

As a result, companies will have to live with a cheaper pound and learn how to manage international supply chain costs even more tightly. Given increasing living costs due to higher import prices for food the purchasing power of British households will be reduced, which may outweigh any positive short-term effects on the level of demand. The uncertain investment climate, too, is expected to last until a final Brexit negotiation result is reached in 2019. The overall economic outlook for the UK is likely to worsen in the next two years (Bastsaikhan, Feli, 2017).

Adam Posen, who worked for both the Federal Reserve Bank of New York and the Monetary Policy Committee of the Bank of England, discussed the damaging effects of Brexit on the British economy at a debate at the Peterson Institute for International Economics, drawing the following conclusions: Brexit will lead to higher inflation, lower purchasing power, a weaker pound, corporate investment will go negative, the government balance sheet will get worse, and the trade balance sheet worse, all due an old-fashioned ideology and unrealistic expectations. (Peterson Institute for International Economics, 19 July 2017).

2.5 THE BENEFITS OF EU CITIZENSHIP

Even as late as 2016 when the referendum took place, a large proportion of the British people were still ill-informed about the benefits of EU membership for the UK, or the value to themselves of EU citizenship and of holding an EU passport. The UK education system is partly to blame for this deficit of knowledge. In the British school syllabus the ancient history of Britain is given priority over EU political education. As late as February 2013, forty years after joining the European Union, Britain's educational authorities published a revised geography curriculum that no longer even referred to it, economically or politically. The history and citizenship curriculum passingly touches on the UK's relationship with Europe, but does not mention the EU as such, or the functioning of the European institutions (Paton, 2013; Gov.uk, 11 September 2013). To compound the fault, the political parties have fallen into a habit over the years of blaming Europe for the many problems that they were unable to solve at home. The Conservative Party in particular has been home to many Eurosceptics, who relentlessly discredit the idea that countries that are geo-political neighbours and share a common cultural heritage could achieve more together as a polity than "every man for himself".

Worst of all, many voters misconceived the referendum as essentially an election campaign, once PM Cameron began campaigning for Remain, and took the opportunity to vote against him; at a minimum they prioritised forcing his resignation over remaining in the EU. This was even after Cameron stated that he would not resign even if Remain lost. Westminster politicians have consistently failed, during the Remain campaign but also long before Remain and Leave had become an issue and a choice, to explain and quantify the actual costs and benefits of EU membership. When the referendum campaign got going, it was easy to continue weaving myth in with facts, and let emotions and propaganda win over reality.

This Section has essayed to supply that deficit by providing the readers a brief overview of the major advantages of EU citizenship, highlighting the benefits for EU passport holders. The European citizens of the Union and their rights are enshrined in Articles 18 through 25 and 45 of the consolidated version of the Treaty on the Functioning of the European Union (TEU).

- *Citizenship of the European Union in addition to national citizenship* (Article 20 TEU): This concept was introduced by the Maastricht Treaty, which was signed in 1992 and came into force in 1993. Every person holding the nationality of a Member State of the European Union is *ipso facto* a citizen of the Union. EU citizenship is only supplemental to national citizenship (Article 20(1). It does not supersede or supplant any of the rights and privileges of citizenship offered by the EU Member State of residence, no matter whether that is the EU citizen's birth country or not. EU citizenship entitles individuals to establish residence in any EU Member State, and to vote there for the EU parliament; to access health, education, unemployment benefits; and to receive pensions from the Member States where they have paid-in contributions. The checklist below elaborates on some of these fundamental rights. Article 20 of the TEU as follows:
  1. Citizenship of the Union is hereby established. Every person holding the nationality of a Member State shall be a citizen of the Union. Citizenship of the Union shall be additional to and not replace national citizenship.
  2. Citizens of the Union shall enjoy the rights and be subject to the duties provided for in the Treaties. They shall have, *inter alia*:
     (a) the right to move and reside freely within the territory of the Member States;
     (b) the right to vote and to stand as candidates in elections to the European Parliament and in municipal elections in their Member State of residence, under the same conditions as nationals of that State;
     (c) the right to enjoy, in the territory of a third country in which the Member State of which they are nationals is not represented, the protection of the diplomatic and consular authorities of any Member State on the same conditions as the nationals of that State;
     (d) the right to petition the European Parliament, to apply to the European Ombudsman, and to address the institutions and advisory bodies of the Union in any of the Treaty languages and to obtain a reply in the same language.
     (TEU, 2012)
- *Right to employment mobility* (Article 45 TEU): The freedom of movement of workers is a policy of the body of law or *acquis Communautaire* ("the *acquis*") of the European Union, and constitutes one of the key principles of the Single Market. It is one aspect of the free movement of persons, and one of the four freedoms of the EU. EU citizenship affords the opportunity to work in any EU Member State without having to apply for work permits or visas. In addition to free movement and residence, this incorporates the right of entry and residency of family members; and the right to work in another Member State entails the right to be treated on an equal footing with nationals of that Member State (although

restrictions apply to certain recent EU Member States). Article 45 of the TEU states:

1. Freedom of movement for workers shall be secured within the Union.
2. Such freedom of movement shall entail the abolition of any discrimination based on nationality between workers of the Member States as regards employment, remuneration and other conditions of work and employment.
3. It shall entail the right, subject to limitations justified on grounds of public policy, public security or public health:
   (a) to accept offers of employment actually made;
   (b) to move freely within the territory of Member States for this purpose; I to stay in a Member State for the purpose of employment in accordance with the provisions governing the employment of nationals of that State laid down by law, regulation or administrative action;
   (d) to remain in the territory of a Member State after having been employed in that State, subject to conditions which shall be embodied in regulations to be drawn up by the Commission.
4. The provisions of this Article shall not apply to employment in the public service.

(TEU, 2012)

- *Right to free movement and residency* (Article 21 TEU): EU citizens may move home to any Member State of their choice. This right was established by the Treaty of Maastricht in 1992, and paralleled the gradual phasing-out of internal borders under the Schengen agreements. The UK did not sign Schengen and still maintains border controls with other Member States. The same right of free movement and residency also applies to pensioners who decide to retire in another Member State whilst drawing pensions from the States where they paid-in contributions.[12] The provisions governing the free movement of persons are laid out in Directive 2004/38/EC on "the right of EU citizens and their family

---

12   Private pensions should be still be able to be moved to another country after Brexit. British or foreign nationals with a British private pension can transfer their entitlement into QROPS (Qualifying Recognised Overseas Pension Scheme). This is a pension scheme established outside the UK which is similar to a UK pension scheme. QROPS legislation was established in April 2006 and as QROPS provider must be recognised for tax purposes in the country that the QROPS is established, their might be new tax regimes enforced on British expats living in the EU after Brexit.

The state retirement plan says that individuals qualify if they have worked and paid national insurance in the UK for 10 years or more (this does not have to have been ten qualifying years in a row). However, as part of Brexit, the UK might have to negotiate reciprocal arrangements with individual EU countries to maintain the status quo and people retiring to those countries could see their state pension payments frozen. There is nothing to suggest existing pension entitlements you have built up will be affected.

members to move and reside freely within the territory of the Member States". The legal basis for this right is Article 21 of the TEU, which states:

1. Every citizen of the Union shall have the right to move and reside freely within the territory of the Member States, subject to the limitations and conditions laid down in the Treaties and by the measures adopted to give them effect.

2. If action by the Union should prove necessary to attain this objective and the Treaties have not provided the necessary powers, the European Parliament and the Council, acting in accordance with the ordinary legislative procedure, may adopt provisions with a view to facilitating the exercise of the rights referred to in paragraph 1.

3. For the same purposes as those referred to in paragraph 1 and if the Treaties have not provided the necessary powers, the Council, acting in accordance with a special legislative procedure, may adopt measures concerning social security or social protection. The Council shall act unanimously after consulting the European Parliament.

(TEU, 2012)

- *Right to access the Single Market* or *European Common Market* (The Single European Act): The four economic freedoms descend from the earlier free movement of persons (or workers), goods, services, and capital. The free movement of goods was the first to be established through the Customs Union before the Union as such was formalised – Member States removed all customs barriers and agreed a common customs policy respecting goods made within the Common Market. It was extended by the Directive on "services in the internal market" (2006/123/EC). The Single European Act (SEA) which under the Delors Commission mandated a Single Market by 31 December 1992, lifted trade barriers (that were still left) and harmonised and competitivised the Member States. Its provisions permitted entrepreneurs, organisations, or indeed anybody, even individuals, who would act on opportunities to sell goods or services, or who would move capital (either as financial investment or as the business activity itself), freely to do so within the territory of the Member States. Article 8a of the SEA states:

The Community shall adopt measures with the aim of progressively establishing the internal market over a period expiring on 31 December 1992, in accordance with the provisions of this Article and of Articles 8b, 8c, 28, 57(2), 59, 70(1), 84, 99, 100a and 100b and without prejudice to the other provisions of this Treaty.

The internal market shall comprise an area without internal frontiers in which the free movement of goods, persons, services and capital is ensured in accordance with the provisions of this Treaty.

(TEU, 2012)

- *Political rights* (Article 22 TEU): The right to vote and stand in elections to the European Parliament in any Member State in which an EU citizen resides is provided for too:
  1. Every citizen of the Union residing in a Member State of which he is not a national shall have the right to vote and to stand as a candidate at municipal elections in the Member State in which he resides, under the same conditions as nationals of that State. This right shall be exercised subject to detailed arrangements adopted by the Council, acting unanimously in accordance with the special legislative procedure and after consulting the European Parliament; these arrangements may provide for derogations where warranted by problems specific to a Member State.
  2. Without prejudice to Article 223(1) TEU and to the provisions adopted for its implementation, every citizen of the Union residing in a Member State of which he is not a national shall have the right to vote and to stand as a candidate in elections to the European Parliament in the Member State in which he resides, under the same conditions as nationals of that State. This right shall be exercised subject to detailed arrangements adopted by the Council, acting unanimously in accordance with a special legislative procedure and after consulting the European Parliament; these arrangements may provide for derogations where warranted by problems specific to a Member State.
- *Right to diplomatic protection of consular authorities of any Member State* (Article 23): If EU citizens travel outside the EU and their own country has no diplomatic representation there, they can seek assistance from the embassies of other Member States to the same extent as that provided for nationals of their own Member State. Article 23 articulates this right as follows:

  Every citizen of the Union shall, in the territory of a third country in which the Member State of which he is a national is not represented, be entitled to protection by the diplomatic or consular authorities of any Member State, on the same conditions as the nationals of that State. Member States shall adopt the necessary provisions and start the international negotiations required to secure this protection.

  The Council, acting in accordance with a special legislative procedure and after consulting the European Parliament, may adopt directives establishing the coordination and cooperation measures necessary to facilitate such protection.

  (TEU, 2012)
- *Right to submit petitions to the European Parliament or contact the Ombudsman in one's own language* (Article 24): EU citizens have the right to submit a petition (*viz.*, a complaint or a request) on any issue that falls within the scope of EU competence. The legal basis for this is Article 24 TEU:

> The European Parliament and the Council, acting by means of regulations in accordance with the ordinary legislative procedure, shall adopt the provisions for the procedures and conditions required for a citizens' initiative within the meaning of Article 11 of the Treaty on European Union, including the minimum number of Member States from which such citizens must come.
>
> Every citizen of the Union shall have the right to petition the European Parliament in accordance with Article 227.
>
> Every citizen of the Union may apply to the Ombudsman established in accordance with Article 228.
>
> Every citizen of the Union may write to any of the institutions or bodies referred to in this Article or in Article 13 of the Treaty on European Union in one of the languages mentioned in Article 55(1) of the Treaty on European Union and have an answer in the same language.
>
> (TEU, 2012)

- *Rights contained in the Union's 'social agenda'* (Articles 9 and 12): Many are the EU Regulations, Directives, Decisions and Opinions which aim to protect employees, consumers, young people in education, and other disadvantaged citizens. The social dimension of European integration has been deeply elaborated through the years, and is a key aspect of the Europe 2020 strategy and governs the enactment of new or amendment of existing EU laws. Article 9 TEU [on employment] states:

> In defining and implementing its policies and activities, the Union shall take into account requirements linked to the promotion of a high level of employment, the guarantee of adequate social protection, the fight against social exclusion, and a high level of education, training and protection of human health.
>
> (TEU, 2012)

Article 12 [on consumer protection] of the TEU sets the policy objective that:

> Consumer protection requirements shall be taken into account in defining and implementing other Union policies and activities.
>
> (TEU, 2012)

- *Right to protection of personal data* (Article 16): Among the many individual rights protected by the EU Charter of Fundamental Rights, the protection of personal data is exceptionally strong compared to other parts of the world. As everybody is obliged to provide personal data on a daily basis, from making a bank transfer to applying for a mortgage or even just signing up for a loyalty card scheme, rights of protection of personal data of EU citizens and residents has been given high priority. Article 16 of the TEU states:

1. Everyone has the right to the protection of personal data concerning them.
2. The European Parliament and the Council, acting in accordance with the ordinary legislative procedure, shall lay down the rules relating to the protection of individuals with regard to the processing of personal data by Union institutions, bodies, offices and agencies, and by the Member States when carrying out activities which fall within the scope of Union law, and the rules relating to the free movement of such data. Compliance with these rules shall be subject to the control of independent authorities.

    The rules adopted on the basis of this Article shall be without prejudice to the specific rules laid down in Article 39 of the Treaty on European Union. (TEU, 2012)

- *Right to health care*: EU citizens on holiday or at work in another Member State holding a European Health Insurance Card (EHIC), has a right to access state-provided healthcare whilst sojourning or travelling in the EU, the European Economic Area (EEA), or Switzerland.
- *Right to property investment*: EU citizens may purchase property without hindrance in all 27 EU Member States.
- *Right to qualify for EU Research Funding*: EU citizens who are students, lecturers or researchers are eligible to apply for EU academic grants equally. These are offered under the mobility programme, the Research Framework programmes, and other grant schemes. Many of them are only available to EU citizens.
- *Right to educational benefits*: EU citizens who move home individually or with family to another EU Member State may attend school and university without discrimination (*e.g.* overseas student fees do not apply).
- *Right to legal equality*: EU citizens have the same legal rights as natural-born citizens in any of the 27 EU Member States.

The enjoyment of reciprocal rights independent of national citizenship is considered one of the major benefits of European Union citizenship. EU citizens have equal legal rights in all EU Member States and full access to the Single Market, by being employed or employing others, or by offering goods and services. Company and individual investments and profits may be freely transferred between the EU Member States without cost (additional to ordinary bank charges *etc*.) (European Commission, DG Justice, August 2016).

2.6   THE RESULT EXPLAINED: WHY DID THE 'LEAVE' CAMPAIGN WIN?

More reasons are needed to fully explain why the Leave campaign won the EU Referendum than can be derived from the socio-demographic data analysed above. These reasons have been widely discussed in the media and are summarised under the following headings.

2.6.1 A vote against the Establishment

The Leave campaign presented an "out" vote as a vote against the Establishment. European politics was always presented in the UK as something alien, un-British, and emanating from a remote power that now rules the once-glorious British Empire. The older generation, especially, considers Britain to be a ruler, not a country that gets ruled. This explains why the "Take Back Control" slogan got such a warm reception from many elderly voters. Most British are more comfortable and familiar with the House of Commons, even the unelected House of Lords in Westminster, than with the elected European Parliament located on foreign soil. Brussels and Strasbourg were branded as 'temples of bureaucracy' – which may well be true, but applies equally to public services bureaucracies in the UK. The European Parliament was branded as an institution undermining everything that is *Great* about Britain. It was a given for the Leave campaign to position the referendum as a vote against the Establishment and for ending "foreign rule" over the British Isles.

It is ironic that key figures of the Leave campaign are also part of the Establishment. For example, Alexander Boris de Pfeffel Johnson (known to the public as Boris Johnson) is not only a "populist" British politician, an historian, author and journalist. He also studied at Eton, the "public school", the British term for an elite boarding school for the aristocracy, and read Literae Humaniores, a four-year course of study of the Classics, at Balliol College, Oxford. Michael Andrew Gove studied English at Lady Margaret Hall, Oxford, where he served as President of the Oxford Union. Nigel Paul Farage was a City commodities trader before he joined politics. In 2016 Farage got involved in the United States Presidential elections and formed a friendship with the newly elected President Donald Trump, who even suggested in a Tweet that "Many people would like to see @ Nigel_Farage represent Great Britain as their Ambassador to the United States. He would do a great job!". All have been full-time politicians for most of their lives, and some are trying to work out how they can take their careers to the next level. There is nothing wrong with a decent career path, but they presented the referendum as a "vote against the Establishment" while being part the Establishment.

2.6.2 The bleak pessimism of the Remain campaign

Remain bombarded the public with dire warnings that leaving the EU would make everybody poorer. Institutions like the CBI, IMF, and OECD chimed in, dutifully predicting economic decline, higher unemployment, and a fall in the value of the pound. The Bank of England warned of recession, and the Treasury announced the income tax would have to be raised to afford the NHS, schools and defence. "Project Fear" dominated the Remain campaign for too long, whilst the Leave campaign flogged the negativism with the cheery image of a Britain that would be "Back in Control". The Leave campaign were able to omit all the achievements of the EU-28 in regards to trade, employment, the social agenda, environment, industry, politics and on and on – without a response from Remain.

2.6.3 An entertaining campaign and simplistic claims attracted voters to Leave

The Leave campaign was more entertaining: The Three Brexiteers – Boris Johnson, Michael Gove, and Nigel Farage – travelled up and down the country on the Vote Leave bus. The face of Euroscepticism in the UK, particularly UKIP leader Nigel Fararge, provoked controversy and, as the Streisand Effect would predict, both galvanised the undecided and the politically disengaged, and mobilised No-voters. It was a classic example of telling people what they wanted to hear, ignoring facts, and emphasizing emotions without making binding promises and taking no determinate responsibility. Some Leave events seemed more about taking the mickey out of all the stuffy Remain blacksuits than debating specific issues. The Leave campaign in the end turned into an X-Factor or Britain's Got Talent show than a strategic political movement.

Catchy, populist slogans like "We want our country back" and "We send the EU £350 million a week. Let's fund our NHS instead" prevailed. The figure of £350 million emblazoned on Leave's "battle bus" was burned into people's minds and even though both the Treasury Select Committee of the House of Commons and the Chairman of the UK Statistics Authority, Sir Andrew Dilnot, dismissed the figure as wrong, nobody cared because nobody trusted or believed them. In an open letter to the Rt. Hon Norman Lamb MP dated 21 April 2016, Mr Dilnot clarified that this calculation was based on "the ONS Pink Book 2015, and converted into weekly amounts using either an average of payments over the last 5 years or using the latest year's [2014's] data". The Leave campaign claim was based on the UK's gross contribution to the EU, which was £19.107 billion (in 2014, or £365 million per week), and not on the contribution *after the rebate*, which was £14.691 billion in 2014, or £285 million per week (£80 million less).

The UK public sector also receives a significant amount of funds from EU programmes, so that after these monies are deducted, the UK's net contribution was £9.872 billion in 2014, or £190 million per week (£175 million less). Taking into account an estimate of the receipts flowing to UK non-public sector bodies from the EU would knock down the estimated average between 2010 and 2014 even further, to £8.889 billion, around £170 million per week (Letter of Sir Andrew Dilnot of the UK Statistics Authority, sent on 21 April 2016). The Office for National Statistics (ONS) estimated that 64.6 million people lived in the UK in 2014. Depending on how it is calculated, as a 5-year average (2010-2014) or at the latest year (2014), *per capita* contribution to the EU was £137.60 or £152.82 per year; £2.65 or £2.94 per week; or 38 pence or 42 pence per day, respectively. The staggering figure of "billions" of UK pounds going into the EU budget translates to an amount per person per week which would not even buy a latte at Starbuck's. The Treasury estimates that the UK private sector received payments (*e.g.*, as research grants) of £1.4 billion which is not included in the ONS statistics, shrinking the estimated net contribution to £8.4 billion in 2014, which would translate into £2.50 *per capita* per week (36 pence per day or £130.03 per year) to the EU budget. Figure 11 breaks this calculation down in detail.

Figure 11: UK net contribution to the EU (excluding payments to non-public sector bodies)

UK contributions to EU budget (breakdown)	Net contribution 2010 to 2014 (millions)					5-year average (millions)			2014 alone (millions)		
	2010	2011	2012	2013	2014	2010-2014	weekly (*)	weekly per person	2014	weekly (*)	weekly per person
[1] Gross contribution before rebate	15,999	16,075	16,441	19,377	19,107	17,400	335	£5.18	19,107	365	£5.69
Less UK rebate	3,046	3,144	3,110	3,675	4,416	3,478	65	£1.04	4,416	85	£1.31
[2] Gross contribution after rebate	12,953	12,931	13,331	15,702	14,691	13,922	270	£4.14	14,691	285	£4.37
Less EU payments to the UK public sector	5,728	5,388	4,795	4,431	4,819	5,032	95	£1.50	4,819	95	£1.43
[3] Net contribution, public-sector bodies only	7,225	7,543	8,536	11,271	9,872	8,889	170	£2.65	9,872	190	£2.94

Source: ONS Pink Book 2015 Table 9.9. Gross contribution before rebate = GCSM, rebate = FKKL, gross contribution after rebate = GCSM-FKKL, EU payments to the public sector = GSCL-FKKL, net contribution = BLZS.

(*) Weekly figures are annual divided by 52 and rounded to the nearest $5 million.

(**) Weekly figures *per capita* are based on 64.6 million UK population (ONS statistics for 2014).

2.6.4 Payment of 'large sums of money' (which is small if put into perspective)

Incomprehensibly outsized figures look enormous (particularly government budgets) until they are broken down and explained. As laid out in the previous Section, the UK net contribution to the EU budget of £8.5 billion in 2014 translates to just £130.03 *per capita* per year or £2.50 per week or 36 pence per day. Most people pay that much or more just for coffee (let alone something big like insurance) without even thinking about it.

The UK government is very good at explaining its own spending to UK taxpayers, but the Cameron Government and the Remain campaign did nowhere near as good a job of explaining the EU budget and the benefits British citizens received from it. Once a year UK taxpayers receive an Annual Tax Summary from HM Revenue & Customs, which details how their Income Tax and National Insurance contributions (NICs) are calculated and how their money is spent by the government (HM Treasury, 13 December 2016; HM Treasury, 15 December 2016).[13] The Tax Summary, which is based on the Official

---

13   Guidance in how the Annual Tax Summary is calculated is available at HM Treasury website: https://www.gov.uk/guidance/annual-tax-summary. Around 30 million UK taxpayers get a personalised Tax Summary every year, which provides an overview of the personal tax and National Insurance contributions (NICs) and how they're spent by the government.

Statistics published by the Government in the Public Expenditure Statistical Analyses (PESA) series, shows that public spending by the UK in Fiscal Year 2015-16 on the UK contribution to EU budget was 1.1% of the total budget (£7.7 billion) at its lowest.

Figure 12: Government spending Fiscal Year 2014-2015

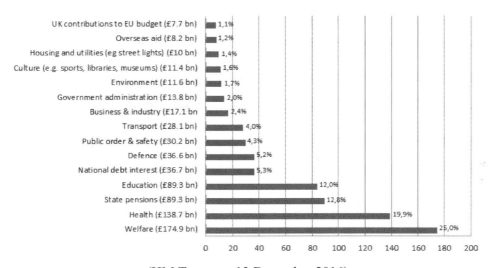

(HM Treasury, 13 December 2016)

In 2015 the average annual net earnings of individuals in the UK were €26,860.40, compared to average EU-28 net earnings of €17,296.22. Average net earnings were at their highest in Luxembourg (€28,799.55) and at their lowest in Bulgaria (€3,485.82) (Eurostat, Labour Market, 2017). The net contribution of £130.03 for the average Briton will obviously not capture the cost to other nationals due to variance across the EU of average individual earnings in the several Member States. In Fiscal Year 2015-16 (the *tax* year ends on 5 April), the tax bands for UK taxpayers were as follows:

- Starting rate limit (savings income):   £5,000 (0% tax rate)[14]
- Basic rate band: £0 – 31,865 (basic rate 20%)
- Higher rate band: £31,866 – 150,000 (high rate 40%)
- Additional rate band: Over £150,000 (additional rate 45%)
  (HM Treasury, 4 March 2015; HM Treasury, 2016b).

An individual with gross earnings of £20,000 per year paid just £33 (or £2.75 per month) in *per capita* net EU contribution per year based on financial year 2015-16 figures.

---

14   See UK Government website at https://www.gov.uk/government/publications/issue-briefing-
      starting-tax-rate-for-savings-interest/issue-briefing-starting-tax-rate-for-savings-interest
      (accessed June 2017).

Someone who earned £30,000, which is above average, paid £55 in net EU contributions, while somebody who earned £100,000 paid £357.79 in net EU contributions.

Figure 13: UK contributions to the EU by income brackets (2015/16 tax year)

Annual income of UK resident/ taxpayer	Starting rate limit £5,000 (0%)	Basic rate band £0 – 31,865 (20%)	Higher rate band £31,866 – 150,000 (40%)	Additional rate band, over £150,000 (45%)	Total tax paid	Net EU contribution (per person/ year)	Net EU contribution (per person/ months)	Net EU contribution (per person/ day)
£0	£0	£0	£0	£0	£0	£0	£0	£0
£5,000	£0	£0	£0	£0	£0	£0	£0	£0
£10,000	£0	£1,000	£0	£0	£1,000	£11	£0.92	3.01 pence
£20,000	£0	£3,000	£0	£0	£3,000	£33	£2.75	9.27 pence
£30,000	£0	£5,000	£0	£0	£5,000	£55	£4.58	15.45 pence
£40,000	£0	£5,373	£3,253	£0	£8,626	£94.90	£7.91	24.23 pence
£50,000	£0	£5,373	£7,253	£0	£12,526	£137.79	£11.48	38.71 pence
£100,000	£0	£5,373	£27,253	£0	£32,526	£357.79	£29.82	£1.01
£200,000	£0	£5,373	£47,253	£22,500	£75,026	£825.29	£68.77	£2.32

(*) Weekly figures are annual figures divided by 52 and rounded to the nearest $5m.
(**) Weekly figures *per capita* are based on a UK population 64.6 million (ONS statistics for 2014).
(***) Daily figures are annual figures divided by 356.
EU net contribution was 1.1% on tax income in financial year 2015-16.
(Dilnot, 21 April 2016; Office of National Statistics, Pink Book 2015)

2.6.5 The exclusion of an estimated 6 million voters who would have been likelier to vote Remain

Some fascinating data emerges from analysing who was eligible to vote in the EU Referendum. Combining this with the statistical information provided in Chapter Two, and comparing this electorate to the Scottish Independence referendum electorate, some amazing conclusions can be drawn. If the Scottish eligibility rules had applied to the EU Referendum, an additional 4.8 million people could have voted, who might well have changed the outcome, giving Remain the victory. Moreover, if all 1.2 million British citizens living abroad in other EU countries had been allowed to vote, the outcome would have been decisive for Remain.

The list below is evidence that, based on eligibility to vote and voter mobilisation, the outcome of a referendum does not always reflect the views of the whole body of the residents or citizens of a country. It only reflects the views of the electorates who were made eligible to vote *and* actually did vote, who formed their opinions based on the information provided and promises made (something which is of course difficult to weigh and reckon-in). Based on the statistical information provided in Chapter Two, if the Scottish rules had applied, an additional 4.8 million voters could have voted and might have led Remain to victory.

Electorates in the EU Referendum

- Commonwealth citizens from 52 countries who were resident in the UK were allowed to vote (as in the Scottish referendum). It is estimated that around one million migrants from the Commonwealth have the right to vote in UK Parliamentary elections, despite not being British citizens. Voting rights for the whole Commonwealth are an anachronism from the days of the British Empire. Critics argue that it should be ended except for citizens of those few Commonwealth countries which grant British citizens reciprocal voting rights (Migration Watch UK, 2016a).
- Irish citizens living in the UK were allowed to vote. The ONS estimate that in 2014 382,000 Irish living in the UK were born abroad.

Not eligible to vote in the EU Referendum

- People aged 16 or 17 were not allowed to vote (unlike in the Scottish referendum where anyone over 16 was eligible to vote). The "UK in a Changing Europe" Initiative calculated that "in 2014, there were 1,534,192 16- and 17-year-olds in the UK, while the number aged 18 or over was 50,909,098, putting 16- and 17-year-olds at 2.9% of the 16+ population" (The UK in a Changing Britain, 2015).
- EU citizens were not allowed to vote (unlike in the Scottish referendum and the European Parliament elections, where EU residents in the UK are eligible to vote). Although it could be argued that EU citizens have a conflict of interest in voting in the EU Referendum as they care more about their own national interest than the UK's. If Remain had won, the Leave camp could have declared the result invalid just for this reason, and the referendum would not have put the matter to rest. On the other side, Remainers can argue that the estimated one million Commonwealth citizens should have had no right to vote, as they have few ties with the EU, skewing the result toward Leave.

    The ONS Labour Force Survey has estimated in 2015 that "there are 3.3 million EU citizens in the UK – 1.6 million from the EU-14, 1.3 million from the EU-8, 300,000 from Romania and Bulgaria and the remainder from the other EU countries of Malta, Cyprus and Croatia" (Migration Watch UK, 2016b). Only EU citizens from Ireland (around 382,000), Malta (37,000) (Balzan, Juergen, 27 June 2016) and Cyprus (estimated 59,000) (Chrysostomou, 19 June 2016) were allowed to vote (because they are Commonwealth countries).

- People of British descent living outside Great Britain were not eligible to vote (as in the Scottish referendum). An estimated 5.5m British people live permanently abroad, almost one in 11 of the UK population. Out of these 5.5m it is estimated that around 1.2m live in EU countries.
- British citizens living overseas to be eligible to vote must have been registered in a UK constituency less than 15 years ago. The number of British people living in the EU is 1.2 million. The largest communities are in Spain (309,000), Ireland (255,000), France (185,000), and Germany (103,000) (United Nations, 2015). Although no statistics exist to track for how long British expatriates have been living abroad, due to the high percentage of pensioners in countries like Spain and marriages with EU citizens, it has been estimated that 700,000 to 800,000 expats have lived for more than 15 years abroad (*The Telegraph*, 28 April 2016). David Cameron's 2015 Conservative manifesto promised a clear commitment to scrap the 15-year rule for overseas voters in favour of "votes for life" for British expats; this was not enforced, however. A group of British citizens brought a legal challenge against the government, claiming they had been wrongly disenfranchised, but the UK High Court ruled that the law was that they had not the right to vote. (Croft, 28 April 2016).

2.6.6 Many voters treated the referendum like an election and stopped listening

PM Cameron put himself on the frontline of the Remain campaign. By many he was seen as its leader, and this gave the campaign an election-like flavour, although the referendum was about much more than voting for a new government for the next five years. It was about defining the UK's relationship to its neighbour countries potentially for ever. The Eurosceptics in his own party demonstrated to the public that voting Conservative does not mean voting for Remain. Floating voters did not buy into the PM's campaign either.

2.6.7 Labour failed to take a position

The Remain campaign was depending on Labour voters to win the referendum. The Labour Party not only declined to position itself or make strong arguments, until the very end most voters were unclear if Labour was for Remain or not. Jeremy Corby was always a Eurosceptic, like the genuinely Marxist Left has always been. This was evident in the 1970s where Labour was more Eurosceptic than the Tories.

Gordon Brown, Tony Blair's successor as Prime Minster, and Sadiq Khan, Major of London, participated in the Remain campaign, but with little backing from Party leader Jeremy Corbyn. He mentioned a few times the importance of the "social agenda of the

EU"; however, he failed to explain what exactly this means for the ordinary man on the street.

2.6.8 Many employers took a hands-off attitude instead of explaining to employees the consequences of leaving the EU

Employers seemed to considered the campaign a personal decision, and did not even consider outlining the implications for their employees. One would have thought that Remain would have been a no-brainer for multinational companies in particular, which depend on international transfers of employees, no barriers to the movement of their services and goods to other EU countries, and the free flow of capital between their affiliates. Yet few employers cautioned their employees not only about the implications of leaving the EU, but also the drawn-out process and uncertainty that was bound to accompany it. Possibly many employers did not grasp the full social and economic implications, assuming the British "let's get on with it" attitude, instead of a "let's prepare for it" approach.

2.6.9 First-ever and older voters flocked to polls

More older voters (65 or over) than younger ones (18 to 24 years) went to the polls. Polls showed support for Brexit was higher amongst those aged 55 and over than amongst younger age groups. Three out of every five voters aged 65 or over said they preferred Leave. The older generation of British citizens perceived the Establishment and politicians as one of the root causes of their problems, in particular their poverty and government's unresponsiveness to their needs, such as social care and cost of accommodation. Politicians in the Remain camp failed to articulate that the "social agenda" is one of the key achievements of the EU.

PART II

What are the implications of Brexit: An impact assessment

We live in a culture where everyone's opinion, view, and assessment of situations and people spill across social media, a lot of it anonymously; much of it is shaped by mindless meanness and ignorance.

Mike Barnicle (1943-)

CHAPTER 3

IMPACT ASSESSMENT OF BREXIT

The question that has puzzled researchers for generations is why lemmings jump from cliffs. Lemmings are small, furry rodents, mammals like us, which periodically run in herds off cliffs into the sea. Although there are many theories about why, this behaviour continues to puzzle scientists. Equally puzzling behaviour is observed when reviewing the UK's EU Referendum: Why do herds of voters decide to run after the path of uncertainty, and why do others choose to play it safe? Who told told the former it is best to jump? Or is it because they expect the herd to jump and fear being left behind? Or do they get a thrill out of it? Or maybe they see no good alternatives?

Perhaps the most puzzling feature of the referendum campaign was the poor analysis and absence of impact scenarios throughout. Of course, plenty of *economic* impact reports were published (see Section 2.4 What is the economic impact), but the implications of Brexit are farther-reaching and the remote implications were almost never addressed. The campaigns on both sides, the Government, and the media in particular took a very narrow view. All-important policy domains like science and research, education and culture, environment and consumer protection were hardly discussed by either campaign. Some voters seemed surprised to learn – after the referendum was over of course – how dependent students, teachers and researches are on EU grants. And most students aspire to more than a gap year when starting their careers: they want the chance to live and work in 27 other countries to widen their horizon. Though places at European Universities are not guaranteed, EU programmes facilitate Europe-wide exchange programmes and grants. And, obviously, the freedom of movement allows graduates more easily to pursue an international career. It was therefore a shock that most of the age group who would have benefited the most from having 28 passports instead of one (*i.e.* European citizenship) failed to vote. Maybe it was politics fatigue, or simply that the younger generation expected nothing to change and naively expected their elders to get it right. However, they were wrong: as PM David Cameron said quite rightly, the EU membership referendum was more important than any general election and a "once in a generation" decision.

No doubt, the campaigns of both camps generated passion and divisiveness. What both campaigns neglected in the months before and after the referendum was an attempt at an assessment of the implications of Brexit for specific policy sectors. This Chapter fills that gap, providing a Policy Impact Assessment (PIA) of Brexit. It follows the structure of the *acquis Communautaire* or code of European law that is brought to bear when accession candidates are starting the process for applying for EU membership. The 35 policy domains covered in the *acquis* are far-reaching: they span the four principles (free movement of goods, people, services and capital); public procurement procedures; company and competition law; industry-specific regulations; taxation; economic and monitory policy; regional policy and its instruments; justice, freedom and security; scientific research, education and culture; the environment; consumer and health protection; Customs Union; external relations; security and defence policy; fiscal controls and budgetary provisions; institutions; and other matters.

A comprehensive analysis would of course call for teams of experts with in-depth knowledge of all aspects of the matters in each of these domains. The authors of this book and the network of legal, business and policy experts in the UK and in Europe to which they belong have a competent grasp of most of these domains; nevertheless, the reader should understand that a detailed analysis would require more resources than any two authors could have, that would produce massive reports for each policy domain, not readably few pages in summary as is provided in this book. Even a massive compendium would be incomplete without a forecasting dimension, which to be "scientific" would need not yet existent software to simulate the various possible economic and social scenarios following on Brexit. This Chapter provides an *approach* and template for such an analysis, and offers a modest but high-level impact assessment. Having said this, to the authors' knowledge no one else to date has attempted a similar synoptic overview using the *acquis* itself as a framework.

3.1 IMPACT ON EU POLICY SECTORS

The following Policy Impact Assessment (PIA) across all 35 EU policy domains is the most compendious ever to the authors' knowledge. It follows the structure of the *acquis Communautaire* (or just *acquis* for short),[15] which is the cumulative body of European Union legislation, acts of state, and court decisions which constitute the body of European Union law from 1958 to the present day. Although there is no official count of valid EU legal acts, it is estimated that the complete *acquis* comprises more than 108,000 documents. It includes:

- the content, principles and political objectives of the Treaties
- standards mandated and referred-to in EU law (treaties and legislation – Directives, Regulations and Decisions, Declarations and Resolutions), and formulated and adopted thereafter

---

15   *Acquis* can mean "treasure" in French. See Europa Chapters of the Acquis: Europa Neighbourhood Policy and Enlargement Negotiations website at http://ec.europa.eu/enlargement/policy/conditions-membership/chapters-of-the-acquis/index_en.htm (accessed August 2017).

- Declarations and resolutions taken by the EU supranational organs
- legislation made pursuant to the EU Treaties, and the consequent case law of the European Court of Justice
- international agreements concluded by the Community, and those ntered into by the Member States themselves within the sphere of the European Union's activities
- legal instruments in the domain of freedom, security and justice, and under the Common Foreign and Security Policy
- legal instruments in the domain of justice and home affairs (*i.e.*, asylum policy, immigration and external borders, police and judicial authorities, fight against terrorism and organised crime).

(EU ABC.com website; Miller, 26 April 2011)

The term *acquis* is also used to refer to laws adopted under the Schengen Agreement before it was integrated into the EU legal order by the Treaty of Amsterdam. New EU Member States must accept all the existing *acquis* and institute mechanisms to incorporate amendments and additions as they are legislated. (Certain elements may be implemented over a transitional period.) The European Court of Justice (ECJ) has ruled that the *acquis* takes precedence over national law in case of conflict, and may have a "direct effect" on citizens of the Member States' and its legal orders.

The authors of this book found that the *acquis* provided a perfect template for constructing an impact assessment. There is no pre-established framework for transacting the exit of a country from the EU, and understandably this is uncharted territory for both the UK and the EU. As the *acquis* has already successfully served as a robust framework for joining the EU, it should also be able to serve equally well for leaving countries – and understanding its implications.

The UK's exit will be not a single event but a process spread over many years (although the official period allocated for it is just two years). Brexit is therefore a case of unprecedented character, triggering the UK to negotiate with the EU for most favourable withdrawal terms, its future relationship with the EU, and its position in the EU's international trade deals (Oliver, 2016). However, the UK cannot keep access to the Single Market unless it accepts the Four Freedoms, as defined in Article 26(3) of the Treaty on the Functioning of the European Union (TFEU): "The internal market shall comprise an area without internal frontiers in which the free movement of goods, persons, services and capital is ensured in accordance with the provisions of the Treaties". Furthermore, the Four Freedoms are also essential features of the European Economic Area (EEA) Agreement. Besides EU Member States, the three European Free Trade Association states parties to the EEA (EFTA EEA states) – Iceland, Liechtenstein and Norway – are contracting parties to the EEA Agreement and as bound by it as the Member States (Shearman and Sterling, 2016).

For the sake of Europe's political, legal and economic stability a well-crafted exit agreement between the UK and the EU must be reached. The PIAs for all 35 EU policy domains indicate the points of impact for the UK; they direct attention to important areas of negotiable policy and open a pathway to a partnership model that could include other countries.

Our impact assessments, below, are based on the assumption that the UK will leave the Common Market, which would mean that the four freedoms of movement – of goods, people, services and capital – would apply to the UK-EU relationship no more. Based on these assessments, the authors believe that the impact of Brexit on the several policy domains will be as followed:

Figure 14: Summary – Impact assessment of Brexit decision on EU *acquis* policy domains

Ref	EU Policy areas as per the *acquis Communautaire*	Impact assessment for the EU and UK
1	Free Movement of Goods	High
2	Free Movement of Workers	High
3	Right of Establishment and Freedom to Provide Services	High
4	Free Movement of Capital	High
5	Public Procurement	Medium
6	Company Law	High
7	Intellectual Property Law	Medium
8	Competition Policy	Medium
9	Financial Services Law	High
10	The Information Society and Media Law	High
11	Agriculture and Rural Development	High
12	Food safety, Veterinary and Phytosanitary Policy	Medium
13	Fisheries	High
14	Transport Policy	High
15	Energy	Medium
16	Taxation	Medium
17	Economic and Monetary Policy	High
18	Statistics	Low
19	Social Policy and Employment Law	High
20	Enterprise and Industrial Policy	High
21	Trans-European Networks	High
22	Regional Policy and Coordination of Structural Instruments	High
23	Judiciary and Fundamental Rights	Medium
24	Justice, Freedom and Security	High
25	Science and Research	High
26	Education and Culture	High
27	Environment	Medium
28	Consumer and Health Protection	Medium
29	Customs Union	High
30	External Relations	High
31	Foreign Security and Defence Policy	High
32	Financial Control	Medium
33	Financial and Budgetary Provisions	High
34	Institutions	High
35	Other Issues	Unknown

The following Sections overview each of the 35 policy domains of the *acquis Communautaire*, by (1) identifying the Directorate General responsible and/or the law that governs this domain; (2) outlining what the policy domain includes; (3) assessing how a hard Brexit or No Deal would impact the UK in general, and business and citizens specifically. Each Section concludes with an Impact Assessment Summary.

Although the following Brexit impact assessment is the most comprehensive that has been published to date and it presents a balanced view outlining the pros and cons, the authors would like to stress that it is not complete; each Section could easily take up a book of its own. With this in mind, our aim is to present to the reader the enormity of Brexit, how it impacts every aspect of our life. For politicians and businesses the following Sections provide a template on how they can assess the impact of Brexit.

3.1.1 Free movement of goods

Definition: *The principle of the free movement of goods implies that products must be traded freely from one part of the Union to another. In a number of sectors this general principle is complemented by a harmonised regulatory framework, following the "old approach" (imposing precise product specifications) or the "new approach" (imposing general product requirements). The harmonised European product legislation, which needs to be transposed, represents the largest part of the acquis under this chapter. In addition, sufficient administrative capacity is essential to notify restrictions on trade and to apply horizontal and procedural measures in areas such as standardisation, conformity assessment, accreditation, metrology and market surveillance.*[16]

The free movement of goods makes part of an economically Liberal programme called the Single Market intended to abolish trade barriers and physical customs requirements within the European Union, reducing the costs associated with the cross-border trade of goods. As an EU Member State, the UK has access to the Single Market. The legal basis for the free movement of goods is Articles 26 and 28-37 of the Treaty on the Functioning of the European Union (TFEU), one of the fundamental principles of the which (Article 28) is the right to free movement of goods originating in Member States, and in third countries which are in free circulation within the Member States.[17] Defined and agreed procedures, standards

---

16 All Chapters of the acquis are available on the European Commissions' "European Neighbourhood Policy and Enlargement Negotiations" website. See the "Europa Chapters of the Acquis", website at http://ec.europa.eu/enlargement/policy/conditions-membership/chapters-of-the-acquis/index_ en.htm (accessed August 2016).

17 Detailed information on the free movement of goods is available at "Fact Sheets on the European Union" website http://www.europarl.europa.eu/atyourservice/en/displayFtu. html?ftuId=FTU_3.1.2.html (accessed August 2016) as well as at "Guide to the application of Treaty provisions governing the free movement of goods", Ref. Ares(2013)3759436 – 18/12/2013. (accessed August 2016).

and rules common to all Member States ensure businesses in the EU have unhindered access to the EU's vast internal market, with its 500 million consumers and 21 million small and medium-sized enterprises (SMEs). The European Commission regulates and monitors the internal market to guarantee the application of EU law, launching infringement proceedings against non-compliant Member States (EC Growth, 2016). The Commission and the ECJ both assure that benefits materialise for consumers, such as free movement of goods in the internal market, high product safety standards, and environmental protection *inter alia*. The Commission assures in particular that Single Market rules are promulgated and implemented and not undermined by other barriers. Where legalisation criteria are not yet harmonised, the free movement of goods is facilitated by the principle of "mutual recognition" of other Member States' criteria for lawfully marketed products.

To unlock the benefits of economic integration for both consumers and companies, the EU addresses various strategic programmes that will boost the Single Market (EC Growth, November 2016):

- *Digital Single Market*: Introduce a fully functional digital Single Market to promote innovation, contribute €415 billion to the EU economy each year, and create hundreds of thousands of new jobs.
- *Standardisation*: Formulate technical specifications for various products, materials, services and processes. Standards reduce costs, improve safety, enhance competition, facilitate acceptance of innovations, and avoid tariff jungles.
- *Barriers to trade*: Promote free trade in the EU and beyond by abolishing barriers, quantitative restrictions on imports and exports, and various technical notification procedures and rules.
- *CE marking*: Meet high safety, health and environmental protection requirements within the EU for manufacturers, and importers and distributors.
- *Public procurement*: Ensure fair, competitive and conductive public procurement of goods and services acquired by public authorities within the Single Market.

Besides the removal of internal tariffs, the EU implements common external tariffs on goods imported from non-EU countries. This Customs Union guarantees the free movement of individuals and services as well as goods, together with the right of business establishment within the EU. Any new negotiated partnership model by the UK will determine the scope of access to the Single Market EU (Shearman and Sterling, 2016).

The UK's trade with the EU reached 44% of its exports in goods and services in 2015, representing £220 billion out of £550 billion total exports; whereas on the other side of the international trade ledger, 53% of the UK's imports, or £290 billion, came from fellow EU Member States (thus, the UK runs a trade deficit with the EU). In goods trade, the UK's major trading partners are the US, Germany, Netherlands, France, Ireland and China. This means the UK has an interest to continue trading with the EU, the world's largest economy, and to have control in negotiating regulations with EU or EEA Members in a post-Brexit scenario. Moreover, the UK benefits from EU trade agreements with over 50 states outside the EU. Brexit would require the UK government to rebuild all of its future cross-border trading arrangements and agreements, including potentially introducing tariffs between the UK and the EU; and negotiating them in parallel with the exit agreement. Given the UK will be 3.5% of world GDP rather than part of 23% of world GDP, which is the EU bloc, the UK's negotiating position will be weak and achieving favourable new tariffs will be correlatively difficult. Finally, Brexit will result in the loss of trade agreements now in the offing, like the EU-Japan agreement, worth an estimated £13 billion to the EU (Barnard, 2016).

In any kind of post-Brexit world, the free movement of goods will be affected and this will impact on consumers and businesses: customs procedures, administrative burdens, and other complexities of trading with the EU could increase for UK companies, due to complying with local and EU standards. UK-based companies' whole supply chains may need to be reconsidered for product and process standards in a Brexit aftermath. Any additional customs or taxes on goods will have a negative impact on trade flows. UK companies will have to factor-in the newly higher costs of EU-based suppliers or redirect shipping to avoid UK customs.

Loss of access to the Digital Single Market with its strategies to facilitate cross-border commerce and allow businesses better access to online services and content will burden UK e-commerce companies and exact extra effort to anticipate EU technical standards for ICT and interoperability, the modernisation of intellectual property rights enforcement, parcel delivery, e-commerce, and the "collaborative economy" of old and new, with the prospect to create new services for customers. UK manufacturers supplying products to EU countries will still need to adjust their product standards to EU norms. Retail and consumer businesses importing goods into the UK will suffer increased handling costs and lower exchange rates, which will affect pricing and consumer spending (Welfare, Klinger, 2016). There is the risk that public procurement on EU standards could exclude UK bidding and supply to public authorities within the EU. In face of higher tariffs and lower pound/euro exchange rates, the economic damage will be high for the exporting industry, and could result in elimination of many manufacturing industries. Such industries as design, marketing and hi-tech may have to leave or merge with EU companies, which maybe ought not to scare the UK (Minford, 2016) but would require structural changes and governmental support to manage a socially smooth transition process in the UK.

Impact Assessment Summary

- The free movement of goods, as one of the fundamental rights of the internal market, is anchored in Articles 26 and 28 through 37 of the TFEU. The European Commission and the European Court of Justice govern compliance with the rules of unhindered trade of goods.

- The harmonisation of legal criteria and the mutual recognition principle assure free exchange of goods despite different regulations amongst Member States of the EU. The lowering of trade barriers and implementation of product standards benefit EU consumers in terms of lower costs and product safety. Businesses benefit from fair competition and easier enforcement of their rights.
- With Brexit, UK businesses will be limited or even excluded from access to a market of 500 million consumers and 21 million enterprises. UK businesses and consumers will be liable to new standards and trade barriers as well as exclusion from new market developments like the Digital Single Market.
- Brexit affects the cost of doing international business, as UK companies will be exposed to export and import regulations and administrative burdens they were previously exempt from. Higher costs will increase product prices for entrepreneurs and consumers.
- UK businesses have to reconsider product and process standards for their supply chains – investments are essential for adapting to a new regional and international market situation.
- UK government will be challenged to provide funds for a smooth transition process to strengthen its internal and export market economy.

3.1.2 Freedom of movement for workers

Definition: *The acquis under this chapter provides that EU citizens of one Member State have the right to work in another Member State. EU migrant workers must be treated in the same way as national workers in relation to working conditions, social and tax advantages. This also includes a mechanism to coordinate national social security provisions for insured persons and their family members moving to another Member State.*

The legal basis for free movement of workers in the EU is guaranteed by Article 3(2) of the Treaty on European Union (TEU) and Articles 4(2)(a), 20, 26 and 45-48 of the Treaty on the Functioning of the European Union (TFEU). Specific legal instruments include Directive 2004/38/EC on the right of citizens of the Union and their family members to move and reside freely within the territory of the Member States; Regulation (EU) No 492/2011 on freedom of movement for workers within the Union; and Regulation (EC) No 883/2004 on the coordination of social security systems and its implementing Regulation (EC) No 987/2009. [18]

Free movement of workers between the 28 EU countries is one of the four freedoms of the Single Market: if you find a job in Rome, Amsterdam or Paris, you can just go for it; nobody can stop you moving to another EU country, which is a great achievement! Currently 3.3 million EU citizens live in the UK, as well as more than 5 million foreign-born people. Likewise, 2.2 million Britons live in EU countries (one million in Spain alone). British pensioners and expatriates are worried that Brexit will also mean that they lose their expatriate healthcare and pensions, potentially forcing an exodus of UK expatriates from Europe, pushing thousands back into Britain. How patriotic is it to destroy the existence of Brits abroad?

The UK never signed up to the Schengen Agreement and so kept its internal border controls and visa policies. What the Leave campaign never admitted (or possibly never knew) is that four non-EU Members are even part of the Schengen Area: Iceland, Liechtenstein, Norway and Switzerland. Looking at levels of total immigration (EU and non-EU) alone, Liechtenstein is leading with 33.1%, followed by Switzerland with 28.9%, Norway with 13.8%, and Iceland with 10.7% (UN, 2015). Compared with 11.3% immigration into the UK, Boris & Co ought seriously to have revised their key argument.

Out of the UK's 32.01 million-strong workforce in July 2017 (175,000 more than December 2016 to February 2017 and 324,000 more than a year earlier), around 3.55 million or 11% are non-UK born workers based on ONS statistics. The employment rate (of people aged from 16 to 64) was 74.9%, the highest since comparable records began

---

18   Detailed information is available at "Fact Sheets on the European Union: Free movement of workers", European Parliament website at http://www.europarl.europa.eu/atyourservice/en/displayFtu.html?ftuId=FTU_3.1.3.html (accessed September 2017).

in 1971. Looking at changes in non-UK nationals working in the UK over the 20-year period from January-to-March 1997 (when comparable records began) to January-to-March 2017, their number increased from 928,000 to 3.55 million, or from 3.5% to 11%. This reflects the admission of several new and poorer Member States to the European Union with its influx from certain East European countries. Looking in more detail at non-UK nationals working in the UK, between January-to-March 2016 and January-to-March 2017, their number increased by 171,000 to 2.32 million, whilst non-UK nationals from outside the EU working in the UK increased by 35,000 to 1.23 million. The ONS calculated that in the January-to-March 2017 period, 5.64 million people "born abroad" were working in the UK, yet non-UK nationals working in the UK was much lower, at 3.55 million. This is because people born abroad working in the UK include many UK nationals. (Office for National Statistics, July 2017).

The share of immigrant workers has indeed been rising sharply in recent years; however, an analysis by the *Independent* newspaper concluded, "EU migrants are more likely to be in work than natives, with the participation rate for the group at just below 80%, refuting the idea that most immigrants do not 'contribute'." British natives' employment rate is 76%; the lowest employment rate (67%) is of immigrants from the rest of the world (due to the lower rate of employment of women in this group; the male rate for this group is similar to others'). Another observer has concluded, "The high and rising labour force participation rate for the UK native population also undermines the idea that immigrants are 'taking' jobs from Britons." (Chu, 5 October 2016).

Inquiry into the importance of immigrant workers to certain industrial sectors of the UK economy, the following facts were found:

- *Manufacturing of food products*: 38% of the workforce are migrants (ONS Labour Force Survey statistics)
- *Scientific research and development*: 22% of the workforce are migrants (ONS statistics)
- *Air transport*: 22% of the workforce are migrants (ONS statistics)
- *Computer programming and consultancy*: 21% of the workforce are migrants (ONS statistics)
- *Health services*: 19% of the workforce (235,000 out of 1,220,000 in total) in National Health Service (NHS) hospitals and community health outlets in England were not British. The share of nursing staff who were non-British was 21%, whilst for doctors it was 30% (NHS statistics). The Institute for Public Policy Research (IPPR) reported that about 55,000 out of this figure were EU nationals, as was one in 10 of the UK's registered doctors. The report noted, "Without them, the NHS would collapse", and concluded, "EU migrants who are already here should get indefinite leave to remain. In particular, EU NHS workers should get the automatic right to citizenship. If they left, it would be a crisis for the NHS." (IPPR, July 2017).

- *Construction industry*: 10% of the UK's 2.1 million construction workers are immigrants (The Chartered Institute of Building, 2015). The UK construction industry relies heavily on European labour. The Royal Institute of British Architects (RIBA), the Royal Institution of Chartered Surveyors (RICS), the Chartered Institute of Building (CIOB), and the Royal Town Planning Institute (RTPI) have outlined their concerns (about skilled labour shortages, for example) in a joint statement to Brexit Secretary David Davis.
- *Education sector*: Each year around 500,000 students from 200 countries come to the UK to study, and 600,000 come to attend English language classes. The ExEdUK NGO estimates that total UK education exports total more than £20 billion, making it the UK's fifth-largest services export. It is also estimated that overseas students directly contribute around £11.8 billion to the UK economy. (ExEdUK, June 2016)

Impact Assessment Summary

- Currently about 3.3 million EU citizens live in the UK, along with more than 5 million foreign-born non-EU people. About 2.2 million Britons live in the EU – one million in Spain alone. Brexit has caused expatriates to worry about losing their health care and pensions, potentially forcing an exodus of expats from Europe back into Britain (and *vice versa*).
- Four European countries not EU Member States are presented as post-Brexit models for the UK; however, all have signed the Schengen agreement and have lost sovereign control of migration from the EU. Consequently, levels of immigration (from all countries of origin) are higher than in the UK (11.3%). Lichtenstein leads with 33.1%, followed by Switzerland with 28.9%, and Norway with 13.8%. Only Iceland is lower with 10.7%.
- EU migrants are more likely to be in employment than natives, with a participation rate of just below 80%. Native British have an employment rate of 76%, non-European immigrants of 67%; yielding an average employment rate of 74.9%.
- Immigrants are employed in manufacture of food products, scientific research and development, air transport, computer programming and consultancy, health services, the construction industry, and the education sector.

3.1.3 Right of establishment and freedom to provide services

Definition: *Member States must ensure that the right of establishment of EU national and legal persons in any Member State and the freedom to provide cross-border services is not hampered by national legislation, subject to the exceptions set out in the Treaty. The acquis also harmonises the rules concerning regulated professions to ensure the mutual recognition of qualifications and diplomas between Member States; for certain regulated professions a common minimum training curriculum must be followed in order to have the qualification automatically recognised in an EU Member State. As regards postal services, the acquis also aims at opening up the postal services sector to competition in a gradual and controlled way, within a regulatory framework which assures a universal service.*

The legal basis for these fundamental freedoms of setting up business and providing services within the EU is stipulated in Articles 26 (internal market), 49 to 55 (establishment), and 56 to 62 (services) of the Treaty on the Functioning of the European Union (TFEU).[19] The TFEU and ECJ case law guarantee the mobility of businesses and professionals within the EU. Self-employed persons or professionals and legal persons operating in one Member State are free to carry on economic activity in another Member State or to provide their services in other Member States on a temporary basis from their country of origin without any further authorisation than what their home country required (Maciejewski, Pengelly, 2016). The prohibition of national discrimination and harmonised access standards facilitate business operations across the EU; large international companies based in the UK providing services to the EU countries, in particular, benefit from dealing with a single set of regulatory standards. The financial services industry appreciates their hub-and-spoke model having a single headquarters and conducting business in every other Member State in Europe *via* branches. Capital reserves can be kept efficiently in the EU home country rather spread over each and every Member State (QBE, 2016).

In a post-Brexit area, the loss of the passport regime will make multinational companies question the UK as a headquarters base, and UK companies trading with the EU have to rethink their corporate structure, incorporation, reporting places for tax and regulation as well as location of their headquarters (QBE, 2016). Companies like Goldman Sachs, Nissan, Siemens *etc.* will have to consider relocating their EU hub away from the UK after Brexit. Insecurity over UK's future partner model with the EU will even multiply the number of companies seeking a new safe haven benefiting from the fundamental freedoms in Europe, as for instance Vodafone is considering. In consequence, jobs and investments will be lost to the UK. A CityUK survey found that about 37% of financial services

---

19   Detailed information on freedom of establishment and freedom to provide services is available at http://www.europarl.europa.eu/atyourservice/en/displayFtu.html?ftuId=FTU_3.1.4.html (accessed August 2016).

companies[20] are ready to relocate staff if the UK leaves the Single Market (Barnard, 2016); for instance, VISA is considering cutting hundreds of jobs due to Brexit. Brexit will accelerate the transfer of jobs to other EU countries like France, Germany, Ireland or the Netherlands. Moreover, investments in the UK will be put on hold, as Siemens announced for its wind power investment plans. Investors are even withdrawing from the UK, like China's investment community (Davies, Treanor, 2016).

The technology industry in the UK is also reassessing its future position, and major technology firms have put their investment plans on hold; the financial technology sector in particular will suffer from Brexit as new employees from foreign universities as well as entrepreneurs will likely move to a more favourable EU location like Berlin. Relocation has also to be considered not to lose access to the future Digital Single Market (Hern, 2016). Uncertain capital regulation is poison for the investment industry and venture capital, not to mention human capital, which is needed for the technology sector growth and transition to the new industry 4.0.

In reference to the recognition of qualifications and diplomas, students planning to study in the UK or in other EU countries are affected by Brexit. Non-EU students will be exposed to higher tuition fees in the absence of EU-funded exchange programmes and other financial subventions such as the Erasmus scheme, and it is unclear if British will qualify for full participation in Erasmus after Brexit. Moreover, it will become more difficult for UK students to move to an EU country for a longer stay than three months. The EU has rules on the admission of non-EU students which provide for an application for a residence permit up to three months in advance upon paying a fee. Particularly, the recognition of qualifications may be a problem. Neither British employers are bound to accept diplomas from EU schools nor are EU employers obliged to evelled British diplomas. There will probably be new agreements on mutual recognition, but overall there will be fewer legal guarantees of recognition as a result of non-acceptance of free movement of persons by the UK (Peers, 2016).

The freedom movement of teachers and cross-border education will also be affected by Brexit. The academic mobility that modern economies have come to depend on – *inter alia* the academic recognition of diplomas and courses of study – and the development of youth exchanges will be have to be renegotiated from scratch to replace Article 165 of the TFEU, or else all of the foregoing will be cramped. The Erasmus programme best known for exchanges of university students, school pupils and apprentices is based on EU law; the UK cannot qualify for full participation in this programme after Brexit ends UK participation in the free movement of people (Peers, 2016).

---

20   See the report on "The impact of the UK's exit from the EU on the UK-based financial services sector", published by Oliver Wyman and commissioned by TheCityUK, 5 October 2016, website at https://www.thecityuk.com/research/the-impact-of-the-uks-exit-from-the-eu-on-the-uk-based-financial-services-sector/ (accessed October 2017).

Finally, withdrawal from EU will affect the transferability of professional credentials and services to Europe from the UK and *vice versa*. This will impact free movement of services and increase doubt about recognisable service quality. The result will be a shortage of qualified, specialised professionals (financial experts, architectures, *etc.*) as well as highly skilled workers (nurses, IT-services, *etc.*). The recognition and expertise has to be checked for each country hosting employees within the EU, a complex post-Brexit task.

Impact Assessment Summary

- The right of (business) establishment and freedom to provide services as one fundamental right of the internal market is stipulated in Articles 26 (internal market), 49 to 55 (establishment), and 56 to 62 (services) of the TFEU. The ECJ guarantees the mobility of businesses and professionals within the EU; accordingly, businesses and entrepreneurs registered in any EU Member State are free to carry on business or to provide services in any and all other Member States.
- Brexit will have a significant impact on the business operation due to the loss of the passport system stemming from these freedoms of movement; in particular, the financial industry and multinational companies will consider expatriating their incorporation from the UK to an EU Member State. Most likely, the UK will haemorrhage jobs.
- Moreover, the limitation or even loss of the right to provide multiple services from the UK to the EU Member States left will alienate current and future businesses in the technology sector – investments will be put on hold or even shunted to other EU Member States.
- The loss of reciprocal recognition of professional qualifications and diplomas in the EU will impede the free establishment of businesses and provision of services. The UK will attract fewer investments and related knowledge transfer will suffer and affect the development of UK businesses in the future.
- The loss of mobility of qualified, specialist workers will cause labour shortages in science and in the services industry in the UK. Higher costs and prices will be faced by consumers and businesses.

3.1.4 Free movement of capital

Definition: *Member States must remove, with some exceptions, all restrictions on movement of capital both within the EU and between Member States and third countries. The acquis also includes rules concerning cross-border payments and the execution of transfer orders concerning securities. The directive on the fight against money laundering and terrorist financing requires banks and other economic operators, particularly when dealing in high-value items and with large cash transactions, to identify customers and report certain transactions. A key requirement to combat financial crime is the creation of effective administrative and enforcement capacity, including co-operation between supervisory, law enforcement and prosecutorial authorities.*

Under the Four Freedoms the free movement of capital is the latest of all Treaty freedoms yet the broadest due to its unique third-country dimension. The global significance of capital movements and the necessity to coordinate monetary policies within the Economic and Monetary Union has led to the Treaty prohibiting any restrictions on capital movements and payments – not only between EU Member States but also with third countries (Kolassa, 2016).[21] The legal basis for the free movement of capital is stipulated in Articles 63 to 66 of the TFEU, supplemented by Articles 75 and 15 for sanctions. The objective is the creation of a liberalised market that encourages economic progress with efficient conditions of investment as well as the promotion of the euro currency underpinning the EU's role as global player.

Brexit will cramp the free movement of capital: capital and currency transfers with the Single Market will have to be registered and will lose its privilege of free circulation in the Single Market once registered. UK business will face higher charges and fees for capital transactions and lose tax benefits on cross-border capital transactions like those granted to EU capital transfers. Consumers will pay higher fees for payment transfers into the EU and have to adjust to new regulations to assure monetary safety and prevent money laundering. Complexity and transaction costs will hamper capital movements and ultimately investments.

Foreign direct investment into the otherwise attractive UK market, with about 55 million consumers, will not benefit from tariff-free access or a single regulatory regime; investment into the UK risks declining due to legal complexity and fees. Particularly, the financial sector will suffer, as almost one third of foreign direct investment comes from overseas banks and other financial services institutions. The UK has been attracting investment from China and other emerging markets in recent years. According to fDi Markets, an FT data service[22], 153 companies headquartered in emerging markets made

---

21   Detailed information on freedom of capital movement is available at http://www.europarl.europa. eu/atyourservice/en/displayFtu.html?ftuId=FTU_3.1.6.html (accessed September 2016).

22   fDi Markets, a service from the *Financial Times*, is the most comprehensive online database of cross-border greenfield investments available, covering all countries and sectors worldwide (see website at https://www.fdimarkets.com/ (accessed September 2016).

greenfield investments in the UK totalling US$7.9 billion in 2015. Since 2003, the UK has attracted about US$83.2 billion in capital investment in greenfield projects from companies headquartered in emerging markets. India as a top source country (having invested US$14.4 billion in 352 projects since 2003) regards the UK as their gateway to the EU market. Based on fDi Markets data recorded since 2003, 4,300 companies have invested in 11,525 projects with a special market focus. Europe or a particular market in Europe is targeted by more than 56% of companies as the end-market for their investment. About 58% of emerging market investors share this market access motive, whereas only 33% cited the domestic market as the primary investment motive (Fingar, 2016). In case of a Brexit, these multinational companies will lose access to the EU markets through the UK, and most of them will have to at least reconsider further investment and/or capital redirection. The uncertainty will put investment and hiring plans on hold, and make companies adjust sales plans and manage rising costs for debt and equity.

Brexit will hit the cross-border lending industry hard, which in the UK accounts for 17% of business of cross border bank lending as compared to 9% in Germany and 9% in France. Brexit will also hit the payment processing system SEPA – Single Euro Payment Area – in Europe that is supported by all 28 EU countries and the EFTA members. If it would continue in the SEPA system, the UK would have to join EFTA (as matters currently stand) and so accept the *acquis*. Moreover, FATF – Financial Action Task Force – the EU setup for an international anti-money laundering framework, would have to persist to assure a trusted, non-infected payment system in the UK. The PSD – payment services directive – regulates payment services and payment service providers throughout the European Union (EU) and the European Economic Area (EEA). The directive's purpose is to make cross-border payments easy, efficient and secure in the EU, and so even non-EU countries may be members of PSD. However, Brexit entails a loss of influence in determining new PSD standards (Pathak, 2016). In particular, the planning of security in the development of mobile payments, of virtual currency applications, and of online payment processing systems without guaranteed UK input may cause a shift of financial transactions and the Fintech industry to European financial centres like Luxembourg or Berlin.

If the UK wants to benefit from the EU's planned Capital Markets Union (CMU), it must retain its free access to EU capital markets. The CMU is to facilitate the raising of capital for firms and cross-border investing. An expansion of alternative lending sources should be welcomed by the UK mid-market,[23] as the lack of long-term finance is a major barrier to business growth. The CMU action plan is to be implemented by 2019 and foresees the following major capital issues (Hogan Lovells, 2016):

- Shortage of long-term infrastructure finance
- Need for improvement of the securitisation market
- Lack of EU-wide bond framework

---

23   Companies with revenue of between £10 million and £300 million.

- Investment barriers to be reduced
- Disclosure rules to be amended
- Lack of funding choices for European businesses, esp. SMEs
- Too few choices for retail investors

The facilitation of securitisation in particular should improve diversification in funding sources and reduce mid-market firms' dependence on equity and bank finance. Firms will benefit from lower costs of capital due to keener competition between all forms of funding (Caroll, 2016). Given the fact that, collectively, the UK's 3000 mid-market businesses contributed £59 billion to the UK economy between 2010 and 2013, it is economically reasonable to support the mid-market (CBI, BDO, 2016). The assurance of free movement of capital across Europe has been and will be essential for development of the UK economy.

Impact Assessment Summary

- The last of the Four Freedoms is free movement of capital as stipulated in Articles 63 to 66 of TFEU, supplemented by Articles 75 and 15 for sanctions. The object was to create a liberalised market for efficient investments and a strong euro currency to heighten the EU's role as global player.
- Brexit will cramp the free movement capital between the UK and EU Member States. UK businesses as well as consumers will face higher capital costs and fees for payment transfers.
- Legal complexity and higher transaction costs will discourage investment in the UK. The loss of a functional gateway for companies to the EU market will redirect investments to EU Member States.
- Capital movement uncertainty will retard investment and likely increase transaction costs. Brexit will hit the cross-border lending industry in particular. It will mean a loss of influence on the determination of new EU payment standards as well, such as PSD, mobile payment, and online payment processing systems.
- The UK will somehow have to retain free access to capital markets to benefit from the EU's Capital Markets Union plan to facilitate capital raising, esp. for mid-market firms, and cross-border investing.
- The assurance of free and efficient movement of capital across Europe has been and will continue to be essential for the British economy to adjust to changes and developments.

3.1.5 Public procurement

Definition: *The acquis on public procurement includes general principles of transparency, equal treatment, free competition and non-discrimination. In addition, specific EU rules apply to the coordination of the award of public contracts for works, services and supplies, for traditional contracting entities and for special sectors. The acquis also specifies rules on review procedures and the availability of remedies. Specialised implementing bodies are required.*

The Directorate General for the Internal Market, Industry, Entrepreneurship and SMEs is tasked with regulating public procurement in the EU: this includes the procurement strategy, legal rules and implementation, e-Procurement, international public procurement, the commissioning of studies and expert groups, and enforcement and implementation.[24]

Public procurement refers to the process by which public authorities – government departments and local authorities, for example – purchase labour, goods or services from private companies on a contractual basis. Things procured can be anything from building work for a local council to stationery and office furniture for bureaux, to catering services at a public university, to cleaning services for a ministry.

The European Commission has calculated that every year about 250,000 public authorities in the EU spend about 14% of GDP on the purchase of services, works and supplies. In a number of economic sectors public authorities are the principle buyers: transport, waste management, social protection, and provision of health and education services.

In the UK the Crown Commercial Service (CCS) is responsible for the legal framework of public sector procurement and leads the development and implementation of policies for the government. Public procurement is currently subject to the EU Treaty principles of non-discrimination, and the free movement of goods and services, and freedom of establishment. The UK follows EU law so as to keep the EU public procurement market open and competitive where suppliers from anywhere in the EU are treated equally and fairly.[25]

---

24   Detailed information is available at "Growth: Internal Mrket, Industry, Entrepreneurship and SMEs" website https://ec.europa.eu/growth/single-market/public-procurement_en (accessed August 2016) and Your Europe: Tendering rules and procedures website at http://europa.eu/youreurope/business/public-tenders/rules-procedures/index_en.htm (accessed August 2016).

25   Detailed information on the UK's public procurement law, including the Directives, regulations, policies and guidance relating to the procurement of supplies, services and works for the public sector, is available on the UK's Crown Commercial Services website at https://www.gov.uk/guidance/public-sector-procurement-policy (accessed August 2016).

The type of public procurement procedures that the EU mandates may be summarised as follows: (Your Europe, August 2017)

- *open procedures*: Any business may submit a tender with a minimum time limit for submission of 35 days.
- *restricted procedures*: Participants are pre-selected from the publication of a contract notice, from whom the public authority selects at least 5 candidates who have 40 days to respond.
- *negotiated procedures*: The public authority must invite at least 3 suppliers with whom it negotiates the terms of the procurement contract.
- *competitive dialogues*: The public authority must invite at least 3 candidates to a dialogue in which the final technical, legal and economic aspects are defined; after which candidates submit their final tenders.
- *electronic auctions*: The public authority may auction off its contract electronically, which requires an initial evaluation to screen out evelledici tenders; then sa start date and time is set, along with the number of bidding rounds and the formula that determines the automated rankings. In each round the tenderer must be able to see its ranking compared to competitors (without knowing their identity).

Public procurement in the EU is thus open to tender by private enterprise. The EU tendering rules and procedures mandate that companies registered in any EU Member State have a right to compete for public contracts in other Members. EU law sets minimum rules applicable to tenders over a certain value (more than €135,000 for central government authorities and more than €209,000 for other public authorities, excluding VAT). For lower valued tenders, national rules apply, which nonetheless have to respect the general principles of EU law; however, "below threshold" procedures may be simplified compared to EU-wide tenders.

For all tenders, public authorities in the EU:

- may not discriminate against businesses registered in another EU country
- may not refer to specific brands, trademarks or patents when describing the characteristics of products and services they wish to purchase
- may not refuse to accept supporting documents (certificates, diplomas, etc.) issued by another EU country, as long as they provide the same level of guarantee
- must make all information regarding tenders available to all interested companies, regardless of the EU country they are registered in
  (Your Europe, September 2017).

Public procurement rules require the following:

- *publish the tender nationally, but also send it to the EU Publications Office:* tenders will be published in a notice in full in one official language of the EU, and a summary translated into other languages.
- *be clear about the technical specifications*: the public authority must transparently define the technical specifications of the supplies it intends to purchase, including aspects of environmental performance, design, safety, quality assurance, or conformity assessment. For public works contracts this may also include tests, inspections and construction techniques.
- *have clearly defined award criteria*: various criteria may be adopted for evaluating tenders, such as the lowest price offered, technical characteristics or environmental considerations. All applicants must be informed of the weighting given to the various criteria.
- *be transparent in the evaluation results and the winning bidder*: public authorities may only begin evaluating tenders after the deadline for submission has expired. Tenderers have a right to be informed as soon as possible whether they have won the contract or not. If they have not, they are entitled to a detailed explanation of why their tender was rejected. The public authority is obligated to observe strict confidentiality regarding the exchange and storage of bidders' data.
  (Your Europe – Tendering, 2017).

The TED (*Tenders Electronic Daily*) is the online version of the "Supplement to the Official Journal" of the EU dedicated to public procurement. TED publishes 460,000 procurement notices a year, and 175,000 calls for tenders which are worth approximately €420 billion. Every day from Tuesday to Saturday, a further 1,700 public procurement notices are published on TED. The homepage Supplement to the Official Journal of the EU[26] attracts thousands of UK big businesses and SMEs.

The key advantages for the UK to have access to this EU-wide public procurement evelled process are:

(1) it is transparent, non-disciminatory, and easily accessible.
(2) it is uniform across all EU Member States and the notices and procurement documents are published in all 24 EU languages.

---

26   Website at http://ted.europa.eu/TED/main/HomePage.do (accessed August 2017).

(3) it is simplified as to submission of responses to tenders by the European Single Procurement Document (eESPD) service for contracting authorities and economic operators.[27]

Brexit will mean that the UK may be excluded from involvement in EU public tenders. UK companies and researcher may lose the right to submit tenders in any EU Member States. UK public authorities too may lose the ability to publish notices in the Official Journal (OJEU) and to select the best provider based on price, quality and delivery. For the public, who is the receiver or end user of these supplies, prices will go up (though possibly hidden in taxes or service charges). That said, if EU bidders are excluded from UK public tenders, UK companies will benefit, as those competitors will be excluded from the process. But economists would argue that less competition is damaging, and also that UK industry will have to find new markets elsewhere in the world to compensate for the loss of business in the EU.

Impact Assessment Summary

- The UK's currently public procurement law and regulations are subject to EU Treaty principles of non-discrimination, and the free movement of goods and services, and freedom of establishment. The Member States can participate in this competitive process EU-wide.
- The TED (*Tenders Electronic Daily*) publishes 460,000 lucrative procurement notices a year, and 175,000 calls for tenders worth approximately €420 billion. Depending on the Brexit negotiations outcome, UK companies may no longer be able to participate in EU tenders.
- UK public authorities may be excluded from publishing notices in the Official Journal (OJEU), and so may be unable to select the most competitive provider based on price, quality and delivery.
- Less competition in the UK tendering process may mean that the cost of public services will go up and their quality decline.

---

27   Website at https://ec.europa.eu/tools/espd?lang=en (accessed August 2017).

3.1.6 Company law

Definition: *The company law acquis includes rules on the formation, registration, merger and division of companies. In the area of financial reporting, the acquis specifies rules for the presentation of annual and consolidated accounts, including simplified rules for small- and medium-sized enterprises. The application of International Accounting Standards is mandatory for some public interest entities. In addition, the acquis specifies rules for the approval, professional integrity and independence of statutory audits.*

The Directorate General for Justice is tasked with implementing EU company law *inter alia*. In fact, DG Justice covers policy domains from family matters and successions, civil and commercial matters, financial crimes, access to justice, judicial cooperation, European judicial training, and company law and corporate governance.[28] The purpose of EU rules in the company law policy domain is to:

- enable businesses to be set up anywhere in the EU
- protect shareholders and other parties with a particular interest in companies
- facilitate businesses being more efficient and competitive
- encourage businesses based in different Member States to cooperate with each other.[29]

The two key policy domains – company law and corporate governance – may be broken down into these topics:
Corporate governance

- *Directors and board members*: Directors have a crucial role in corporate governance: ensuring proper management of the company and looking after investors' interests. Directors have defined duties and liabilities. EU norms (*e.g.* Recommendation 2005/162/EC) deal with non-executive or supervisory directors, rules of independence, and the setup of committees on the (supervisory) board.
- *Shareholders*: EU regulation strives to protect minority shareholders, employees, and other interested parties and stakeholders. Directive (EU) 2017/828, for example, facilitates shareholder engagement, especially in the long term. It mandates rules governing identification of shareholders, transmission of information, exercise

---

28 Detailed information is available at the "European Commission – DG Justice – EU company law" website http://ec.europa.eu/justice/civil/company-law/eu-company-law/index_en.htm (accessed October 2017).

29 European Commission, Justice, Company law and corporate governance website at http://ec.europa.eu/justice/civil/company-law/index_en.htm (access October 2017).

of shareholders rights, transparency to institutional investors, asset manager and proxy advisor roles, remuneration of directors, and related-party transactions. Certain rights for shareholders in listed companies were defined by Directive 2007/36/EC. Directive 2004/25/EC set minimum standards for takeover bids (or changes of control) involving securities of EU companies.

- *Sustainable investment*: Various surveys and public consultations have been done to identify ways of sustainable investment.
- *Remuneration policies*: Remuneration for board members is a key area where managers may have a conflict of interest and shareholder interests must be reckoned in. For example, Recommendation 2009/385/EC furnishes guidelines for performance-based remuneration and stakeholder involvement.
- *Transparency*: Full disclosure of corporate governance arrangements is useful for investors and adds reputational value to businesses. Recommendations on the quality of corporate governance reporting by listed companies essay to enhance transparency. Directive 2013/34/EU imposed the obligation for EU-listed companies to provide a corporate governance statement in their annual reports.
- *Financial institutions*: Following the 2008 financial crisis, the EU enacted binding rules for corporate governance and remuneration on credit institutions and investment firms, now reflected in the Capital Requirements Directive (CRD) IV package. Directive 2013/36/EU (Capital Requirements Directive) and Regulation (EU) No 575/2013 (Capital Requirements Regulation) laid down rules for banks and investment firms, which include effective risk management, requirements for boards, remuneration of executives (bonuses) and employees, and disclosure related to corporate governance.

EU company law

- *Formation, capital & disclosure requirements*: Directive 2009/101/EC covers disclosure of company documents and the validity of obligations entered into, and applies to all public and private limited liability companies. Directive 2012/30/EU covers the formation of public limited liability companies and puts rules on maintaining and altering their capital. Directive 89/666/EEC (the 11th Company Law Directive) imposes disclosure requirements on foreign branches of EU companies. Directive 2009/102/EC (the 12th Company Law Directive) provides a framework for forming a single-member company.
- *Domestic mergers & divisions*: Directive 2011/35/EU governs mergers of public limited liability companies in the same EU Member State. Directive 82/891/EEC (the 6th Company Law Directive) regulates the division of public limited liability

companies in a same EU Member State. It gives protections to shareholders, creditors and employees.

- *Business operations involving more than one country*: Directive 2005/56/EC (the 10th Company Law Directive) lays down rules to facilitate mergers of limited liability companies across more than one Member State (cross-border mergers). Directive 2012/17/EU governs the interconnection of central, commercial and companies registers (business registers).
- *EU legal entities*: Regulation 2157/2001 is the statute for the European Company (Societas Europea or SE). Regulation 2137/85 is the statute for European Economic Interest Groupings (EEIGs).

EU company law is designed to facilitate companies in setting up subsidiaries in other EU Member States, protect shareholders, and improve collaboration. The UK has a strong culture of corporate governance; and Brexit is unlikely to weaken this position. As the Government aims to promote business and trade beyond Europe, it seems likely that the UK will keep and possibly improve on many of the EU company law rules and norms.

Impact Assessment Summary

- The Directorate General for Justice is tasked with implementing EU company law, which is designed to enable businesses to be set up anywhere in the EU; provide protection for shareholders; make business more efficient and competitive; and encourage EU-wide business collaboration.
- Corporate governance rules cover directors and board members, shareholders, remuneration policies, transparency, and the special responsibilities of financial institutions.
- EU law covers formation, capital and disclosure requirements, domestic mergers and division, cross-border business operations, and EU legal entities like the European Company (*Societas Europea* or SE) and European Economic Interest Groupings (EEIGs).
- Brexit could weaken the legal vehicles currently available to pan-European companies and protecting stakeholders.

3.1.7 Intellectual property law

Definition: *The acquis on intellectual property rights specifies harmonised rules for the legal protection of copyright and related rights. Specific provisions apply to the protection of databases, computer programs, semiconductor topographies, satellite broadcasting and cable retransmission. In the field of industrial property rights, the acquis sets out harmonised rules for the legal protection of trademarks and designs. Other specific provisions apply for biotechnological inventions, pharmaceuticals and plant protection products. The acquis also establishes a Community trademark and Community design. Finally, the acquis contains harmonised rules for the enforcement of both copyright and related rights as well as industrial property rights. Adequate implementing mechanisms are required, in particular effective enforcement capacity.*

The Directorate General for the Internal Market, Industry, Entrepreneurship and SMEs is also tasked with regulating intellectual property, including patents, trade mark and industrial design protection, geographical indications, trade secrets, intellectual property in general, and enforcement.[30]

Immediare substantial legal changes are unlikely; however, inevitably and undeniably Brexit will have a major impact on intellectual property. The UK government and UK business will seek to ensure that the protection of intellectual property remains intact and robust.

Trade Marks/ Designs

The EU trade mark regime is likely to be significantly affected by Brexit in the long term. EU trade marks ("EU TMs") and Community-registered designs ("CRDs") will no longer provide any protection in the UK absent parallel registration in the UK. It is expected that transitional arrangements will allow owners of EU TMs and EU CRDs to convert to or reapply for UK trade marks and design protection, by claiming their original Community registration or priority date. Owners who convert their existing rights into UK rights "may consider supplementing new applications for EU TMs and CRDs with corresponding UK marks and designs until the conversion of EU TMs/CRDs is confirmed" (Everscheds, 2016:16). It is obvious that this puts administrative burdens and unnecessary costs on trade mark and design holders. As these are oftener owned by individuals than companies, the extra burden will be all the more, especially for designers and individuals working in the creative industries. Some may not be able to afford legal advice and additional costs

---

30   Detailed information is available at "Internal Market, Industry, Entrepreneurship and SMEs: Intellectual Property" website https://ec.europa.eu/growth/industry/intellectual-property_en (accessed August 2016) and "Your Europe: Intellectual property rights" website http://europa. eu/youreurope/business/start-grow/intellectual-property-rights/index_en.htm (accessed August 2016).

for conversions or duplication of applications, thereby either weakening or even losing their existing rights.

Patents

The EU patent regime has been set up outside of the EU and EEA, and allows patent holders to protect their IP globally. The European Patent Office issues a bundle of national patents and their enforcement will not be effected by Brexit. However, the proposed Unitary Patent ("UP"), a European patent which can offer protection across participating countries will likely be affected. Ratification of the United Patent Court Agreement would be required to determine what role the UK may play in this process in the future.

Copyright

Copyright is the area of IP law likely to be the least affected by Brexit. This is because no territorial right and no registration regime in the UK or anywhere in the EU exists. Most copyright is enshrined in treaties that far transcend national or EU borders. The principles of the applicable EU Directives have already been implemented in the UK. It is expected that these will remain unchanged, unless repealed or amended by the UK Parliament. Some divergence between UK and EU copyright law may occur over time, as the UK will not be bound to follow future EU legislation or case law.

Impact Assessment Summary

- No immediate legal changes are evelled; however, Brexit will have a major impact on intellectual property rights.
- Trade Marks and Design Protection: EU trade marks ("EU TM") and Community-registered designs ("CRDs") will no longer provide any protection in the UK. Owners of EU TMs and CRDs will have to convert to or reapply for UK trade marks and design protection, increasing administrative burdens and costing more money. If individuals cannot pay, they may lose their IP rights.
- Patents: While the European Patent Office will continue to protect IP globally, UK participation in the EU's new Unitary Patent ("UP") offering protection of participating countries around the world is likely to be affected.
- Copyright: Likely the least affected area of IP law, most copyrights are enshrined in international treaties that far transcend national and even EU borders.

3.1.8 Competition policy

Definition: *The competition acquis covers both anti-trust and state aid control policies. It includes rules and procedures to fight anti-competitive behaviour by companies (restrictive agreements between undertakings and abuse of dominant position), to scrutinise mergers between undertakings, and to prevent governments from granting state aid which distorts competition in the internal market. Generally, the competition rules are directly applicable in the whole Union, and Member States must co-operate fully with the Commission in enforcing them.*

The fundamental objective of competition policy is to assure a legal framework for fair competition within the European Union. The distortion of competition must be prevented to achieve a free and dynamic Single Market able to promote economic welfare for everyman. To this end Community competition rules target five major regulatory objectives (Honnefelder, May 2016):

- Comprehensive ban on anti-competitive agreements (Article 101 TFEU)
- Ban on abuse of dominant market position (Article 102 TFEU)
- Merger control procedure (Council Regulation (EC) No 139/2004
- Prohibition on state aid under Article 107 TFEU
- Regulation of public services, services of general interest, and services of general economic interest (SGEIs)

The Commission reassesses tax rulings in the Member States in the light of state aid rules. The application and enforcement of competition rules is essential for a level playing field to attract overseas businesses to EU Member States.

The impact of Brexit on competition policy will depend on the agreement negotiated between the UK and the EU. If the UK joins the EEA, doing business will be based on common rules and equal conditions of competition – in fact, two separate legal systems are already applied in parallel in the EEA. However, in mergers the European Commission has exclusive jurisdiction in all cases in the EEA having a Community dimension. Further major impacts on the application of UK competition policy are not expected *if* the UK joins the EEA, except that it will lose all influence on shaping EU competition law (Petropoulos, 2016).

In the case of bilateral trade agreements between the UK and the EU (and Switzerland), competition policy has to be accommodated by close collaboration of the authorities enforcing the trade agreements. A full Brexit, however, without any agreements in place shifts competition policy power to the Competition and Markets Authority (CMA), which applies only UK law. Granted that the principles of free markets and undistorted competition are the basis of UK competition policy, there is no bond of CMA to EU company law anymore. Two parallel systems of enforcement will be responsible for dealing with mergers where the market shares straddle the divide. Brexit will thus end the one-stop-shop principle of merger control under the EU Merger Regulation. Companies have to comply with the CMA and European competition authority, both, a duplication, which imposes on companies higher administrative costs, longer investigation processes, and higher risks due to conflicting views and disagreements between the two authorities. A hard Brexit will further require adjustments to deal with double jeopardy for offenders liable to pay anti-competition fines twice, and to assure amnesty for whistle-blowers through joint leniency programmes (Petropoulos, 2016). Finally, Oxera estimates that the incremental costs to the UK public sector for 80-90 extra staff at the CMA could be up to £4.8 million per year (Oxera, 2016).

Following a full Brexit, claimants in competition cases have to run risks of jurisdictional uncertainty as between courts on both sides of the UK-EU divide, an uncertainty that could make it uneconomical to pursue a claim in the UK against EU-domiciled defendants. The status of Commission decisions as factual evidence in UK private damages claims is, in particular, legally questionable for applicability in UK courts in a hard Brexit scenario. Thus, the number of claims brought in the more favourable jurisdiction of the UK will decline, so that uncertainty over jurisdiction or the legal status of European Commission decisions will have diverted litigation to other countries (Oxera, 2016). As many EU merger notifications are handled in London in behalf of non-UK parties as well as standalone and follow-on actions based on infringements, Brexit would have significant affected competition law and practice (Whish, 2016): just a 10% reduction in UK-based competition advisory work would subtract £167 million from UK gross value added (GVA) per year by 2030 (Oxera, 2016).

The risks to international M&A transactions in the UK are related to that contractual risks that would stem from the forgone backstop of the European legal framework, hence planned as well as existing cross-border M&A-contracts need to be evaluated for Brexit impact. Transactions will have to be verified and checked for adjustments for the following major issues: avoidance of UK law as choice of law and place of jurisdiction; assurance of the application of accepted arbitration clauses; integration of *force majeure* clause and material adverse change clause to protect transactions from essential market and corporate asset deterioration; involvement of two jurisdictions for public M&A-transactions; assessment and integration of additional restructuring costs into purchase price calculation by factoring-in corporate law and abolition of freedom of establishment. In sum, cross-border transactions involving the UK will have to be checked continually for structuring and compliance challenges by M&A-advisors (Scherer, Söhnchen, 2016).

Brexit will set the UK free to give more state aid and grant preferential tax treatment to international companies, as the EU's state aid control system would not apply; in retaliation, EU authorities could easily limit market access by companies significantly supported by state aid (Petropoulos, 2016). After Brexit, the UK will leave the European

Competition Network, terminating its role in the elaboration of EU competition law and policy. The loss of the UK as positive contributor to a more liberal competition law will be missed among liberal EU Member States, and although it can be heard in the OECD and ICN and even negotiate agreements with the EU, this more remote influence is much weaker (Whish, 2016).

To avoid protectionism for industries or national champions, close collaboration between the CMA and European competition authorities is necessary. The maintenance of efficient, well-functioning markets will assure an efficient allocation of resources, so that companies and consumers may benefit from lower input and output prices.

Impact Assessment Summary

- The fundamental objective of competition policy is to assure the legal framework for fair competition across the entire European Union. The EU Commissions assesses and monitors the application and enforcement of competition rules to ensure a level playing field in the Single Market.
- In case of hard Brexit the EU loses exclusive jurisdiction over competition policy and has to involve the Competition and Markets Authority (CMA) of the UK. Two parallel systems of enforcement will then be responsible for competition issues, rendering the treatment of cross-border disputes complex and difficult as well as expensive.
- Brexit will terminate the one-stop-shop principle for merger control under the EU Merger Regulation. Duplication of investigation processes will increase administrative costs and risks for mergers. M&A transactions have to be assessed for contractual risks.
- Jurisdictional uncertainty in competition cases that span the UK-EU divide may result in litigation being forced to be shifted from the more favourable jurisdiction of the UK to other countries.
- Brexit empowers the UK government to provide state aid to its industry, which is liable to provoke EU reactions like product tariffs or further limitations on the UK's market access.
- The CMA and European competition authority will have to collaborate to avoid protectionist, unfair measures from disadvantaging companies and consumers all over Europe.

3.1.9 Financial services

Definition: *The acquis in the field of financial services includes rules for the authorisation, operation and supervision of financial institutions in the areas of banking, insurance, supplementary pensions, investment services and securities markets. Financial institutions can operate across the EU in accordance with the 'home country control' principle either by establishing branches or by providing services on a cross-border basis.*

Responsible for making and implementing policy in the domain of Banking and Finance is the Directorate General for Financial Stability, Financial Services and Capital Markets Union (DG FISMA). According to DG FISMA, financial services policy has to provide stable, secure and efficient markets. Financial services policy must assure coherence and consistency between different policy domains such as banking, insurance, securities and investment funds, financial markets infrastructure, retail finance and payment systems (EC, June 2016). In response to the financial crisis of 2008, the European Commission is pursuing several initiatives on new rules for the global financial system to enhance the financial sector in Europe and create a Banking Union to strengthen the euro.[31] The EU Commission has committed itself to overhauling the regulatory and supervisory framework of the financial sector and has proposed more than 40 legislative and non-legislative measures. The new rules form a single rulebook for all financial actors in the EU and must be implemented by the Member States, laying the basis for a Banking Union. In order to strengthen the banking and finance sector, the EU has adapted the Establishment of a single supervisor for banks led by the European Central Bank (EC, June 2016). The initiatives so far passed create a safer and sounder financial sector for the Single Market and contribute to stability for planning and long-term efficiencies for companies and consumers.

If the UK steps out of the financial stability mechanism set by the EU, Brexit could mean terminating the leading role of London as the financial centre of Europe. London provides wholesale financial services to Europe and its wider economy, including derivatives, foreign exchange trading, private and public bond trading, equity trading, and commodities trading. Any fragmentation of these markets will result in higher administrative and financing costs for the financial sector, trickling down to transaction costs for companies and finally consumers (Schoenmaker, 2016).

The UK finance industry will suffer from restricted Single Market access due to loss of *passporting* rights that will require UK-registered companies to establish or acquire a regulated subsidiary in the EU in order to keep market access; likewise, EU-registered companies will have to establish or acquire a regulated subsidiary in the UK. In consequence of doing business in the financial sector in both the UK and EU, the costs

---

31   See for detailed information the "Progress of financial reforms" published by the European Commission at website http://ec.europa.eu/finance/general-policy/policy/map-reform/index_ en.htm (accessed September 2016).

of compliance with different regulations and the complexity of transactions will increase (Fry, 2016). Operating duplicate entities will waste effort and separate banking services such as coverage and sales from trading and clearing. In particular, European banks will have to adapt to a Brexit situation as 70% of their capital market operations go through London (Noonan, 2016). Finally, there is a risk that the UK financial industry will lose up to 232,000 jobs – a significant shake up of this powerhouse (Woods, 2017).

Staffing for newly established entities in the EU will require transfer or recruiting of management or staff in the new jurisdiction, and even the settlement of outsourcing arrangements between group companies (Fry, 2016). Brexit will relieve financial services providers in the UK of EU regulation in remuneration and bonuses (*e.g.* CRD IV) and will put additional pressure in retaining and recruiting management and staff for the EU-regulated financial services industry. The search for staff and talents will cause labour shortages in the financial sector. London could loosen regulation and lower taxes to counter financial institutions' relocation plans and attract new business to London (Moshinsky, 2016).

According to a BCG report, European banks may need to lay away as much as €40 billion of extra capital to capitalise and finance business activities after Brexit. There will be an estimated 8% to 22% rise in annual operating costs for banks' capital markets divisions making lenders withdraw from some business opportunities. A JPMorgan report concluded that Brexit could cost investment banks US$1.5 billion a year each. There is also a chance that some banks may re-engineer their operating models to reduce costs and restore performance (Noonan, 2016). Financial institutions have to reconsider providing financial services needing a passport such as (retail) banking (CRD IV), insurance (Solvency II), and investment (MIFID). Euro clearing and settlement are also at risk, as the European Central Bank could limit euro transactions to the EU/EEA area under the so-called location requirement (Schoenmaker, 2016).

The financial services sector in both the UK and the EU must adapt their business models to whatever scenario emerges from Brexit. There is the opportunity for investment banks to consider new business set-ups by focussing on the following key issues (Morel *et al.*, 2016):

- *Business portfolio*: create a simpler and more efficient bank by reducing products, clients and locations
- *Organizational redesign*: complement front office cuts with organizational reforms
- *Simplify IT*: unplug applications and move onto a modern and efficient IT infrastructure
- *Cloud/outsource*: outsource infrastructure and application development to the Cloud
- *Smart compliance*: smart compliance and risk management at a limited cost as differentiator
- *Utilities*: leverage utility models for non-differentiating business processes.

A more fragmented business with provision of focussed services could emerge and rationalize the financial services industry. A more liberal, less regulated and tax friendly UK financial sector can gain new global business for London. Nevertheless, the EU will counteract this UK policy by aggravating access to the single market and future Banking Union with extra regulatory and supervisory requirements. However, banks have to be prepared for London's centre for international trade and finance to end.

Impact Assessment Summary

- The Directorate-General for Financial Stability, Financial Services and Capital Markets Union (DG FISMA) is responsible for initiating and implementing policy in the area of Banking and Finance. The objective is to provide stable, secure and efficient markets as well as to improve and enhance the financial sector in Europe and the euro.
- The creation of the banking union sets a new framework for the financial industry to stabilise the financial sector with long-term efficiency for companies and consumers. With the Brexit, the UK will be excluded from working on and benefiting from the new regulations.
- Furthermore, the Brexit could mean UK's step out of the financial stability system as well as fragmentation of the financial wholesale market. As a result, administration and finance cost for corporates and finally consumers could increase.
- The loss of passport rights will increase operating costs for the financial industry doing either business in the EU or in the UK in the future. Moreover, the loss of jobs in London and creation of new relocated jobs in the EU will induce social frictions and competition for talents in the UK.
- The Brexit is a catalyst for streamlining the financial sector's business models to maintain a competitive advantage. In particular, investment banks have to reconsider customized service solutions.
- Finally, the fight for global capital has to bear in mind transaction costs, customers' needs and compliance rules denying any unilateral British government actions.

3.1.10 Information society and media

Definition: *The acquis includes specific rules on electronic communications, on information society services, in particular electronic commerce and conditional access services, and on audio-visual services. In the field of electronic communications, the acquis aims to eliminate obstacles to the effective operation of the internal market in telecommunications services and networks, to promote competition and to safeguard consumer interests in the sector, including universal availability of modern services. As regards audio-visual policy, the acquis requires the legislative alignment with the Television without Frontiers Directive, which creates the conditions for the free movement of television broadcasts within the EU. The acquis aims to the establishment of a transparent, predictable and effective regulatory framework for public and private broadcasting in line with European standards. The acquis also requires the capacity to participate in the community programmes Media Plus and Media Training.*

The Information Society and the media are intrinsically borderless. Immediately after the EU Referendum authorities both public and private tried to boost business confidence that the UK would continue to adapt to and meet the adequacy requirements of EU regulatory regimes. It is a policy domain that spans a wide range of regulatory regimes. This Section provides a general overview and some insights into electronic commerce and the Digital Single Market, audio-visual media services, and data protection.[32]

The Directorate General for Communications Networks, Content and Technology (DG CONNECT)[33] is responsible for developing the Digital Single Market.[34] Its aim is to generate smart, sustainable, inclusive growth in Europe. CONNECT focusses on policy making for the digital economy and the information society, and their impact on research

---

32 For further information, see Guido Reinke (July 2015) "The Regulatory Compliance Matrix: Regulation of Financial services, Information and Communications Technology, and Generally Related Matters" (GOLD RUSH Publishing).

33 Detailed information is available at "Communications Networks, Content and Technology (CONNECT)" website at https://ec.europa.eu/info/departments/communications-networks-content-and-technology_en (accessed October 2017).

34 This Directorate General has renamed a number of times, and is also known as:
    -   from 1 July 2012: DG for Communications Networks, Content and Technology (DG CONNECT)
    -   1 Jan 2005 – 30 June 2012: DG for Information Society & Media (DG INFOSEC)
    -   1986 – 31 Dec 2004: DG Telecommunications, Information Market, and Exploitation of Research (DG XIII), shared responsibilities with DG Enterprise (DG XII)

and innovation, business and industry, and culture and media. CONNECT is even involved in foreign affairs and security policy, public health, finance and the euro, and education and training.

The Internet and digital technologies are transforming the global markets. The European Commission has therefore set it as a top priority to develop a Digital Single Market and set up DG CONNECT to manage the transition. CONNECT works with counterparts across the EU wrestling with the digitalisation of the economy to achieve growth and jobs. It facilitates citizens, businesses and public administrations to give access to and provide digital goods, content and services. In doing so, it seeks to conserve Europe's cultural diversity and values, its creativity, and its respect for intellectual property rights during the transformation process to the new digital environment. It supports the drive for digital innovativeness and the development of digital skills. Investments in potential technological breakthroughs are supposed to boost the competitiveness of the European economy as a whole as well as in key sectors. To render the Single Market fit for the digital age, trade barriers must be superseded and regulations harmonised to achieve the digital integration that could contribute as much as €415 billion per year to the European economy and create hundreds of thousands of new jobs. CONNECT aims to open up opportunities for new start-ups and facilitate small and medium enterprises in growing and innovating in a market of over 500 million people. To enhance the EU's competitive position, the following major objectives have been set (EU, December 2017):

- Boost eCommerce in the EU
- Modernise EU copyright
- Update EU rules on audio-visual media and technology platforms
- Strengthen the European Union Agency for Network and Information Security (ENISA), the EU's cybersecurity agency dedicated to preventing and addressing network security and information security problems
- Create a single regulatory framework for the data economy
- Adapt ePrivacy rules for the new digital environment
- Facilitate technology usage by large and small companies alike, as well as by researchers, citizens and public authorities

---

- 1983–1986: Task Force Information Technology (TFTI) for various programmes, including ESPRIT (European Strategic Programme for Research Information Technologies), TFTIT (Task Force Technologies de l'Information et Télécommunications) and RACE (Recherche Avancée dans les Communications en Europe).

Electronic commerce and the Digital Single Market strategy

The Digital Single Market (DSM) strategy[35] was adopted on the 6 May 2015 and includes 16 specific initiatives, which are structured under the following three pillars:

- *Pillar I: Better access for consumers and businesses to digital goods and services across Europe,* comprising rules that facilitate cross-border eCommerce, enforcement of consumer protection rules, more efficient and affordable parcel delivery, and that end unjustified geo-blocking (discriminatory practice treating customers unequally by location); conducting an antitrust competition inquiry into the eCommerce sector; reviewing European copyright law; and reviewing the Satellite and Cable Directive and the several VAT regimes.

- *Pillar II: Creating the right conditions and a level playing field for digital networks and innovative services to flourish,* overhauling EU telecommunications rules including spectrum coordination and high-speed broadband; reviewing the audio-visual media framework; analysing the role of online platforms; reinforcing trust through security and EU data protection rules; and facilitating a partnership with industry on cybersecurity in the domain of technologies and solutions for online network security.

- *Pillar III: Maximising the growth potential of the digital economy,* proposing a "European free flow of data initiative" and the launch of a European Cloud initiative which would define priorities for standards and interoperability and support an inclusive digital society where citizens have the right skills.

Brexit will change the European eCommerce ecosystem just as new laws for payment and geo-blocking of products come to the final stages of adoption. UK businesses plying eCommerce channels will have to change as well. The depreciation of the pound against the euro has made it dearer for them to purchase eCommerce merchandise from the EU. UK-based eCommerce may have a chance to earn new revenues from international and US sales if the pound decreases value against the dollar. According to Ecommerce Europe and the Ecommerce Foundation's joint 2016 European B2C e-commerce report,[36] British eCommerce shoppers spent in average €3,625 a head in 2015. The upshot is, eCommerce merchants in the UK may have to consider relocating their base to the EU if the UK loses market appeal for a skilled workforce. The increased costs of tariffs on goods and services as well as shipping merchandise due to Brexit puts businesses based in the UK at a competitive disadvantage on cross-border eCommerce. The current skill shortage may worsen if visas are harder to obtain

---

35   Detailed information is available at "Digital Single Market" website https://ec.europa.eu/digital-single-market/en/policies/shaping-digital-single-market (accessed November 2017).

36   European Business Review (June 2016) "Brexit and the e-commerce market in Europe", website at http://www.europeanbusinessreview.eu/page.asp?pid=1536 (accessed November 2017).

for workers qualified to do multi-lingual customer service after the UK has left the Single Market. International merchants and companies may decide to set up business in EU Member States, or even leave the UK, due to increased costs of operation and administration. On the other hand, UK merchants focussed on the UK market will undergo hardly any changes. Service providers to UK merchants, however, may have to adjust to cost changes in their supply chains as well as to the business uncertainty. If customers change their consumption habits regarding cross-border shopping, EU-based merchants may have to reconfigure their supply sources. Trust in eCommerce services may be impacted by Brexit, as UK businesses may well not benefit from the Digital Single Market achievements, such as the availability of a pan-European certificate for online shops like the Ecommerce Europe Trustmark or any harmonised consumer protection rules. Customer trust might sink, if facing limited competitive choices and confronted with new pricing and product offers required by merchants, suppliers and manufacturers (Laubscher, 2 May 2017).

Audio-visual media services

The impact of Brexit on the television and film industries will be shaped by the UK's future relationship with the EU, whether through a free trade agreement and/or under WTO rules. The EU's Audio-visual Media Services (AVMS) Directive, which is under review at the moment. The UK has highly benefited from access to the Single Market in the last decade; for example, the British Association for Screen Entertainment (BASE), which represents the interests of video distributors, was securing a sustainable and successful future in the Digital Single Market to the benefit of consumers and the creative economy. It is estimated that the European audio-visual (AV) media sector is worth around €97 billion a year and employs between 0.7 and 1.1 million people (Oxera and O&O, May 2016).

On Brexit's positive side, it could lead to greater flexibility in setting TV advertising policy and could change the frequency and length of advertising breaks to benefit commercial broadcasters. There nevertheless remain some critical implications for the sector. First, the UK's success as a European audio-visual hub has been built partly on its ability to attract and retain skilled staff from across the EU. The sector now fears a significant loss of talent. Secondly, EU funding totalling millions of euros has in the last decade financed the production and/or distribution of influential British content, including *Great Expectations*, *Slumdog Millionaire* and *The King's Speech*. It remains uncertain whether Chancellor of the Exchequer Philip Hammond is committed to fiscally substituting EU-funded projects after 2020. Thirdly, British audio-visual media exports to the EU account for over 50% of earnings, and Western Europe is BBC Worldwide's second largest overseas market after the US (D'Arcy, 26 September 2016). British content has benefited from AVMS rules, which obligate outlets to broadcast a portion of European programming at a minimum, and allow channels based in the UK to broadcast across Europe under the rule of origin. This has led to significant export opportunities and incentives for US producers, too, to use the UK as their European headquarters. Fourthly, the European Commission has proposed a revision of the AVMS Directive that would allow Member State governments to charge levies on online streaming services. The UK criticism of this plan has staved it off so far, yet British influence is rapidly diminishing because of Brexit. Also implicated are the provisions of the EU Regulation 2017/1128 "on cross-border portability of online content services in the internal market" (Portability Regulation), another key regulatory domain in which the UK will lose essentially all influence.

The new Data Protection framework

Directorate General JUSTICE is responsible for any reform of the data protection legal framework.[37] The current reform is seen as "an essential step to strengthen citizens' fundamental rights in the digital age and facilitate business by simplifying rules for companies in the Digital Single Market". It is expected that overcoming the current fragmentation and its costly associated administrative burdens will lead to savings for business. A proposed EU Regulation, COM (2012)11 "on the protection of individuals with regard to the processing of personal data and on the free movement of such data" (General Data Protection Regulation or GDPR), was published on 25 January 2012. After a public consultation of more than four years, the GDPR became law in May 2016 as (EU) 2016/679. The Member States, including the UK, have until 6 May 2018 to transpose the GDPR into national law, to be applicable from 25 May 2018. The new regulation will supersede the more than 20-year-old Data Protection Directive 95/46/EC and the UK's Data Protection Act 1998.

The UK Department for Digital, Culture, Media & Sport introduced the Data Protection Bill 2017 to the House of Lords on 13 September 2017. It is expected that the

---

37   Detailed information on this topic is available at the "European Commission – DG Justice – Protection of personal date" website http://ec.europa.eu/justice/data-protection/index_en.htm (accessed September 2017).

The Director General Justice is responsible for EU company law. DG Justice covers policy domains such as family matters and successions, civil and commercial matters, financial crime, access to justice, judicial cooperation, European judicial training, and company law and corporate governance. The purpose of EU rules in this area is to:

- enable businesses to be set up anywhere in the EU;
- provide protection for shareholders and other parties with a particular interest in companies;
- make business more efficient and competitive; and
- encourage businesses based in different EU countries to cooperate with each other.

(Justice – Company law and corporate governance website).

EU regulation will be discussed in the House of Commons and receive Royal Assent in early spring 2018.[38]

The EU-wide collaboration on data protection is evidenced not only by the elaborate regulatory framework, but also by its institutional setup. The Article 29 Working Party (Art. 29 WP) was made up of the data protection authorities of each Member State. Ever since it was set up, its members have followed their mandate to advise their data protection regulators and businesses, promote the consistent application of EU law in Member States (as also Norway, Liechtenstein and Iceland have done), and make recommendations (as on standard contractual clauses). Art 29 WP will be superseded by the European Data Protection Board (EDPB), which will lead to even further integration. GDPR mandates a new independent supervisory authority, the European Data Protection Board, which will replace the Article 29 Working Party on the protection of individuals with regard to the processing of personal data established by Directive 95/46/EC. The new authority will be responsible for issuing guidelines and opinions, adopting legally binding decisions, as in case of disputes between national supervisory authorities, collate certification mechanisms, and provide for consistent application of the new Regulation. Brexit is likely to require new national authorities, although most EU authorities have been mirrored at national level. But setting up new authorities will put additional administrative and financial burdens on the UK. It is unclear how the UK will be interact with supranational regulatory authorities like the European Data Protection Board once it has left the EU.

The upcoming EU ePrivacy Regulation "concerning the respect for private life and the protection of personal data in electronic communications and repealing Directive 2002/58/EC (Regulation on Privacy and Electronic Communications)" was proposed in January 2017. It will be an update of the EU's existing ePrivacy legal framework (also know as the Cookie Law) under the EU ePrivacy Directive of 2002 (revised in 2009), which required prior consent to receive "cookies": businesses in Europe must get explicit consent to use cookies and for electronic (direct) marketing (which includes the Web, email, apps, telephone, instant messaging and so on) and to provide clear opt-outs to users under the proposed new law.

It is expected that after Brexit, the vast majority of data privacy, data retention and public access to information rules and regulations of the EU will continue unchanged in the UK. Many EU concepts, even before being captured by UK statutes, statutory instruments or regulations, were already embedded in UK law *via* court decisions. UK companies operating or just selling in the EU, or monitoring the sales activities of EU citizens from the UK, must comply with data protection rules governing how they collect, store and

---

38   Detailed information is available at "Gov.uk – Data Protection Bill 2017" website: https://www.gov. uk/government/collections/data-protection-bill-2017 and "Parliament.uk – Data Protection Bill 2017-19" website https://services.parliament.uk/bills/2017-19/dataprotection.html" (accessed November 2017).

share customer, employee and third-party data. Since the Referendum, the Information Commissioner of the UK has been encouraging civil society and business to prepare for GDPR regardless of Brexit. The UK's Data Protection Bill 2017 entering into force next year mirrors the GDPR. However, once the UK has exited the EU (and assuming it is outside the EEA), the same rules used for non-EU countries will apply, and the UK may be required to meet "adequate safeguard" standards for data transfers to be lawful. If the UK ends up in a hard Brexit scenario, it will be treated like a third country, which would entail an assessment for adequacy.

Impact Assessment Summary

- Directorate General for Communications Networks, Content and Technology (DG CONNECT) is the Commission's department responsible for developing the Digital Single Market. Directorate General Justice is responsible for the reform of the data protection legal framework. The Information Society and electronic media are intrinsically borderless, and the UK would have to continue to adapt to and meet the adequacy requirements of the EU's regulatory regimes to get frictionless access to the market and consumers.
- Electronic commerce and the Digital Single Market (DSM): With the launch of the DSM strategy in May 2015, the EU has launched a new Single Market for better access for consumers and businesses to digitalised goods and services. Regulatory overhauls to the telecom rules, the audio-visual media framework, cybersecurity, data protection, and clearer definitions of standards and operability will oblige players outside the DSM to adapt to the new EU regime if they want to partake in the EU market. Benefits accrue to those partaking in DSM, like industry partnerships to offer cybersecurity, a European Cloud solution, and funded development programmes.
- Electronic Commerce in Europe is likely to become dearer for UK consumers and businesses due to the depreciation of the pound amongst other factors. The average UK eCommerce shopper spent €3,625 in 2015, which highlights the importance of an active participation in eCommerce by businesses.
- Audio-visual media services: the British TV, film and creative industry has benefited greatly from the European audio-visual media market, which is estimated to be worth around €97 billion a year and employs between 0.7 and 1.1 million people. By leaving the Single Market, it is expected that the UK will lose talent; millions in funding to finance productions and/or distribution; (easy) access to its most important market (over 50% of British exports to the EU); and its influence on key regulations, such as online streaming. The UK has been also able to attract major US producers who use the UK as their European headquarters. On the positive side, Brexit could lead to greater flexibility in setting TV advertising policy.

- Data Protection: data protection is currently undergoing a major regulatory reform through the EU General Data Protection Regulation (GDPR, EU 2016/679). The current EU regulatory body (Article 29 Working Party), on which all Member State data protection regulators are represented, will be superseded by the European Data Protection Board (EDPB). This raises questions about the UK's future relationship to this regulatory body. It is expected that UK law will continue to mirror the GDPR, although in case of a hard Brexit it would nonetheless be treated like a third country, which would entail an assessment for adequacy.

3.1.11   Agriculture and rural development

Definition: *The agriculture chapter covers a large number of binding rules, many of which are directly applicable. The proper application of these rules and their effective enforcement and control by an efficient public administration are essential for the functioning of the common agricultural policy (CAP). Running the CAP requires the setting up of management and quality systems such as a paying agency and the integrated administration and control system (IACS), and the capacity to implement rural development measures. Member States must be able to apply the EU legislation on direct farm support schemes and to implement the common market organisations for various agricultural products.*

The Directorate General of Agriculture and Rural Development is the department responsible for EU policy in this sector and deals with all aspects of the Common Agricultural Policy (CAP). This includes preparing draft laws and policy proposals, conducting research and innovation, and administering funding and grants.[39] The European Commission defines its objective for the agricultural sector as follows:

- helping farmers to produce sufficient quantities of safe food, in conformity with EU norms on sustainability, the environment, animal welfare, traceability, *etc.*
- providing farming enterprises with support systems to help stabilise their incomes in the face of less predictable production conditions
- facilitating investment in a sustainable, modern farming sector
- maintaining viable rural communities, with diverse economies
- creating and maintaining jobs throughout the food chain
  (Agriculture and rural development website)

The agricultural sector is one of the hardest hit by Brexit. Exit from the EU internal market regulated by the Common Agricultural Policy (CAP) will have a significant impact on the UK's imports and exports of agricultural products. CAP offers mechanisms to protect farmers ranging from import tariffs and export subsidies to direct income support. The UK will not only have to negotiate a trade regime with the EU and other countries too, which the EU had covered, but also develop a new agricultural policy of its own. The first step would have to be that the UK establishes a schedule of commitments which would include import tariffs and a checklist of which trade volumes the UK will grant market access at lower (or zero) tariffs (so-called tariff rate quota) to other countries;

---

39   Detailed information is available at "Agriculture and Rural Development" website https://ec.europa. eu/info/departments/agriculture-and-rural-development_en (Accessed September 2017).

which would have to be negotiated with all 128 WTO members. At the same time the UK will have to negotiate market access to other countries. Currently the sector receives extensive subsidies from the EU, which account for 50% of British farm incomes. The UK will also have to come up with a policy framework on how it will manage its domestic agricultural sector.

The UK agricultural sector is relatively small (output of €28 billion in 2016) compared to Germany (€50 billion), France (€70 billion), Italy (€53 billion), Spain (€46 billion) and even the Netherlands (€27 billion), and the UK is not self-sufficient and is obliged to import (Smit, March 2017:2). In 2016 the UK imported food and agricultural (F&A) products worth £47.5 billion (€52.25 billion), of which £33.6 billion (€36.96 billion) or 71% were from EU countries. The top three imports were animal protein, fresh produce and consumer foods from the Netherlands, France, Spain, Germany and Ireland. On top of that, 32% of the UK's food and agriculture workers also come from EU countries; thus, it is expected that Brexit will cause a labour shortage. In the same year the UK's F&A exports amounted to £22.5 billion (€24.55 billion) , of which £13.6 billion (€14.96 billion) or 60% goes to EU countries (Smit, March 2017).

Currently animal products can only be imported from a country with which the EU has an agreement and only at specific inspection points. From British ports the two most accessible Continental ports are Le Havre and Dunkirk; however, these would need major capacity upgrades to check products exported from the UK under non-EU rules (Zeffman, 14 October 2017:11).

Although Brexit is not expected to cause food shortages, it bears huge implications for availability of items in demand and for price increases. Some analysts expect that prices of imported fruit and vegetables will rise by up to 8% after Brexit, irrespective of what trade deal is struck. Brexit supporters counterclaim that food prices will fall as high tariffs on goods from outside the EU are abolished (Smit, March 2017). For example, sugar producer Tate & Lyle claim that its raw materials bill is inflated by €40m a year due to EU tariffs and quotas.

For nearly 50 years the EU's Common Fishery Policy (CFP) has dictated where UK fishing boats can operate and how much they can catch. Fishermen operating from other EU countries have been able to get into British territorial waters. Leaving the CFP will have a dramatic impact on coastal communities in the UK. One of the key arguments in the Brexit debate was that the British fishing industry will hugely benefit from leaving the EU. (Blitz, 3 July 2017). The fishing industry, however, is only a tiny fraction of the UK economy, contributing less than 0.5% to the annual GDP. There are also good reasons for quotas: they help prevent overfishing. How promising, then, is withdrawal from CFP, really, and does it herald a new future for British fishing? A report from the House of Lords (House of Lords, 17 December 2016) argues that the UK by setting its own fishery rules will have a louder voice alongside the EU and Norway in setting annual Total Allowable

Catches. The report concludes, "Withdrawing from the CFP gives the UK the opportunity to develop a fisheries management regime that is tailored to the conditions of UK waters and its fleet." The flipside is that the UK will still have to reach an agreement with the EU on quotas and access to each other's territorial waters after Brexit. The report rightly summarizes the dilemma: "fish are a vulnerable resource, prone to over-exploitation. They know nothing of political borders [or Brexit] and many species move freely between national territorial waters throughout their life cycles".

Andy Lebrecht, UK Deputy Permanent Representative to the EU and former Director General of food and farming in the UK Department for Environment, Food and Rural Affairs – where he gained significant experience of EU negotiations through his work on the CAP, – argued that four challenges lie ahead for the UK: (Lebrecht, 2 November 2016).

(1) The English fleet traditionally catches its fish in Irish, French, Norwegian not just UK waters. Unlike the Scottish fishing fleet, which depends relatively little on non-UK waters, the rest of the UK will be obliged to negotiate to retain access to these non-Ukwaters.

(2) The allocation of catch quotas is based on historical records dating back to 1973. The UK accepted and has defended these quotas since they were introduced in 1983. The EU is likely to resist strongly any attempt by the UK to reset this well-established basis for quota allocation. The negotiations to agree a different allocation principle will be difficult.

(3) The UK fishing industry depends heavily on exports to the EU, and tariffs could damage the industry significantly. In 2015 Britain exported to the EU £921 million worth of fish (including £224 million salmon), whereas total fish imports to the UK were worth £775 million excluding salmon. France and Spain in particular will have every incentive to demand high tariffs on fish imports from the UK. In future negotiations, access to markets and access to waters will be interlinked.

(4) UK vessels benefit from rights to access Norwegian waters where high stocks, of cod particularly, are of great value. As Norway is an EEA country, the UK must negotiate to have continued access to these waters; however, the odds of agreeing any access quota regime that differs significantly from the *status quo* looks slim.

Environment Secretary and Brexiteer Michael Gove announced in July 2017 that the UK would leave the 1964 London Fisheries Convention that allowed vessels from six EU countries to fish within six and 12 nautical miles of the UK coastline. He said Britain will go further and "take back control" of its territorial waters up to 200 nautical miles and that as a result the UK will be able to "dramatically increase the amount of fish that we catch". In fact, the expectation that the fishing industry will thrive on Brexit is flawed and room for radical improvements is limited. If the UK should choose the path of a hard Brexit, the

EU will do the same. Setting higher quotas will result in overfishing and damage existing stocks. Neither Norway restricting UK vessels' access to North Norwegian cod nor the UK demanding hundreds of fishermen from the eight countries that traditionally fish in UK waters stay in port and lose their livelihoods would be easy to enforce. The national authorities would have to step up their enforcement and ongoing monitoring, potentially damaging UK-EU relations with arrests and clashes at sea. It is likelier the UK would avoid going that route merely to support an industry that contributes less than 1% to the UK's economy.

Impact Assessment Summary

- Brexit forces the UK to think about how to replace the EU's Common and Agricultural Policy and its protectionist mechanisms, such as import tariffs, export subsidies, and direct income support, with a new policy and tariffs and trade volumes to be negotiated perhaps with each of 128 WTO members.
- 50% of British farm incomes consist of EU subsidies; what will replace that?
- 71% (£33.6 billion or €36.96 billion) of the UK's domestically consumed food and agricultural products are imported from the EU and 60% (£13.6 billion or €14.96 billion) of the UK's farming output is exported to the EU.
- The UK is not self-sufficient in food and is under necessity to import. Brexit will not change this.
- It is expected that prices will rise significantly after Brexit, irrespective of what trade deals are struck. For example, imported fruit and vegetables may rise by up to 8%.
- The UK fishing industry's advantage from Brexit is exaggerated. Much the same fishing quotas will continue to exist, access to Norwegian waters in particular where high stocks of cod are caught is still problematic, and a trade deal to avoid tariffs for trade with the EU (and non-EU countries) will still have to be negotiated with no guarantee of UK advantage.

3.1.12   Food safety, veterinary and phytosanitary policy

Definition: *This chapter covers detailed rules in the area of food safety. The general foodstuffs policy sets hygiene rules for foodstuff production. Furthermore, the acquis provides detailed rules in the veterinary field, which are essential for safeguarding animal health, animal welfare and safety of food of animal origin in the internal market. In the phytosanitary field, EU rules cover issues such as quality of seed, plant protection material, harmful organisms and animal nutrition.*

DG Health and Food, *a.k.a.* DG Sante, owns the remit to improve the health and safety of European citizens and to create jobs within the EU. DG Sante's specific goals are to assure the safety of food and medicinal products, and to protect animal health and welfare, and plant sanitation. To achieve these goals, DG Sante develops and implements policies, laws and programmes for better regulation in the EU and worldwide; assures compliance with existing legislation; and keeps citizens and stakeholders informed (EU, July 2015).

EU food safety policy focusses on maintaining a well-functioning, safe food chain in Europe whilst supporting the food industry – Europe's largest manufacturing sector and biggest employer – with high standards and regulations for safety. It also controls animal diseases and plant pests; promotes technologies for economic development; and streamlines the legal framework for developments in the domains of food safety, animal health, plant sanitation, and animal welfare. Besides enforcing legislation, DG Sante works with international partners to secure high levels of protection and safety standards in the EU (EU, July 2015).

The UK's Brexit out of Europe's regulations will have a serious impact on the food industry. Any separate bilateral treaties with the EU will lead to significant costs and to a loss of competitiveness for the food industry in the UK, if manufacturers have to operate under dual food standards. Food safety and hygiene regulations will have to comply with EU criteria, both so that foods may move freely across the EU Single Market without import costs and delays, and may be manufactured and processed in the EU by UK companies (Morris, 2016). An overhaul of existing food law is thus not reasonable. International standards like Codex Alimentarius would apply to the UK, which harmonise standards for companies manufacturing and developing food (Staniforth, 2016). Given the commercial uncertainty for the food industry, companies should review business agreements and processes, and consider health changes and adjustments to food. In addition, companies must examine dual-sourcing for improved supply-chain resilience, changing sources, and exploiting new exchange rate advantages and labour-rate differentials across Europe (Staniforth, 2016). The integration of value chains in the food industry makes necessary that companies reassess development scenarios and value chains' composition continually.

For consumers EU food standards assure food safety along the whole food chain along with proper food labelling. Common food rules also make detection of food poisoning easier, increase the variety of goods for buyers, and protect the appellations of traditional European food products (ITV, 2016). The EU also promotes integrated food value chains, due to food control cost, and protects the EU food market from cheaper imports (ITV, 2016). Overall, consumers have benefitted from food safety development in the EU, avoiding a downgrade and adjustment to lower food quality and safety standards. A hard Brexit endangers EU food standards: the UK could be tempted to lower standards to more liberal US levels. And loss of the EU's protected designation of origin could mislead British consumers' choices, requiring them to verify traditional foods. Companies selling such foods will have to differentiate products at higher marketing cost and also legal expenses for registration under international trademark law.

According to Tim Lang, Professor of Food Policy at City University London, Brexit will raise food prices, water down safety standards, let big business dictate food law, and negatively impact public health. The fact that the UK must import about 40% of its fruits and vegetables from the EU will make consumers and industry to pay more for food. It is estimated that the UK will need about ten years to become self-sufficient in food (Michail, 2016).

Brexit may require replacing 43 years of co-negotiated food legislation comprising about 12,295 EU regulations. Taking into account that UK food law consists 98% of EU law, the renegotiation of new trade agreements, safety regulations, product labelling, *etc.* will require expert negotiators whom the UK Food Standard Agency (FSA) does not have (Michail, 2016). The future negotiations will have to be monitored by an independent authority to prevent the food industry influencing downgrading of food safety standards. According to the UK's food trade group, Food and Drink Federation (FDF), the country is facing "a period of chaos" and the food industry will be facing a time of profound uncertainty (Michail, 2016).

The Irish food industry, reliant on exports to the UK, has called for state support lest it lose thousands of jobs because of Brexit-born pound sterling weakness. According to the Food and Drink Industry Ireland (FDII), subsidies of €25 million for market diversification and product innovation is needed to save the cost competitiveness of Irish labour, energy and insurance. With exports to the UK worth €4.4 billion, Ireland is facing many adjustments to prepare itself for Brexit and a lower pound sterling, not excluding the risk of loss of confidence in a competitive supply base, if Ireland is excluded from the restructured UK food supply chain (Morrison, 2016). A significant risk for suppliers to the UK food industry that needs to be addressed is how to maintain cost competitiveness in the long run.

Impact Assessment Summary

- The Directorate General for Health and Food (DG Sante) protects the health and safety of European citizens. The regulatory scope of DG Sante encompasses food and medicinal products, animal health and phytosanitation. EU food safety policy assures a well-functioning, safe food chain in Europe.

- A hard Brexit will significantly impact the food industry. Changes to food regulations will raise production and distribution costs for the cross-linked food industry, and UK food companies must examine dual sourcing alternatives, review business agreements, processes and standards.
- Brexit may put EU food standards at risk and/or downgrade them to the neo-liberal US level. New food supply choices may harm the quality and even safety of consumers.
- Food prices may be expected to rise indefinitely due to the fact that the UK imports about 40% of its fruits and vegetables from the EU.
- The renegotiation of more than 12,000 EU regulations will require the UK FSA to employ qualified people it does not yet have, to avoid a period of uncertainty and chaos. The UK government is well advised to keep changes to EU food regulations to a minimum.
- The Irish food industry will suffer from a depreciated pound sterling due to its dependency on exports of about €4.4 billion to the UK. Suppliers of food to the UK face a challenge in becoming more competitive. Brexit negotiations must consider its impact on neighbouring countries.

3.1.13 Fisheries

Definition: *The acquis on fisheries consists of regulations, which do not require transposition into national legislation. However, it requires the introduction of measures to prepare the administration and the operators for participation in the common fisheries policy, which covers market policy, resource and fleet management, inspection and control, structural actions and state aid control. In some cases, existing fisheries agreements and conventions with third countries or international organisations need to be adapted.*

The EU's Common Fisheries Policy (CFP), once linked to its Common Agricultural Policy, has been made more independent since the reforms of 2002. Rectification of the imbalance of the fleet capacity and catch potential was the initial focus of CFP, but the 2002 reforms refocussed it on preserving the fragile balance of marine ecosystems. CFP defined its main goal to assure sustainable fisheries and guarantee incomes and stable jobs for fishermen. To this end, fisheries management was further developed to include stabilising fish stocks and biological systems. Measures were also applied to improve safety and working conditions on board fishing vessels, regulate product quality, and control fishing techniques. Finally, the Community Fisheries Control Agency was established in Vigo to assure effective, transparent, fair controls on fishing (Marti Dominguez, 2016). In 2009 the Commission initiated a reform of the CFP, and by May 2013 a new fisheries regime for the future had been reached for environmentally sustainable fishing and aquaculture as well as economic, social and employment benefits, which features the following highlights: multi-annual ecosystem-based management of multi-species fisheries plans; new discard policy for regulated species till 2019; adjustment of fleet capacity to fishing opportunities; extension of the exclusion zone of 12 nautical miles until 2022 for traditional fleets; rules to align with EU policy EU fishing fleets in third countries and international waters; sustainable aquaculture; information sharing and decentralization of governance in the fishing grounds of the Member States. Additionally, new regulations for labelling, quality and traceability will enhance consumer choice. Finally, establishment of the new European Maritime and Fisheries Fund will help absorb the losses inherent in implementing the new CFP in the EU littoral (Marti Dominguez, 2016).

The Leave campaign, spearheaded by Nigel Farage, a member of the European Parliament Fisheries Committee, promised that the UK fishery industry would benefit from the abandon of both CFP and CAP. One obvious CFP argument for leaving the EU was that Britain would regain sovereignty over its Exclusive Economic Zone extending 200 miles from its coast. Public opinion in the UK considers the CFP (and the EU in general) to be well in favour of other EU states, giving to French and Dutch fishermen one-sided access to UK waters beyond the six mile zone, subsidising other Member States to expand and modernise their fleets, harming small scale fishing, and winking at "quota hopping" – the practice of registering ships from other Member States for British quota – at the expense of the UK's fishery. The introduction of Total Allowable Catch (TAC) under the CFP to limit the catch of certain fish species forced fishermen to discard fish of the wrong species, resulting in environmental disaster and financial catastrophe (Matthews, 2016). According to the Business for Britain report,[40] leaving CFP would enable the UK's fishing communities to recover if fish stocks are sensibly managed, and reduce foreign access to the UK's fishery zone. But even this revitalisation of the fishery industry depends on successful Brexit negotiations, and the impact will not be felt but over a generation (Elliott, 2016).

In any event, the UK is bound to international agreements for regulation fishing quotas to protect fish ecosystems and species. The UK's geopolitical position also complicates ring-fencing its fish resources, as its shares fish stocks with other countries. In the meantime, the UK is bounded to the agreed UK quota, and fishing after Brexit will surely entail renegotiated agreements with the EU (Harvey, 2016).

New fishery arrangements carry costs for trade-offs of new quota shares and access arrangements for the UK's fishermen, versus what probably consumers will have to bear in higher import prices for fish, or government through subsidising the fishing industry. The EU subsidises small fisheries by state aid to purchase fishing boats. Only about 11,800 people are directly employed in the UK fishery industry, about half of whom live in Scotland, which voted to stay in the EU. Scottish political leaders fear Brexit will cut their fishing quota and negatively impact its fishery sector. Any new renegotiation of quotas will take time and fishermen cannot expect a quick change of their economic situation after Brexit. In fact, renegotiation with the EU as well as effective management of fishing stocks will require the UK to pass a new plan to maintain and conserve the marine environment for its consumers and industry, requiring new international cooperation. To avoid further disadvantage to and protect the livelihoods of its small-scale fishery, the UK government – the real culprit in the decline of small fishery, not the EU – must quit privileging a few large companies by allocating its quotas to the Spanish fleet (Harvey, 2016).

According to Parliament Energy and Environment Sub-Committee debates on Brexit and Fisheries, scientists stressed that Brexit would give back to the UK control over the discard of species in the North Sea, and cause renegotiation of quotas among regional fleets and between EU countries for shared fishery stocks. At the same time, the UK exports two-thirds its fish to the EU, which Brexit could interfere with. Leaving the EU and its CFP is likely to cause budget cuts for fishery management, a new structure and renegotiation of quotas, and capitalisation of the European Maritime and Fisheries Fund

---

40   See House of Lords - European Union Committee, 8th Report of Session 2016–17, HL Paper 78, Brexit: fisheries, 17 December 2017, website at https://publications.parliament.uk/pa/ld201617/ldselect/ldeucom/78/78.pdf (accessed October 2017).

(EMFF) for the conservation of the marine environment and economic growth and jobs in coastal communities[41], presenting challenges to the UK. New international agreements must be negotiated particularly with neighbouring countries, as there are no real "British" fish. After Brexit the UK is well advised to join the North East Atlantic Commission, as Norway did. Even so, according to the Parliamentary Sub-Committee, the UK fishery system ought to be aligned with CFP standards because of its well-known practice and acceptance. Fishing has to adjust its boats and equipment to the new fishing patterns planned to be introduced by the UK, which will necessitate new investments by the industry (Energy and Environment Sub-Committee, 2016).

Impact Assessment Summary

- The EU Common Fisheries Policy (CFP) is aimed to assure sustainable fisheries and stabilise income for fishermen by setting sustainable fishing quotas for Member States. The reformed CFP improves the markets for fishery and aquaculture as well as subsidises CFP measures.
- Brexit from the CFP might be a chance to revitalise small-scale fishing and fish stocks by reducing foreign access to British waters. However, fish do not obey national boundaries and an extension of the fishing zone will be a result of Brexit negotiations. There is a need for international agreements on fisheries.
- The UK must align its neighbouring country interests and also consider regional interests such as Scotland's fishing industry, where about half of the UK fishery industry works. There is the general fear of Brexit's impact on its fishery industry due to quota cuts. The UK might also suffer a significant loss of its fish exports to the EU.
- The UK will have to negotiate anew its international cooperation, including fisheries. If it would save its small-scale fishery, the UK must quit privileging large fishing companies and protect fishery livelihoods.
- The UK is well advised to join the North East Atlantic Commission and to introduce new fishing patterns through investment funds for adjusting fishing rig to promote the local fishing industry.

---

41   For more details see https://www.gov.uk/guidance/european-maritime-and-fisheries-fund-emff-apply-for-funding (accessed October 2017).

3.1.14 Transport policy

Definition: *EU transport legislation aims at improving the functioning of the internal market by promoting safe, efficient and environmentally sound and userfriendly transport services. The transport acquis covers the sectors of road transport, railways, inland waterways, combined transport, aviation, and maritime transport. It relates to technical and safety standards, security, social standards, state aid control and market liberalisation in the context of the internal transport market.*

The Directorate-General for Mobility and Transport is responsible for the gamut of transport, especially inter-modal transport, issues. This includes strategic oversight, but also passenger rights, security and safety, clean transport development/ sustainable transport, urban transport, intelligent transport systems, research and innovation, international relations, public service obligations, logistics and multimodal transport, and related social issues.[42]

The EU is the only area in the world were citizens have full protection weather they travel by air, rail, ship, bus or coach. If something goes wrong with passengers trips, if certain requirements are met they can claim compensation. Disabled passengers with reduced mobility have specific rights as well. The key 10 passengers rights include (Europa 10 passenger rights, August 2016):

1. non-discrimination
2. access and assistance for disabled passengers and passengers with reduced mobility
3. information
4. choice to cancel trips due to disruption
5. retouring or rebooking
6. assistance in event of long delay
7. compensation
8. carrier liability
9. easy complaint handling
10. effective enforcement of rights

Privatisation of transport in the UK, in particular of railway systems, is one of the most advanced in Europe. British Rail privatisation started under the government of Margaret Thatcher and was completed by 1997. Whoever has been a daily commute on British trains will agree that most of the private train operators did not deliver on the promise of

---

42   Detailed information is available at "Europa Mobility and Transport themes" website http://
ec.europa.eu/transport/themes/index_en.htm (accessed August 2016).

lower fares, improved customer services and more investment. Leaving the EU could also mean that private operators will reduce by using the argument of increased administrate and financial burdens, some of these passenger rights that the EU currently guarantees. This will not happen immediately, but over time customer protection could dilute.

The UK travel industry has benefited from the European Common Market, especially the aerospace industry. Air traffic across Europe is controlled by the EU's Open Skies Agreement and the EU-US Air Transport Agreement of 25 and 30 April 2007 that created a trans-Atlantic Open Aviation Area: a single air transport market between the EU and the US with free flow of investment, no restrictions on air services, and access to the domestic markets of both parties (European Commission – Mobility and Transport, 2017). Without negotiating the UK's access, flights between airports in the UK and the EU-27 would default to the more limited bilateral agreements that pre-existed the US-EU arrangement. British airlines would lose the right to operate flights between any two Member States. Airlines from EU countries would likewise be barred to operate services between their home countries and the UK, and would have no right to fly from the UK to a third country. For example, Irish Ryanair could continue to fly from Dublin to London, but not between London and continental Europe. Airlines must arrange schedules well in advance, which requires legal certainty. The expected economic impact on the industry as gauged by investors is obvious by looking at the share prices of the two main airlines in the UK. British Airways' price dropped by 22% within one month (from 515.81 pence on 23 June to 403.40 on 25 July) and evelle's price lost 33% of its value (from 1,533 pence on 23 June to 1,022 on 25 July).

Budget airlines like EasyJet, Ryanair and Eurowings owe their existence to EU deregulation. If the UK leaves the European Common Aviation Area, British airlines would have to renegotiate both intra-EU and transatlantic flight rights. Everyone with industry insight understands what implications this has for BA and evelle. On 20 April 2012 International Airlines Group (IAG) (the holding company of BA) bought out British Midlands International (BMI) to integrate into their organisation, despite its increasingly heavy losses exceeding £100 million per year by 2012. There were also rumours that Virgin Atlantic was preparing to bid to acquire full control of BMI. Flight routes and airport slots are expensive and limited, and BMI owned some profitable flight routes, which explains the interest in a loss-making airline company.

Almost 70 million passengers flew with evelle in 2015 to 136 airports in 31 different countries, operating on 735 routes, a +18% annual passenger growth between 2000 and 2015 (evelle annual report and accounts, 2015). Leaving the Common Market would mean renegotiation of many routes, and this could affect fares. Considering the competition in the industry, British airlines could lose intra-EU routes for good.

For travel by road, British companies that run commercial vehicles on the Continent would still have to comply with EU rules. Brexit will also affect British ports and lorries carrying goods between the UK and the Continent, and EU companies trading with the

UK would receive similar treatment. As exporters would have to pay import duties and VAT on these goods, checks at ports like Dover would be required. The White Paper "Customs Bill: Legislating for the UK's future customs, VAT and excise regimes" (HM Treasury, October 2017) suggests that instead of putting custom checkpoints at ports, the government would have to purchase land further inland to accommodate the backlog. (Blitz and Houlder, 9 October 2017). The shipping industry and the UK Chamber of Shipping, which represents more than 170 freighter, tanker and cruise liner companies, warned that a catastrophe looms unless a frictionless border is in place when Britain leaves the EU. It was suggested that ports like Dover, the busiest truck port in the UK, could face up to a 30-mile-long queue if Brexit yielded back the traditional custom checks. The port handles 2.6 million trucks a year, while the Eurotunnel caters for another 1.6 million a year (O'Carroll, 12 April 2017).

Impact Assessment Summary

- Passenger rights, including compensation claims, may be compromised in highly competitive transport sectors (such as railways) where major investments are required in the coming years.
- The UK will be excluded from EU-funded research and innovation projects that lead to efficiency and environmental improvements. For instance, EU funds enabled Transport for London to provide the greener, cleaner technology of hydrogen buses over the entire London system.
- Better value for taxpayers' money requires that public procurement procedures allow bidders from all EU Member States to submit public tenders. For example, the New Routemaster – one of London's red double-deckers, also known as the *Boris Bus* (after the colourful Mayor of London who brought them back) – operates on a hybrid diesel-electric engine and is manufactured in Northern Ireland by Wrightbus; nevertheless, five non-UK companies were invited to bid for the contract.
- Airlines will have to negotiate both intra-EU and transatlantic flight rights, which could be extremely costly, and some existing routes may be lost. Fares are likely to increase, and this could lead to the end of UK-based low-cost airlines.

3.1.15 Energy

Definition: *EU energy policy objectives include the improvement of competitiveness, security of energy supplies and the protection of the environment. The energy acquis consists of rules and policies, notably regarding competition and state aids (including in the coal sector), the internal energy market (opening up of the electricity and gas markets, promotion of renewable energy sources), energy efficiency, nuclear energy and nuclear safety and radiation protection.*

The EU's Directorate General for Energy is responsible for disseminating information and regulating the oil and gas market, nuclear energy, coal, fusion power, and renewable energy. The importance of this sector is underlined by the EU's high dependency on crude oil (more than 90%) and natural gas (66%) from abroad. The total import bill for these two resources is more than €1 billion per day. DG Energy defines the energy strategy; regulates the market, as by unbundling energy supply and generation from transmission networks; provides consumer rights and protections (*viz.* open and fair retail markets; Citizen's Energy Forum and the Vulnerable Consumer Working Group); fosters innovation and transparency, as by replacing at least 80% of electricity meters with smart meters by 2020; increases security of imported supplies through diversification of energy sources and regulations; promotes renewable energy and a low-carbon economy (the EU aims to achieve its 20% renewables target by 2020) whilst enforcing energy efficiency (the EU has set itself a 20% energy savings target by 2020); assures the efficient, responsible use of fossil fuels (oil, gas, shale gas and coal); makes safe nuclear power, including radioactive waste, radiation protection, and decommissioning of nuclear facilities; is building a reliable infrastructure by connecting energy markets and regions; stimulates international cooperation; accelerates the energy transition through technology and innovation; and enforces respewct for EU energy law.[43] In the energy policy domain DG Energy collaborates with Euratom Supply Agency (ESA), Agency for the Cooperation of Energy Regulators (ACER), Fusion for Energy (F4E), and Innovation and Networks Executive Agency (INEA).

The core of EU energy policy is to achieve an integrated energy market, security of energy supply, and the sustainability of the energy sector. Energy markets in the EU are exposed to many risks: increasing import dependency, high and volatile energy prices, competition from growing global demand, security risks for producing and transit countries, and the growing threat of climate change. Besides that, EU energy policy is challenged to improve energy efficiency, share renewables, yield transparency and manage further integration and interconnection of world energy markets. EU energy policy derives from

---

43   Detailed information is available at "Europa Energy" website https://ec.europa.eu/energy/ (accessed October 2016).

Article 194 of the TFEU, which undergirds the integration and regulation of an internal market for energy having regard for preserving the environment. The Single Market fully applies to energy, allowing Member States to supply energy across borders, which is of particular importance in case of shortages.

Although there are pooled competences in a common energy policy, each Member State retains the right to realise its own energy policies (Mellar, 2016). Major achievements of the EU are the integrated climate and energy policy goals to be reached by 2020 for reduction of greenhouse gas emissions, share of renewable energy and an improvement of energy efficiency. Other energy policies agreed by the EU are: completing the internal energy market; improving security of external energy relations; improving security of energy supply; boosting energy efficiency; making the best use of the EU's indigenous energy resources (including renewables); and supporting research, development and demonstration projects (Mellar, 2016).

Besides the Member States' agreement on energy rules, there is the Energy Community, which tries to stabilise an integrated energy market between the European Union and its immediate neighbours. The Energy Community Treaty has since 2006 been extending EU internal energy market rules and principles through a legally binding framework. The remit of the Treaty is to establish a stable regulatory framework; integrate the larger energy market; enhance the security of supply; improve the environmental situation; and foster supply competition. To achieve the liberalisation and integration of energy markets, the contracting parties have agreed to the Energy Community Treaty and to adopt core EU energy legislation (the so-called *acquis Communautaire*) in the following areas: electricity, gas and oil, renewable energy, energy efficiency, the environment, competition, statistics, and infrastructure. The institution is headed by a Ministerial Council tasked with establishing priorities and guiding Treaty implementation. The decision-making procedures are supported by other institutions: a Parliamentary Plenum, Regulatory Board, Permanent High Level Group, Energy Group Secretariat, and three advisory Fora in the policy domains of electricity, gas and oil. Finally, the Energy Community takes account of the needs of its outside stakeholders, including civil society, investors and donors (Energy Community, 2015).

The overall purpose of energy policy is to create stability, security and environmental protection for industry and consumers in the EU, particularly through long-term investment in capital-intensive energy projects. A hard Brexit would affect energy investment, especially interlinked, cross-border, jointly funded energy projects; for example, the Connecting Europe Facility and the European Investment Bank (EIB) are major supporters and investors in UK energy, but they would be obliged to reconsider projects with the UK, thus impacting UK energy market development in the long run (Energy and Environment Sub-Committee, 2016). About €3.5 billion were invested by the EIB in energy projects in 2014. Brexit would require these energy projects to be checked as to credit and terms and conditions (Norton Rose Fulbright, 2016), any of which could increase gas bills for industry and consumers, as could lower exchange rates and the fact that half of the UK's gas is imported. Although gas prices have been increased in the past, twelve gas suppliers have already announced an increase in prices since Brexit, which may be significant.

Brexit will have an impact on the UK's adherence to the EU energy governance framework and will challenge several EU directives' application such as EU Industrial Emissions Directive 2010 (IED), which controls and reduces greenhouse gas emissions and the generation of waste. The UK's plans to close all unabated coal-fired power stations by 2025 implies that IED will continue to apply. The UK is well advised to become a partner of the EU and to comply with relevant EU law to avoid divergence of the UK and EU energy regulatory regimes (Norton Rose Fulbright, 2016) and to keep adjustment costs low for the industry.

Brexit from the EU energy market, where the UK has steadfastly promoted liberalism, may not only entail negotiation of a new energy market framework for the UK, but also precipitate a review of European energy policy for better or worse. Disentanglement from environmental regulations originally mandated by EU directives would result in more un-certainty for industry due to the complicated legislative operations of EU Energy Policy arrangements with their long lead times. It is estimated that it could take up to ten years to change-over just UK domestic legislation (Energy and Environment Sub-Committee, 2016). Further complications arise with the limitation of free movement of employees in the energy sector, such as oil platform workers in the North Sea.

A hard Brexit could give the UK freedom to subsidise its energy industries and increase energy capacity as well as to avoid infringement proceedings for missing such EU targets as the 2020 renewable energy target. Subsidies would still have to comply with the WTO subsidy regime, however, which is similar in objectives to the EU state aid rules (Norton Rose Fulbright, 2016).

In addition, Brexit could constrain trading and exchange opportunities for UK-generated electricity in the Single Market. Consequently, the industry may suffer a lack of planning security for new capacity, burdening new energy plants construction in the UK (which is mainly provided by foreign companies like EDF, Toshiba, Hitachi and CNC). The UK, as an island, must also compensate for loss of grid stability due to loss of access to Europe's meshed grid, as energy is hard to store and requires large-scale infrastructure. Although the WTO has a zero-cap principle on energy trade, the EU could impose transmission charges or other non-tariff barriers to the UK's energy trade after Brexit, meaning more costs for energy suppliers and ultimately consumers.

Assuring the UK's energy supply will require more investment in the energy sector: renewables and low-carbon resources as well as pipelines and interconnectors. As interconnection is essential to stability, the UK should maintain access to the EU energy market and remain part of the North Seas Countries' Offshore Grid Initiative (NSCOGI).

Brexit generally should not alter the UK's climate change goals: its environmental protection regime is based on the UK Climate Change Act, which mandates defining its Nationally Determined Contribution targets under the United Nations Framework Convention on Climate Change (UNFCCC). The 2030 target for the purpose of the Paris Agreement is included in the fifth carbon budget already passed by Parliament. If the UK withdraws from the Single Market, the EU's collective targets have to be redistributed amongst the Member States. Brexit should require consideration of membership of the Emissions Trading Scheme (ETS) of the EU, which regulates the defined allocation of targets amongst the non-traded sector, domestic emissions, and the traded sector, including heavy industry and power generation (Energy and Environment Sub-Committee, 2016).

Over and above this, the UK is already committed to supporting negotiation and implementation of international carbon reduction targets to help with energy supply efficiency and renewable growth. There is huge uncertainty about the UK's future international energy position and its energy policy interrelation with the EU. This puts investment stability in the energy sector at risk and energy price developments too, in the end. In particular, the development of 25 gigawatts of new productive capacity by 2030 at the latest would require further investment in the UK, and non-planned adjustments would raise capital costs for investors. Given the fact that €100-200 billion over the next decade must be invested for the UK's energy transition, any uncertainty would challenge investors' timelines, valuations and ultimately energy supply stability.

Impact Assessment Summary

- The core of EU energy policy is to integrate its energy market, secure its energy supply and make the sector sustainable. To achieve these objectives the EU has adopted an energy strategy setting clearly defined targets in regards to market liberalisation, transparency, renewable energy, the low-carbon economy, and energy efficiency. It provides incentives, funding, and a regulatory framework.
- Brexit risks energy stability, security, and environmental protection for industry and consumers if the UK should change its energy policy (for the worse). Uncertainty about future energy policies raises the cost of long-term and capital-intensive energy projects.
- There is a risk that energy prices will secularly increase for business and consumers due to a weaker pound sterling and the UK's necessity to import half of its gas supply. As a result, the UK's location attractiveness for industrial investors may deteriorate.

- Brexit will challenge the UK government to disentangle itself from EU directives that have been enacted into UK law in the next years, with the possibly unintended consequence that energy trading, the sector, and investors are made insecure. Overall, there is a certain risk of destabilising the British energy supply.
- The UK must take a clear position on its future energy needs and energy policy interrelations with the EU so as to smooth its energy transition and boost its supply.

3.1.16 Taxation

Definition: *The acquis on taxation covers extensively the area of indirect taxation, namely value-added tax (VAT) and excise duties. It lays down the scope, definitions and principles of VAT. Excise duties on tobacco products, alcoholic beverages and energy products are also subject to EU legislation. As concerns direct taxation, the acquis covers some aspects of taxing income from savings of individuals and of corporate taxes. Furthermore, Member States are committed to complying with the principles of the Code of Conduct for Business Taxation, aimed at the elimination of harmful tax measures. Administrative co-operation and mutual assistance between Member States is aimed at ensuring a smooth functioning of the internal market as concerns taxation and provides tools to prevent intra-Community tax evasion and tax avoidance. Member States must ensure that the necessary implementing and enforcement capacities, including links to the relevant EU computerised taxation systems, are in place.*

The Directorate General for Taxation and Customs Union is in charge of developing and managing the Customs Union, the foundation of the European Union, and implementing tax policy across the EU for the benefit of citizens, business, and the Member States. The DG's activity addresses the following issues: simplifying and modernising tax rules and administration; supporting the correct application of the EU tax and customs *acquis*; managing and securing international supply chains; crafting a coherent VAT system; working toward a coherent direct tax strategy; improving international transparency and the exchange of information; monitoring accession candidates' application of the customs and tax *acquis*; adapting energy taxation to the needs of a low-carbon economy; and assisting Member States to detect and combat fraud and tax evasion. Under the Customs 2020 and Fiscalis 2020 programmes, the Directorate General is supposed to assure efficient interaction between the Member States' tax and customs administration and promote the adoption of modern, efficient computer-based systems and IT in order to facilitate legitimate trade and find out fraudulent activities.[44]

The EU addresses the issue of harmonising indirect and direct taxes to enable a smoothly running internal tax market. Although the Member States have all the sovereignty to levy taxes, the EU objective is to maintain a fair competition and tax system, focussing on the fight against tax evasion. Any EU tax rules must be adopted unanimously by the Member States, making such agreements difficult. The legal basis of them in the tax articles of the TFEU provides for a harmonisation of national laws on turnover taxes, excise duties, and other indirect taxes which have the effect of taxing the Establishment of the internal market, as on free movement of persons, services and capital, the environment and

---

44   Detailed information is available at "European Commission Taxation and Customs Union" website https://ec.europa.eu/taxation_customs/home_en (accessed November 2016).

competition. Direct taxes comprise taxes levied on income, wealth and capital whether personal or corporate. Although EU action on corporate income tax is more developed, it focusses mainly on the principles of the Single Market. "Indirect taxes" denote not taxes levied on income or property, but refer to value added taxes, excise duties, import levies, and energy and other environmental taxes. EU harmonisation of indirect taxes has advanced more than of direct taxes due to the former's promotion of internal market trade. National tax policy is subject to each member state complying with EU rules; the main priorities of EU tax policy are the elimination of tax obstacles to cross-border economic activity, the fight against harmful tax competition (the "race to the bottom"), and the promotion of cooperation between national tax administrations in assuring prevention and combating fraud. The Europe 2020 strategy for smart, sustainable, inclusive growth, the harmonisation of tax policy supports the achievement of EU-wide policy goals (Paternoster, 2016). The European Commission has defined the major tax issues to be the following: direct and indirect taxation, tax evasion, fiscal state aid, and infringement procedures. The Commission's focus is on removing cross-border tax obstacles like discrimination, double taxation, difficulties in claiming tax refunds, and lack of information on foreign tax rules. The Commission has major achievements in the savings taxation directive and the directives on mutual assistance between tax administrations; however, its priority is the fight against evasion of both for direct and indirect taxes. Combined efforts on the national, EU and global levels, facilitating exchange of tax-related information, must be expanded to stop tax evasion and fraud. In 2017 the Member States will apply the new OECD global standard (GS) for the "Automatic exchange of information" (AEOI), now incorporated into EU law, doing just that (Paternoster, 2016).

Brexit will heighten uncertainty for UK businesses during the time the UK government is negotiating exit terms and terms of trade with the EU. No specific tax impacts are expected during this time, but one of the principal risks of taxation issues must be considered in UK's companies' strategic report of their annual accounts. In case of a hard Brexit, the UK would be no long part of the EU's Customs Union and exports between the UK and the EU would be liable for customs, which for companies would be cumbersome and administratively costly. The EU's customs duties on imports from the UK would make it less attractive for companies and consumers in the Single Market to source goods from the UK. The UK government itself would impose customs duties and tariffs on imports, increasing the cost of both raw materials and finished goods for UK companies relying on EU suppliers. The UK would further lose the benefit of 34 existing trade agreements with non-EU countries which the EU has negotiated over years. Finally, Brexit will raise more non-tariff barriers for exporting and importing UK companies, due to customs clearance adding time, complexity and cost to UK companies' value chains (BDO, 2016).

The EU harmonised VAT in 1977 to avoid distorting competition with different tax rates in Europe, which promotes free trade. Brexit will empower the UK government to change the VAT rate, even replace it with an entirely different tax. Given the high and unnecessary adjustment costs of UK businesses to a new VAT system, a change in the architecture of VAT seems unlikely in the short term. To avoid the risk of double taxation or double non-taxation in a post Brexit era under two different VAT systems, making tax payments and refunding complicated, the UK will be motivated to keep its VAT system materially aligned with the EU's. The imposition of VAT on imported goods from the EU to the UK and *vice versa* would impact on businesses. Although VAT might be often recoverable, there would be a cash flow cost for the period between import and recovery for many businesses (Allen & Overy, 2016).

When the UK exits the EU, businesses will need to adapt to corporate tax regulations for EU business activities. The withholding taxes on foreign dividends from subsidiaries or on royalties from overseas will have to await negotiation in a tax treaty. The EU's Parent-Subsidiary Directive and Interest and Royalties Directive preventing withholding tax from being a cost would cease to be available as an additional layer of protection for UK businesses. And UK legislation providing for relief from tax charges triggered by cross-border mergers or restructuring within the EU – for instance, the transfer of a UK business to an EU entity in exchange for shares – would not be applicable anymore (BDO, 2016).

A hard Brexit would give the UK more flexibility in tax regulations in the absence of the European Court of Justice nullifying UK domestic tax law on the basis that it is discriminatory, obstructs one or more of the fundamental freedoms, or constitutes state aid. It would also have more scope to set tax incentives to make a more competitive tax regime (Allen & Overy, 2016). It might reintroduce new tax rules in the long term that have been held to be contrary to EU law. However, some UK rules that remain on the statute books even though they have been held to be contrary to EU law would likely become effective automatically were the UK to leave the EU, like stamp duty on UK shares issued into clearing systems like Euroclear, Clearstream, or DTC (Allen & Overy, 2016).

The UK would be free to grant state aid and incentives in a post-Brexit era, for example granting tax advantages for attracting investments and promoting innovative growth. The raised investment amount and company age could be increased for Venture Capital Trust and Enterprise Investment Schemes. The UK can amplify R&D relief and assign both grants and SME R&D tax credits to the same company to support innovations without its being notified as state aid. Regional corporate tax rate reductions to attract foreign direct investment will be possible. Nevertheless, tax reductions generally must be paid for, and state aid will induce retaliation measures by affected states' imposing higher tariffs and customs regimes for UK importers and exporters (BDO, 2016).

Brexit would also benefit the EU insofar as making it easier to reach unanimity on the introduction of a Common Consolidated Corporate Tax Base (CCCTB), where the rules for computing taxable profits can be set at the Continental level. The CCCTB would eliminate unfair tax advantages for multinationals and yield a single corporate tax regime. With the CCCTB's main opponent gone, harmonisation of corporate taxation could proceed.

Though regaining fiscal sovereignty, the UK supports the OECD recommendations on Base Erosion and Profit Shifting (BEPS) that assure international cooperation on unfair tax advantages (Allen & Overy, 2016). The UK must therefore assess the benefits of tax changes in a post-Brexit era and weigh up the potential costs of implementation, financing, and countermeasures by its international trading partners. Results will be hard to predict in a volatile, uncertain, complex and ambiguous business operating environment!

Impact Assessment Summary

- The EU promotes harmonisation of taxation to assure an efficient Single Market in the EU as well as international cooperation in the domain of taxation.
- A hard Brexit will return sovereignty in fiscal matters to the UK to attract investment. Nevertheless, state aid and tax incentives will complicate the position of the UK in its future trade negotiation with the EU.
- UK companies will have to consider tax changes for ERP systems as well as compliance processes for VAT, imports and exports. Additional adjustment costs will have to be integrated into the post-Brexit processes of businesses.
- In particular, multinationals will have to scrutinise complex tax withholding issues regarding interest, royalties and dividends. Double-taxation treaties will have to be reviewed and business operations may have to be restructured for tax purposes.
- Both manufacturers and retail businesses will have to learn to comply with new customs duty rates and VAT compliance rules in cross-border trade of goods.

3.1.17 Economic and monetary policy

Definition: *The acquis in the area of economic and monetary policy contains specific rules requiring the independence of central banks in Member States, prohibiting direct financing of the public sector by the central banks and prohibiting privileged access of the public sector to financial institutions. Member States are expected to co-ordinate their economic policies and are subject to the Stability and Growth Pact on fiscal surveillance. New Member States are also committed to complying with the criteria laid down in the Treaty in order to be able to adopt the euro in due course after accession. Until then, they will participate in the Economic and Monetary Union as a Member State with a derogation from the use of the euro and shall treat their exchange rates as a matter of common concern.*

The Directorate General for Economic and Financial Affairs (DG ECFIN) concentrates on the improvement of EU citizens' well-being. DG ECFIN's policies aim to support sustainable economic growth, a high level of employment, stable public finances, and fiscal stability. Its major focus currently is on the recovery of the European economy from the economic and financial crisis,[45] by endeavouring to achieve two of the European Commission's general objectives: boosting jobs, growth and investment, and a deeper and fairer Economic and Monetary Union (EMU),as well as supporting three key Pillars of EU economic policy: raising investment, carrying out structural reforms, and ensuring fiscal responsibility. To boost investor confidence, all three Pillars need attention. DF ECFIN must also take international economic development into account for the sake of the EU's prosperity and stability. DG ECFIN's strategic plan provides for the following five specific objectives and measures (EC, June 2016):

1. to promote growth- and employment-enhancing policies in the euro area and the EU (through policy guidance to Member States, implementation of structural reforms, external factor)
2. to promote macroeconomic and fiscal stability in the euro area and the EU (through coordination of policies in a multilateral surveillance framework)
3. to promote investment in the EU (by creating an investment plan for the EU for strategic investments, projects and technical assistance)
4. to promote prosperity beyond the EU (through a efficient and stable monetary and financial system at home, and global economic governance and comity)

---

45   Detailed information is available at "European Commission: Directorate General for Economic and Financial affairs (DG ECFIN)" website at http://ec.europa.eu/dgs/economy_finance/index_ en.htm (accessed September 2017).

5. to improve the efficient functioning of the Economic and Monetary Union (through completing the EMU, and financial assistance programmes to Member States)

So far, the EMU has achieved a greater coordination of economic policies at European level and secured Member States' commitment to budgetary discipline *via* the Stability and Growth Pact. The completion of the EMU led to the introduction of the euro, and since 1 January 1999 the European Central Bank (ECB) has been in charge of steering European monetary policy and keeping prices stable. Following the financial crisis of 2007, the EU installed a system of economic governance, improving coordination and surveillance of economic policies and establishing a funding mechanism for Member States facing economic problems (Verbeken, 2016). Today the euro has been adopted by 19 Member States who seek to benefit from lower-cost financial and foreign-exchange transactions and the Establishment of an European international reserve and payment currency. The European System of Central Banks (ESCB) is committed to maintaining price stability, for the achievement of which the ECB relies on standard instruments like open market operations, standing facilities, and the holding of minimum reserves. In response to the financial crisis, the ECB took a number of non-standard monetary policy steps, including purchases of assets and sovereign debt from the secondary market, aiming to secure price stability and the effectiveness of the monetary policy transmission mechanism (Verbeken, 2016). The EU has also set up a new framework for coordinating and surveilling Member State fiscal policies, supported by the Stability and Growth Pact, diverse Stability or Convergence Programmes, and the Excessive Deficit Procedure. As financial, fiscal and macroeconomic imbalances are strictly interrelated, macroeconomic surveillance has been introduced to identify and correct imbalances at an early stage through a Macroeconomic Imbalance Procedure (MIP). Financial assistance programmes, such as the European Financial Stabilisation Mechanism (EFSM), the European Financial Stability Facility (EFSF) and European Stability Mechanism (ESM), have been designed to shore up the financial stability of the Single Market and the euro area as well. Finally, the regulation and supervision of banking had to be harmonised to assign responsibility for supervision, resolution and funding at EU level, and to enforce compliance with the same rules by banks across Europe. The resultant Banking Union comprises the Single Supervisory Mechanism (SSM), the Single Resolution Mechanism (SRM), the Single Resolution Fund (SRF), the Bank Recovery and Resolution Directive (BRRD), and the European Deposit Insurance Scheme (EDIS), supplemented by stricter capital requirements and a comprehensive assessment, and stress tests for banks (Magnus, 2016). This integrated banking framework aims to restore economic and financial stability in the EU, to bring back investment and well-being for both businesses and individuals.

The UK opted out of the part of the Maastricht Treaty 1992 that would have required it to complete the EMU; however, the financial crisis and the decline of the pound since

Brexit bids to revive the debate over the costs and benefits of joining the euro. To replace the pound with the euro, the UK would have to qualify for the EMS over a two-year period. Given the likely post-Brexit scenarios, UK would have great hardship in meeting the convergence criteria. Members of the European Exchange Rate Mechanism benefit from the European Financial Stability Facility that helps stabilise euro-zone economies undergoing credit crunches, recessions, and sovereign debt crises. The EU intends to strengthen the EMU and the stability of the EMU by enhancing convergence of the economic, monetary and fiscal policies of the Member States. The Five President Report gives a two-stage roadmap from 2015 to 2025 to coordinate economic policies ever more closely in order to establish a smooth-functioning and resilient Economic and Monetary Union. The report underlines that the euro is more than just a single currency, it is a political and economic long-term project (EC, October 2015).

The UK, being outside the European Exchange Rate Mechanism, has kept its economic sovereignty, and so the Bank of England has the ability to use interest rate policy to reach independent macro-economic objectives. The uniquely British housing market and financial sector as well as the UK's interdependency on the US business cycle would make full convergence with the Eurozone difficult.[46] Further arguments against euro-isation bring up the inadvisability of setting a single interest rate to apply to the economic and structural diversity in the EU (Economics Online, 2016).

Moreover, the UK never signed the 2013 Treaty on Stability, Coordination and Governance in the Economic and Monetary Union. This intergovernmental agreement is a new stricter version of the Stability and Growth Pact, which stipulates criteria for its signatories to achieve a balanced budget. It introduced an EU financial transaction tax and projected future regulations effecting UK's financial industry, which made the UK baulk (Falola, 2011). Consequently, it is not eligible to apply for bailout money from the ESM (Connelly, 2012).

The new Banking Union aims at stabilising and enhancing EU financial institutions and markets. For this purpose, the SSM is a mechanism useful directly to oversee the 120 or so banks with a presence in or partnership with the EMU, representing 82% of bank assets. The SRM additionally lays the foundation of a common template for a pan-European bank insolvency law. For the protection of deposits, the EU plans to harmonise national systemic guidelines for deposit insurance, assuring deposits to the amount of €100,000, funded by financial institutions (Hüffel *et al.*, 2015). Given the planned strong harmonisation of financial regulations and the ECB's ongoing empowerment, the UK has been reluctant to support a Banking Union; stressing instead its special financial structure and larger stock market relative to GDP, compared with other Member States. The unique characteristics of UK financial industry include the strong growth of the peer-to-peer and alternative

---

46   See Economics Online (2016) "Monetary Union", website at http://www.economicsonline. co.uk/Global_economics/Monetary_Union.html (accessed October 2017).

lending market, the orientation of UK banks beyond EU markets, and more non-EU banks' holding the sector's assets (Davies, 2016). The Banking Union is nonetheless pivotal to London as an international financial centre and the gateway to Europe for international banks. The UK is the centre of the major European banks' wholesale operations as well. Central coordination of supervisory banks could avoid national supervisory failures and their cross-border externalities, achieving a more integrated banking sector. The Banking Union would thus provide a solid arrangement for managing financial stability (Hüttl, Schoenmaker, 2016).

Joining the Banking Union would facilitate cross-border banking in the Single Market that would go beyond the single currency in supporting the functioning of the Single Market. Following a hard Brexit, the UK's trade and economy will suffer from economic uncertainty. Trade statistics show that UK exports of goods and services to the EU accounted for 44% (£222 billion) of this trade and 53% of its imports from the EU (£291 billion). Future projection of trade flows between the UK and the EU depends on future trade agreements and the treatment of tariffs and trade barriers under WTO rules. The impact on the UK will be manifold due to uncertainty of trade flows, foreign direct investment, business transfer adjustments, budget deficits, and finally exchange rate stability. The direct impact on the economy of size and spillover effects of new capital inflows due to a more favourable regulatory regime for new investors as well as the savings of the UK's contribution of an estimated £8.5 billion (in 2015) to the EU budget is hard to predict (Miller, 2016). Based on an IMF estimate, the savings of the budget contribution (0.33% of GDP) will be offset by trade barriers, resulting in output losses that may exceed 1% of UK GDP; moreover, its trade losses were estimated to fall in the range between 1.5% and 9.5% of GDP (Burke 2016). Following the leaked papers, the UK Treasury predicts that due to the hard Brexit, GDP would fall between 5.4% and 9.5% within 15 years. In the same period, the net impact on public sector receipts will result in a loss of between £38 billion and £66 billion per year due to the smaller size of the economy (*The Guardian*, 2016). On top of leaving the EU, the UK will have to pay costs of as much as £20 billion to the EU to cover Britain's share of the multi-year payment liabilities of about €300 billion from pension pledges and multi-annual contracts to commit to fund infrastructure projects, which Brussel will request from the UK (Barker, Parker, 2016).

A hard Brexit and the pound's depreciation could not only combine to send investors running from sterling-denominated assets, but also precipitate a property market correction of a "finance-property bubble" become overvalued. The UK has attracted speculative international capital which has inflated the finance-property bubble and therewith sterling's value, resulting in an overvalued pound for all other sectors. With lowered incentives to invest, UK producers lost competitiveness at home and abroad, leading to a poor productivity performance. The UK's outsize current account deficit has inflated external debt to 300% of GDP as at the end of 2014. About two-thirds was short-term, which intensified sterling's plunge. Brexit has exposed the pound as overvalued by about 20-25%, and it has depreciated by 15% since Brexit. It is estimated that it will have to depreciate another 5-10% before it stabilises at around US$1.1 per pound. A lower pound will help the UK's trade and productivity recover in the long run (Mody, 2016). An economic recovery and an uptick in exports needs to be seen in Britain's new future, and may require state-initiated investment funds, programmes and incentives.

Impact Assessment Summary

- DG ECFIN aims to support sustainable economic growth, a high level of employment, stable public finance, and banking stability. To recover from the financial crisis, the Five President Report defines a road map up to 2025 to deepen the EMU and make it more resilient to external shocks.
- The UK, to maintain its independence and safeguard its financial market position in Europe and due to stronger relations outside of Europe, did not follow the EMU; thus it is not eligible to benefit from the EMS and the established EMU framework of the Banking Union.
- The financial industry in the UK would benefit from joining the EMU and trading with the European wholesale banking business in one currency. The Banking Union would provide a solid arrangement for managing financial stability.
- A hard Brexit would impact the UK respecting the uncertainty of trade of goods and services, foreign direct investment, business transfer adjustments, the budget deficit and finally exchange rate stability.
- According to leaked memos, the UK Treasury predicts GDP will fall between 5.4% and 9.5% within 15 years and result in a possible loss of between £38 billion and £66 billion annually.
- Brexit precipitated a pound devaluation as a consequence of economic uncertainty and an overvalued economy due to the speculative finance-property bubble.
- The impact on the real economy will probably be seen after a hard Brexit is implemented. A weak pound will nevertheless put importing companies under cost pressure and increase prices of imported goods for UK consumers.

3.1.18 Statistics

Definition: *The acquis in the field of statistics requires the existence of a statistical infrastructure based on principles such as impartiality, reliability, transparency, confidentiality of individual data and dissemination of official statistics. National statistical institutes act as reference and anchor points for the methodology, production and dissemination of statistical information. The acquis covers methodology, classifications and procedures for data collection in various areas such as macro-economic and price statistics, demographic and social statistics, regional statistics, and statistics on business, transport, external trade, agriculture, environment, and science and technology. No transposition into national legislation is needed as the majority of the acquis takes the form of regulations.*

Eurostat is the EU's statistical office and is situated in Luxembourg. Its mission is to provide high quality statistics for Europe and to promote the values of respect and trust, excellence, technical innovation, service orientation, professional independence. It provides the EU with European statistics that set up comparisons between countries and regions, allowing decision-makers at levels of governance, Union, Member State and local, and the private sector too, with reliable data to make informed decisions. Furthermore, the public and media is given matchless access to accurate data on society whereby to evaluate political performance .

Eurostat provides specific data (the so-called euro-indicators) for a wide range – general and regional statistics, economy and finance, and evelledi and social conditions: housing price index, inflation, interest rates, labour cost index, unemployment, employment, job vacancies, and public deficits and debt. Sectors covered include industry, trade and services; agriculture and fisheries; transport; environment and energy; science, technology and the digital society; and topics covering include industrial producer prices, industrial production, international trade in goods, service turnover, and retail trade. This information is published in statistical books, manuals and guidelines, working papers, statistical reports, leafelets and brochures, and online databases.[47]

National statistics in Member States are nevertheless important for national purposes to make decisions and evaluations at European level.

Impact Assessment Summary

- Eurostat is the EU statistical office responsible for providing high-quality statistics for Europe and for promoting the values of respect and trust, excellence, technical innovation, service orientation, and professional independence.

---

47   Detailed information is available at "Eurostat - Your key to European statistics" website http://ec.europa.eu/eurostat (accessed September 2017).

- It provides specific data for a wide range – general and regional statistics, economy and finance, and socio-demographic data.
- These EU-wide comparable data help governments, regions and businesses make informed decisions.

3.1.19 Social policy and employment

Definition: *The acquis in the social field includes minimum standards in the areas of labour law, equality, health and safety at work and anti-discrimination. The Member States participate in social dialogue at European level and in EU policy processes in the areas of employment policy, social inclusion and social protection. The European Social Fund is the main financial tool through which the EU supports the implementation of its employment strategy and contributes to social inclusion efforts (implementation rules are covered under Chapter 22, which deals with all structural instruments).*

The general principles of social and employment policy address the socio-economic dimension of European integration in face of the social and economic challenges in the EU-28. The Europe 2020 strategy focusses social and employment policy on assuring inclusive growth with high levels of employment, reducing the number of people living in poverty or at risk of social exclusion. The common objectives of the EU and its Member States in the social and employment policy domains are stipulated in Article 151 of TFEU (Kraatz, 2016).

Ever since the 2008 financial crisis, the Member States' labour markets and households have faced higher levels of unemployment and poverty. Economic stagnation cries out for development of solutions to excessive public and private indebtedness in the EU. The imminence of globalisation and digitalisation and robotics all call for profound adjustments and a more skilled labour force to maintain competitiveness. The new growth agenda of the EU stresses jobs, growth, fairness and democratic change. With EU support, the Member States are undertaking to modernise their social protection systems.

The Directorate General for Employment, Social Affairs and Inclusion (EMPL) pursues initiatives to build a highly competitive social market economy. The Europe 2020 Strategy is to create more and better jobs; promote skills and entrepreneurship; improve the functioning of labour markets; confront poverty and social exclusion; modernise social protection systems, including pensions and particularly long-term health care; facilitate the free movement of workers; promote their rights, health and safety at work; and protect persons with disabilities (EC, January 2015). DG EMPL manages several social funds to support the realisation of the Europe 2020 Strategy, as controlled by key performance indicators. These include the European Social Fund (ESF) and the Youth Employment Initiative (YEI), the Fund for European Aid to the Most Deprived (FEAD), the European Globalisation Adjustment Fund (EGF), and the Employment and Social Innovation Programme (EaSI). The Europe 2020 strategy relies on the two Pillars of the integrated policy-making and a thematic approach to reach clear-cut goals in the domain of employment (75% employment for the 20-64 age group) and social policy (supporting 20 million people at risk of poverty). DG EMPL originates policy guidance and initiatives for employment and social policies, champions better working conditions and free movement, and supports policies favouring employment and social policy innovation. The

EU provides the enabling legislative framework. EMPL's applies its funding instruments according to a thematic approach to impact on employment, mobility, education and training, social inclusion, and the fight against poverty (EC, January 2015). Three out of the seven flagship initiatives fall within its responsibility and are addressed by the Agenda for New Skills and Jobs, Youth on the Move and the European Platform against Poverty and Social Exclusion (Kraatz, 2016).

The impact of Brexit on employment and social policy in the UK may be high. Although the UK had always a critical attitude to the Continental concept of a social market economy, the demand for a balanced income distribution could increase among the British population. Brexit could widen the gap between rich and middle class due to the uncertain continuation of EU employment rights and economic development in the future. Albeit a devaluated pound may create employment, there is no sustainability without economic policy measures. The impact of Brexit on economic performance may well be temporary, but the impact on social policy could be much longer-lasting. Given the return of UK sovereignty to the domain of social and employment legislation following Brexit, an exit from EU employment rights is most likely. Standards of employment and social policy, regional development, and even education risk being softened or abolished by Brexit (Andor, 2016).

At present, the EU guarantees to workers rights to paid holidays, parental leave, equal treatment for part-timers, and other EU employment rights. Brexit could tempt the UK to test and alter substantive EU rights of the UK workforce: paid annual holidays, improved health and safety provisions, a right to unpaid parental leave, a right to time off for urgent family reasons, a right of part-time, fixed-term and agency workers to equal treatment, outsourced workers' rights, and information, consultation and significant health and safety protections. Without the backup of EU law, UK employees are exposed to losing their hard-won benefits and protections from employers (TUC, 2016). Following Brexit, the CBI and TUC issued a joint statement urging both the government and companies, unions and other stakeholders to take action toward securing jobs and investments, and to reassure workers worried about the potential negative implications of Brexit on their employment and social protection rights (CBI; TUC, 2016).

Most likely, the UK will consider changing unpopular EU employment regulations, working time and agency working in particular. The transfer of undertaking (TUPE) regulation, rights relating to transferred staff, and the right to information and consultation in the course of job changes would be weakened (Heyes, 2016). Regarding the financial sector, the UK could repeal or amend the Capital Requirements Directive IV provisions regulating variable remuneration to attract and keep top talents (Bronstein *et al.*, 2016).

ECJ rulings in policy domains like TUPE and discrimination have become part of UK legislation and case law, and UK law has been further influenced by ECJ rulings from the past (Emmott, 2015). However, after Brexit the ECJ will have no more jurisdiction in the UK; its future judgments will be binding on no one, though UK courts might continue to regard them as persuasive authority (Bronstein *et al.*, 2016). The ECJ's recent controversial decisions illustrated the incapacity of trade unions to organize industrial actions in disputes that cross borders (Viking and Laval cases), and their limited capacity to negotiate improved pay and conditions for posted and outsourced workers (TUC, 2016).

Any social dumping and cutting back on legal rights for UK workers in order to enhance competitive advantage is likely to meet Member States' and other trading partners' fierce resistance and demands for UK adherence to legal protections for its workers (Emmott, 2015). After Brexit, EU nationals would likely no longer have the right to remain; some industries would suffer a lack of skilled workers, leading to wage rises and delays to projects. Free employee movement would be difficult for UK staff in Europe and limited by the terms negotiated with EU Member States (Lock, 2016).

The social care system in particular will be hit by limits on the free movement of social care workers, including about 80,000 EU emigrants or 6% of the jobs in this sector in England. The replacement of the European Convention on Human Rights with a "British bill of rights" would jeopardise future equality and human rights protections agreed by the EU, which might even have an impact on social care. Respecting diversity, promoting equality, and assuring human rights is a core purpose for care workers and are assured by the adherence to the European convention on human rights and distinct from EU membership. Brexit might result in dissolving bindings to any future equality and human rights agreed by the EU (Campbell *et al.*, 2016). Disabled people, too, fear for their historic gains, anti-discrimination laws and workplace rights, but also future benefits. Brexit could undermine the EU-prompted rights of disabled workers such as the draft EU Accessibility Act, which would impose on EU states common access requirements for goods and services from computers to banking, transport, telephones and e-commerce (Campbell *et al.*, 2016).

The EU is determined to maintain the same standards for its Member States for the sake of a levelled playing field across Europe that provides security for employees in the UK economy. The EU Parliament has called for more action to boost upward social convergence and combat unemployment. Enhancement of existing financial instruments like the ESF and EGF,[48] by supporting laid-off workers, will help mitigate structural changes and steer workers to other jobs or to set up their own small business. The new European Progress Microfinance Facility, set up in 2010, provides microcredit to small businesses and unemployed workers aspiring to go into business for themselves. EU financial support helped cities in North England like Manchester to modernise its central city neighbourhoods, and to improve the quality of life and of the environment; thus, by funding regional development projects, the EU added value to the UK's membership (Andor, 2016). Brexit will eliminate structural and personal support of laid-off workers in

---

48   See for further fund application rules website at http://ec.europa.eu/social/main.jsp?catId=326&langId= en (accessed November 2016).

the UK. The EU benefits will disappear and the real economy will prevail – social welfare will probably be consolidated into fewer hands than before Brexit.

Impact Assessment Summary

- The Directorate General for Employment, Social Affairs and Inclusion (DG EMPL) pursues policy, legislative and financial initiatives to build a highly competitive social market economy in the EU. Improvement of employment, and reduction of poverty risk and social exclusion are defined as major goals.
- The EU's new growth agenda stresses the agenda for jobs, growth, fairness and democratic change. Social Funds are applied to mitigate structural changes caused by globalisation and the technological revolutions.
- The UK has adopted many EU laws that guarantee workers rights to paid holidays, parental leave, equal treatment of part-timers *etc.*, and nudge toward improvement of life conditions for the disabled.
- Brexit has created a risk of softening or even abolishing employment rights and social assistance for the British workforce. There is the reality that UK courts will regard the ECJ's and may also come to regard the EctHR's judgments as persuasive authority, but not binding.
- Labour rights will probably not change overnight, but will be modified or changed in the medium and longer term. There is also a risk of devolution from and ignorance of any future equality and human rights protections agreed by the EU.
- EU-funded projects for the unemployed in the UK will be stopped. In the end, society could even be more strongly polarised than before Brexit.
- Brexit and its risk of "social dumping" will challenge EU institutions and Member States to regulate and enhance competition on a social market basis.

3.1.20   Enterprise and industrial policy

Definition: *EU industrial policy seeks to promote industrial strategies enhancing competitiveness by speeding up adjustment to structural change, encouraging an environment favourable to business creation and growth throughout the EU as well as domestic and foreign investments. It also aims to improve the overall business environment in which small and medium sized enterprises (SMEs) operate. It involves privatisation and restructuring (see also Chapter 8 – Competition policy). EU industrial policy mainly consists of policy principles and industrial policy communications. EU consultation forums and Community programmes, as well as communications, recommendations and exchanges of best practices relating to SMEs aim to improve the formulation and coordination of enterprise policy across the internal market on the basis of a common definition of SMEs. The implementation of enterprise and industrial policy requires adequate administrative capacity at the national, regional and local level.*

The Directorate General Growth is in charge of the Internal Market, Industry, Entrepreneurship and SMEs, and is tasked with creating a growth-friendly framework for European enterprises. DG Growth was set up in 2015 by merging the ex-DG for Enterprise and Industry with parts of the ex-DG for Internal Market and Services and one unit of the ex-DG for Health and Consumers. The reshuffle illustrated the new priorities of the Juncker Commission to promote economic growth, as witness furthermore the allocation of €315 billion to the plan to invest in Europe's economy. The remit of the new DG compasses five major goals: completing the internal market for goods and services; implementing the Europe 2020 Agenda of smart, sustainable and inclusive growth; fostering entrepreneurship and the growth of small businesses; generating policy on the protection and enforcement of intellectual property rights; implementing the EU's space policy *via* the two large-scale programmes Copernicus (earth observation satellite) and Galileo (global navigation satellite system).[49] In cooperation with other DGs, DG Growth has set up project teams to address the most important issues: jobs, growth, investment, competitiveness; the digital Single Market and Energy Union; the euro and social dialogue; better regulation and interinstitutional affairs; budget and human resources. For the realisation of DG Growth's objectives, a budget of almost €16 billion has been committed for fiscal period 2014-2020 (EC, 2016).

Industry is the backbone of the European economy, producing about 80% of Europe's exports and accounting for 80% of private research and innovation, not to mention providing high-skilled jobs. Given its manufacturing decline of 15.1% of GDP and loss of 3.5 million jobs since 2008, the EU must strengthen its productive base to spark an

---

49   Detailed information is available at "European Commission: Directorate General Growth for Internal Market, Industry, Entrepreneurship and SMEs" website at http://ec.europa.eu/growth/ (accessed September 2017).

economic renaissance in manufacturing, construction, mining, raw materials, tourism, creative industries, and business services. To achieve the modernisation, the EU has been defining its policy priorities for supporting industry; communication; implementation of competition policy; and task forces targeted on problem areas. The European Commission is determined to whet EU competitiveness and open up new markets for industry with measures like the conclusion of the Comprehensive Economic and Trade Agreement (CETA) with Canada and the Transatlantic Trade and Investment Partnership (TTIP) with the USA. Small and medium-sized enterprises (SMEs) representing 99% of all businesses in the EU and entrepreneurship are well understood to be key to prodding economic growth, innovation, job creation, and social integration. The Commission supports SME development with several programmes: the Small Business Act for Europe to create a business friendly environment; the Entrepreneurship Action Plan to foment innovation; the Enterprise Europe Network to ease access to new markets and internationalisation; Access to Finance to facilitate capital formation; Horizon 2020 to help SMEs compete internationally; Your Europe Business Portal, SME Internationalisation Portal etc. to provide support networks and information for SMEs (EC, 2016). The Juncker Commission got enacted a €315 billion investment plan for Europe that is intended to stimulate investment by providing visibility and technical assistance to projects and making smarter use of new and existing finances. The EIB and the European Investment Fund (EFI) have already raised €116 billion in the first year of operation in 2015. Because of EFI's signal success, the Commission is committed to doubling the lifespan of the Fund and its financial capacity to provide a total of €500 billion of investment capital by 2020 (EC, November 2016).

The Brexit vote was strongly supported by the UK's Rust Belt that hopes to hold the government to revitalising the manufacturing economy especially. UK industrial policy, however, has a toxic legacy from in the 1960s and 1970s of trying forlornly to arrest the nation's manufacturing decline. The state ought to attend only to create a legal and fiscal framework attractive to foreign direct investment, which is essential to tackling structural changes, increasing competitiveness, and creating new jobs in industry (James, 2016). The new Department for Business, Energy and Industrial Strategy (BEIS) is claimed to have re-introduced "industrial strategy" into British public policy, and was one of Theresa May's first acts as Prime Minister. Since then, her Government has indicated elements of that strategy: stricter merger and acquisition rules, new corporate governance principles, productivity growth, infrastructure projects, increased house-building, and support for regional development. Brexit will definitely impact aspects of industrial policy such as the application of state aid rules, trade agreements, and the labour market (Rhodes, 2016). Brexit challenges domestic and foreign industry and UK entrepreneurs to cope with higher costs from having to reorganise supply chains (resulting in higher prices for consumers). The Centre for Business and Economics Research (CEBR), Hitachi Capital and online pollsters YouGov found through market research that businesses have abandoned or delayed investments of an estimated £65 billion since Brexit (Euractiv, 2016).

A review of the building of Britain's first nuclear plant by the French utility EDF in conjunction with Chinese partners highlights the Government's new industrial policy approach, which comprehends foreign partnerships (James, 2016). Another example is the commitment got by the UK from the car maker Nissan to investment more in its Sunderland plant to secure 7,000 jobs in the North East in the near future. There is nonetheless an ineluctable investment risk and a loss of UK government credibility if it should fail to secure tariff-free access to the Single Market after all (Excell, 2016).

Industrial policy after Brexit reflects the Government's expressed design in intervene in mergers on grounds of the public interest. At present, mergers are subject only to EU Merger Regulation (EUMR) that gives the European Commission exclusive jurisdiction to review mergers with an EU dimension. The one-stop merger control principle forbids Member States to investigate or intervene in such mergers; they must comply with the Commission's decision to clear or block the deal. A hard Brexit will enlarge the scope of the Government to prohibit acquisitions by foreign companies in order to protect national champions or to reflect social considerations like employment (Cleary Gottlieb, 2016). In a post-Brexit world, this subjects EU mergers to the UK's jurisdiction and a potential veto, as Theresa May has vowed that industrial strategy will step in to defend important sectors like pharmaceuticals (May, 2016).

Economic freedom and stability is essential but not to jeopardise and dry up inward investments. The High Value Manufacturing Catapult, an innovation and technology centre, concludes that the UK must continue to drive productivity gains in manufacturing to stay globally competitive. Economic activity that adds value must be promoted by industrial policy. The promotion of an innovation translation model with the support of companies must be adhered-to to attract investment and position British industry favourably in a competitive world market. The maintenance of world-class research and innovation capabilities to bring new products, processes and services to market as well as provision of skilled worker are pivotal to success (Elsy, 2016).

The Brexit decision will also impact the collaborative dimension of research and funding for British science. The EU budgeted about €120 billion to fund research and innovation projects from 2014 to 2020, of which the UK was a major beneficiary. From 2007 to 2013, the UK contributed about €5.4 billion to the EU's research and development budget and received back from the EU €8.8 billion funding for research, development and innovation activities during this time (The Royal Society, 2015). Science associations are now afraid of losing their role as major players in international scientific research which sprang from the positive synergies of funding and collaboration between the EU and UK (Toor, 2016). The collaboration essential for space exploration is also in doubt (albeit the European Space Agency (ESA) is an inter-governmental organization separate from the EU). It is joint EU-ESA initiatives like the €4.3 billion Copernicus earth observation programme that are put in limbo. Overall, scientists apprehend a negative effect on the UK space industry (Toor, 2016).

Then there is the risk of Brexit forfeiting the financial support of the European Fund for Strategic Investments (EFSI). Although the UK is one of the biggest contributors to the Juncker Plan (at €6 billion), it is also the biggest beneficiary with €1.473 billion of approved financing. UK access to EFSI's total fund of €21 billion must be redefined after Brexit. At present, EFSI aims to mobilise €315 billion between 2015 and 2018 for projects linked to the environment, infrastructure, innovation and SME across Europe. So far, the sum of €116 billion has been mobilised in slightly more than one year. Juncker is targeting a total fund of €630 billion up till 2022 to support demand and fight deflation (Da Rold, 2016). The UK has obtained about €835 million so far, for three infrastructure projects. The EIB has promised that signed and approved investment projects for the UK will be carried out, but future projects have been put on hold; indeed, Brexit will not only compromise Juncker's Plan but also EIB's whole investment policy. In recent years, the UK has received €43 billion of long-term investment from the EIB, compared to a total of just €1 million for the European Free Trade Agreement (EFTA) countries (Switzerland, Liechtenstein, Norway and Iceland). Loss of the UK's 16% share of capital in the EIB means that funding for long-term investments in the UK has become exposed to higher financing costs, and leaves the UK with no public investment structure (Barbière, 2016).

Prime Minister May in her speech to business leaders ahead of the Autumn Statement said she means to give Britain the lowest corporate tax of the world's top 20 economies (15% or lower). Her Government is also planning to invest £2 billion per year in research and development, and a further sum of £1.3 billion is dedicated to roads and projects. Finally, the Treasury will review the corporate tax system (Dominiczak, Hughes, 2016) and face the challenge to refinance these tax reductions and funding losses.

Carolyn Fairbairn, Director General of the CBI, says industrial strategy must be sector-specific to get abreast of competitors' thinking and doing. Of importance is co-funding from Government and business in a partnership of equals (CBI, 2016). The interaction of industrial policy with other policy domains calls for a more general economic framework. To rebalance the UK economy, an appropriate monetary policy must manage the overvalued currency that underpins the increase in competitiveness of UK manufacturing firms. The Establishment of an appropriate technical system is needed to provide higher value added services to international markets and key industries such as telecommunication, aerospace, defence, life sciences and energy (Aubrey, Reed, 2016).

Impact Assessment Summary

- The Directorate General Growth has set wide-ranging goals and has a budget of €16 billion to support industries and SMEs for jobs, growth, investment and competitiveness. The Digital Single Market, Energy Union; Euro and Social dialogue;

Better Regulation and Interinstitutional Affairs; Budget and Human Resources are its remit.

- Brexit cuts off support by the EU for investing in SMEs and industrial projects, of which the UK has been the biggest beneficiary so far.
- With Brexit the UK enters a new industrial policy era for boosting productivity and developing new industries like biotechnology. Yet at the same time, the UK is losing access to funding for public infrastructure investment as well as the benefits of collaboration in scientific research.
- Existing pharmaceutical industries will be protected and stricter merger and acquisition rules will be introduced as industrial policy yardsticks in the post-Brexit area. Further, the UK is set to challenge the EU as corporate taxes cuts are planned to attract investment.
- Brexit will challenge both domestic and foreign industries and entrepreneurs to cope with higher costs from the necessity of reorganising supply chains (with higher prices for consumers).
- A post-Brexit United Kingdom will be obliged to find replacements for EU investment support of large infrastructure projects and SMEs; in particular, alternative public funding structures must be set up.

3.1.21   Trans-European networks

Definition: *This chapter covers the Trans-European Networks policy in the areas of transport, telecommunications and energy infrastructures, including the Community guidelines on the development of the Trans-European Networks and the support measures for the development of projects of common interest. The establishment and development of Trans-European Networks and the promotion of proper interconnection and interoperability of national networks aim to take full advantage of the internal market and to contribute to economic growth and the creation of employment in the European Union.*

The Treaty on the Functioning of the European Union (TFEU) carries over from the Maastricht Treaty the duty to develop Trans-European Networks (TENs) in transport, energy and telecommunications. The legal bases are Articles 170-172 and 194(1)(d) of the TFEU. Regulation (EU/1315/2013) of 11 December 2013 on "Union guidelines for the development of the trans-European transport network and repealing Decision No 661/2010/EU" reformed TENs fundamentally in 2013. The objective is to support the connection of all the regions of the EU. These networks are intended to contribute to the growth of the internal market and to full Continent-wide employment, while pursuing environmental and sustainable development goals.[50]

In its 1993 White Paper on Growth, Competitiveness and Employment, the European Commission stressed the fundamental importance of the TENs to the internal market, and in particular to job creation – not only through the actual construction of infrastructure. The TENs focus is on the following three sectors:

1. *Trans-European Transport Networks* (TEN-T): to support the construction and upgrade of transport infrastructure across the European Union. (Since 2014 it has been put under the jurisdiction of the EU's Innovation and Networks Executive Agency or INEA.)
2. *Trans-European Energy Networks* (TEN-E or TEN-Energy): to link the energy infrastructure of EU countries.
3. *Trans-European Telecommunications Networks* (eTEN): to "promote the interconnection of telecommunications networks, the setting-up and the deployment of the interoperable services and applications and the necessary infrastructure; to facilitate the transition towards the information society; to improve the competitiveness of European industry; to strengthen the single

---

50   Detailed information is available at "European Parliament: Trans-European Networks" website at
      http://www.europarl.europa.eu/atyourservice/en/displayFtu.html?ftuId=FTU_5.8.1.html (accessed
      September 2017).

market; to increase economic and social cohesion; to accelerate the development of new growth area activities".

TENs has led to the founding of the European Information Super-Highway. Article 155 of TFEU stressed the importance of measures "to ensure the interoperability of the networks, in particular in the field of technical standardisation", and mandated guidelines to set the priorities and objectives of the Super-Highway, and to support projects of common interest, through pioneering pilot programmes and feasibility studies, and loan guarantees and interest-rate subsidies.

Brexit would most likely mean the UK's exclusion from the TENs if it does not contribute to this programme fiscally. In the long term, the UK could fall behind in these areas, not necessary due to a lack of funding, but to the fact of being excluded in key initiatives and strategic projects.

Impact Assessment Summary

- The Treaty on the Functioning of the European Union (TFEU) carries over Trans-European networks (TENs) in the areas of transport, energy and telecommunications from the Maastricht Treaty.
- TENs are considered of strategic importance to the internal market, in particular to job creation, not only through the actual construction of infrastructure.
- Brexit could lead to the UK's exclusion from these strategic projects, which could impact the UK's improvements to its outdated transport infrastructure and energy network (National Grid). The knock-on effect could contribute to a decline in innovation and competitiveness.

3.1.22 Regional policy and coordination of structural instruments

Definition: *The acquis under this chapter consists mostly of framework and implementing regulations, which do not require transposition into national legislation. They define the rules for drawing up, approving and implementing Structural Funds and Cohesion Fund programmes reflecting each country's territorial organisation. These programmes are negotiated and agreed with the Commission, but implementation is the responsibility of the Member States. Member States must respect EU legislation in general, for example in the areas of public procurement, competition and environment, when selecting and implementing projects. Member States must have an institutional framework in place and adequate administrative capacity to ensure programming, implementation, monitoring and evaluation in a sound and cost-effective manner from the point of view of management and financial control.*

The Regional Policy is the EU's major social investment policy.[51] The financial vehicles that support this policy are the European Structural and Investment Funds (ESIF). They aim to reduce regional disparities in income, wealth and opportunities. Europe's poorest regions receive most of the support, but some financial support is in principle available to all European regions under one or other of the policy's funds and programmes. The current Regional Policy framework is set for a period of seven years running from 2014 to 2020.

From the ESIF, the UK was allocated around €16 billion in 2014-2020. Of that, England has been allocated roughly €10.6 billion, Wales €3 billion, Scotland €1.8 billion, Northern Ireland €741 million and Gibraltar €11 million. Other funds were also allocated to projects and industries spanning the whole of the UK. (Institute for Fiscal Studies, April 2016) The ESIF focus on five key areas: (1) research and innovation, (2) digital technologies, (3) the low-carbon economy, (4) sustainable management of natural resources, and (5) small business. (European Commission – European structural and investment funds, 2017).

The European Structural and Investment Funds are five:

1. *European Regional Development Fund (ERDF)*: to strengthen economic and social cohesion in the European Union by correcting imbalances between its regions.

---

51   Detailed information is available at the "European Commission - Regional Policy" website at http://ec.europa.eu/regional_policy/en/policy/what/investment-policy/ (accessed September 2017).

2. *European Social Fund (ESF) (including the Youth Employment Initiative)*: to invest in people, with a focus on improving employment and education opportunities across the EU. It also aims to improve the situation of the most vulnerable people at risk of poverty. More than €80 billion is earmarked for human capital investment in select Member States between 2014 and 2020, and at least €3.2 billion is allocated to the Youth Employment Initiative.

3. *Cohesion Fund (CF)*: to help Member States whose Gross National Income (GNI) *per capita* is less than 90% of the EU average, with the objective to reduce economic and social disparities across the EU and to promote sustainable development. In 2014-2020 the targets are Bulgaria, Croatia, Cyprus, the Czech Republic, Estonia, Greece, Hungary, Latvia, Lithuania, Malta, Poland, Portugal, Romania, Slovakia and Slovenia.

4. *European Maritime and Fisheries Fund (EMFF)*: to help fishermen in the transition to sustainable fishing, support coastal communities in diversifying their economies, finance projects that create new jobs and improve quality of life along European coasts, and make it easier for applicant fishermen to access financing.

5. *European Agricultural Fund for Rural Development (EAFRD)*: to encourage through finance projects from tourism to internet coverage in rural areas, to organic conservation. These projects are usually partly financed by the EU and partly through national, regional or private funds.

The Structural Funds and the Cohesion Fund together with the Common Agricultural Policy (CAP) make up the great bulk of EU funding, and the majority of total EU spending. The main source of all EU funding to the UK is through CAP. Records held by Defra show how much was paid out to beneficiaries of the scheme by each of the four Paying Agencies around the UK. In 2015 this amounted to €1.9 billion in England, €283 million in Wales, €612 million in Scotland, and €319 million in Northern Ireland. (UK Co-coordinating Body, 2017) Treasury figures show that in 2015 70% of all EU money received by the UK private sector came from two funds, the European Agricultural Guarantee Fund and the European Agricultural Fund for Rural Development. (HM Treasury, December 2015). The European Agricultural Guarantee Fund is designed to help stabilise farmers' incomes when agricultural markets are volatile. This money makes up around 70% of CAP and is fully funded by the EU.

The UK public sector receives also regional funding: The fact is that the EU transferred more than £4.4 billion (€5.7 billion) in public sector receipts to the UK in 2015. This money came mainly from large funding programmes: the European Agricultural Guarantee Fund (EAGF, which primarily finances direct payments to farmers and takes measures regulating or supporting agricultural markets), EAFRD, ESF, and ERDF. There are also other sources of funding from the EU, such as research funding and funding from the European Investment Bank, but they make up a much smaller fraction of the funding received by the UK. (HM Treasury, December 2015).

These are large funds which will not be available after Brexit. Rural communities, researchers and students, fishermen and small business will suffer the most if these funds are not replaced by funding by the UK government. In times of tight budgets it is most likely that regional funding will be nowhere near as generous as the EU's. Advocates of cutting funds argue that reduced funding will increase competitiveness, but disadvantaged and economically weaker communities naturally need greater state support than the more thriving urban communities. Cutting all these funds will have an unknown, but possibly drastic effect.

Impact Assessment Summary

- The Regional Policy is the EU's main investment policy, which is supported by the Structural Funds and the Cohesion Fund. It aims to reduce regional disparities in income, wealth and opportunities.
- €16 billion of the European Structural and Investment Funds were allocated to the UK for 2014-2020, with roughly €10.6 billion for England, €3 billion for Wales, €1.8 billion for Scotland, €741 million for Northern Ireland, and €11 million for Gibraltar.
- European Structural and Investment Funds (ESIF) focus on 5 areas: (1) research and innovation, (2) digital technologies, (3) the low-carbon economy, (4) sustainable management of natural resources, and (5) small business.
- If these funds do not get replaced by UK funding, the impact on rural communities, researchers and students, fishermen, and small business could be drastic.

3.1.23 Judiciary and fundamental rights

Definition: *EU policies in the area of judiciary and fundamental rights aim to maintain and further develop the Union as an area of freedom, security and justice. The establishment of an independent and efficient judiciary is of paramount importance. Impartiality, integrity and a high standard of adjudication by the courts are essential for safeguarding the rule of law. This requires a firm commitment to eliminating external influences over the judiciary and to devoting adequate financial resources and training. Legal guarantees for fair trial procedures must be in place. Equally, Member States must fight corruption effectively, as it represents a threat to the stability of democratic institutions and the rule of law. A solid legal framework and reliable institutions are required to underpin a coherent policy of prevention and deterrence of corruption. Member States must ensure respect for fundamental rights and EU citizens' rights, as guaranteed by the acquis and by the Fundamental Rights Charter.*

The Directorate General for Justice and Consumers (DG JUST) is responsible for EU policy concerning justice, consumers and gender equality. The EU's open borders means that the citizens of many nations are increasingly involved in cross-border disputes. In order to ensure easy access to courts and authorities, the EU has passed more than 20 legal instruments. The core principles guaranteeing access to cross-border justice are: mutual recognition, based on mutual trust between EU countries; and direct judicial cooperation between national courts. To this end, the European Commission promotes and supports the training of legal practitioners in EU law and in the national law of (other) Member States. Judicial cooperation in civil matters means clear rules on jurisdiction, court competence, applicability of law, and mutual recognition of judgments and enforcement. The business climate benefits from better enforcement of commercial claims, simplified enforcement of judgements, rules to assist creditors to recover cross-border debt, and modernised insolvency proceedings. Furthermore, the EU has taken the initiative in the domain of sales law, insurance contract law, and cloud computing contracts to reduce trade barriers derivative of differences among the EU Member States in national contract law.[52] In regards to Justice Policies, the Commission is committed to preserving the EU-promoted values of human dignity, freedom, democracy, equality, the rule of law, and respect for human rights, including the rights of minorities. The Charter of Fundamental Rights of the EU subsumes the protected rights under six titles: Dignity, Freedoms, Equality, Solidarity, Citizens' Rights, and Justice. This Charter is legally binding on EU institutions and national governments, and entered into force with the Treaty of Lisbon in December 2009. The major objectives of the EU are respect of fundamental rights, equal treatment, protection

---

52   For further information see the EC on Justice at website http://ec.europa.eu/justice/index_en.htm (accessed December 2016).

of personal data, equal access to justice, and protecting and empowering consumers anywhere in the EU (EU, December 2016). Moreover, suspects and accused persons must be guaranteed a fair trial in all Member States. Thus, the Commission promotes legislative proposals that complete its roadmap of procedural safeguards. The European Council and Parliament are finding agreement on rights for suspects and accused persons.

Brexit will have an impact on the British legal system in the long-term. The opportunity of the UK government to repeal EU directives, which were implemented through Parliamentary enactment, will cause legal uncertainty for business in the post-Brexit era. By contrast, EU Regulations are directly applicable in national law without the need for enabling legislation; thus Brexit precipitates a needless, instant, automatic destruction of a current regulatory regime, resulting in potentially a lowering of protections for consumers and business (Prochaska, 2016). At present, the European Communities Act 1972 (ECA) gives primacy to the European Court of Justice in matters of EU law. A complex body of British case law has also arisen to complement EU law. Estimates of how much UK law was influenced by EU law between 1993-2014 vary from around 13% to 62% (Heywood, 2016). In fact, the UK has much EU-derived law and precedent from EU mandates and influence already on the statute books that raises the question how current and future EU law will impact trade and business transactions with the EU in a post-Brexit era. To make matters worse, no experience with negotiating post-secession agreements exists. After Brexit is done, the UK will no longer be subject to the EU treaties; however, many of those treaties as well as EU Regulations related to local legislation will have to be disentangled in left-over laws. Further, ECJ rulings integrated into UK law will continue to apply until reversed or repealed. New EU legislation and the ECJ's jurisdiction will not apply to the UK after Brexit (Heywood, 2016). In practice, it is expected that UK law will be changed only slightly in order to avoid non-compliance with EU law, the better to trade with EU Member States. There is a low risk that laws for data protection, consumer protection, financial services and product liability will change. Lest the UK is precluded to trade with EU Member States in future, its courts and administrative organs must take into consideration ECJ rulings on applicable legislation. The interpretation of EU law also implicates EU-derived legislation integrated into UK law. There are ECJ decisions that can affect any non-EU country, as in the area of data protection in the *Google Spain* and *Schrems* decisions (Heywood, 2016). In sum, Brexit is expected to trigger complex legal ramifications and cause legal uncertainty in the short and medium term. Adaptation will put demands on resources, cost money and time, and might require a review of legal changes to assure an efficient and a fair judicial system in terms of the transaction costs (contract and enforcement costs). Brexit is likely to result in only superficial sovereignty for the UK, as EU law will affect the EU-derived UK law that the UK government will have no capability to influence any more.

In reference to international private law, important judicial consequences would ensue from a hard Brexit once Article 50 is officially invoked and the two-year transition period is complete. Before then, the UK will still be under EU rules. According to the Brussels I Regulation and its Recast of 2012, with a few exceptions, "a judgment given in a Member State shall be recognised in the other Member States without any special procedure being required", while mechanisms for the enforcement of judgments in civil and commercial matters have been simplified (Philippe, 2016). Brexit will end this regime; indeed, new treaties will have to be negotiated between the UK and EU to provide for the enforcement of UK judgements in the EU and *vice versa*. Absent such treaties, the UK might enact the same EU rules into national law, or apply ancient rules which were valid before the EU membership. Even so, the multiplicity of the determination of jurisdiction and enforcement of judgments will result in complexity and may have a negative impact on the international attractiveness of the UK courts, while benefitting EU Member State courts (Philippe, 2016). The scope of regulation of the enforcement of judgments to be renegotiated includes, besides the Brussels I Recast Regulation for civil and commercial matters and specific Regulations on insolvency and family matters, for example, also the Regulations on the European Enforcement Order of 2004 and on the Order of Payment of 2006. For the last two, no non-EU equivalent exists, and will have to be negotiated in bilateral and possibly tough negotiations. As a result, the enforcement of judgments between countries will become more complex still. As for cooperation between Member State courts (under the Evidence Regulation of 2001 and Service Regulation of 2007), Brexit will entail national enactment of similar or different rules or negotiation of cooperation agreements with the EU; otherwise, the UK should have to rely on The Hague Convention on the Recognition and Enforcement of Foreign Judgments in Civil and Commercial Matters of 1971. Hence, contractual relationships will have to be reconsidered and renegotiated for contractual clauses that are UK-related, such as choice of law or jurisdictional provisions and clauses relating to the territorial application of the contract (Philippe, 2016).

Fundamental rights in the UK are currently protected by three interlinked regimes: EU law and the EU Charter of Fundamental Rights; the European Convention on Human Rights (ECHR), the effectiveness of which has been enhanced by the Human Rights Act 1998; and domestic rights (Murkens, Trotter, 2016). Leaving the EU would relieve the UK of the obligation of complying with any human rights provisions in EU treaties and other sources of EU law. The Charter of Fundamental Rights would not apply and the ECJ would lose all jurisdiction over the UK (Parliament UK, 2016). This means that Brexit could jeopardise the protection of important rights like labour and anti-discrimination. Albeit bound still to the ECHR, the UK government by introducing a British Bill of Rights could put at risk core rights of British protected under international law, like privacy and family life. The ECHR is outside EU law, and the jurisdiction of the European Court of Human Rights which authoritatively interprets it depends on accession to the ECHR by the UK and other signatories, including non-EU countries (Heywood, 2016). British politicians, however, may be prone to leave the European Court of Human Rights due to unpopular decisions such as on prisoner voting rights. Theresa May has affirmed, "that whatever happened to the Human Rights Act, the UK would be staying in the ECHR" (Ward, 2016a). The measurable increase in hate crimes since the referendum calls for further clear commitments as to how to deal with immigration in the UK (Ward, 2016b).

Finally, Brexit has created a mood of economic uncertainty and possibly political instability that will complicate the struggle against lower ethics standards. The fear is that if British companies, particularly in the financial industry, face fiercer competition, it could translate into laxer anti-money-laundering checks, even an increase in corruption. EU anti-corruption experts thus consider Brexit a worry. Given that Britain has deliberately set its course against common European political values and goals, it has limited the basis for the working and impact of transnational law enforcement, and ultimately the fight against corruption in Europe. Hence, the Government and civil society organisations, journalists and concerned individuals will have to set priorities and stand up for official enforcement of laws against corruption and organised crime (OCCRP, 2016).

Impact Assessment Summary

- The Directorate General for Justice and Consumers (DG JUST) concerns itself with protecting rights and freedoms under the six titles of Dignity, Freedoms, Equality, Solidarity, Citizens' Rights, and Justice, which must be considered by the Member States under binding agreements in the EU.
- Brexit allows the UK to change EU-derived law on the statue books, but that is raising uncertainty for the economy of unpredictable repeals in the short and medium term. Complex legal ramifications will require resources, money and time to sort out, and will in any case entail a loss of governance and co-sovereignty powers to influence future EU law.
- There is a low risk that laws for data protection, consumer protection, financial services and product liability will be adulterated, entailing a risk of lower standards for consumers and businesses.
- Brexit will require EU regulations on the enforcement of judgments in civil and commercial matters to be renegotiated. Contractual relationships will therefore have to be reviewed, such as choice of law or jurisdiction provisions and clauses relating to the territorial application of contracts.
- The UK is still bound to the ECHR, but a British Bill of Rights would introduce a risk of weakening core rights of British protected under international law, such as privacy and family life, and contracts will no longer be subject to the EU Charter of Fundamental Rights.

3.1.24   Justice, freedom and security

Definition: *EU policies aim to maintain and further develop the Union as an area of freedom, security and justice. On issues such as border control, visas, external migration, asylum, police cooperation, the fight against organised crime and against terrorism, cooperation in the field of drugs, customs cooperation and judicial cooperation in criminal and civil matters, Member States need to be properly equipped to adequately implement the growing framework of common rules. Above all, this requires a strong and well-integrated administrative capacity within the law enforcement agencies and other relevant bodies, which must attain the necessary standards. A professional, reliable and efficient police organisation is of paramount importance. The most detailed part of the EU's policies on justice, freedom and security is the Schengen acquis, which entails the lifting of internal border controls in the EU. However, for the new Member States substantial parts of the Schengen acquis are implemented following a separate Council Decision to be taken after accession.*

The broad scope of DG JUST ranges from guaranteeing fundamental rights to cooperation between judicial authorities to asylum and immigration. To establish an EU security strategy, the EU has improved internal security by cooperation on law enforcement, border management, civil protection and disaster management. The enforcement of the EU's four freedoms requires coordination between national policies, especially in the framework of the European Police Office (Europol), to handle global crimes like money laundering, cybercrime, *etc*. Thus, efficient judiciary systems across the EU is a pivotal point for the functioning of the internal market. The Treaty of Lisbon lays a solid foundation for the development of a criminal justice area of European integration – a judicial cooperation in criminal matters to tackle international crime. Based on the mutual recognition of judicial decisions in all EU Member States, fighting crime and protecting rights of victims, suspects and prisoners are stipulated as a core principle of EU citizenship. A key objective of strategic guidance in the domain of freedom, security and justice is the development of judicial cooperation in criminal matters. Measures developed by the EU to tackle crime include mutual legal assistance, mutual recognition of judicial decisions, and the European arrest warrant. Further, harmonisation of legislation and setting minimum rules encourages legal texts and penalties to converge across the EU. A common criminal justice regime must encompass organised crime, trafficking in human beings, exploitation of children and child pornography, terrorism, financial crime (fraud, money laundering, corruption), environmental crime, counterfeiting, cybercrime and racism. The EU established Eurojust to stimulate and improve cross-border mutual legal assistance and the coordination of investigations and prosecutions between EU authorities. The setup of the European Judicial Network (EJN) in criminal matters improves the carrying-out of cross-border investigations and prosecutions by national judges and prosecutors. In order to fight trafficking in drugs and human beings, as well as terrorism, the Tampere European Council called for Joint Investigation Teams (JITs) to be set up by two or more Member States, which may include representatives of Europol and Eurojust. The Council aims to strengthen the right of accused persons to a fair trial by a framework decision on procedural safeguards in criminal proceedings. In September 2011 EU-wide minimum rules on criminal law for the protection of citizens from criminal acts were promulgated. Furthermore, the European Commission published a Communication titled "Towards an EU Criminal Policy", which listed policy principles for a coherent EU role in criminal law (Milt, 2016).

Brexit may also affect regulatory enforcement in respect of economic crime. Changes are expected in legislation, concerning the prevalence of economic crime during times of economic uncertainty as well as concerning European law enforcement bodies and their roles in prosecuting economic crime. It is unlikely, however, that after Brexit UK laws will change in the time frame of its two-year transition period. Howbeit the UK is bound by international obligations to implement UN and EU measures over trade and economic sanctions, the UK could be tempted to review sanctions on trade and economy after Brexit; for instance, to increase exports to emerging markets. It might also quit implementing European Directives like the Fourth Money Laundering Directive (weakening its prosecution of crime). Anti-corruption being the priority that it is, a relaxation of financial regulation would harm the UK's global financial market position and subvert economic stability and commercial relations with the EU (Harris *et al.*, 2016). The financial industry, with close ties to offshore jurisdictions like the British Virgin Islands and Guernsey, manage about $1.65 trillion in total client assets; the ownership of which, as a result, is often masked. According to the National Crime Agency, "hundreds of billions of US dollars of criminal money almost certainly continue to be laundered through UK banks, including their subsidiaries, each year" (NCA, 2015). Furthermore, London, as home of the financial industry, pays about one third of the UK's total tax take. This scale of it all presents a strategic threat to the UK's economy and reputation. To avoid a loss of global standing, particularly of the financial sector, the NCA has prioritised money laundering in the National Security Strategy (NCA, 2016). Finally, Brexit may affect the UK's relationship with EU law enforcement bodies – the intelligence sharing between the Serious Fraud Office (SFO) and National Crime Agency (NCA) and the EU to fight against corruption. Formal mutual assistance could be delayed; particularly, joint investigations involving the UK and EU may suffer and impact law enforcement and intelligence sharing. For instance, notifications of certain persons crossing the border from the EU into the UK would be less efficient, as well as the restraint, confiscation and recovery of assets (Harris et al., 2016).

Given the fact that the financial markets have become global, the power of collective action, which the EU exemplifies, is necessary to continue the fight against crime. However, the hardening competition in the financial sector risks tempting the UK to lower compliance standards to attract capital inflows by offering a safe haven for corrupt assets.

The May Government's ambition to cut corporate tax rates to 15% signals a move to turn the UK into a super-offshore haven – a "Singapore on stilts". This could well stultify anti-corruption plans (OCCRP, 2016).

The UK has achieved progress in fighting corruption in recent years, yet the consequences of Brexit and the search for new international partners may result in a decline of its anti-corruption standards. Taking back control of Britain favours reliance on the quality of parliament and the government, now that checks and balances by supra-national bodies have been cut out. New anti-corruption legislation could be delayed (like Unexplained Wealth Orders), causing a failure to prevent economic crime for lack of a register of the beneficial owners of UK property held by foreign companies. The government's commitment might even be lost sight of due to the challenges of Brexit to negotiate a "good deal" for the UK. There is a need to strive for more transparency, accountability, and basic ethics in politicians' conduct more than ever, particularly because, with increased economic pressure on companies, managers may be becoming more willing to cut ethical corners. Business leaders and politicians are now expected by citizens to take measures not only to fight corruption but also inequality. The rest of the world is watching how the UK will handle corruption in the post–Brexit world, which leaves the government, companies, entrepreneurs and SMEs, and consumers alike to wrestle with a challenging environment (Barrington, 2016).

Companies registered or linked to the UK must take into account the changeability of laws subject to Brexit, and deal accordingly with compliance standards (as with the UK Bribery Act of 2010). There is no reason for companies to believe that the Directive concerning politically exposed persons, risk assessments, beneficial ownership transparency, trusts and tax crimes, will not be implemented as well by the UK during the two-year transition period as by EU Member States by as of 2017. As signatory to the Financial Action Task Force ("FATF"), the UK could cause the FATF Mutual Evaluation taking place in 2018 to evaluate the UK negatively if there is any softening of the EU Money Laundering Regulations. The UK is likely to stand for good compliance as long as Article 50 is not triggered; in particular, it is interested in keeping *passporting* access to the Single Market for its financial industry and in safely sharing information between countries' Financial Intelligence Units. Companies dealing in the UK or with the UK must obey changes to the UK's criminal and regulatory measures including to the Fourth EU Anti-Money Laundering Directive, Reform of AML Law, UK Bribery Act 2010, Europol and European Arrest Warrant, Sanctions, Overseas Bribery and Corruption Prosecutions, and Deferred Prosecution Agreements ("DPAs"), which ensured both national and international compliance standards (Delahunty, 2016).

Brexit may make it harder for British police to handle crime, according to the head of Europol, the EU law enforcement agency. As a second-tier member of it, the UK policy and intelligence community has direct access to the European security database, which could be lost, jeopardising the UK's prosecution of cross-border crime, including terrorism, money laundering and human trafficking. Missing the link to EU police cooperation and use of the Schengen information system may harm counter-terrorism policy. The UK will be under legal pressure to negotiate a parallel arrangement for post-Brexit EU police cooperation (Rankin, 2016).

Impact Assessment Summary

- The Directorate General for Justice and Consumers (DG JUST) works on freedom, security and justice in the European Union through coordination of law enforcement, border management, civil protection and disaster management. International cooperation between national police forces are essential to tackle international crime via Europol and Eurojust.
- Brexit will create economic uncertainty and political instability in the sense of a risk of "infecting" other economies – one cause of the prevalence of crime. In the post-Brexit era, the UK will likely lighten trade and economic sanctions, and may modify and delay the implementation of the Money Laundering Directive.
- The challenges of Brexit could distract the UK's attention from the fight against corruption. There is a risk of lowering compliance standards to attract capital inflows, and the introduction of anti-corruption law could be delayed.
- Companies registered in or linked to the UK must take into account the changeability of laws subject to Brexit, and be careful to keep up with the regulatory environment to ensure their compliance with both national and international standards in the field of crime.
- British police will lose direct access to European security databases, complicating law enforcement against terrorism, money laundering and human trafficking.

3.1.25 Science and research

Definition: *The acquis in the field of science and research does not require transposition of EU rules into the national legal order. Implementation capacity relates to the existence of the necessary conditions for effective participation in the EU's Framework Programmes. In order to ensure the full and successful association with the Framework Programmes, Member States need to ensure the necessary implementing capacities in the field of research and technological development including adequate staffing.*

The Directorate General Research for Science and Innovation is tasked with supporting scientific research and technological innovation.[53] European research and development programmes are a prime example of how Europeanisation works in practice. The network idea – that bringing divers actors together can foment innovation and stimulate scientific progress and economic development – is one of the foundations of EU R&D. EU-funded programmes incentivise companies and other stakeholders to collaborate and to network with each other as a condition of receiving subsidies and funding.[54] Many of these programmes support or lead to new regulatory initiatives, thus providing a platform for discussion and evaluation of Information Society policies and standards.

The authors have discovered that EU funding is an important enabler of stakeholder collaboration, bringing together industry and research organisations with common interests. European R&D programmes lead to collaboration for more than the limited project period; often they bring stakeholders with different skills and resources together into long-term partnerships.

EU funding for technology companies and academic institutions is formatted in consecutive four-year programmes. These Framework Programmes (FPs), as they are called, for research and technological development (RTD)[55] are designed to encourage technological uptake and to support the EU's ICT policy objectives.[56]

---

53 Detailed information is available at the "European Commission – Research & Innovation" website http://ec.europa.eu/research/index.cfm (accessed August 2017).

54 See Framework Programmes for Research and Development, and the EUREKA (European Research Coordination Agency) programme to support RTD on the basis of establishing joined ventures between firms of more than one country.

55 The European Commission in its policy papers uses the term "Research and Technological Development" (RTD). In this book, the more generic term Research and Development (R&D) will be used throughout.

56 The Framework Programmes were as follows (The EU Framework Programme for Research and Innovation, website http://ec.europa.eu/programmes/horizon2020/en/what-horizon-2020

FPs are EU's main means of supporting leading-edge RTD. The budget has increased steadily with each new FP, and the EU has focussed on ICT as a top priority. The Fourth FP (FP4), running from 1994 to 1998, allocated more than a quarter of its total budget to ICT programmes; e.g., IT, telematics, and advanced communication technologies and services (ACTS). While FP4 focussed on technology, the themes of FP5 (1998-2002) reflected the social dimensions of the Information Society policy agenda, whereby funding was allocated for ICT systems and services for citizens; new methods of work and electronic commerce; multimedia content and tools; and socially essential technologies and infrastructure, e.g., the "User-friendly Information Society" programme. The overarching goal was to involve more European citizens in using ICTs, boosting the rate of economic growth and creating new jobs in Europe. Another main objective of FP5-funded programmes was to stimulate the innovativeness of European industry, to enhance their global competitiveness, and to support the policy of sustainable development (the "Competitive and sustainable growth" programme). FP6 (2003-2006) prioritised research on the Information Society and eEurope Action Plan. The projects featured medium- and long-term R&D in the next generation of technologies integrating computers and communications networks into everyday life; e.g., the "Information Society Technologies" (IST) programme. Horizon 2020 is the biggest EU Research and Innovation programme ever, with nearly €80 billion of funding available over seven years (2014 to 2020). This sum is not counting the private investment that this money will attract. It promises more breakthroughs, discoveries and world-firsts by taking great European ideas from the lab to the market.

The Commission stressed that the FP7, which had spanned 2007-2013, "provides new impetus to increase Europe's growth and competitiveness. The programme places greater emphasis than in the past on research that is relevant to the needs of European industry, to help it compete internationally, and to develop its role as a world leader in certain sectors" (Framework Programmes Website – FP7, 2007). FP7 was deployed in four thematic sub-programmes: "Cooperation", to promote European leadership in key technologies through the cooperation of industry with diverse research institutions; "Ideas", to consolidate the excellence of Europe's science base by stimulating Europe-wide competition; "People", to open up career prospects and mobility (or "free movement") for researchers; and "Capacities", to amplify Europe's R&D capacities. The largest single portion of the FP7 budget was allocated to ICTs: €9.11 billion, or 17% of the total budget of €53.3 billion.

(accessed October 2017)): FP4 (1994-1998, budget of €13 billion); FP5 (1998-2002, budget of €15 billion); FP6 (2003-2006, budget of €19 billion); and FP7 (2007-2013, budget of €53.3 billion) and Horizon 2020 (2014-2020, budget of €80 billion).

These research programmes provide many opportunity for researchers and small business to get their innovation and collaboration funded. There have been wide concerns that Brexit would not only bring the UK's participation in frameworks to an end, but also end the opportunity for UK businesses to develop EU-wide business and research networks. This could undermine the competitiveness and output of IP by UK universities and businesses.

Impact Assessment Summary

- The Directorate General for Research, Science and Innovation is tasked with science and research support. European research and development programmes are stimulating collaboration, innovation, and scientific and economic development.
- The latest Framework Programme, Horizon 2020, is the biggest EU Research and Innovation programme ever, with nearly €80 billion of funding available over seven years (2014 to 2020).
- A hard Brexit means that UK research and business will be excluded from future EU programmes, which will have a lasting impact on innovation and competitiveness.

3.1.26 Education and culture

Definition: *The areas of education, training, youth and culture are primarily the competence of the Member States. A cooperation framework on education and training policies aims to converge national policies and the attainment of shared objectives through an open method of coordination, which led to the "Education and Training 2010" program, which integrates all actions in the fields of education and training at European level. As regards cultural diversity, Member States need to uphold the principles enshrined in Article 151 of the EC Treaty and ensure that their international commitments allow for preserving and promoting cultural diversity. Member States need to have the legal, administrative and financial framework and necessary implementing capacity in place to ensure sound financial management of the education, training and youth Community programmes (currently Leonardo da Vinci, Socrates, Youth).*

The Directorate General of Education and Culture (DG EAC) is tasked with managing many aspects of this important policy domain. It is responsible for initiating policy on education, culture, youth, languages and sports.[57] Examples of how DG EAC does promote these activities include:

- *Education and Training*: These undertakings concentrate on policy cooperation: bringing Members together to learn from one another and EU-wide collaboration to improve education. It covers topics such as productivity and skills marketability (in Commission terms "growth and jobs"), social inclusion, and expanding education through new technologies.
- *Culture and Media*: These undertakings promote cultural diversity and intercultural dialogue. Culture as seen as a catalyst for creativity, and European cultures constitute a "soft power" that plays a vital role in external relations.
- *Youth*: These undertakings try to give young people a voice in shaping society, by including them in dialogues with policy makers and having them represented in the EU policy-making process.
- *Languages*: The EU has 24 official languages and another 60 regional and minority languages at least; therefore, a policy and strategy to promote language learning and linguistic diversity is adopted to give all citizens more equal opportunities and to shore up the riches of regional and minority cultural identities.
- *Sports*: These undertakings are designed to encourage popular participation in physical culture and to broaden the availability of sporting opportunities. This

---

57   Detailed information is available at "European Commission – DG Education & Culture" website http://ec.europa.eu/dgs/education_culture/ (accessed August 2016) and at "European Commission – Education and Training" website at http://ec.europa.eu/education/ (accessed August 2016).

includes provision of sporting facilities for the handicapped and disadvantaged. DG EAC also promotes the fight against doping and organised crime in sports.

DG EAC supports its policies through a number of projects and programmes:

- *Creative Europe*: This programme finances hundreds of projects supporting artists, actors, musicians and others that work in the creative industry.
- *Erasmus+*: This programme has existed for 30 years to improve education and training in Europe and to provide people with learning opportunities at any stage of life. It also supports youth initiatives that promote the ideals of citizenship, solidarity, and tolerance among citizens from 13-30 through a variety of projects, voluntary activities and exchange programmes. With a budget of €14.7 billion for 2014-2020 it provides opportunities for over 4 million Europeans to study, train, gain experience, and volunteer abroad.
- *Marie Sklodowska-Curie Actions (MSCA, 2018-2020)*: This programme helps European researchers at all stages of their careers. All disciplines, from life-saving health care to "blue sky" fundamental research, are eligible for funding. It also helps industrial doctorates who combine academic research and study with work for companies, and other innovative training frames that enhance employability and career development. Along with funding, the programme helps scientists with opportunities to gain experience abroad and in the private sector.
- *Other programmes and policies*: Multiple programmes mainstream multilingualism and other kinds of educational and cultural training, teaching and skills activities. The EU sees this as one of its main social and integration responsibilities, as it allows citizens from diverse, possibly disadvantaged backgrounds to access funds and opportunities in a typically underfunded sector. Examples of specific initiatives are (Europa Education and Training, October 2017):
    - *HEInnovate*: a free self-assessment tool for all types of higher education institution
    - Study in Europe: a portal to information on studying in over 30 European countries
    - *U-Multirank*: a platform for comparing the performance of higher education institutions
    - *European Institute of Innovation and Technology* (EIT): supports innovation by promoting entrepreneurial talent and new ideas
    - *We Mean Business*: to support organisations in identifying potential trainees
    - *European Language Label*: an award for language teaching and learning initiatives
    - *Electronic Platform for Adult Learning in Europe* (EPALE): a virtual community for teachers, trainers, researchers, academics, policy makers, and professionals active in adult learning

- *e-Twinning*: a platform on which for remote school staff to communicate, collaborate, develop projects and share experiences
- *School Education Gatewaylink* (outside the European Commission domain): a single point of entry for teachers, schools, experts and others in the school education field.
- ESCO: a multilingual scheme for classifying European Skills, Competences, Qualifications and Occupations
- *Europass*: a set of five official documents to make your skills and qualifications clearly and easily understood in Europe
- *Learning Opportunities and Qualifications in Europe*: an initiative providing information on courses, work-based learning, and qualifications in the EU.

Member States are responsible for their own education and training system, yet as national budgets become overstretched and education and culture goes un- or underfunded in many countries, EU policies can create otherwise impossible opportunities and level playing fields. Private education is not affordable for most students, while EU programmes and initiatives are open to everybody, and have been going beyond the traditional school, apprentice and university systems to supply skills deficits in the workforce, technological developments in education, and global competition. A new framework – Education and training 2020 (ET 2020) – will foment political reforms for cooperation in education and training.

A Hard Brexit or No Deal could see all these opportunities for young *or* old vanish overnight. If they cannot access funds and partake in these programmes any more, they must rely entirely on funding from the UK government or private funds. Unfortunately, the UK education budget is not so forthcoming as in most EU countries, and students leave university thousands of pounds in debt. The biggest loss, however, is for all European citizens: it will be more difficult for British students to study in the EU, and European students coming to the UK could see their tuition fees double if they are treated like overseas students from outside the EU. As at academic year 2015-16 (the latest year for which statistics are available) 127,440 students of EU Member States were studying in UK higher education, or 6% of the total enrolment. An exodus of any appreciable size would be felt in terms of declining fees and employment in an already anaemic sector (Higher Education Statistics Agency, 12 January 2017).

There is also the risk of "brain drain" at British universities. A recent analysis by the Russell Group, which represents 24 of the UK's leading universities, found that 24,860 members of staff at UK universities hail from other EU States, or 23% of the total. Since Brexit, EU staff members have been leaving in much larger numbers than in previous years. Tim Bradshaw, the Russell Group's Acting Director, has had to call for reassurances for EU students and staff. "Students, lecturers, researchers and professional services staff from across Europe have helped make our higher education sector a world leader," he said. "We want them to stay after the UK leaves the EU. We need an immigration system that lets us recruit and retain the best minds from around the globe." If the trend of more EU citizens leaving UK's education continues, it could have big repercussions for the whole sector. This concern was shared in an Article 50 open letter by Russell Group Chair, Professor Sir David Greenaway, and Acting Director Dr Tim Bradshaw which called for urgent assurances from UK ministers of the rights of citizens of other EU member states to work and reside in the UK, and reiterated the commitment of Russell Group universities to maintaining research ties with partners across Europe (Russel Group, 29 March 2017).

Impact Assessment Summary

- The Directorate General of Education and Culture (DG EAC) is responsible for policy on education, culture, youth, languages and sports. These are usually underfunded assets in many countries, and so the EU has allocated funding that can be accessed by otherwise disadvantaged EU citizens.
- The 30-years-old Erasmus programme has been allocated a budget of €14.7 billion for the 2014-2020 cycle alone, to provide opportunities for over 4 million Europeans to study, train, gain experience and volunteer abroad.
- A study found that an estimated 23% of all academic staff are from EU countries. There is a risk that an increasing number of them will leave, which could constitute a brain drain and damage the UK as a world leader in the higher education sector.

3.1.27 Environment

Definition: *EU environment policy aims to promote sustainable development and protect the environment for present and future generations. It is based on preventive action, the polluter pays principle, fighting environmental damage at source, shared responsibility and the integration of environmental protection into other EU policies. The acquis comprises over 200 major legal acts covering horizontal legislation, water and air quality, waste management, nature protection, industrial pollution control and risk management, chemicals and genetically modified organisms (GMOs), noise and forestry. Compliance with the acquis requires significant investment. A strong and well-equipped administration at national and local level is imperative for the application and enforcement of the environment acquis.*

The Directorate General for Environment works under the political leadership of the Commission for Environment, Maritime Affairs and Fisheries. DG Environment is responsible for the EU's environmental policy to protect, preserve and improve the environment for present and future generations. It proposes and implements policies for high standards of environmental protection and the preservation of the quality life of EU citizens. Moreover, it monitors Member States' compliance with EU law and represents the EU on environmental matters in international meetings.[58] According to its mission statement, EU policy assures European citizens life in accord with ecological limits so as to enable an innovative economy, alongside a protected biodiversity and minimised environment-related health risks, to enhance society's resilience and economic growth decoupled from resource exploitation. The Member States' environmental achievements within a common legislative framework are quite successful so far, including declines in sources of air and water pollution, falling greenhouse gas emissions, a transformation in waste management, *etc.* (IIEP, 2016). The General Action Programme to 2020 guides European environment policy for living well within the limits of our planet. At the same time, the EU promotes a level environmental standards playing-field and fairer competition across the Single Market.

The competence to make environmental policy is shared between the EU and its Member States, but environmental degradation is a borderless challenge that demands international cooperation as much as or more than national action. The EU environmental regulatory regime relies on the multi-level governance structure comprising the Member States, various public and private bodies, the EU itself, and international organisations. Environmental concerns exact EU participation in international agreements and programmes providing funding. The Establishment of *L'Instrument Financier pour l'Environnement* (Programme for the Environment and Climate Action) or LIFE in 2013 is the only programme funding environmental action at national level. But environmental

---

58   See for further information the Directorate-General for Environment at website http://ec.europa. eu/dgs/environment/index_en.htm (accessed December 2016).

protection is secured by integration into other EU spending programmes like the European Maritime and Fisheries Fund (EMFF), European Regional Development Fund (ERDF), and European Agricultural Fund for Rural Development (EAFRD). Further, DG Environment works with other agencies in developing and implementing environmental policy. For the implementation of the 2030 Sustainable Development Goals, DG Environment and DG International Cooperation and Development are to integrate environmental considerations and funding programmes into the other Directorates General (EC, March 2016).

The EU is authorised to make environmental policy in domains such as air and water pollution, waste management, and climate change. In fiscal matters, town and country planning, land use, quantitative water resource management, choice of energy sources, and structure of energy supply, Brussels respects the principle of subsidiarity and the necessity of unanimity in Council. Since the Treaty of Maastricht (1993) the environment has been an official policy domain, and since then it has been integrated into EU sectoral policies and extended to sustainable development, including relations with third countries (Ohliger, 2016). EU environmental policy principles include precaution, prevention and rectifying pollution at source, and "polluter pays". The last principle is implemented by the Environmental Liability Directive (ELD), which aims to prevent, remedy or sanction environmental damage to protected species, natural habitats, water and soil. The scope of polluter-pays encompasses transport of dangerous substances, discharge into waters, the safety of offshore oil and gas operations, *etc.* The integration of the environment into EU policy domains like energy policy and pollution emissions secures the shift to a competitive low-carbon economy by 2050. In tandem with economic and social policies, the sustainable development strategy is integrated into the Europe 2020 strategy so as to point the way toward sustainable growth and a resource-efficient, low carbon-economy. Environmental impact assessments and public participation assure that a high standard of environmental protection is reached before public projects are approved or authorised. The EU has entered into numerous global, regional and sub-regional environmental agreements on a wide range of issues like nature protection and biodiversity, climate change, and transboundary air and water pollution. Partnership agreements and cooperation strategies with neighbouring countries and regions round out the EU panoply of environmental protection measures. Enactment of minimum standards of environmental inspection and criminal sanctions by the Member States is mandated by EU law to enforce the environmental *acquis*. The European Union Network for the Implementation and Enforcement of Environmental Law (IMPEL) and the Environmental Implementation Review are policy mechanisms for achieving simple and cost-effective implementation of EU environmental law and regulations (Ohliger, 2016).

Given that there are several hundred directives, regulations and decisions of the EU in force relating to the environment, UK, EU and international environmental law are closely integrated. A hard Brexit will decouple them and reintroduce challenge and uncertainty into the green sector of the economy. The UK could be tempted to ease environmental product rules as well as processes and standards to boost industries incurring high environmental protection costs in matters of air pollution, recycling and nature conservation. In particular, trading companies as well as green technology companies, which are exposed to strict product standards and tariffs, could exploit lower UK standards after Brexit. Laxer environmental product rules and process standards compared to EU policies endanger health, nature and commerce in the UK. Relaxation of environmental regulations post-Brexit would affect other EU policies like agriculture, fisheries, research and development, international trade, overseas development, and foreign affairs. Finally, Brexit will exclude the UK from influence over environmental law on climate and energy policy, and the development of better environmental regulations and a recyclical economy in the EU. There are several policy areas that might be deregulated by the UK, like the quality of air, water and waste; nature reserves; climate policy; and agricultural and fisheries policies. More than likely, Brexit will leave the UK environment in a more vulnerable and uncertain position than it would as a Member State (IIEP, 2016).

Up till now, UK membership of the EU has been a boon for the environment. As one example, EU environmental regulations undergirded lawsuits that compelled the UK government to comply with air pollution standards and to clean up its sewage-strewn beaches. The EU reinforced the resort by industry to recycling and waste treatment. On the other hand, the UK installed world's first carbon trading scheme in 2002, and recently set up an advisory body on government carbon budgets called the Committee on Climate Change. British environmentalists have criticised EU policy on agriculture and fisheries for not being more progressive and sustainable. The Common Fisheries Policy is criticised for its quotas and severe controls (although the EU improved CFP by introducing a discard ban on 1 January 2016). The CAP is blamed for incentivising large-scale farms that maximise the output of food at the expense of the environment. The precautionary principle prevents the reckless use of new technologies and of genetically modified crops in CAP. After Brexit, the UK may create a more agile, adaptable environmental policy. The UK may spend money more effectively on farmers and the environment. Following a simpler and broader environmental stewardship, even wildlife habitats and higher animal welfare standards could be enhanced. Theoretically, the UK could keep the best EU environmental legislation and improve the worse ones (Johnston, 2016). On the other hand, once outside the European Union, the UK can never push for better agricultural and fishery policies for Europe nor reshape international environmental rules and regulations at the same level.

Unstable post-Brexit financial markets will also make it harder to attract and allocate investment in the creation of a cleaner, safer environment, harming the UK's growing green economy. Environmental policy has negative and positive effects on employment, yet new jobs in the green market are expected with the advent of the recyclical economy (IEEP, 2016). Given the intensifying competition for foreign direct investment, Brexit could throw the UK back to weaker environmental regulation than the EU. Greenpeace considers the UK government "one of the most obstructive and regressive in Europe on environmental issues" (Johnston, 2016). Brexit could turn out to be a real danger to the UK environment, as Brexiteers like Boris Johnson and Nigel Farage are climate change sceptics (Carrington, 2016). The departure of the UK also weakens the EU's negotiation position internationally, as the it can never be sure the UK will be on board, which probably bodes ill for achieving global environmental agreements (Johnston, 2016).

Under current environmental law, businesses must be in compliance with environmental regulations beyond the UK, including *e.g.*, the EU Emissions Trading System (EU ETS) and producer responsibility regulations like Restriction of Hazardous Substances (RoHS), and Registration, Evaluation, Authorisation and Restriction of Chemicals (REACH). The emissions reduction targets in the Climate Change Act 2008 and its own carbon reduction schemes are unlikely to change; the validity of ETS allowances after Brexit, however, is questionable, especially continuation of the emissions trading scheme. Even the UK's commitment to the UN Framework Convention on Climate Change and the Paris Agreement is in doubt. And the development of the renewable energy sector has depended on observance of the EU's Renewable Energy Directive, which may cease to be in force after Brexit. On the other hand, the UK is likely to stick to EU recycling and waste targets due to the UK's strong recycling industry. As for REACH and the Classification, Labelling and Packaging (CLP) Regulations that govern the environmental safety of products, the UK would be not legally bound to adhere to them after Brexit. In order not to jeopardise trade and export with EU countries and to protect end-users from hazards, UK should be interested in complying with these standards and obligations. Overall, Brexit will have a far-reaching, complex effect on the British environmental legislation. There is an opportunity to set up a more UK-specific regime in the long run, but there is also a risk of medium-term uncertainty for the green economy (Kettely; Rudd, 2016).

Internationally, tackling cross-border environmental issues as a unilateral negotiator will have been complicated. International cooperation is needed both for the protection of environmental resources and for the development of efficient and sustainable environmental technologies, as the management of limited resources is essential for qualitative economic, social and political wellness. The EU system of strategic planning after periodic reviews of future challenges provides predictability for business and creates trust in the economy – which British government will have to consider when defining a new environmental policy after Brexit. Taking into account the policymaking interests of the governments of Scotland, Wales and Northern Ireland in Brexit negotiations on environmental protection, agriculture and fisheries, the UK has to expect and overcome severe tensions.

Impact Assessment Summary

- The Directorate General for Environment has contributed to improving the environment, and with its General Action Programme seeks to protect and preserve it for present and future generations. Any borderless environmental protection requires multi-level governance that includes the Member States, the EU and international organizations, and coordination of several EU policies areas to be effective.

- Brexit necessitates a lengthy and laborious process of extrication from EU law in force in the UK. There is a risk of lowering environmental product standards and process regulations to unduly benefit industry and investors.
- Green investments are becoming less attractive to investors, which will set back development of more efficient environmental technologies and resources in the UK. In the post-Brexit era, the UK has neither voice nor vote to influence EU environmental policy.
- The UK's obstructionism to EU environmental policy endangers environmental protection measures, and creates uncertainty for the economy and investments.
- UK businesses will have to re-evaluate their compliance with the regulations and standards of both their domestic and foreign markets, resulting in higher monitoring, legal and adjustment costs.
- The UK would be well advised to establish a clear environmental policy planning procedure to create stability for the several economies of its Union.

3.1.28 Consumer and health protection

Definition: *The consumer protection acquis covers the safety of consumer goods as well as the protection of the economic interests of consumers in a number of specific sectors. Member States need to transpose the acquis into national law and to put in place independent administrative structures and enforcement powers which allow for effective market surveillance and enforcement of the acquis. Appropriate judicial and out-of-court dispute resolution mechanisms as well as consumer information and education and a role for consumer organisations should be ensured as well. In addition, this chapter covers specific binding rules in the area of public health.*

The Directorate of Health and Food Safety (Sante) endeavours to make Europe a healthier and safer place for citizens. DG Sante reduces and manages risks to public health, Europe's food and farm animals, crops and forests. In particular, Sante monitors implementation of EU laws on food and product safety, consumer rights, and public health by national, regional and local governments. Stakeholders' interests must be taken account of and advocated in relation to other EU policies on trade, competitiveness and the environment.[59]

Consumer policy is a main strategic objective of the EU for improving the quality of life, and is part of EU legislative considerations in all relevant areas. The EU promotes consumer protection, as it regards economic demand by its 500 million consumers as the central factor driving innovation and enterprise. Consumer spending accounts for 56% of the EU's GDP.[60] The European Consumer Agenda encapsulates the EU's strategy for consumer policy in line with the its growth strategy Europe 2020. It defines several objectives of a well-functioning internal market: consumer safety, knowledge and enforcement of consumer rights, integrating consumer interests into key sectoral policies, and consumer empowerment. Most of the 62 items on the Consumer Agenda have been fulfilled, based on the Report on Consumer Policy for 2012 to 2013.[61] The Consumer Programme 2014-2020 is budgeted at €188.8 million to strengthen consumer policy in four key areas of the Single Market: safe, competitive products; professional consumer organisations; consumer right claims; and collaboration between national bodies for

---

59   See for detailed information „European Commission DG Health and Food Safety", website at http://ec.europa.eu/dgs/health_food-safety/about_us/who_we_are_en.htm (accessed December 2016).

60   European Commission 'A European Consumer Agenda – boosting confidence and growth', website at http://ec.europa.eu/consumers/archive/strategy/docs/consumer_agenda_2012_en.pdf (accessed January 2017).

61   European Commission 'Report on Consumer Policy 2012-2013', at website http://ec.europa. eu/consumers/strategy-programme/policy-strategy/documents/consumer_policy_report_2014_ en.pdf (accessed January 2017).

consumer rights enforcement. Funds are provided to all 28 Member States as well as the non-EU EEA members. A set of proposed measures for consumer rights has been reviewed, including alternative dispute resolution, collective redress, passengers' rights, bank account fees transparency and switching, and better access to digital goods and services. The better to make an effective consumer protections policy, the EU supports consumer civil society, consumer education in schools, consumer information *via* setup of European Consumer Centres (the ECC-Network), and enforcement of consumer rights *via* EU-wide networks for consumer protection information and laws (Maciejewski, Hayer, 2016a). The EU's consumer protection measures furnish European citizens a high common level of protection against risks and threats to health, safety, and economic and legal interests wherever they live, travel or shop in the EU, and greater ability to defend their interests (Maciejewski, Hayer, 2016b).

As regards public health, the EU pursues the three strategic objectives to foster good health, to protect citizens from threats to health, and to support a dynamic health care system. EU health agencies address cross-border diseases, biological and chemical agents, and environmental hazards posing significant risks to public health and international trade. Crisis coordination and management in particular are imperative for tackling global health threats. European health systems, moreover, need improvement to be more effective, accessible and resilient in order to answer to the rising cost of healthcare, an ageing population and chronic diseases, the shortage of health professionals, *etc*. (OECD, EU, 2016). DG Sante assumes the coordination of all health-related domains. This includes pharmaceutical products wherein DG Sante is supported by the European Medicines Agency (EMA) and the European Centre for Disease Prevention and Control (ECDC). EU health strategy also supports the larger Europe 2020 strategy by promoting good health and preventative medicine. The EU's Health for Growth programme is challenged to improve access to medical treatment, medicines and provisions, as well as the adoption of information technologies like use of mobile devices and artificial-intelligence applications for more efficient systems (Sosa-Iudicissa, Tejedor de Real, 2016).

Brexit's impact on UK consumer policy is hard to predict given the complex consumer protection regime in the UK. As EU consumer policy became an integral part of internal market policy as well as of UK national law, covering a wide range of goods and services. Recent EU-driven but also national changes in UK consumer policy have led to the transposing of the Directive on Consumer Rights (2011/82/EC) and implementing its requirements through the Consumer Contracts (Information, Cancellation and Additional Payments) Regulations 2013. The Government revised the UK consumer law for dealing with consumer rights and remedies in relation to the supply of goods, digital content, and services, as embodied by the Consumer Rights Act (CRA) 2015 (Miller, 2016). In case of a hard Brexit, the UK would have a chance to adopt, stop or replace EU legislation to improve economy, for instance in the domain of retail finance. The repeal of the European Communities Act 1972 (ECA) has consequences for EU directives on retail finance and consumer protection as incorporated in primary UK legislation, including EU law in force on consumer credit, consumer protection, data protection and privacy, consumer dispute resolution, e-banking, insurance, mortgages, and public enforcement of consumer interests (Allen, Thorley; 2016). Changes will be hard for a post-Brexit UK to achieve, as both policy domains and levels of governance are entangled; compounded by the difficulty of replacing the high level of consumer protection guaranteed by the EU Charter of Fundamental Rights, EU Treaties, and EU legislation in force in the EU and the UK.

Following a hard Brexit, a significant impact on the consumer protections that UK citizens currently enjoy under EU under competition and consumer law is expected eventually. This includes protection from unfair practices, unsafe goods, misleading marketing practices, distance selling, *etc*. The achievements of EU law in curtailing restrictive practices and monopolies on subjects as diverse as roaming charges, internet search engines and tied contracts could fall victim to deregulation. There is even the risk that EU consumer protection law might be rolled back; for instance, passengers' right to compensation and care after delayed or cancelled flights could be replaced to ease the burden on UK airlines of Regulation 261/2004 (Erkelens *et al.*, 2016). Given that a huge amount of UK consumer protection regulation is derived from the EU, the UK has an opening to repeal it all after Brexit, if it is felt that it hampers the trade and production of UK companies. The consequence could be that if British companies no longer have to comply with EU product standards, other companies whose main trade is with the EU would be disqualified to trade with companies in the EU. This is a cost challenge for British export companies who will have to adjust their supply chains to meet EU product and trade requirements. Business is already worried about adjusting to and complying with new consumer policies after the recent adoption of changes in the UK. The British Consumer Rights Act 2015 (CRA) – dealing with consumer rights and remedies in relation to the supply of goods, digital content and services – might have to be supplemented to implement the EU's planned, more comprehensive Digital Content Directive and Online Goods Directive. Further to that, UK businesses trading with EU consumers must keep tabs on EU requirements for data protection, product liability, governing law and jurisdiction, not just marketing and advertising. UK businesses would be well advised to continue to comply with whatever EU consumer law is in force and to monitor developments just as if Brexit had never happened. UK companies must bear in mind that in a post-Brexit era UK consumer law could veer away from EU consumer law in the long term. Defending claims may be more expensive as EU consumers under current law are authorised to take action against traders in their local courts (Taylor, Wessing, 2016). For their part, consumers dread a watering down of their existing rights and protections. Any long-term implications for to commercial and consumer standing are difficult to predict. On the plus side, consumer protection, privacy and product liability law is considered unlikely to change (Miller, 2016).

Brexit will have an impact on the law of public health and health care. Although health care systems are the EU Member States' responsibility, the EU regulates several aspects of health care: reciprocal access, pharmaceuticals, working hours of doctors, and mutual recognition of qualifications. A hard Brexit would require the NHS, and public health and medical research regulation to be reviewed concerning movement and qualification of health professionals, procurement rules, medicines and devices, cross-border patient entitlements, and certain public health measures (Miller, 2016). Loss of access to the European Centre for Disease Control and Prevention (ECDC) is a risk. It monitors, communicates and provides expertise and responses to communicable disease developments. The UK puts its leadership role in public health at risk, for example, in outpacing antimicrobial resistance, in securing better standards in pharmaceuticals, and in tobacco control (FPH, 2016).

According to the NHS, there are about 130,000 people from the EU working in health and social care in the UK, amounting to 10% of doctors and 5% of nurses (NHS Confederation, 2016). A hard Brexit will challenge the NHS hospital and community health service to replace about 55,400 EU nationals. NHS leaders are even worried that it will be difficult to attract new recruits from EU countries. According to the European Directive on the recognition of qualifications, health and social care professionals automatically get recognition for the qualifications from accepted medical schools in the EEA that are assigned to them by the relevant regulatory body in any EEA country. After Brexit, however, British health care regulators might apply stronger criteria on health and social care professionals from the EEA. The introduction of stronger pre-registration checks of EEA-trained healthcare professionals as to medical language skills and professional competence might improve services quality on one hand; but on the other, it complicates the provision of sufficient healthcare services. Moreover, work outside of the EU is most likely to be restricted for UK doctors after Brexit, too, given the spirit of retrenchment it represents (Miller, 2016).

The EU Working Time Directive that sets a general limit of 48 hours in the work week and mandates 11 hours of rest between shifts for health services staff will be subject to critical review, especially touching junior doctors. Brexit will enable NHS to ignore the Working Time Directive to give greater employment and training flexibility to medical staff, but at the same time the widely accepted Directive could meet with labour union opposition in the UK (Miller, 2016).

Brexit will hinder access to healthcare systems for EU citizens residing in the UK and UK nationals living in the EU. Other reciprocal healthcare schemes are likely to be at risk, such as the European Health Insurance Card scheme, including access rights to health care and reimbursement of treatment costs for visitors or state pensioners living in another part of the EEA – even in the case that the UK remains in the EEA (Miller, 2016). This will in practice restrict freedom of movement for British citizens.

The harmonized approach to medicine regulation in the EU is jeopardised by the Brexit. At present, pharmaceutical companies benefit from one centralised authorisation from the European Medicines Agency (EMA) for therapeutic, scientific or technical innovation and public or animal health products. Companies may apply simultaneously to national marketing authorities or take advantage of the mutual-recognition procedure (EMA, 2016). In case of a hard Brexit, pharmaceutical companies intending to offer a medicine in the UK would have to apply to the UK Medicines and Healthcare Products Regulatory Agency (MHRA), separately, for marketing authorisation (Miller, 2016). After the EU Referendum, the MHRA confirmed its commitment to contributing globally to improving public health through effective regulation and medical devices (MHRA, 2016), yet there is the risk of higher authorisation costs for companies and slow access to new medicines for the British themselves. Certainly, the duplicative registration work of the UK national MHRA will put up administrative costs, whence prices for medicines are likely to go up (Castle, 2016).

The risk of a hard Brexit is pushing EMA to consider relocating to a Member State of the EU. The dislocation of EMA and concomitant loss of qualified staff members risk setting back the licensing of new drugs and the monitoring of existing ones. The surveillance of globalised drugs supply chains in liaison to other international regulators and market interventions for product quality might be affected, constituting a risk to public health. Besides that, moving EMA could threaten the power of the UK life science industry, which has benefited from EMA's proximity (Castle, 2016).

Impact Assessment Summary

- DG Health and Food Safety (Sante) improves the quality of life of EU citizens, reduces risks to the public's health and monitors implementation of EU law by Member State governments. The EU assures its citizens' health, safety and economic and legal interests as well as defends their rights.
- A hard Brexit affords the UK the choice to adopt, stop or replace EU legislation to benefit economic interests at the expense of consumer rights in product safety, fair competition, digital rights, *etc.*
- Trading companies are well advised to comply with current EU consumer law and to watch it for developments in data protection, product liability, governing law and jurisdiction, and marketing and advertising. Additional transaction costs will likely be charged to consumers.
- A hard Brexit will affect the legislation of public health and healthcare. The NHS will be hard put to regulate the migration and qualifications of health professionals, increasing transition costs for the entire health system.
- Loss of access to the ECDC undercuts UK leadership in developing health products. The harmonised medicines regulation of the EU will also be cut off. Higher authorising costs and longer timetables for launching medicines in the UK will raise costs for pharmaceutical companies and delay consumer access to new medicines.

3.1.29 Customs Union

Definition: *The customs union acquis consists almost exclusively of legislation which is directly binding on the Member States. It includes the EU Customs Code and its implementing provisions, the combined nomenclature, common customs tariff and provisions on tariff classification, customs duty relief, duty suspensions and certain tariff quotas, and other provisions such as those on customs control of counterfeit and pirated goods, drugs precursors, export of cultural goods as well as on mutual administrative assistance in customs matters and transit. Member States must ensure that the necessary implementing and enforcement capacities, including links to the relevant EU computerised customs systems, are in place. The customs services must also ensure adequate capacities to implement and enforce special rules laid down in related areas of the acquis such as external trade.*

The EU Customs Union unifies 28 national customs services into one uniform system for handling goods (imported, exported and transiting) under a common set of rules (the Union Customs Code). Thus, goods are traded freely within the Customs Union, whether they are made in the EU or imported from outside. The Customs Union was founded in 1958 by the six Member States of the European Economic Community. It mandated in stages convergence on common rates of customs duties and the application of common trade provisions as to third countries. The instalment of the Common Customs Tariff abolished restrictions on internal trade and created the Common Market. Implementation of the Community Customs Code in 1994 provided a common framework for import and export procedures. There are nowadays no customs controls for trade inside the Single Market, but common tariffs and trade measures are applied at the EU's frontiers in line with unified customs management legislation (UIA, 2017). All Member States of the EU and some territories of the UK, not part of the EU (Akrotiri and Dhekelia, Bailiwick of Guernsey, Bailiwick of Jersey, and the Isle of Man), form the contemporary European Union Customs Union (EUCU). The EU also has separate agreements forming a Customs Union with the three countries Andorra, San Marino and Turkey, with the exception of certain goods. The European Commission negotiates international trade deals on behalf of Customs Union members, for example with the World Trade Organisation (EC, July 2017). Initially, the Customs Union was confined to the coal and steel sector, but was rapidly extended to all products and services with the ECC Treaty. The Commission's main purpose was to complete the Single Market, promoting its four principles for the benefit of businesses and consumers (Moussis, 2011).

The EU's Customs Union obliges Member States to allow goods, if legally produced and marketed in other Member States, to be placed on their domestic markets; a Common External Tariff falls on goods imported from third countries. Goods imported into the EU must comply with Single Market law, which mandates harmonisation of product standards and safety requirements, and the principle of mutual recognition of certification and conformity practices among the Member States. For goods imported into the EU mutual recognition agreements are in place ensuring the complex determination of levied duties in accordance with rules of origin based on origin of materials, value added process and final substantial production phase (HoL, 2016). The European Commission's Directorate General of Taxation and Customs Union (DG TC) aims to manage, defend and develop the Customs Union *inter alia* by protecting the EU's external borders. It also tackles tax obstacles so that individuals and companies can operate freely across borders within the internal market. To this end, tax systems are adjusted to serve competitiveness and sustainable development and respond to international challenges concerning customs and tax policies: EU enlargement, international agreements on customs co-operation, and trade facilitation, among others. Cooperation between Member States is facilitated to fight tax and customs fraud. Finally, DG TC engages in open dialogue with stakeholders and interested parties to assure prevailing and effective tax and custom rules (EC, July 2017). Briefly, DG TC's mission is to develop and manage the Customs Union, the bedrock of the European Union, and to monitor and implement EU tax policy. Thus, it prepares legislative and non-legislative strategic initiatives and effects information sharing between Member States, including development of a modern, efficient computer-based and IT system in the EU to facilitate and survey trade as well as detect fraudulent activities (EC, July 2017).

Aside from the United States and China, the EU is one of the largest traders in the world, with a 16% share of the global volume of €21.5 trillion on trade and supply chain logistics in 2014. In 2015 the value of EU trade with other countries amounted to €3.5 trillion, more than the total yearly retail sales in the EU. Its main trade partners were the United States, China, Switzerland and Russia. It underlines the importance of an efficient established EU customs system that more than 2,000 EU customs points working 24 hours a day and 365 days a year should handle almost 293 million customs declarations annually (EC, July 2017). The objective of 113,000 customs officers is to protect Europe's society and consumers from international trafficking and smuggling, goods presenting a risk for safety and health, and to protect the financial interests of the EU and its Member States. About 4.8 million business operators are registered in DGTC's Economic Operations Identification and Registration System (EORI), enabling them to import and export goods in the role of consignee, declarant or representative. Operators with Authorised Economic Operator (AEO) status enjoy favourable treatment in trading simplification and facilitation, provided certain criteria are met, like legal compliance, record-keeping, financial solvency, *etc*. As 98% of customs declarations are submitted to Customs electronically, AEOs are crucial to electronic interlinks and international supply chain functioning. Member States do not require separate accompanying documents, so, about 91% of declarations are cleared within one hour. At the end of 2015 almost 39,000 valid authorisations for the use of simplified procedures at import and export were in effect. In 2015 customs duties contributed 13.6% to the EU budget of about €137 billion, the second-ranking EU revenue source behind Gross National Income (GNI) contribution by each Member State and VAT-based resources (EC, July 2017).

Figure 15: The UK's top ten trading partners

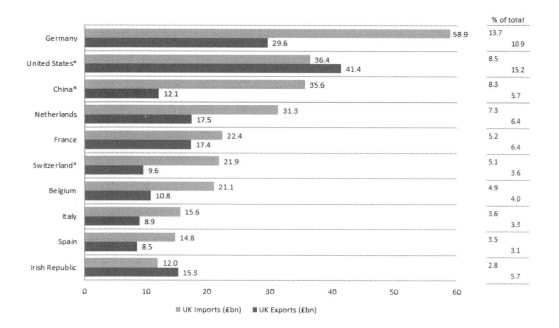

After Brexit, the UK should consider remaining part of the Customs Union, given the fact that seven out of ten of its major trading partners are Member States. However, the Customs Union is part of the foundation of the EU, enshrined in the Treaty of Rome; after Brexit the UK is only qualified to join a Customs Union of the Customs Union, such as the agreement with Turkey from 1995. This agreement differs from Customs Union membership in that not all Turkey-EU trade is tariff-free, and it is subject to customs checks; and technical barriers to trade and liability to anti-dumping duties burden trade between the two. Turkey must also give tariff-free access to goods from third countries with which the EU has a free trade agreement. Finally, customs revenue is not shared between Turkey and the EU; each trading partner collects common customs tariff revenue and the collector keeps it. Thus, Brexit could result in a radical change for handling customs and a reduction of benefits for customers in terms of supply and prices (HoL, 2016).

Leaving the Customs Union will impose costs on the UK's trading partners, as rules of origin must be checked for complex producer supply chains, not just imported consumer goods. A new bureaucracy must be set up to manage the introduction of a new customs code, control procedures, the training of customs officers, *etc*. According to an estimate by Open Europe, leaving the Customs Union could cost 1%-1.2% of the UK's GDP (Ruparel, 2016), and traders could be facing customs costs amounting to 4%-15% of the cost of goods sold due to administration of and compliance with rules of origin (HoL, 2016; CEPR, 2013). Another challenge is trade in services, which are making separate tariff-free treatment ever more difficult by being ever more bundled-in with products. At first glance, Brexit from the Customs Union might give back some independent external policy competence, to facilitate the closing of new free trade agreements not only with third countries but also EU Member States; because, by remaining in the Customs Union, the UK would be sacrificing its freedom to choose its own trading partners and to impose its own tariffs. Brexit particularly allows the UK to negotiate free trade agreements and other deals with non-EU countries – a trade policy independent of the EU. Nevertheless, the British must consider the implications of leaving carefully, in order to minimise the costs of administrative delays, compliance with customs checks, and the rules of origin. This would include new trade agreements with the Republic of Ireland. Additionally, simultaneously negotiating with the EU for remaining in the Customs Union whilst pursuing a new trade policy is a challenging and risky balancing act. The House of Lords recommended that the UK aims to remain an interim member of the Customs Union until a new trade agreement with the EU (over and above Brexit) can be concluded. The practical challenge is to find a reasonable arrangement till March 2019 so as to develop new trading relations almost from scratch (HoL, 2016).

In case no agreement can be reached ("No Deal"), after two years UK-EU trade would fall under WTO rules, by which UK would have to renegotiate with the EU its share of tariff rate quotas and subsidies. The Government should therefore focus on its future trading relationship with the EU and WTO schedules, and reach a transitional agreement about Customs Union membership. At the same time the UK needs to batch industrial interests in order to define new trading frameworks under WTO rules (HoL, 2016). The two-year timetable is tight, however, and the UK's political position weak both domestically and internationally. On top of that, negotiating capacity in terms of administrative knowhow is low and industry is yearning for a stability in lieu of which it is willing to leave the country. Under the banner "protect British producers", there is evidence that HMRC would reintroduce import duties for some consumer goods, such as cars, dairy products and electronics. Such protectionism will harm the economy and consumers. The risks encompass not only imposing costs on business and taxpayers, but also slapping consumers with fewer choices and higher prices for lower quality goods as result of ignoring complexity and mixing-in national sovereignty in pursuit of a shiny new global, independent trading policy. Any idea of leaving the Customs Union and then renegotiating tariff exemptions for free movement of services is illusory (Roberts, 2017). As long as the UK does not respect common market rules and the dispute resolution mechanism that is the European Court of Justice, it is dreaming to presume on reaching an agreement with the EU on a new Customs Union. Just a free trade agreement could take years and would be the hardest form of Brexit. Border controls would have to be erected between Ireland and Northern Ireland, and fresh impetus for Scotland to break away from the UK. Brexit might therefore begin the end of the United Kingdom.

Impact Assessment Summary

- The Customs Union obligates Member States to allow goods that are legally produced and marketed in other member states to be placed on their domestic market. A common external tariff is applied to goods imported from third countries. In 2015 customs duties collections contributed 13.6% to the EU budget of about €137 billion.
- The European Commission's Directorate General, Taxation and Customs Union (DG TC) is in charge of managing, defending and developing the Customs Union by protecting the EU's external borders. DG TC also tackles tax obstacles, readjusts tax systems, and fights tax fraud to maintain fair market competition for the benefit of customers and businesses.
- Brexit gives the UK the opportunity either to stay in the European Union Customs Union or to set up a new customs union with the EU, meaning no tariffs, free trade on all goods, customs checks and technical barriers to trade. Exiting the EU Customs Union will result in loss of free movement of goods into and out of seven out of the UK's ten top trading partners.
- Brexit may cause radical change in handling customs and higher costs for businesses and consumers: a new customs code, customs controls, training of customs officers must be set up. Exiting from the EU Customs Union could cost as much as 1%-1.2% of UK's GDP.
- Brexit will allow the UK to develop a trading policy independent from the EU, but totalling the costs to business of administrative delays, compliance with customs checks, and the rules of origin ignores the long time it takes close new trading agreements, which is itself a high cost.
- In case no agreement is reached, after two years the UK-EU trade would fall under WTO rules so that the UK would have to renegotiate with the EU its share of tariff rate quotas and subsidies. The UK should therefore consider remaining an interim member of the Customs Union and batching industry interests so as to define new trading frameworks under the WTO rules after March 2019.
- The UK is well advised to remain in the Customs Union to avoid backsliding into protectionism that imposes costs, limited choices, and higher product prices on producers and consumers.

3.1.30 External relations

Definition: *The acquis in this field consists mainly of directly binding EU legislation which does not require transposition into national law. This EU legislation results from the EU's multilateral and bilateral commercial commitments, as well as from a number of autonomous preferential trade measures. In the area of humanitarian aid and development policy, Member States need to comply with EU legislation and international commitments and ensure the capacity to participate in the EU's development and humanitarian policies. Applicant countries are required to progressively align its policies towards third countries and its positions within international organisations with the policies and positions adopted by the Union and its Member States.*

The European Union is inspired to create, develop and enlarge principles of freedom and common values, such as are enshrined in the United Nations Charter and international law. A key aspect of this is to prepare for human rights and democracy by promoting economic prosperity and integrating economies into a Single Market. The EU is committed to broaden its strategic interests and objectives in the international arena, and so it extends and enhances political and trade relations with other parts of the world. Regular summits with EU's strategic partners – North America, Japan, Russia, India and China – undergird development, co-operation and political dialogue. The EU's "dialogues" for fostering and intensifying relations include the Mediterranean, the Middle East, Asia, Latin America, Eastern Europe, Central Asia and Western Balkans (EP, 2017).

External relations covers a multitude of policy areas, like foreign policy, external trade, development policy, human rights and democracy, EU enlargement, and the EU "Neighbourhood", and relations with countries outside the Neighbourhood. Foreign relations is still an intergovernmental matter in the EU, meaning that the Member States control their own foreign policy to a large degree. Yet it is still true that negotiation as a partner in a bloc is more effective in achieving goals and representing European values. The predecessor Directorate General for External Relations (DG RELEX) managed an effective, coherent EU external relations policy. Under the Lisbon Treaty DG RELEX was merged into the European External Action Services (EEAS), formally launched 1 January 2011. The EEAS has a key role in foreign relations and sends 139 delegations to represent the EU around the world. They are in charge of all policy domains between the EU and the host countries. Delegations are diplomatic missions to foreign countries as well as to international organisations like the United Nations and the World Trade Organisation. EEAS is headed by the EU's High Representative who is the Vice-President of the European Commission and its personnel includes Member State diplomats. This the chief diplomat is charged with initiating and carrying out EU foreign, security and defence policies (EEAS, 2017).

EU trade relations policy promotes open market access and helps shape global trade systems adopted by the World Trade Organisation (WTO). To accelerate the transition from labour-intensive, low-value products to higher-value, branded products, the EU negotiates free trade agreements and defends European interests in international trade disputes. But in addition, through its trade strategy "Trade for ALL" it also promotes European values like human rights, sustainable development, good governance and environmental protection. The EU regards external economic relations as the occasion for catalysing growth, job creation and investment. Free trade agreements help integrate countries into global economic systems and expand economic welfare and growth in the long term. CETA or the EU-Canada Comprehensive Economic Trade Agreement (2016), the EU-Singapore FTA (2014), and the EU-Vietnam FTA (2015) were important trade policy achievements. Further FTAs are to be concluded with the USA, Japan, Australia, New Zealand and Tunisia, finalisation of which may take several more years (Viilup, 2016).

Following the Generalised Scheme of Preferences (GSP), the EU offers preferential access to the EU market to developing countries. GSP has been replaced by the Economic Partnership Agreements (EPA), which align better with WTO rules; *e.g.*, the EPA between the EU and the African, Caribbean and Pacific (ACP). The Aid for Trade (AfT) programme, too, part of Official Development Aid (ODA), assists trading capacities in developing countries to create growth and reduce poverty by free and fair trade (Imbert, 2016). The EU offers external financing instruments of various focuses, formats and sizes to support development policy in partner countries. EEAS specifies the strategic direction of EU development cooperation, and it administers the financing instruments along with the Commission. Besides eradicating poverty, the EU is committed to defending human rights and democracy, promoting gender quality, and addressing climate and other environmental challenges by its external financing instruments (Ramet, 2016).

With the British decision to leave the EU, a key driver for such foreign policies as enlargement, trade liberalisation and climate change mitigation has been lost – (although the UK changed its position towards enlargement policy). As holder of a permanent seat on the United Nations Security Council and obstructer of the EU's overcentralisation, the UK will be missed as a challenging and revising partner of EU policy. Even so, Brexit will not derail the EU. For starters, enlargement has had to be put on hold anyway due to the persistent effects of the financial crisis in several EU member states as well as institutional crisis within the EU. Secondly, trade liberalisation and climate change have become second nature to an EU that boosts trade as growth driver by negotiating new FTAs. Although the UK was a stumbling block to an integrated EU foreign policy, any push toward it is now in doubt owing to the climate across much of Continental Europe. One thing Brexit will likely affect is both the UK's and EU's global standing. The EU is in the throes of its inadequate management of the Eurozone and the refugee crisis. Institutional changes are ineluctable. But the UK has forfeited its credibility as a responsible partner in this, respecting foreign and security policy in particular (Weilandt, 2016).

Brexit will result in loss of preferential access to the EU Single Market, UK's largest trading partner. The UK therefore has strong incentives to reach a trade deal with the EU in order to regain access to 500 million consumers and over \$18 trillion worth of GDP purchasing power. Absent agreement, UK exports will be subject to the EU's external tariff system after 2019. Trade with the EU will suffer as well as trade access through the more than fifty preferential trade agreements with other countries negotiated by the EU and the new bilateral trade and investment agreements currently being negotiated by the EU with Japan, the Philippines, Mercosur, Morocco and India (HoL, 2016; McBride, 2017). Furthermore, loss of the UK's bridgehead to the EU market might easily drive foreign investors out of its major financial services and industrial sectors. Whether lower corporate taxes can compensate for loss of free market access and movement of qualified workforce remains to be seen. Rhetorical affirmation of the special relationship of the UK with the US by new President Donald Trump and Prime Minister Theresa May must be followed up by some kind of trade deal. Any optimism about reaching an astute trade agreement must be tempered by realism, in addition to the necessary implication that seeking closer trade support from the US constitutes a disruptive act aimed at the EU, which will hardly help negotiations with the EU (*The Guardian*, 2017).

Brexit will require the Government to achieve not just one single deal, but at least a set of six interlocking deals. The Brexit negotiations will include following major issues (Grant, 2016):

1. Britain's legal separation from the EU
2. a Free Trade Agreement (FTA) with the EU
3. interim status for the UK till the FTA takes effect
   accession to full membership of the WTO (likely also necessary to an interim UK-EU arrangement)
4. new FTAs to replace the bilateral preferential trade deals between the EU and about 53 countries
5. co-operation with the EU on foreign, defence and security policies

Brexit negotiations will take longer than the two years provided for by Article 50 of the Treaty on European Union due to the complicated interlinkage of policy domains and lack of experience with such proceedings. The UK must change at last 20,000 laws to effect a real separation from the EU (von der Burchard, 2017). A hard Brexit will challenge the Government to negotiate a new FTA for each country. But its negotiating power is weak and industrial interests are involved in allowing UK companies to enter a new market where their competition is feared. And completion to ratification of a new FTA with the EU and negotiation of an interim deal will take several years in itself. Yet by the end of that two-year period, and directly following exit from the EU, ideally, the UK is supposed to have negotiated and obtained the approval of all 163 WTO members to the new tariff agreements, and then replace the EU's current FTAs with 53 other countries. As if that was not enough, the UK will have to renegotiate its future relations with the EU in policy domains like foreign affairs and defence, policing and judicial co-operation, and counter-terrorism (Grant, 2016). In general, the UK is legally entitled to negotiate and conclude trade deals with non-EU countries before exit during the two years stipulated by Article 50. On the other hand, whether leaving the EU and adopting a liberal tariff and trade policy will bring prices down and boost GDP (Lawyers for Britain, 2017) is hard to predict, given the potential for long-term trade impacts such as new regulations and other non-tariff barriers imposed by EU Member States. Lost negotiating leverage in world markets will make it harder to close new FTAs probably lasting for four to ten years (Foster; Kirkup, 2016). The Government will have to build up a currently almost non-existent trade negotiating capacity to be able to deal simultaneously on multiple trading issues over many years. UK-based firms will thence be exposed to material uncertainties over the negotiating period and finally as to the quality of the outcomes.

Given the protracted period of Brexit negotiations, there are heightened political risks, even so far as the breakup of the United Kingdom itself. Scotland's governing National Party will be tempted to secede. Powerless to influence the Westminster Parliament's decision to honour the Brexit referendum, Scotland as a Remainer will be apt to hanker after another independence referendum. On the other hand, the collapse of the oil industry, a lagging economy, and the circumstance that two-thirds of its trade is with the rest of the UK would challenge an independent Scotland (Jefferson, 2017). Brexit will also affect Northern Ireland's trade relations with the Republic of Ireland as to economic integration, political stability and border controls. About two-thirds of Northern Ireland's imports from the EU and about half of its exports to the EU are with the Republic of Ireland, and Brexit-imposed trade barriers will hurt Northern Ireland's economy significantly. Between 23,000 and 33,000 border-crossing employees will be exposed to new Common Travel Area rules and EU Social Security Coordination in the post-Brexit era. As the second-largest beneficiary of EU funding as a percentage of regional GDP, Northern Ireland will be hit in its agriculture sector particularly hard by this loss of funding access. Given its structural fragilities such as a sluggish recovery from the last recession and the prevalence of small firms, Northern Ireland has more to lose from a bad Brexit deal than the rest of the UK (Biondi, Goncalves Raposo, 2016). Even worse is that Brexit may undermine the Good Friday Agreement due to a massive constitutional change – exit out of the EU – without the support of a majority of the Northern Irish. Dual Irish citizenship, EU investment in the peace process and European economic investment there will be affected by Brexit. The consequence may be that Northern Ireland will suffer a "devastating" impact on its economy and politics (Fenton, 2016).

On the other side of the border, the Republic of Ireland is committed to the EU, yet is economically deeply intertwined with the UK. It is thus in line to feel Brexit's impact more sharply than any other EU Member State. Its agricultural sector, with about 40% of its produce exported to the UK, will be the most highly exposed to Brexit and its likely tariffs. On top of that, the devaluation of the British pound has put the euro-denominated prices of Ireland's exports under pressure. Above all, Ireland must worry about its key economic advantage for overseas investors – a 12.5% corporate tax rate – being seriously diluted due to the UK lowering its own rate to 15% to keep itself attractive to investors even after Brexit (Doyle, Champion, 2016). The hardening of the border with Northern Ireland will disrupt business supply chains and free movement of employees and tourists. Although Ireland might benefit from potential relocations of financial services companies from the City of London or from renewed foreign investment in Irish industry, the ratio of detriments to benefits of needs only change marginally for the Brexit balance to tip the wrong way. In any case, Ireland is facing a big crisis in trade, commerce and migration from a hard Brexit (Taylor, 2016). Ireland's government is sounding the alarm, too, that Brexit's Protestant nationalism and the complication of its border with Northern Ireland imperil the peace settlement (McBride, 2017). The House of Lords has pointed out that Anglo-Irish relations feature "a special set of historical, geographical, economic, social and cultural ties" that cannot be ignored (Boland, 2017). It may nevertheless be that the relationship has passed the moment of psychological liberation, meaning Ireland must now focus on its economic relations with the Continent and beyond (Boland, 2017).

Finally, Brexit may set the stage for more populist and nationalist movements across the Continent jeopardizing European values and the EU's political stability. Anti-EU parties like France's National Front, Germany's Alternative für Deutschland, and Hungary's Jobbik embolden eurosceptics to vote to trigger the EU's leaving mechanism. The potential success of Brexit's aftermath for the UK threatens Europe's unity ((McBride, 2017), which is needed to deal with present and future international and global problems.

Impact Assessment Summary

- The EU's external relations are performed by the EEAS based on developing and enlarging the principles of freedom and democracy. The EEAS pursues free trade agreements as a key driver of economic prosperity, defends the EU's interests in international trade disputes, and catalyses growth, job creation and investment in the EU and its trading partners through external economic relations.
- Brexit should not have a severe impact on the EU's external relations, though the UK's critical voice will be missed. It is rather the UK that will lose credibility as external partner, not the EU as united global partner.

- Brexit will challenge the UK government to negotiate not one but six interlocking sets of agreements to effect Britain's legal separation from the EU, redefine applicable trade arrangements and assure co-operation on foreign, defence and security policy.
- A hard Brexit would oblige the Government to build up its presently woefully inadequate capacity to negotiate simultaneously on multiple trading (and other) issues. UK-based firms will be exposed to great economic uncertainty and may be disappointed with the quality of the negotiated outcomes.
- A hard Brexit would seriously impact the economy and politics of Scotland and Northern Ireland. It risks motivating another independence referendum in Scotland. A hardening of the border between Northern Ireland and the Republic of Ireland could destabilise the weak peace settlement in Northern Ireland between Catholics and Protestants. Brexit could precipitate a breakup of the UK (even beyond Scottish secession).
- The mismanagement of Brexit's aftermath by either the EU or the UK's could motivate eurosceptics to undertake more exits from the EU, or it could serve to reunite the EU in the future.

3.1.31   Foreign, security and defence policy

Definition: *The common foreign and security policy (CFSP) and the European security and defence policy (ESDP) are based on legal acts, including legally binding international agreements, and on political documents. The acquis consists of political declarations, actions and agreements. Member States must be able to conduct political dialogue in the framework of CFSP, to align with EU statements, to take part in EU actions and to apply agreed sanctions and restrictive measures. Applicant countries are required to progressively align with EU statements, and to apply sanctions and restrictive measures when and where required.*

The Common Foreign and Security Policy (CFSP) was enshrined in the Treaty on European Union of 1993 which aims to preserve peace; strengthen international security; promote international co-operation; and develop and consolidate democracy, the rule of law and respect for human rights and fundamental freedoms. CFSP was started in 1999 as an essential tool of EU foreign policy. It empowers the EU to intervene outside its own territory on civilian and military crisis management missions / operations for peace-keeping, conflict prevention and international security. The 2009 Treaty of Lisbon created the High Representative of the Union for Foreign Affairs and Security Policy (who also serves as Vice-President of the Commission) and the permanent President of the European Council to be the main actors of the new CFSP. The EEAS (see previous section) was also created and as an integral part of the CFSP the Common Security and Defence Policy (CSDP) was updated. The European Security Strategy (ESS) was reviewed and a new Global Strategy on Foreign and Security Policy (EUGS) was prepared to provide a broad strategic framework for the CFSP. On 28 June 2016, the EU's High Representative for Foreign Affairs and Security Policy presented its Global Strategy for a Common Foreign and Security Policy, which stressed the value of a cohesive, pragmatic approach to security, and strategic autonomy. The Global Strategy set five priorities for EU foreign policy: the security of the Union, state capacity and social resilience in the EU's East and South, an integrated approach to conflicts, co-operative regional projects with regional organisations (to spread the European idea at sub-national level), and global governance for the 21st century. A sectoral strategy will further define the civil-military level of ambition: tasks, requirements and capability priorities. On 14 November 2016, a CSDP Implementation Plan for defence and security issues was presented to the Foreign Affairs Council. Three sets of priorities were identified to which each CSDP peace keeping mission should contribute amid realising the Global Strategy with regard to defence and security issues: responding to external conflicts and crises; capacity building of partners; protecting the Union and its citizens. This Implementation Plan sets out 13 proposals for Member States to implement the EUGS, which comprises a coordinated annual review of defence spending; a better EU Rapid Response by use of

EU Battlegroups; and a single permanent structured cooperation (PESCO) framework for Member States willing to undertake more onerous commitments to security and defence (Troszczyńska-van Genderen, Legrand, 2016). The ambition of the Implementation Plan is to be fully complementary to NATO and the UN. At present, the EU has 16 military operations and civilian missions outside its territory. These are executed in accordance with the international law of UN mandates and/or national invitations by the country on whose territory it happens (EEAS, 2016).

Given the fraught security climate in and around Europe, Brexit shock, and an unpredictable US foreign policy, the European Council has urged fast implementation of a security and defence policy plan by EU institutions and Member States. Forty-two concrete proposals for bettering EU-NATO co-operation were given to the Council, from countering hybrid threats and cyber security to operational cooperation in the Mediterranean. The EU aims to avoid duplicating structures or competing with the NATO, but to streamline and improve the functioning of existing security and defence structures in the EU. To achieve all this, a common defence policy needs to align political wills and create mutual trust among Member States to agree upon increased defence budgets. The annual €500 million military R&D budget may help harmonise standards and requirements for a Single Market for the EU defence industry. There are doubts that the funds will be sufficient only to creating a military-industrial complex (Solana, Blockmans, 2016). The Implementation Plan is a step in the right direction of defining the EU security and defence policy, but no defined level of input has been given so far to meet effectively current and future changes. The reality is that the Member States will be obliged to reconfigure their armed forces in the short term, and combine military capabilities in the long term. The fixed-costs plans for realisation support the commitment to a European Defence Union (Solana, Blockmans, 2016). The European Council will evaluate the initial progress of the three Pillars – Implementation Plan for security and defence as part of the EU Global Strategy, European Defence Action Plan, and concrete proposals for an enhanced EU-NATO Joint Declaration – in March 2017.

Part of EU foreign policy, the European Neighbourhood Policy (ENP) governs relations with 16 states on the EU's southern and eastern flanks. The ENP offers political association, economic integration, and greater mobility of people. The European Council, made of the heads of state of the EU's Member States, is the final decision body. The High Representative chairs the monthly meeting of the Foreign Affairs Council made of the Foreign Ministers of the EU 28. In making its foreign and security policy more consistent, the High Representative is supported by the External Action Service (EEAS) (EU, 2017; EEAS, 2017).

Brexit has meant the loss of one of only two Member States with global strategic ambitions, significant armed forces, a nuclear deterrent, and a permanent seat in the United Nations Security Council. The authors nonetheless appraise Brexit as having no major impact on external affairs or the Common Security and Defence Policy. Britain had lost its interest in the CSDP, unlike France who was the initiator of an EU defence policy. Given that the EU's current missions abroad are rather unambitious, the loss of Britain's personnel and equipment contributions will not be noticed (Weilandt, 2016). Withdrawal from the CSDP is unlikely to affect the UK even in terms of cost savings. In contrast, the British defence industry is being affected indirectly by the Brexit-driven fall in sterling's value in the context of dollar-based procurement systems for industries such as defence (Raczova, 2017).

Brexit will also weaken another tool of security policy. The EU imposes targeted economic sanctions in lieu of military involvement in foreign disputes, which it wishes to avoid. Sanctions have been used for objectives as diverse as nuclear non-proliferation, counter-terrorism, conflict management, and democracy and human rights promotion. Even after Russia violated sovereign Ukraine's territorial integrity, the EU preferred measured economic sanctions upon the Crimea and Sevastopol, and finally sanctions targeting trade with Russia in specific sectors (European Council, 2017). In recent years the UK has pro-actively advocated sanctions against Russia, Syria, North Korea and Iran. Brexit may affect sanctions both supplemental to UNSC sanctions and unilateral (without UN sanctions; *viz.*, Syria, Russia, Myanmar). All types of sanctions regimes presuppose a consensus of the Member States, and the strong support of the UK has led to unanimity before. A united EU sanctions policy is both an effective foreign policy tool and an economic instrument for the Member States (in that it limits trade competition. Post-Brexit, collaboration with the EU toward unanimity likely becomes costlier and more complicated for the UK. Plus, the rigour of the sanctions supported by the EU – the world's largest trade bloc – and by the UK – the fifth-largest economy and home of Europe's financial heart – may be lessened. Finally, the UK will lose influence over the EU's sanctions policy and whether it will be diplomatic or severe execution of sanctions. Thus, Brexit will harm both the UK's foreign policy and the EU's sanctions policy. The EU will consequently have to cast about for alternatives for its toolbox of security instruments (Moret, 2016).

It is possible that the UK might use its diplomatic, intelligence and military assets to reach foreign objectives – such as providing the security undergirding for reaching favourable new free trade agreements. The commitment to defend the Baltic states and Poland insofar as it entails a political link between security and any future EU-UK trade agreement might redefine the UK's military role. Finally, the UK will have less influence on EU policy-making, including on defence and security (Grant, 2016). Given the increasing costliness of military budgeting, the UK has an interest in a stronger EU military force after it has left the Union. After committing his Government to invest more than £178 billion in capabilities to support special forces and in deployable armed forces, former Prime Minister Cameron underlined defence as strategic priority for the UK (Raczova, 2017). Even PM May has lobbied for all Nato states to raise their spending levels, defence equipment spending in particular, to meet the Nato target of 2% of each Member State's GDP, which is also in line with US expectations (*The Guardian*, 2017).

Brexit is likelier to impact the politics and governance of the CSDP. The UK ranks only fifth among contributors to CSDP military operations, deploying only 4.19% of the personnel provided by Member States. The fall of the New Labour Government and the new political formation of David Cameron's coalition cabinet as well as the unsuccessful impact of small-scale operations on the ground had persuaded the UK gradually to withdraw from the CSDP after 2010. The exit of Britain cries out for another Member State to fill the governance vacuum. A closer cooperation between France and Germany might be politically opportune for founding an integrated common security and defence policy and an EU-wide defence industry. A new European Defence Union is needed to tackle international and global conflicts with more efficient, cohesive defence structures and capabilities. Border controls and regional stability, too, require a pan-European approach to security and defence. Accordingly, the UK should be considered by the EU a cooperative partner after Brexit on the one hand, and it should contribute to CSDP operations and access the defence market of the EU as a third party on the other. This will stabilise Europe's security architecture (Faleg, 2016).

In face of the cross-border nature of terrorism and cybercrime, EU-UK defence and security cooperation are essential. The British intelligence services are amongst the best in the world and a key strategic priority for security and stability. Former PM Cameron moved investing £2.5 billion and employing 1,900 additional staff to implement counter-terrorism policies. The Government Communications Headquarters (GCHQ), MI5, and counter-terrorism police must also be beefed up with new equipment like unmanned aircraft. Security cooperation with the EU entails intelligence cooperation and data sharing through the EU's security network and infrastructure. With Brexit, the UK loses inside, automatic access to these platforms to tackle internationally organised crime, cyber threats, and terrorism. Despite the value of the "five eyes" intelligence cooperation between Britain, America, Canada, Australia and New Zealand, lost access to the European Arrest Warrant and informal exchanges with Eurojust and the Anti-Fraud Office complicates security cooperation for the UK after Brexit, as it is excluded from decision making in the CSDP related to intelligence sharing. The UK could be an important anchor of security and stability for the European continent *via* NATO and the Organization for Security and Co-operation in Europe (OSCE), this is queered by the now-distorted relationship with the EU (Raczova, 2017).

Impact Assessment Summary

- The Global Strategy of the European Union Foreign and Security Policy aims to take responsibility for five priorities of EU foreign policy: security of the Union; state and social resilience in its East and South; integrated approaches to conflicts; cooperative regional orders; and global governance for the 21st century.

- The CSDP Implementation Plan complements NATO and the UN in tackling external conflicts and crises, capacity building of partners, protecting the Union and its citizens. The Member States must commit themselves to higher defence expenditure on EU security and defence policy, they must reconfigure their armed forces and capabilities and develop their defence sector.
- Brexit will probably have less of an impact on the CDSP due to the UK's already low involvement in missions. Nevertheless, British defence will be affected indirectly by Brexit due to a weak pound in the context of a dollar-based procurement regime.
- Brexit diminishes the effectiveness of the foreign policy tool of unified sanctions. Any collaboration with the EU will likely be costlier and more complicated for the UK. Brexit will weaken both UK foreign policy and EU sanction practice.
- UK will continue to invest in defence to support special forces and deployable armed forces, as well as to offer defence industries shelter from future trade agreements.
- UK withdrawal from the CSDP will require France and German to collaborate to develop a cohesive defence structure for the EU.
- Finally, Brexit will exclude the UK from major decisions in the CSDP, related to loss of access to the European Arrest Warrant and exchanges with Eurojust and the Anti-Fraud Office, developments that complicate international security cooperation for the UK.

3.1.32 Financial control

Definition: *The acquis under this chapter relates to the adoption of internationally agreed and EU compliant principles, standards and methods of public internal financial control (PIFC) that should apply to the internal control systems of the entire public sector, including the spending of EU funds. In particular, the acquis requires the existence of effective and transparent financial management and control systems (including adequate ex-ante, ongoing and ex-post financial control or inspection); functionally independent internal audit systems; the relevant organisational structures (including central co-ordination); an operationally and financially independent external audit organisation to assess, amongst others, the quality of the newly established PIFC systems. This chapter also includes the acquis on the protection of EU financial interests and the fight against fraud involving EU funds.*

The Directorate General for Budget (DG BUDG) is tasked with executing the EU's full budgetary cycle – from preparation of the draft budget to its implementation and discharge by the European Parliament. DG BUDG has a staff of 490 who provide expertise in accounting, economics, finance, business, programming, audit, law, communications, human resources, European administration, and other fields. Besides budget support services, DG BUDG provides guidelines and frameworks to manage the budget process, including the multiannual financial framework for managing EU expenditure; the budgetary regulatory framework as it concerns financial regulation; public internal financial control (PIFC) systems; and corporate IT systems for financial management and accounting (ABAC). The European Commission informs the high budgetary authorities – the Parliament and the Council – each month about the implementation of the annual budget. By the end of March, each Directorate General must produce an annual activity report to be examined by the Commissioners as part of their assessment of the Commission's financial situation. They then review the internal auditors' annual report and internal control system documents. Their synthesis report proposes measures to correct identified weaknesses. Finally, the report was sent to the Parliament and Council, and is used by the European Court of Auditors to evaluate the EU's management of its resources (EC, 2017).

The formal budget control process ensures the formal legality, accuracy, and financial management of budget operations and financial control systems. To ensure best practices, the European commission developed the PIFC model to assist national governments in re-engineering their internal control environment and upgrade public sector control systems.[62] Budgetary control of economy, efficiency and effectiveness prevents waste of funds and fraud. The final output is scrutinised by the Court of Auditors and the achieving of objectives

---

62 European Commission (2006) "Welcome to the world of PIFC – Public Internal Financial Control", EU Commission, DG Budget, website at http://ec.europa.eu/budget/library/biblio/documents/control/brochure_pifc_en.pdf (accessed February 2017).

(performance criteria) by the European Parliament. The Member States are the first instance of control of operational expenditure under the European Agricultural Guarantee Fund (EAGF), European Agricultural Fund for Rural Development (EAFRD), and the Structural Funds. Internal control is executed by certified officers and accountants and by the institution's internal auditor. National audit institutes and the European Court of Auditors (ECA) carry out the external control. The ECA provides a detailed annual report to the budgetary authority, and also reports on lending and borrowing operations and the European Development Fund. Controlling is executed at political level by the European Parliament's Committee on Budgetary Control. It prepares Parliament's position on the implementation control of the EU budget and European Development Fund, the EU's financial statements, the financial activities of the European Investment Bank, the cost-effectiveness of various forms of EU funding, and fraud and irregularities in connection with the implementation of the EU budget. The European Parliament prepares the decision on whether to discharge the Commission in respect of implementation of the budget (Gay, 2016).

Following the June 2016 EU Referendum, he financial balance between the UK and the EU will be recast with essential impact on many sectors of the UK economy. At present, the UK is a net contributor to the EU budget, contributing more funds than it receives back from the EU in grants and subsidies. The UK is in the first place at the lower end of the net contributors – behind the Netherlands, Germany and Sweden. In the second place, the immaterial benefits are higher than the material ones, such as access to the internal market and EU-related policies and co-operation. Since the activation of Article 50 of the Treaty of the European Union in March 2017, it has become a matter of urgency for the British Government and the EU to find answers to the treatment of the budget contribution up till April 1, 2019: how much for how long can the UK claim from or contribute to EU assets. From a budget perspective, the following main negotiation domains must be addressed (Sánchez-Barrueco, 2017a):

- UK claim on EU assets such as buildings, budget, EIB
- UK payment of its share of EU liabilities like multiannual commitments, pensions, long-term loans
- UK payment in exchange for market access
- UK budget-contribution and application periods for EU spending programmes

In case of No Deal between the EU and the UK, the Member States would have to decide how to deal with the treatment of mutual liabilities and even how to fill the contribution gap left by the UK's exit. Continued EU financial support for UK projects and the UK's legal obligation to remit to the EU budget require legal certainty for government and economy's sake. However, the already negotiated multiannual agreements of the Multiannual Financial Framework between the UK and the other Member States are assumed to run, at latest, until late 2020 (Sánchez-Barrueco, 2017b). There are different legal perspectives whether the UK is legally obligated to continue its financial contributions to the EU budget after this period or not, which are presented as follows. Of the principles which govern the interpretation of treaties in public international law, *pacta sunt servanda* and *bona fides* are two of the main ones (Sánchez-Barrueco, 2017b). Applying the Vienna Convention on the Law of Treaties (VCLT), Article 43 VCLT provides, "The [...] denunciation of a treaty, the withdrawal of a party from it [...] shall not impair the duty of any State to fulfil any obligations embodied in the treaty to which it would be subject under international law independently of the treaty." The contrasting legal opinion is that the EU as an international organisation is not legally bound to the VCLT, and Article 50 TEU would prevail as the relevant rule over other provisions of a more general scope. Without rejection of the Vienna Convention as the legal basis for future obligations and provisions, failure to reach agreement after Article 50 has been triggered would nullify the application of the Treaties to the UK. The consequence would be that the Multiannual Financial Framework, the Financial Regulation, and lower-level regulations governing EU spending programmes would collapse for the UK.[63] Even individual spending decisions adopted by the Commission and other institutions and agencies would collapse (Sánchez-Barrueco, 2017b). The Treaty provisions would collapse for the UK too, who would no longer enjoy standing to defend its interests before the ECJ (Sánchez-Barrueco, 2017b). Such a theoretical interpretation of the law entails that triggering Article 50 withdraws the UK not only from the EU but also from the obligation of previous budget commitments and remittances to the EU, following on the loss of jurisdiction of the ECJ (Sánchez-Barrueco, 2017b). On the other hand, the UK would instantly lose all material and immaterial benefits of EU membership and undermine its reputation as serious partner in all future negotiations. For the sake of the comity of nations the UK should not push its advantage to the maximum, and the Government have been acting as if they understood that. Because, besides the damage to the UK's international prestige, the logic of Article 50 is unprecedented, and its legal interpretation and application is practically unachievable within the given time frame of two years. Any pending law case drawing on the lack of jurisdiction of the ECJ or any other internal jurisdiction would increase legal uncertainty for the British economy and hamper any negotiation for a potential transition period for the UK's financial industry.

According to the British ONS, the annual net British contribution to the EU between 2010-14 was £7.1 billion. In addition to this amount, the UK should be prepared to pay a "exit bill" to the EU ranging from €20 billion to €60 billion as part of reaching moral, favourable negotiation results with the EU (The House of Lords, 2017). To finesse future payments, the Government might consider contributing more to EU security programmes or EU projects from the aid budget. British minsters seem to be prepared for further EU budget

---

63   See Sánchez-Barrueco, Maria-Luisa (2017b) "The Brexit budgetary debates II: the budgetary consequences of no agreement", EUFINACCO: Financial Accountability in the EU, 2 February 2017, website at https://eufinacco.wordpress.com/2017/02/02/the-brexit-budgetary-debates-ii-the-budgetary-consequences-of-no-agreement/ (accessed October 2017).

contributions during any transitional period and while concluding any free-trade deal with the EU beyond 2019. Any EU rebates secured by Margaret Thatcher in the 1980s probably will not be allowed to offset the bill (Arnold, 2016). Michel Barnier, Brexit Chief Negotiator for the European Commission, insists that the Brexit scenario covers a narrow four-point agenda of separation issues and will not address broader question of the future EU-UK relationship. The so-called "cheque" will cover the UK's share of continuing payments and other liabilities like EU staff pensions; second, the status and rights of EU nationals and British nationals in the EU; third, the disengagement of EU agencies based in Britain; and fourth, "special situations", referring to Northern Ireland and Gibraltar. Off the agenda are internal market access and *passporting* for the financial industry (McTague, 2016).

The British budget deficit, at 4.1 % of economic output last year, challenges the UK to tackle its "unhealthy" public finances: a budget shortfall of £10.55 billion must be financed in the insecure political and economic environment created by the 2016 Brexit vote. Post-Brexit budget planning is complicated by having to take account of Brexit's potential impact on industry and trade in the immediate future. Brexit could increase public-sector net borrowing by £24 billion or more in 2017-18 (Irish Times, 2016).

The UK is a sizeable net contributor, providing about 12% of the revenues accruing to the EU ledger. However, the current budget contribution of the UK in the annual amount of £10.3 billion is now worth just €11.5 billion – a fall of about €2.5 billion due to the devaluation of sterling since June 23, 2016. Whereas the gap might be closed in the short term by unused revenue from 2016, in the long term the shortfall will have to be refinanced, for example by fines levied against companies and Member States for breaking EU competition rules. So far, these fines have been worth €1.1 billion. Member States are being confronted to pay more into the budget or withdraw less from it, igniting fierce political bargaining within EU institutions and Member States (House of Lords, 2017). The real EU budget change will probably be seen after 2019, in the post-2020 budget plans to be submitted at the end of 2017. The ultimate real impact will depend on the agreements reached between the UK and the EU (Baume, Aries, 2016).

Saving EU credibility before its citizens necessitates a more transparent decision procedure on the EU budget. Revenue flows and benefits must be communicated to the public in a comprehensible format. This essential step is in order if the EU would prevent other countries following the UK example (Kalfin, 2017).

Impact Assessment Summary

- The Directorate General for Budget (DG BUDG) is tasked with executing the full budget cycle and monthly informing the Parliament and Council about implementation of the annual budget. Internal control is executed by certified officers and accountants and by the institution's internal auditor. The national audit institutions and the European Court of Auditors (ECA) execute the external control.

- Budget standards such as PIFC fortify internal control systems and budgetary control, with the objective of imposing efficiency and avoiding waste and fraud in the budget. The budget is reviewed finally by the Court of Auditors and the European Parliament.
- Brexit has impacted the EU budget respecting the revenue and expenditure flows between EU and the UK during the two-year negotiation period following the triggering of Article 50 TEU.
- The legal basis for the UK's obligation to continue remittances to the EU is not clear among lawyers. Accepting that Article 50 prevails over other provisions of a more general scope, such as the Vienna Convention on the Law of Treaties, the UK could not only withdraw from the Union but also declare budget commitments and remittances to the EU to be void (if one ignores the political fallout).
- In reality, the UK is prepared to continue its EU budget commitments even in case of agreement with the EU not being reached. The goal is to negotiate a friendly exit and new agreements with the EU.
- The "exit bill" from EU's financial obligations is estimated to range from £20 billion to £60 billion. Moreover, Brexit negotiations are subject to a formal procedure that leaves out other crucial aspects like internal market access and banking *passporting* rights.
- The Government's budget for 2017-18 must be financed by net borrowings of £24 billion; likewise, the EU must refinance its own budget to the tune of about £14 billion in the long term to make up for loss of the British contribution, which has ignited fierce bargaining within the EU and its Member States.
- The EU ought to make its budget decision procedures and disclosures more transparent to its citizens, if it would forestall other Member States following the UK example.

3.1.33 Financial and budgetary provisions

Definition: *This chapter covers the rules concerning the financial resources necessary for the funding of the EU budget ('own resources'). These resources are made up mainly from contributions from Member States based on traditional own resources from customs and agricultural duties and sugar levies; a resource based on value-added tax; and a resource based on the level of gross national income. Member States must have appropriate administrative capacity to adequately co-ordinate and ensure the correct calculation, collection, payment and control of own resources. The acquis in this area is directly binding and does not require transposition into national law.*

DG BUDG is additionally tasked with managing the European Union budget. This consists of proposing and implementing the financial framework, and collecting the revenues that EU Member States have agreed to contribute. To meet challenges like economic crisis, emigration, border control, evelledicism, terror attacks, *etc.*, DG BUDG allocates funds for investment in key policies and priorities. This enabled the EU to begin to implement the European Agenda for Migration and stimulate jobs, growth and competitiveness, which doubled the EU budget to more than €10 billion between 2015 and 2016. The EU budget also helped farmers, reduced regional disparities, provided liquidity to the financial system, and subvened progress on the Energy Union, Capital Markets Union, and a Digital Single Market to create further growth in the EU. The 2015 budget was met, and no Member States were called upon for more money. The initiative "Budget Focused on Results" (BFOR) assures more benefit from expenditure of taxpayer money (EC, July 2015). By pooling resources at European level, Member States can benefit from budget subventions for transport; exploration of outer space; health, education and culture; consumer and environment protection; research, development and innovation; justice cooperation; and foreign policy. The Structural Funds in particular enabled certain otherwise incapacitated Member States to afford stable growth-supporting investment after the financial crisis of 2008. The European Fund for Strategic Investments (EFSI) has helped catalyse private investment throughout Europe (EC, April 2017).

To realise the Commission Work Programme 2017, DG BUDG has been given a budget of €157.9 billion, representing about 1% of EU Gross National Income (GNI). About €74.9 billion has been allocated for jobs, growth and investment programmes, of which €53.6 billion is reserved for the EU Structural and Investment Funds. Moreover, €3 billion of the budget is allocated for guarding EU's external borders and providing security, and another €3 billion for addressing the root causes of migration.

The European Commission initiates the budget decision process. Both the European Parliament and the Council take a position, and in case of disagreement, a Conciliation Committee is convened. Within 21 days the parties are obliged to find a compromise. Finally, the European Council and Parliament approves it. The initial proposal for the 2017 budget was tabled on June 30, 2016; thereafter, the 21-day conciliation procedure ran from 28 October until 17 November. On 17 November the compromise was reached on the 2017 budget (EC, December 2016).

The revenue for the budget currently derives from three main types of own resources:

- customs duties collected at the external borders of the Union, which go directly into the EU budget, Member States retaining 20% to defray collection costs.
- the harmonised VAT bases of all Member States: a uniform rate of 0.3% is levied on each Member State, with some exceptions.
- an "EU membership fee" based on Member States' income level measured by Gross National Income (GNI). In the annual budgetary procedure this rate is fixed, but some Member States, such as the UK, enjoy a reduction.

The maximum annual amount of own resources which the EU may raise during a budget year is limited to 1.2% of EU GNI. This simple calculation has been complicated by negotiated adjustments and rebates by the Member States over many years, as a result of which the financing arrangements have become gnarly and opaque. At present, about 80% of the budget is financed out of national contributions based on VAT and GNI. A comparison of the net contribution of each Member State exhibits the ratio of direct payments into the EU budget to the return on this contribution. Nevertheless, this perspective ignores the functional benefits of pooling resources, access to the Single Market, and more favourable terms with global trading partners (EC, April 2017).

In 2014 the UK was the fourth-largest national contributor to the EU budget, with €11.34 billion, representing 9.73% of the total – behind only Germany, France and Italy (Amaro, 2017). In 2015 the assessed contribution rose steeply to £19.5 billion (€26.5 billion) out of a total of €118.60 billion Reckoning-in the "rebate" negotiated by PM Margaret Thatcher in 1984, the UK budget contribution was reduced to £14,6 billion (€6.6 billion). This is about £225 (€305) for every person in the UK, or around £40 million (€54 billion) a day (Bennet; Kirkup, 2017). In 2015 the UK became the third-largest net contributor to the EU budget after Germany and France. In the same period, the UK was the 6th largest recipient of EU expenditures, but its expenditure share measured as a percentage of GNI was the lowest at 0.30% (Amaro, 2017). Measured *per capita*, the UK is the eighth-largest contributor to the EU budget. The largest payers are the Dutch, of whom everyone sends almost 4 times as much to Brussels (Bennet; Kirkup, 2017).

The UK spends most of its EU money on agriculture and regional development. Brexit will require the entitlements of the 1,800 EU staff in the UK and the relocation costs of EU institutions based in the UK, like the European Medicines Agency and the European Banking Authority, to be settled. However, the UK has already declared that it will not pay a €60 billion bill to leave the EU – even though this money is UK's share of commitments to its EU staff's pensions and funding approval already received for UK-based EU projects. On top of that, the UK has to stand behind its commitment to the current Multiannual

Financial Framework, which regulates annual EU budgetary expenditures over a seven-year timeframe from 2014 to 2020. If the UK leaves the European Union in March 2019, the EU has to decide how it will organise its budget between that time and the end of 2020. There is no automatic mechanism for raising a Member's contribution. Novel alternatives must be considered, such as higher contributions from remaining Member States, the creation of new revenue sources, a reduction of EU expenditure, or a combination of all three (Amaro, 2017).

Given the tougher challenges ahead for all of Europe, the future budget of the European Commission will somehow have to fund more policies and projects with fewer resources. The EU must conserve and in fact expand its leading role on the global stage in a shifting global economy. The unstable situation of the EU and the loss of the UK as major net contributor necessitate an agile and flexible budget policy. An EU White Paper has projected five scenarios affecting future budgets: the EU simply carries on; it does less together; it moves ahead at different levels of intensity; it does less but more efficiently; and it does much more together. Accordingly, the budget must be allocated and funded by reducing spending for the existing policies and/or increasing revenues, as the Union may neither borrow money nor run a budget deficit. As well, the multiannual framework for 2014-2020, encompassing a total investment volume of €1 trillion, will be approved for future funding of supported policies (EC, April 2017). The proposal for the next multiannual framework for a reduced EU-27 must consider the EU's new funding challenges in mid-2018. In addition, the European Commission BFOR initiative of 2015 was important for the future development of the budget. Its review did address and its successors will continue to address new scenarios for European policy development as well (EC, July 2015, 2016, 2017). There are a number of potential own sources of revenue available to fund future budgets of the remaining EU-27: reformed VAT; corporate taxes; financial transaction taxes; electricity and motor fuel surcharges, seigniorage (central bank currency issuance fees); carbon trading revenues; and travel and authorisation system fees (ETIAS) (EC, April 2017). At all events, the new funding of the EU budget will be linked to the future development of the European Union and its Member States' commitment to a stronger global role; thus, there is hope for a closer, more transparent EU membership.

Impact Assessment Summary

- The Directorate General for Budget (DG BUDG) is also tasked with managing the budget, including proposing and implementing the financial framework and collecting revenues. The 2017 budget is about €158 billion, of which €75 billion is reserved for jobs, growth and investment programmes, including €53.6 billion for the Structural and Investment funds.

- The UK is the third-largest out of the ten net contributing Member States (paying in more than gotten back), and the eighth-largest contributor *per capita*.
- Within the current Multiannual Financial Framework 2014-2020, the EU must make up UK's budget contribution of about €17 billion after Brexit in March 2019. The remaining Member States must agree higher contributions, new revenue sources, and/or a reduction of expenditures.
- The directly unmeasurable monetary value of EU membership encompasses the functional benefits of pooling resources, having access to the Single Market, and more favourable terms with global trading partners.
- The EU will demand that the UK stands behind its share of commitments to its EU workers' pensions and funding approval already received for UK-based EU projects. For this part, the UK must figure out how to make up for the lost access to EU revenues such as from the Structural Investment Funds.
- The EU must define a flexible and agile budget sufficiently funded in the long term to conserve and expand its important global economic and security role.

3.1.34 Institutions

Definition:: *This chapter covers the institutional and procedural rules of the EU. When a country joins the EU, adaptations need to be made to these rules to ensure this country's equal representation in EU institutions (European Parliament, Council, Commission, Court of Justice) and other bodies and the good functioning of decision-making procedures (such as voting rights, official languages and other procedural rules) as well as elections to the European Parliament. EU rules in this chapter do not affect the internal organisation of a Member State, but acceding countries need to ensure that they are able to participate fully in EU decision-making by setting up the necessary bodies and mechanisms at home and by electing or appointing well-prepared representatives to the EU institutions. After concluding the accession negotiations, specific rules for the interim period until accession ensure a smooth integration of the country into EU structures: an information and consultation procedure is put in place and, once the Accession Treaty is signed, the acceding country is granted active observer status in the European Parliament and Council as well as in Commission committees.*

The founding Treaties form the basis of European Union institutions and bodies and their conferred powers. The Treaty on the Functioning of the European Union comprises seven EU institutions (or organs) – the principal decision making bodies as listed in Article 13: the European Parliament, the European Council, the Council of the European Union, the European Commission, the Court of Justice of the European Union, the European Central Bank, and the Court of Auditors.[64] Of which the European Council, the Council of the European Union the European Commission, and the European Parliament are responsible for drafting policies and taking decisions. The European Council sets the EU's broad priorities by bringing national EU-level leaders together. It has no formal power to legislate, yet its definitions and agendas in practice may carry the weight of law.[65] Formal legislation requires the European Parliament, the Council of the European Union, and the European Commission. These three institutions set policy and make law by the Ordinary Legislative Procedure. Draft laws are proposed by the Commission, while the Parliament and Council adopt or reject them. The Commission and the Member States then implement and enforce them, the Commission ensuring the proper application and implantation of the laws (EU, November 2017). Two other EU institutions that play vital

---

64 See Council of the European Union (2009) "Consolidated Versions of the Treaty on European Union and the Treaty on the functioning of the European Union", Brussels, 15.03.2008, website at http://register.consilium.europa.eu/doc/srv?l=EN&f=ST%206655%202008%20INIT (accessed November 2017).

65 See the Copenhagen Criteria, agreed at the 1993 European Council summit in Copenhagen, which set the accession standards that governed the entire Eastern Enlargement era. Thus, European Council decisions resemble the "constitutional conventions" of the Westminster system.

roles are the Court of Justice of the EU for upholding the rule of European law and the Court of Auditors for vetting the financing of EU activities. The European Court of Justice constitutes the whole judiciary and monitors whether Community law is being observed. It consists of two separate chambers: the Court of Justice and the General Court. The Court of Justice is a *sui generis* court (meaning "of its own kind" in deciding cases no other court may dispose of), and a supranational institution. In cooperation with the national judiciaries of the Members, the Court of Justice is tasked with the uniform interpretation and application of EU law, and settling legal disputes between the national governments and EU institutions. Private parties (individuals, companies, civil society organisations) may take action against EU institutions alleging infringement of their rights (ECJ, 2017). There is also a Court of Auditors who as independent comptroller looks after the interests of EU taxpayers. It has no binding legal authority, but examines the legality, accuracy and regularity of Union revenue and expenditure (ECA, 2017). The Union's overall powers and decision-making procedures have evolved through successive treaties. The power and responsibilities of these institutions are stipulated in the Treaties along with the principles of the EU's actions and observances of rules and procedures. These Treaties are agreed by the Presidents and Prime Ministers of all Member States, and are ratified by their parliaments (EU, November 2017).

Moreover, there are other institutions and interinstitutional bodies that take on special roles within the EU, such as the European Central Bank, the European External Actions Services (EEAS), the European Economic and Social Committee, the European Investment Bank, the European Ombudsman, the European Data Protection Supervisor, the Publications Office, the European Personnel Selection Office, the European School of Administration, and a host of specialised agencies and decentralised bodies. The Central Bank, which is tasked with keeping prices stable and supporting economic growth and job creation, does not officially draft regulations or take decisions of EU policy. It manages the euro, and sets the frameworks and implementation measures for EU economic and monetary policy (ECB, 2017).

The supranational organs' decisional powers stem from Member States' agreement to transfer some of their sovereign power to these organs in specified policy domains. The EU organs' decisional procedural system encompasses legislative procedures, the budgetary procedure, appointment procedures, procedures for concluding international agreements, and quasi-constitutional procedures (Schonard, 2016). Whereas in the domain of the Common Foreign and Security Policy and in other domains, the decisional procedures differ from regular supranational decision-making: there is a stronger component of intergovernmental co-operation and Member State involvement. For example, the public debt crisis and the need for aid packages for Member States in financial difficulties prompted new decisional mechanisms. These intergovernmental procedures include, *e.g.*, procedures for amending the Treaties or activation of passerelle clauses, accession procedure, withdrawal closure, enhanced cooperation procedure, procedure for decisions in foreign affairs, foreign crisis management, appointment procedure, and a sanctions procedure for a serious and persistent breach of Union principles by a Member State (Novak, 2017). The budgetary procedure was overhauled by the Lisbon Treaty, which gave Parliament an equal say with the European Council on the entire EU budget (Calatozzolo, 2017).

With its Brexit decision, the UK has put in question the efficiency and effectiveness of the European institutions. While the UK may choose to disengage from the EU, the EU is bound to prevent a 'contagion effect' and so is self-interested in the economic imperative of a quick and favourable deal for Britain. In the long term, the EU must repair unbalanced power structures and shore up its democratic values and four freedoms to forestall an uprising of protectionist forces. Additionally, the EU has to unify itself as a bloc to avoid losing its global impact (Patel, Reh, 2016). After Brexit, revision of the Treaties has become pivotal to the EU's solidarity and integration. Future Treaty changes are foreshadowed in the recent adoption of two draft reports by the Committee on Constitutional Affairs (AFCO) of the European Parliament: Report on improving the functioning of the European Union building on the potential of the Lisbon Treaty,[66] and Report on possible evolutions of and adjustments to the current institutional set-up of the European Union[67] (Cremades, Novak, 2017). Flexibility is needed to cope with the increasing heterogeneity of the Member States as well; thus, future projects for deeper integration require flexible setups (Grabbe, Lehne, 2016).

On the occasion of the 60th anniversary of the Treaty of Rome, the European Commission presented a white paper on the future of Europe on 1 March 2017. The five conjectured scenarios foresee the pathways Europe could take to rise to its challenges, ranging from globalisation to the impact of new technologies on society, and from security concerns to the rise of populism. The drafts of the future stimulate reflections on the EU-27's current condition and its possible development by 2025, encompassing carrying on as before or doing much more together. One thing is obvious: the Single Market cannot survive if countries are allowed to stay in it whilst opting out of whole policy domains of the *acquis*. The European Commission plans to contribute to the future development of the EU by publishing reflection papers on the following topics (EC, 2017):

- developing the social dimension of Europe
- deepening Economic and Monetary Union, on the basis of the Five Presidents' Report of June 2015
- harnessing globalisation
- the future of Europe's defence
- the future of EU finances.

---

66   See report 2014/2249(INI).

67   See report 2014/2248(INI).

The first conclusions will be drawn in President Juncker's State of the Union speech at the December 2017 European Council. The European Union must scrutinise its institutional setup and its procedures to manage chances and challenges (EC, April 2017).

Loss of the EU's second-biggest economy epicentres the current risk of a cycle of disintegration, as has been threatened by Poland and Hungary, and by opposition parties like Marine Le Pen's Front National in France. The EU's crisis of euro integration, economic stability as well as Schengen and the control of its external borders calls for clear action to consolidate the EU's standing and reputation. On the British side, there is a risk of relative poverty and international obscurity if the UK fails to create an effective economic and political relationship with the EU. The loss of market access to and political influence in the EU, but also the uncertainty of the outcome of the Brexit negotiations may destabilise the domestic economy – to say nothing of strategic considerations about the financial sector and neighbouring countries like Ireland, all which may finally push businesses and jobs out of the country. The Government must coordinate with the Bank of England to stabilise markets and to promote small and medium-sized enterprises so as to be able to absorb economic shocks in future. Unilateral moves that might destabilise the EU must be avoided, lest it jeopardise constructive negotiations; and pursuit of a proven partnership model ought still to be considered. In parallel, the EU must induct its Members into an overarching European spirit by continuing integration in key domains, but with a sensible balance of powers and greater emphasis on practical projects among different decentral or regional sub-groups of nation states to keep the EU in contact with the deeps of its Member States. Reasonable international business links with Britain must be maintained for mutual benefit as with defence and finance. Finally, the EU should concentrate on practical integration projects to continue the deepening process and to claim unity in security, tax transparency, central border control, *etc*. (Leonard, 2016).

The UK and the EU must find a clear position for dealing with exit negotiations; otherwise, time for facing global challenges is wasted on disputes that threaten to hinder EU reforms and further protectionism. For instance, the EU institutions have a chance to change the composition of Parliament and the rules on the financing of the EU (Cremades, Novak, 2017). The shift of power in the EU after Brexit will likely boost Germany's strong voice in the Council and strengthen a more regulative approach to future EU decisions. On the other hand, France's economically weak position makes any phalanx against the emerging stronger Member States' interests for centralisation in the EU unstable. There is a great chance to force the EU to advance in its integration process, by focussing on European citizens, benefits of the EU beyond the economic benefits of free trade, EU and globalisation, and the value of a liberal European national identity and culture. Finally, EU institutions and influential Member States must take up a decisive leadership role to complete the Economic and Monetary Union, fight against terrorism, and defend European democratic values.

Impact Assessment Summary

- The founding Treaties form the basis for the 7 main European institutions: the European Council, the Council of the European Union, the European Commission, and the European Parliament, which are responsible for drafting policies and taking decisions within in the EU. The EU Court of Justice enforces competition within the internal market and is the guardian of the rule of EU law.
- Supranational decisional procedures for the conclusion of international agreements will significantly impact the EU's ability to negotiate new treaties with trade blocs or dominant trading nations. The intergovernmental cooperation in the EU will suffer from Brexit, and will make the EU and the UK more vulnerable to foreign crisis and terrorism.
- The EU institutions face the challenge of repairing the EU's power structures, promoting its four freedoms, and strengthening its bloc solidarity in order to avoid losing its global negotiating power. Flexibility on the part of Member States will deepen the integration process.
- Both Brexit and the 60th anniversary of the Treaty of Rome has driven the EU to rethink the social dimension of Europe, the deepening of the EMU, globalisation, the future of Europe's defence policy, and EU finances.
- The renewal process of the EU will pressurise the UK to align with EU Member States so as to desist destabilising its economy and provoking job flight. The Government must co-operate with the Bank of England in particular to foster stable markets for small and medium-sized enterprises.
- Europe's institutional crisis holds the chance of transforming the EU from an overregulated economy with a taker mentality into a more flexibly regulated, dynamic economy with a can-do mentality. A clear position respecting the variable pace of the EU's integration and development must be accepted to overcome this crisis and to demonstrate a unitary position in the Brexit negotiations.
- The UK ought to re-evaluate its power to reinvent itself *in co-operation* with the EU and ultimately to weigh up the pros as well as the cons of rejoining a preferred trading partnership instead of fighting so hard for an isolated role, harming UK businesses and people – realism and common sense are in high demand!

3.1.35   Other issues

Definition: *This chapter includes miscellaneous issues which come up during the negotiations but which are not covered under any other negotiating chapter. No such issues have been identified for the moment. Chapter 35 is dealt with at the end of the negotiating process.*

Chapter 35 of the *acquis* "Other issues" is an interesting one. This Chapter is currently blank, as officially "no such issues have been identified for the moment".

The *acquis* is the accumulation of all EU norms and rules, but latterly has been adapted to lay down to accession candidates the preconditions for EU membership, giving more transparency to the approval procedures that warrant that new members are not admitted until they have demonstrated that they can play their full part as a Member State. As part of this process, they need to demonstrate their competence:

- to comply with EU norms and rules
- to obtain the assent of the EU institutions and Member States to their accession
- to obtain their citizens' consent expressed through their national parliament or by referendum.

The Treaty of the European Union states that any European country may apply for membership if it respects the EU's democratic values and is committed to promoting them. As defined in by the European Council in Copenhagen in 1993, the key accession criteria are:

- stable institutions guaranteeing democracy, the rule of law, human rights, and respect for and protection of minorities;
- a functioning market economy and the capacity to cope with the competition and market forces that prevail in the EU;
- the ability to take on and implement effectively the obligations of membership, including adherence to the aims of political, economic and monetary union. (Copenhagen European Council, 21-22 June 1993)

The accession negotiations cover the conditions and timing of the candidate's adoption, implementation and enforcement of "the *acquis*", meaning all current EU rules. Other issues may be financial; *viz.*, how much the new Member is likely to give into and take out of the EU budget, and the form of transitional arrangements giving the new Member or existing Members a gradual phase-in timetable to adapt to certain rules.

Despite all the grief of the UK leaving the EU, Brexit not only might fill *acquis* Chapter 35 with content, it could define the rulebook on how a Member State leaves the Union.

As exit procedures are unprecedented, the *acquis* structure and content could be applied in future to both countries that want to join and countries that want to leave. Moreover, a critical review of the *acquis* by the EU indicates its rightfulness to achieve its aim of both shared economic and European values for a stable, enclosed European community with clear procedures. The current malaise consists not only in the UK government's rather chaotic identity-finding and positioning process, but also in uncertainty about how the process involving everybody works overall, and what should come next and then next. The EU Treaties and the Commission have laid a foundation by creating two phases: Phase One is the separation or "divorce" from the EU, and Phase Two is the substitute relationship. The EU and the UK are entering unchartered territory; both are in a learning process, and the *acquis* may become more important than it is already.

Finally, Brexit is a new chance for the EU to rethink and redefine its own balance of powers between the EU's supranational institutions and its Member States and regions. If the European project is to thrive in the future, all parties must aim to keep the Union together and to advance its values of freedom and democracy.

Impact Assessment Summary

- As the last Chapter of the *acquis*, "Other issues", is officially blank because no such issues have ever before been identified, an impact assessment for is strictly impossible.
- The *acquis* was adapted to define the conditions for EU membership, embodying accession criteria for would-be Members to meet, and negotiation parameters (timing and transitional arrangements).
- As the exit rules might be viewed as rules of joining in reverse, the *acquis* could also act as rule book for Member States intending to leave the EU. Chapter 35 might end up defining issues that cannot be neglected.
- The structure and content of the *acquis* could be regularly reviewed by the EU to achieve a stable and democratic European Union and to initiate an evolutionary process for betterment of its people.

3.2 MAIN TOPICS COVERED DURING THE CAMPAIGN

Having presented the foregoing impact assessment, we would like to remind readers what the main points of controversy were between the Remain and Leave camps in the campaign. These were published at the time in the media, often with little analysis or questioning of the accuracy of facts.

As the two camps were highly polarised, information on both sides was "weaponised": incomplete or evell. Relatively few facts were provided, and even when a few were, they were taken out of context (as results from economic forecasts), were wrong (as the claim of money that could be saved when leaving the EU), or overgeneralised (as how much money each household would leave when leaving the EU). Some key memes of both campaigns are summarized as follows.

1. *Regulation that benefits consumers, employees and business*
    The Remain campaign attempted to educate voters that not all EU regulations are "bad", in particular regulation for: (a) the digital economy, like the Roaming Regulation that capped roaming charges for consumers and finally abolished them in June 2017, and the new General Data Protection Regulation (GDPR) that forces business organisations to treat personal information carefully; (b) employment rights, like working hours and job security; and (c) consumer rights, which covers the right to return defective products, and the compensation scheme for "bumped" travellers.

2. *National sovereignty*
    The Leave campaign drew a contrasting picture of British sovereignty undermined by supranational organisation like the European Commission and Council of Ministers; that a sovereign UK would be able to implement regulations benefitting UK citizens and businesses better than EU regulations. It is estimated that more than 50% of UK regulations derive from EU. As we are living in a globalised world, harmonizing regulations for health and safely (such for the medical and nuclear sector), consumers, employees and so on is not necessarily a bad thing. The abolishment of tariffs in the Single Market does reduce the income for HMRC (the UK tax authorities), but at the same time guarantees cheaper prices for UK consumer when they buy French or Dutch dairy produces or German or Italian cars. Furthermore, weak economic regions and industries (such as agriculture) in the UK receive EU subsidies. In the Referendum's aftermath the losers – including whole industrial sectors and even nations (Scotland, Northern Ireland, Wales, and greater London – have complained bitterly that they have felt excluded from any key decisions relating to Brexit. These worrisome signs imply that national sovereignty is not necessarily the best outcome of a shift

of the decisional process from Brussels to Westminster, especially if it ignores regional interests. The unalloyed benefit touted by the Leave campaign seems less attractive now to many in industry and the regions.

3. *The Single Market and our economy*

Both camps made noises acknowledging the desirability of remaining in the Single Market: Leave held out Norway and Switzerland (both of whom signed the Schengen Agreement which allows free movement of people, i.e. unrestricted immigration) as models for maintaining market access. In sum, all sides conceded the advantages of being in the Single Market.

The Remain campaign argued that leaving the EU would harm the economy significantly, in support of which they presented various forecasts and studies. The Treasury estimated Brexit could leave the average UK household worse off by £4300 in an economy 6% smaller by 2030. Bank of England governor Mark Carney warned that Brexit could cause a recession. Christine Lagarde of the IMF predicted that Brexit would cause "severe regional and global damage", which could send UK shares and property prices into a tailspin.

The post-Brexit realisation that the Single Market could be closed off if no compromise about freedom of movement is found aggravated the worries. Suddenly uncertainty increased significantly.

4. *Control of immigration*

This was the battle cry of the Leave campaign; however, soon after the Referendum key advocates of Leave admitted that immigration is needed to grow the economy.

5. *Free trade*

Secretary of State for International Trade Liam Fox was determined to have trade deals negotiated and ready to sign on the day Britain leaves the EU. Boris Johnson promised that Brexit will usher in a new era of free trade deals, claiming it would allow Theresa May to strike deals that would lift bans and lower tariffs on British goods.. He cited the Scottish delicacy haggis, which the US banned on health grounds in 1971, and whisky, on which India imposes a 150% duty, as examples of products that could be exported in volume.

At the same time during the campaign, President Obama was warning that the UK would be at the "back of the queue" waiting for a trade deal with the US if the people of the UK chose Brexit. Trade negotiations are tough, complex and take years. And even when a deal is reached, that does not mean the case is closed. China and India with a population more than 20 times the size of the UK are not easy partners to negotiate with. Few trade deals are one-sided, and whichever is struck could cause damage ranging from the country being flooded with cheap products from Asia, to restrictions on travel being slapped on foreign workers and students. Obviously, when it comes to negotiations, size matters. The EU has been able to secure good deals just because of the value of scale. Of course, nobody wins all the time, and common ground needs to be found. But it is questionable that the UK will be much more successful selling Scotch whisky to India and haggis to the US.

PART III

Lessons learned for the European Union and United Kingdom

If you have ten thousand regulations you destroy all respect for the law.

Winston Churchill (1874 – 1965)

CHAPTER 4

HOW DEMOCRACY AND REFERENDA WORK, AND WHAT THE FLAWS ARE

Winston Churchill once quipped, "It has been said that that democracy is the worst form of government except all the others that have been tried." To which Franklin D. Roosevelt may have been admonishing, "Democracy cannot succeed unless those who express their choice are prepared to choose wisely. The real safeguard of democracy, therefore, is education." A referendum is the most direct form of democracy; however, considering the importance of the subject and the consequences for the people, too little was done to inform the people partaking in the decision.

Some politicians, especially those surprised by the outcome, might have consulted Aristotle beforehand, who noted, "Democracy arises out of the notion that those who are equal in any respect are equal in all respects; because men are equally free, they claim to be absolutely equal." Despite belonging to different political parties, the backgrounds and beliefs of the MPs at Westminster are not very diverse at all. Giving the same weight of vote to the old and the young, to the social benefits taker and the City banker, to the "people that just get on" and the super-rich, can lead to unpredictable consequences. While a very large majority of MPs supported Remain, the much more diverse population across the four nations of the United Kingdom whom they supposedly represented was much more unpredictable in their voting behaviour and in using the power that they were given.

The authors of this book have drawn lessons from recent political developments and concluded that, most importantly, people need to be informed about the implications of their decisions, especially where complex matters are concerned. Nobody would consider putting a complex business law to a referendum, especially not if no effort were made to explain it and evaluate its implications. In this sense, democracy needs to be managed to lead to informed decisions. Haphazard democracy leads to unpredictable and probably undesirable results, uncertainty and polarisation. In the age where large corporations control the media and can make up the news,[68] where social media can spread fake news

---

68   A report by the Media Reform Coalition, titled "Who Owns the UK Media?", reviewed the national newspaper market and claimed that just three companies – Sun and Times owner News UK, Daily Mail publisher DMGT, and Daily Mirror owner Trinity Mirror – control 71% of

within hours, and where many politicians' goal is to win the next election with the attitude "whatever it takes", some control is required. When newspapers and broadcasters are spreading radical and extremely unbalanced views, social media platforms spread fake news, or parties launch manifestoes that are unrealistic, in most cases no watchdog will intervene. The question, which will not be answered in this book, is who can control and intervene in the political debate if things get out of control?

A referendum is "a vote in which all the people in a country or in an area are asked to give their opinion or decide an important political or social question" (Cambridge Dictionary, 2017). The EU Referendum on 23 June 2016 was a form of direct democracy, which should have been managed in the same way as elections and other democratic processes. As discussed in this book (see Section 2.6), there was a deficit in managing the process of the referendum, which did not meet any of the necessary criteria, but also did not set any thresholds. Most importantly, the authors believe that the wrong question was asked. The economic common market has always been preferred in the UK over the political union by both people and parties by a wide margin. Thus, the majority of voters probably would not have voted to leave the Single Market or Customs Union (nor Euratom nor abandon the standards set by the three European standards organisations) if such a choice could have been prescinded from the European Union as a whole, with its political integration project. PM Cameron negotiated such a "special status" for the UK in February 2016. He secured some impressive exemptions and reforms in the 28-nation bloc, within a very short period of time, covering political issues from sovereignty and migrants and welfare benefits to economic governance and safeguards for the interests of countries

---

the national newspaper market. The report shows that six major newspaper groups own 81% of local newspapers. The remaining 56 publishers in the UK have a market share of just 19%. This concentration of ownership threatens viewpoint plurality in the market "crucial in setting the agenda for the rest of the media" (Sweney, 2015). The new UK television broadcasters set up by the Television Act 1954 to break the BBC's monopoly, provided more plurality, as did the advent of satellite television. But plurality of channels is not necessarily plurality of owners, nor therefore viewpoints, and so the pluralism of the traditional media, which still commands the authority, is not enough for the whole truth always to emerge. In regards to television broadcasting, Sky which is controlled by News UK owner Rupert Murdoch, has become (under the influence of his political rivals) the iconic example of this. There are more powerful media moguls than Rupert Murdoch – the ones who have been able to make him controversial whilst continuing themselves to operate in the shadows, Murdoch being unable to turn the tables. The concentration of growing power of ITV, Channel 4 and Channel 5 leads to a concentration in the hands of just a few broadcasters. The report concludes, "We believe that concentration within news and information markets in particular has reached endemic levels in the UK and that we urgently need effective remedies. This kind of concentration creates conditions in which wealthy individuals and organisations can amass huge political and economic power and distort the media landscape to suit their interests and personal views" (Sweney, 2015). In 2012, a report from Ofcom concluded that potential concentrations of media power should be subject to regular, formal reviews (Sweney, 2012).

outside the monetary union. But this brilliant performance was widely underreported, even ridiculed in the press (see Section 1.2).

It is not disputed that referenda are a legitimate vehicle of direct democracy; however, if the specific question and its form of words – (let alone its remote consequences) – misproblematises the issues and/or if it is inadequately grasped by the voter, then a referendum can easily produce results not intended even by the winning majority. To illustrate, an answer to the question if one is "happy" or "unhappy" will depend on the social context, not just the individual as such. An overdosed patient recovering in the hospital who will be returned to incarceration in an insane asylum is likelier to answer "no" than such a patient with prospects of immediate release to his family. In the context of an in-out referendum, this implies that the same or similar voter would respond differently if posed the same question at different times with different information about the (remote) consequences. The very form and scope of the question can both capture the issue and influence the answer differently. The referendum might have been contingent, for example: "If by a date certain the UK may not be permanently exempted from 'ever closer political union' whilst maintaining the Single Market, shall the Government be directed to trigger Article 50?" Questions of the same kind could have been posed about immigration as well, and other issues of overriding importance.

This Chapter will analyse and present some viewpoints on democracy and referenda. Section One explains how stereotypes and incomprehensible numbers can play tricks with our minds when we make decisions. Section Two questions how it is possible that candidates that do not have a popular majority can win an election, and discusses the need to manage referenda. This Section also summarises the Electoral Commission's recommendation for a standard legal framework for the conduct and regulation of future referenda, and the Electoral Reform Society's recommendations to improve the conduct of future referenda. Section Three describes how facts became almost secondary in the campaign for the EU Referendum, and how psychological factors prevailed. Section Four analyses the role of the media during the campaign, and presents some interesting insights about which sources voters used to make their decision.

4.1 VOTING BEHAVIOUR AND SOCIAL PSYCHOLOGY

The in-out referendum has been different from general elections in many ways. Lines could not be clearly drawn between Labour and Conservatives as both parties were divided between the Remain and Leave camp, nor could any party be made responsible for the *current state of the nation*. At the same time, the younger generations could not remember how life had once been outside the EU more than 43 years ago, nor there was any detailed assessment about what the implications of Brexit for individuals would be. Living on the British Isles and outside the Schengen area always involved some kind of border controls – involving passport controls at either ferry terminals or airports, – so natural borders existed in most peoples heads (unlike in Ireland where people widely reject the border between the North and South of the country).

Chapter Two analysed how different socio-demographics voted; however, the issue is much more complex. The older generation who should have remembered the bad state of the UK economy before joining the EC in 1993 (after a failed earlier attempt) and how the common market helped to boost the UK economy might have been expected to back Remain. They also lived through the post-War era and experienced how East and West Europe's fate was for many years in the hands of the superpowers – the US and Soviet Union. Yet the older generation, which is usually assumed to take more rational decisions than the more impulsive younger generation, voted mostly for Leave. Following the standard assumption, the younger generation, which favours (dramatic) change and displays a dislike of strict rules and regulation (which is the common perception of the European institutions, and any central government) should have voted for Leave. Their age-voting behaviour, too, was the reverse of expected. So there are no simple answers.

Many analysts have tried to explain the outcome, and so have the authors of this book. It is a combination of many factors, and one would need to construct a complicated formula that weights every factor to come anywhere near the right result. Of course, this is impossible. The authors' assumption is that voters in both camps displayed similar behavioural and psychological characteristics. Their decisions were influenced by the same factors, and some voter groups were probably more receptive to certain arguments than others for various reasons. The list below is a summary of some of the factors that are mostly likely to have had an influence on the referendum results.

- *Socio-demographic factors*: Polling statistics indicate that age, education and rural *vs.* urban residence had a big influence on voting behaviour (see Chapter Two). The Remain camp was on average younger and better educated. But older is not necessarily wiser, nor yet is better educated necessarily better informed. The Remain camp, for all its educatedness, proved too ignorant of the EU to explain its advantages to the undecided.
- *Long-term belief systems*: The Euro-sceptic politicians and media have become increasingly strident in recent years in their opposition to the European integration project, which had a major influence on the British people's views on the EU. If you are constantly being informed of the negative aspects of the EU, and are then asked to reconsider the negativity by a late-coming Remain campaign just a few months before the pivotal referendum on continuing membership, this will not be very convincing to many voters.
- *Change of focus from economic to political union*: While the 1975 referendum was all about membership of the common market and a purely economic union, which the British always did and continue to favour, many changes of a decidedly more

political flavour have intervened since Margaret Thatcher revamped the common market. The 2016 referendum was a judgment on a political union. Economic benefits are easier to explain and less controversial than political integration, and thus it was easier for the Euro-sceptics to win ground.

- *Traditional and social media*: The continuing evolution of media from hierarchical to social had a massive impact on the results. Like the population, even the hierarchical ("mainstream") media was polarised on the issue.
- *Poor journalism and populism*: The media neglected distinguishing "news" from scrutinised facts, and some provided a platform for the most vehement of all Euro-sceptics, UKIP. This was arguably poor journalism in that it distributed information uncritically that easily could have been refuted, apparently for the sake of attracting readers and viewers by telling them what they wanted to hear. President Trump has identified the powerful media and inaccurate reporting ("fake news") as one of the biggest challenges of his Presidency, and has taken to communicating with his 110 million followers directly on Twitter. During the referendum campaign, there was hardly any challenge to misinformation.

The following Sections try to explain the results in this context; however, it does not really explain how the different camps were able to mobilise their voters (perhaps differentially), or how important each of these factors were in respect of the overall result.

4.2 WINNING THE DEBATE: STEREOTYPES AND "FACTS"

The world has changed dramatically over the last 20 years, but certain stereotypes remain in people's heads. Some people still think of Russia as Communist country where people are robbed of their personal liberties or of China as a totalitarian system where most people work in rice fields. The media in Western countries too often focuses on shortcomings and stereotypes. People who have visited these countries have seen a very different picture. Moscow's financial district makes London's Canary Wharf look like a hamlet and can match Manhattan's skyline. The tallest freestanding structure in Europe, the Ostankino Tower at 540 meters, and the tallest skyscraper, the Federation Tower at 374 meters, are situated in Moscow. In fact, ten of Europe's six tallest buildings are located in Moscow. Forbes reported in 2017 that the most billionaires live in New York (82), followed by Hong Kong (75), Moscow (73), Beijing (54), and London (50) (Forbes, 2017). China's high-speed rail (HSR) network exceeds 22,000 kilometres and is the longest in the world. With more than 4,500 bullet trains it makes the British High Speed 2 (HS2) with just 560km from London to Manchester and Leeds (to be completed in 2033) look like a toy train. Clearly, this is a very different picture from what many people still have.

The same applies to stereotypes of the European Union and the unrealistic expectations that media and Brexiteers implanted in people's heads. Concerning the

European institutions, many think of them as huge bureaucracy. In 2016 around 33,000 people worked for the European Commission and its departments, known as Directorates General (DGs); 6,000 people worked for the European Parliament and its General Secretariat, working groups, and sub committees; and around 3,500 people worked for the Council of the European Union. In addition, 4,300 translators and 800 interpreters provide services to support the 24 official languages. In total, the EU-28 spend around 6% of its annual budget on staff, administration and facility management (European Union, 2017). In comparison, the UK has 418 principal Councils (353 in England, 22 in Wales, 32 in Scotland, and 11 in Northern Ireland) with 21,050 councillors, which employ around 1 million full-time equivalent staff (in England alone) and has an estimated revenue expenditure of £95.4 billion in 2015-2016 (LgiU, 2017). Another comparison to EU staff provides Derbyshire County Council, which employed around 36,000 public servants in 2013 (Full Fact, 2017). Birmingham City Council is the largest Council in the UK. In 2010 it employed 20,000 staff; however it is planning to reduce this number to 7,000 in 2018 (Elkes, 2014). In the United States, in 2014 the State of California employed more than 883,000 public servants, probably a big reason why the State is so deeply in debt (Governing the State and Localities, 2014). (The EU is not permitted to assume debt.) When presenting figures like these, it is always important to put them into perspective. Cross-comparing the population of the EU-28 (*ca.* 510 million) with the State of California (*ca.* 40 million), against the number of public employees of the EU (*ca.* 47,600) with California's (*ca.* 883,000) yields an eye-opening result. California employs 2,207 public servants per 100,000 citizens, whilst the EU employs just 9 per 100,000! This surely contradicts the widespread perception of the highly efficient Sunshine State *vs* the "stifling" Brussels bureaucracy.

The human mind has its limitations, and the stereotypes and incomprehensible figures used in debates and campaigns to win arguments clearly exploit some of these limitations. The same old canned arguments sound convincing to all too many. So how do we make informed decisions in general, and in regards to politics in particular? The most important thing is to question stereotypes; put numbers in perspective or break them down into smaller digestible units; and always do your own fact gathering and checking. Winning an argument is not the same as a balanced view, but often presents only one side of the story.

4.3 THE REFERENDUM: A DEMOCRATIC TOOL?

Even the oldest democracies (Greece, which introduced the concept of *demokratia* or "rule by the people" in 507 BC), the biggest democracies (India, which is soon to be the most populous country in the world), and the strongest democracies (USA, which promotes democracy around the world) are far from being perfect. Like all democracies, there is no doubt that the EU needs to reform, to continue to reduce bureaucracy, and to review the social agenda. But this requires strong Member States like the UK, France and Germany, who can take the lead.

Even more importantly, democracy does not always mean that the winning candidate got the majority of votes. The first-past-the-post (FPTP) electoral rule is that the candidate who receives more votes than any other wins. This rule, which is widely used in the United Kingdom, United States, Canada, India and most Commonwealth countries, can mean that the winner has less than a majority of votes. The UK's Electoral Reform Society is a civil society organisation advocating abolishing the FPTP for all national and local elections. It argues that it is "bad for voters, bad for government and bad for democracy".

For example, during the UK General Elections held on 7 May 2015, the Conservatives took 51% (331 seats) of the seats with only 37% (11.334 million votes) of the votes. The Liberal Democrats with 8% (2.416 million votes) and the SNP with 4.7% (1.454 million) together received fewer votes than UKIP with 12.6% (3.881 million) but both gained more seats (LibDem 8 seats, SNP 56 seats, UKIP only 1 seat); *i.e.*, with fewer votes, they together managed to win 64 times the number of UKIP seats in Parliament. In the United States presidential elections the winner has lost the popular vote a number of times. The President of the United States is actually elected by an Electoral College, which means that he does not necessarily need a majority of the popular vote. In the 2016 presidential election, the Democratic nominee Hillary Clinton received 65,853,516 popular votes and 227 Electoral College votes, while the Republican nominee Donald Trump received 62,984,825 popular votes and 304 Electoral College votes. Despite Clinton's popular vote lead of 2.1%, or almost three million votes, Trump became the 45th President of the United States.

Important decisions like the EU Referendum are far too important to neglect defining clear rules and to be decided with anything less than an absolute majority of votes. Such a vote can have huge implications not only for individuals but for the country as a whole, and can lead to costly aftermath with an uncertain final outcome. In the lead-up to the EU Referendum, PM Cameron's Government felt sure of winning it and gave little attention to its structure or to any plans for the eventuality of a Leave victory.

MPs declared their EU Referendum stances in advance. 480 MPs declared for Remain, including 185 Tories, 218 Labourites, 54 Scottish Nationalist, 8 LibDems, 1 Green, 3 from the Welsh Plaid Cymru, 7 from various parties in Northern Ireland – Sinn Féin, SDLP, UUP and the Alliance Party – and 4 from other parties. Only 159 MPs declared for Leave, including 138 Tories, 10 Labourites, the 1 from UKIP, 8 from Northern Ireland's DUP, and 2 from other parties. 11 MPs were undecided (Press Association, 2016). Of the 30 Cabinet ministers in office when Theresa May was appointed PM in July 2016, 24 were for Remain and six for Leave. In the vote on the Brexit Bill to trigger Article 50 of the Lisbon Treaty, the MPs were "whipped" into going along with the referendum majority lest they betray the democratic will of the people; even though 56% of Conservative MPs and 73% of all MPs had favoured Remain (as at March 2017). This clearly indicates that MPs do not always reflect the views or opinions of the people. Another such extreme is the gulf between the US capital and the people of America. Surveys and reporters might as well forget about asking people who live in the District of Columbia for their views: 90.9% voted for the Democrats and just 4.1% for President Trump. Clearly, parliaments and capital cities are not always representative of "their" people.

The disparity between the rules of the EU and Scottish Independence referenda as to of electorate eligibility, the unstructuredness of the EU Referendum, and the shortcomings and misleading claims of the debate raise the question whether the people made an informed decision. Other issues are: whether there should be an agreed trigger for referenda; how referenda should be regulated; and how can high-quality public information and debate be ensured before the people go to the polling booth? The Electoral Reform Society is a UK-based pressure group promoting electoral reform, in particular replacing the first-past-the-post system with proportional representation or the single transferable vote. The Electoral Reform Society's (2016) report's main findings were:

1. **Information**: People felt consistently ill-informed – yet this was not for lack of interest: voters expressed high levels of interest throughout the campaign. This shows a need for action in future to ensure that rates of interest are matched by extensive public information campaigns and a vibrant deliberative debate, including the possibility of holding official Citizens' Assemblies during the campaign.
2. **Personalities**: The 'big beasts' largely failed to engage or convince voters to their side, with many voters appearing switched off by the 'usual suspects'. This suggests that far more important than major political figures being wheeled out is having a strong narrative based on policies not personalities, which inspires people to debate the issues for themselves.
3. **Negative campaigning**: As the race wore on, the public viewed both sides as increasingly negative. It is not clear that either side gained from this approach.
   The need for real deliberation: There is an appetite for informed, face-to-face discussion about the issues, but this can only be nurtured within the context of a longer campaign (Breat, 2016).

The Electoral Commission is an independent body set up by the UK Parliament. It regulates party and election finance and sets standards for well-run elections, while being independent of government and answerable to Parliament. The Electoral Commission recommended in its report on the EU Referendum concluded that "the UK government should establish a clear standard legal framework for the conduct and regulation of future referendums". In its recommendations the report said, "Any Government considering providing funding directly to Electoral Registration Officers (EROs) for public awareness ahead of a future referendum or scheduled polls should consult EROs and the Electoral Commission in sufficient time to ensure that effective plans for local and national activities can be developed and implemented." A six-months notification in advance of polling day would allow reasonable time to plan advertising and the organise the logistics of the referendum. It was also suggested, "Electors should be able to check online whether they are correctly registered to vote", which would replace paper-based applications and direct contact with ERO officials to find out about the status of the voter registration. (On the other hand, such paperless voting system could open the risk to voting fraud and manipulation, which is precisely the reason why successive governments of all parties have resisted this reform.) Online services are particularly of interest as helping to address the recommendation that "[a]ccess to the voting process should be improved for overseas electors". There have been numerous complaints by overseas electors that they did not receive their postal ballot packs in time (The Electoral Commission, 2016a). As well, local councils often hire contractors to help process the ballot papers, which outsources a politically sensitive operation whilst shirking responsibility and deflecting the blame to unaccountable third parties for electoral failure.

The Electoral Reform Society, touted as the UK's leading voice for democratic reform, works with political parties, civil society groups, and academics. It aims to empower every citizen to participate in democratic processes. Reflecting on the EU Referendum, the Society concluded that "[d]oing referendums differently after the EU vote" (Will Brett, 2016) was advisable, and that in particular, "the wider debate let voters down". Nine key recommendations were offered to improve the conduct of future referenda:

Laying the groundwork
1. Mandatory pre-legislative scrutiny for any parliamentary Bill introducing a referendum, lasting at least three months, with citizens' involvement
2. A minimum six-month regulated campaigning period to ensure time for a proper public discussion
3. A definitive 'rulebook' to be published, setting out technical aspects of the vote, as soon as possible after the passing of any referendum Bill

Better information
4. Citizenship education to be extended in schools alongside UK-wide extension of votes at 16 to all public elections and referendums
5. A 'minimum data set' or impartial information guide to be published on a website at the start of the regulated campaigning period
6. An official body – either the Electorate Commission or an appropriate alternative – should be given the task of intervening when misleading claims are made by the campaigns, as in New Zealand

More deliberation
7. The government should fund a resource for stimulating deliberative discussion/ debate about referendum

8. An official body should be tasked with providing a toolkit for members of the public to host own debates/deliberative events on the referendum
9. Ofcom should conduct a review into an appropriate role for broadcasters to play in referendums, with aim of making coverage/formats more deliberative rather than combative/binary

(Electoral Reform Society, 2016b).

It is very unfortunate that these insights and recommendations came too late to inform the most important decision that the British people had to make in a generation. But then, referenda are by tradition extremely rare due to the principle of parliamentary sovereignty. As at 2017 only three referenda have ever covered the whole United Kingdom: (1) the *1975 European Communities membership referendum* on the issue of continued membership of the European Communities (EC); (2) the *2011 Alternative Vote (AV) referendum* on the proposal to use the alternative vote system in parliamentary elections; and (3) the *2016 EU in-out referendum*. The UK government has held 11 major referenda within each of the constituent countries of England, Scotland, Wales, and Northern Ireland on issues of devolution, sovereignty and independence; the first such was the Northern Ireland border poll in 1973 and the most recent was the Scottish Independence referendum in 2014.

Under the European Union Act 2011 there is also provision for the United Kingdom to hold future referenda in the event of powers being transferred from the UK to the European Union under any treaty changes. As the UK government prepares the UK to leave the EU by May 2019, this provision is unlikely to be executed, nor does it support an argument for holding a second Brexit referendum. Even so, a second referendum is backed by the Liberal Democrats, the Greens, and the Scottish National Party, and according to a poll by Survation for the *Mail on Sunday*, 53% of the British public back a second referendum and 69% of the respondents disagree with the Prime Minister's "Hard Brexit" plans (Cook, 2017). There are many reasons pro and con that speak for a second referendum, such as:

1. *Provisions in the European Union Act 2011*: If the transfer of powers from the UK to the EU should trigger a referendum, transferring all EU laws onto the British statutory book through the Great Repeal Bill equally should be sufficient to trigger a referendum.
2. *Economic reasons*: When David Cameron announced the EU Referendum, the UK was the fastest growing economy in the Western world. The Leave campaign was convinced that Europe was on the verge of collapse. One year after the referendum, the pound sterling has weakened by more than 15%,[69] and inflation

---

69 The pound sterling continued very volatile and the weakest of the big currencies. In late July 2017, when people were flying in an out of Britain (more on Friday 21 July than any other day in history), it became obvious to holidaymakers that Brexit will have a significant impact on their holiday budget. Airports such as Gatwick, Luton and Birmingham were reportedly offering less

at 2.9%, six times higher than the 0.5% it was a year ago. Food prices have risen noticeably and the wage growth has fallen to 1.7%. Europe is now growing faster than Britain (Bilimoria, 2016).

3. *Broken promises*: Many promises have been withdrawn or are eroding. The £350 million a week promise for the NHS budget and immigration below 100,000 have been abandoned altogether. Trade deal promises are chancy, as the negotiations are long-drawn-out, require tough compromises, and are very unlikely to be as lucrative as the EU's trade deals, due to the UK currently lacking experienced negotiators, whilst the larger EU-27 with their Single Market wield more negotiating leverage than any Member State would have on its own. The Leave campaign oversold the prospects of the UK doing deals with Commonwealth countries in particular. Left out of account is the inconvenient fact that a trade deal is not one-sided: it can mean that cheap products flood the UK market, forcing less competitive companies to close, or that deep compromises on immigration need to be made as in the case of India, which insists on trade partners opening up to accept Indian labour. The new Indian High Commissioner in London, Yashvardhan Kumar Sinha, has said very clearly that India is open to a bilateral trade deal – but there will be no trade deal without movement of people, *i.e.*, higher immigration (Canton, 2017). This could mean that more of the 1.25 billion people in India get easier access to live and work in the UK in exchange for the UK having the privilege to be the tenth country ever and the first Western country to sign a bilateral trade deal with India.

4. *Terms of leaving the EU were not part of the referendum*: The terms of leaving the EU were not discussed in detail during the campaign, nor were they part of the referendum question. Nobody specifically voted to leave the Single Market, the Customs Union or leave non-political organisations that deal with health and safety such as Euratom,[70] the EMA,[71] or the EASA.[72] Furthermore, as there was no exit strategy, no terms agreed on what leaving the EU would mean, many argue that the people should have another referendum on that question once the deal is final. The final deal will be far more consequential than an employment contract. Who would sign a blank employment contract without knowing the job description and responsibilities, and agreeing the pay and benefits?

---

than one euro per pound. With as little as 88 cent for one pound, Cardiff airport offered the worst exchange rate since the inception of the euro currency in 1999 (Bartlett, July 2017).

70   The European Atomic Energy Community (website: http://ec.europa.eu/euratom/).

71   European Medicines Agency (website: http://www.ema.europa.eu/ema/).

72   European Aviation Safety Agency (website: https://www.easa.europa.eu/).

The lessons learned are that Britain has entered unchartered territory. It is the first country to leave the European Union after voting to join it (Greenland had no choice until after it was given home rule by Denmark, having been entailed by the latter's accession), but also has used a democratic tool which it has very limited experience with. Britain must now go through the exit process, and it faces an uncertain future in regards to re-building her relationships with the world. So far, Murphy's Law has been vindicated: "Things will go wrong in any given situation, if you give them a chance." In common parlance, "If it can go wrong, it will." The question remains why not give people a final say over the final deal? In a second referendum, the younger generation who did not engage in the first one would have a second chance, and would be able to make a much more informed decision. The first referendum was like a "pig in a poke". Democracy is not just about voting for representatives, but also informing oneself. This was hardly possible in the first EU Referendum.

4.4 HOW IMPORTANT ARE FACTS IN A CAMPAIGN?

The result of UK's EU Referendum surprised many people – not only outside of the UK. Many subsequent analyses by think tanks, poll predictors, and marketing campaigners tried to find reasonable explanations how it was possible to mobilise so many diverse voter groups. Evidently, the Remain campaign proved to be wrong to trust in the voters to realise the obvious high risks of an exit from the EU. Something apart from the facts of Brexit was carelessly neglected – the psychology of voter groups. Remain solely focussed on economic argumentation about the impacts of Brexit on the UK, ignoring the emotions, social influence, and mental short cuts as more powerful drivers of behaviour than logical arguments. The Leave campaign deployed messages like "getting back control" that triggered emotional responses. They also picked up on topical issues like immigration which voters were worried about and encouraged their discussion (Cole, 24 June 2016).

Other psychological factors that influenced the social creatures who were the voters on both sides include the herd mentality, emotionalism, fear of loss of control, lack of information access, and appeals to misperceptions affected the public's behaviour and the outcome of the referendum. Easy accessible social networks drove voters to align their individual behaviour with anticipated group behaviour, a herd mentality that made voters more receptive to controversial statements than to a more inaccessible rationality.

Emotional messages spread by popular politicians motivated more voters than rational arguments. The relentless emphasis on the costs to the UK of EU membership, the excruciating problems of Europe, the underfinanced NHS, stagnating wages, job losses to immigration, all made Leavers vote to avoid more losses in the future. They were strongly motivated by the thought of being in charge of their own destiny – and to follow the Leave slogan "take back control". Moreover, providing the media with simple messages allowed campaigners to reach and mobilise voter groups ranging from conservative to politically disengaged voter groups. Typically, Boris Johnson confessed to a fellow journalist that he served up to *The Telegraph* made-up Euro-sceptical stories (McKernan, 2016). Such negative messages created fear of change and loss of status that could even scare voters for opening up to the rational arguments of the Remain campaign such as emergency budgets, austerity cuts, *etc*. In such a negatively charged campaign, the Remainers missed opportunities and had difficulties putting the positive arguments for the EU across to the voters. The Remain campaign failed as its Conservative leaders did not understand basic human psychology and motivations (Cole, 24 June 2016).

However, the narrowness of the poll result and its multiple impact factors should foreclose drawing any conclusion that facts did not or will not matter to voters. In fact, presenting evidential and causal claims must be thoroughly prepared by the political parties to properly address its voter groups. Moreover, political leaders have to take a stand for objective, fact-based communication on the EU supported by the media. Given the effects on collective beliefs of decades of negative press coverage of the EU and by the politicians, Euro-myths have been created and have taken deep root in British society; for example, that EU institutions are unaccountable. The Remain campaign did not realise the deficit in public knowledge about the nature of the EU and its benefits for UK citizens, including entrepreneurs (Meyer, 2016).

Finally, the governing elite ensconced in secured, homogeneous evell have lost touch with the real needs of the populace. A group of political and economic leaders put their selfish aims over the general welfare. The Conservative Party and its leader focussed on continued austerity and London and the South East region, ignoring the needs of provincial and rural people. Worse still was that the opposition Labour Party suffered from the ambiguous positioning and lukewarm support of their leader Jeremy Corbyn toward such a significant referendum. The British people took their decision and favoured the unknown, such was their social class discomfort and aversion to the British government.

For the sake of future referenda but also the credibility of the EU institutions, both UK governments and the EU need to invest more in educating the public about what the EU is and how it works for peoples' and nations' benefit. Moreover, the spread of inaccurate information must be fought by credible and responsible politicians including a reasonable press. Finally, the Government has to consider carefully the linkage of democracy, political promises and knowledge in order not to risk the social achievements such as political and economic stability for its citizens (Meyer, 2016).

Thus, a successful marketing campaign for selling the facts and benefits of Europe to its citizens should include a focus on the voters' needs, clear propositions, the relevance of the message, the use of affective stories, credible testimonials, and not just assume the voters will make the wise choice. Marketing has to give voters realistic solutions, not just explanations. The EU's successes must be communicated and should include psychological motivator slogans – "Europe for prosperity". The relevance of the message should touch all voter groups, but should avoid destabilising the *status quo*. Packed into an interesting and emotional story, voters are prompted to share and spread messages by word of mouth or online *via* social media. The press should be more responsible and function as an arbiter of consistent and solid messaging to the citizens by politicians. The media's primary role was simply to be a clear channel between both camps and the public; it failed to scrutinise or sufficiently debate the messages themselves. Voters are more attracted to trustworthy solutions than to evaluating alternatives (Cole, 19 July 2016). Facts have to be delivered in a confident way to win the confidence of the voters to identify and stand up for their European rights. Bearing this people-oriented perspective in mind, the EU institutions should win more acceptance by EU citizens and Member States.

4.5 THE ROLE OF MEDIA DURING THE CAMPAIGN

The result of the referendum reflects the importance of the media and their power to influence voters. An analysis of who took which decision – readers, viewers and listeners – reveals that, according to Ipsos Mori, 64% of 18 to 34-year-olds and 58% of 35 to 54-year-olds voted Remain. About 57% of university graduate and white-collar workers backed Remain versus 45% of manual workers, pensioners, and the unemployed. Only 22% of voters understood "well or very well" what they took their decision on (Preston, 2016). According to BMG Research for the Electoral Reform Society, before the referendum about 34% of UK residents gave the BBC as their chief information source, followed by newspapers (20%), family members (18%), and social media (16%). A more detailed analysis of voter demographics reveals that 24% of 18 to 24-year-olds reported the BBC as their most important information sources, compared to 41% of over-65s. By contrast, 29% of over-65s reported newspapers as their main information source compared to just 16% of 18 to 24-year-olds. Social media was preferred by about 33% of the 18 to 24-year-olds as a major information source compared to just 8% of over-65s (BMG, 2016). Further analysis indicated a gender gap and an education gap as well as an incomprehension gap. About 25% of over 65s reported the Leave campaign to be their most information source, and even 48% of UKIP voters referred to this source. Evidentially, the selection of information sources and media usage differs between the demographic voter groups among the demographics and media usage (BMG, 2016). Thus, politicians, journalists and media are in charge to create a evelled playing field for its voters and ensure a balanced debate with equal access to the different views and facts.

The basis for the Brexit result has been being laid for 40 years in inaccurate reporting about the EU and what it is all about. A comparison of the referendum campaigns of 1975 and 2016 underlines the differences and the evolution of the UK political communication process. The vote for Stay in the EC in 1975 was a forgone conclusion. In advance, the proper terms of UK membership were re-negotiated with the EC by the Labour government.

Therefore, the debates of the major parties referred to economic aspects and restoration of democratic sovereignty. During the 2016 campaign, the multiple uses of media, in particular television timetables, reflected a less respectful communication driven by a populist tenor. Broadcasters neglected a balanced presentation of news and arguments to inform voters about the facts. Moreover, the perceived integrity of the leading political actors in 2016 was low compared to the politicians of 1975, like Roy Jenkins, Ted Heath, Shirley Williams, Tony Benn, Michael Foot, Peter Shore, Margaret Thatcher, and Enoch Powell, who believed in their cause. On top of that, the media informed the voters about the EC in a cognitively appealing way, enabling them to comprehend the meaning of the decision. Thus, ITN short films explained different features of the Common Market workings. The same approach was chosen by British broadcasters for the first direct elections to the European Parliament in 1979. In 2016 no effort was made by the media to give voters essential background information about the European Community. In 1975, the media covered each political campaign. Television news predominated in the 2016 campaign; as a result, news was more filtered and more engineered to affect viewers. The media-coached politicians lost themselves in sound bites and the media neglected to put out information on a factual basis; thus, the media failed as well to prepare the electorate in advance for this meaningful decision, who now have to bear the hard consequences (Blumler, 2016).

The print media affected the referendum result. The *Independent, the Telegraph, The Guardian*, and *the Mirror* newspapers took a more Europhile stance. On the other side, populist messages for leaving the EU were spread more by the tabloids, especially *Sun, Daily Mail*, and *Express*. Their messages reached the over-sixties and less-educated people who supported Brexit the most. Nevertheless, readers of the *Daily Mirror*, the pro-EU tabloid, supported Brexit, reflecting the complexity of demographics and psychological behaviour, where the voters themselves were polarised across all media – illustrating the challenge for media to reach its readers through their social groups. Eurosceptic sentiment arose four decades ago when *The Herald* (*The Sun*) started critically reporting about the European integration and *The Express* opposed the British membership of the EC in the 1960s. However, all major national newspapers supported the pro-EC vote in 1975. Over time, Eurosceptic journalism has become more intense in the UK. The integration debate and Britain's exit from the European Exchange Rate Mechanism (ERM) in 1992 incited tabloids, in particular *The Sun*, to attack the European Commission as well as the European Economic Community. The peak of euro-scepticism was reached in the debate on the re-launch of the Economic and Monetary Union, when *The Sun* warned Tony Blair against committing the UK to joining the Eurozone. On the other hand, during the 2015 election *The Mirror* warned David Cameron against holding a referendum on membership (Wring, 2016). The checks and balances of a responsible media role is the basis for the formation of sound opinion in a democratic system.

Undoubtedly, there is a short-term and a cumulative long-term effect of the mass media on the voters' Brexit decision. The Leave campaign applied simple KISS messages ("keep it simple stupid") like "take back control", whereas the Remain campaign failed to sell their arguments on the benefits of the EU. The media set the agenda of the Brexit debate and focussed on politicians and issues. As a result, media played an important role in how the facts about Brexit were presented. The long-term effect of an Euro-sceptic press might have been more powerful in influencing people's evaluation of the EU. Particularly the link to recent key issues for the press like integration and immigration affected the public's perception of the EU. Reporting on the EU has reflected rather a conflictual than a collaborative relationship. Also, in contrast with the 1970s, the Tories have taken up a Eurosceptic and Labour a more Europhile position in debates about Europe. The public has been primed for a negative attitude towards the EU, so that it was probably easier for the Leave campaign to confound topics like immigration to distract from the real purpose of the referendum. The Remain campaign was missing social currency for their arguments (Berry, 2016).

In fact, the UK experienced power and prosperity during its EU membership, but Brexit will abolish this collective good for the British people. Even worse, during the Brexit campaign media and politicians created a post-rational politics and culture of indignant, self-righteous moralism. The result is distrust and uncertainty about UK's future relationship to the EU and its welfare state (Gifford, 2016). For that reason, it is essential for the media as an important part of democracy to inform the people what the EU is all about – a collective good for its citizens. Plain untruth needs to be corrected by the media and politicians should stand up for the truth, because this is the only chance to give the people balanced information for their decisions.

CHAPTER 5

REFLECTIONS ON BREXIT AND LESSONS LEARNED

This, the final Chapter, draws the ultimate lessons contained in this book from the findings of the authors' observations and experiences in their political and business life.

This Chapter consists of six sections. The first provides an overview of the winners of Brexit: professionals who will be in high demand in the years to come include transformation programme advisors, legal advisors and law firms, accountants and tax advisors, financial services advisors, information technology and infrastructure technologists, Exchange traders, regulators and compliance consultants, and politicians and regulators.

Section Two expounds our vision on Britain in 2026. We have built it on surveys, historical events, and research conducted by accredited authors and publications.

The third Section proceeds with a vision querying whether the European Union will be stronger or weaker by 2026 as a result of Brexit. One year after the referendum, the EU and its Member States seem to be sticking together, the EU-27 economy has started growing, new trade agreements with Canada and Japan have been signed, and the French-German axis is determined to strengthen the Union through progressive reform. So maybe it is a good thing that the UK is finally leaving the EU to re-invent the wheel after undoing 42 years of work, and stops putting the brakes on deepening European integration, so the remaining Member States can get on with sharing military and other resources, and focussing on economic growth.

The fourth section presents a plan for businesses to prepare for Brexit; (1) mobilise cross-company Brexit working groups, (2) followed by pro-active information gathering and external networking, and (3) conduct business impact assessments, identifying key regulations, and create a risk register. Also, develop a Brexit position paper, (4) understand the key stakeholders in the process and the channels to engage with them, and try and influence the government not just individually but through business associations. (5) Stay positive, but be prepared with a contingency plan in these uncertain times.

The fifth Section lays out some possible Brexit scenarios. This is important background information, because if the UK would follow the Swiss example, as suggested by some Brexiteers and media during the campaign, the UK would need to sign up to the Schengen Agreement, stop passport controls immediately and adopt all EU regulations, without having any say over any of it. A reality check of what has been suggested by both sides is clearly called for.

The sixth and final Section summarises the lessons to be learned. *Some* of "the people have spoken", but not all, and many were not even invited to speak (*i.e.* vote) in the referendum. "We want our country back" has been and never will be delivered, as the same people that ruled Westminster politics before the referendum will be still be in charge after leaving the EU. The only difference is that they will be able to rule absolutely, with no checks and balances any more from the European Parliament or the European Court of Justice. It is obvious that vast differences divide Westminster and Brussels. The current UK government has decided to head toward isolation rather than integration. A contradiction subsists between touting openness and "doing business with the world", while indicating by its actions that the UK is planning to cut ties with its most important trading partner. What we have learned is that Brexit is nothing but a massive transformation programme[73], which is something hardly any politicians are able to manage. At the same time, a lot of money is at stake, flowing in both directions. Undoubtedly, Brexit has divided the country and led to turmoil and a constitutional crisis. Nevertheless, whatever people and politicians may decide, the ultimate arbiter will be the marketplace. We also draw some conclusions on immigration, and share some of the studies that immigrants bring benefits so long as they make part of the productive workforce. As evidenced below, EU citizens make on average a higher contribution to the country's economy than British citizens, which means that reducing the ratio of British to EU workers will cause the wealth of the country to decline.

In our final reflections, we summarise what has been researched, analysed and presented in this book. The authors concluded with what could be called the *Brexit Paradox*. Some Brexiteers deceive themselves and misinform the public, that the UK can leave the EU but be still part of the Single Market and Customs Union. This is like

---

[73]   In business terms, a transformation programme describes a complex programme that leads to fundamental changes in how business is conducted. It has clearly defined objectives, such as improving the efficiency of certain operational processes in order to achieve clearly defined cost savings, sales increases, reduction of the number of call-in complaints, reduction of subscriber churn, *etc*. The success of a transformation programme can be measured by a matrix of target numbers.

Unlike a business transformation programme, the Brexit transformation programme has vaguely defined objectives and no matrix of success factors, merely for example the vague intention of reducing immigration, instead of a commitment to reducing net immigration by 45,000 EU citizens by 31 December 2020. It will thus be impossible to measure the success (if any) of Brexit. Costs are also not measured or even estimated, so that positive results in the future might nonetheless come at a higher price than they are worth. From a business standpoint, the first year of Brexit has not inspired confidence in many businesses because of a lack of adequate project planning by the May Government. The Brexit plan read more like a horoscope than a major programme with huge implications for businesses and UK and European citizens.

promising that England can play in the World Cup but negotiate different or better rules compared to the other teams – for unknown reasons, or under the perception that the World Cup can't take place without the UK. To develop this final thought further, if the European Union is the World Football Association (Fifa) for Europe and the UK does not want to follow FiFa rules anymore, it will not only leave the World Cup (Europe), but also the world of football. Like Fifa, the European Union and its members set the rules which hold everything together and ensure that everybody is treated equally. If one team is allowed to be privileged, this means that the whole idea of the EU, where everybody shares the same benefits and obligations, will have been compromised.

5.1   WHO ARE THE WINNERS OF BREXIT?

When the government restructured Whitehall after the Brexit vote, two new departments, the Department for International Trade (DIT) and the Department for Exiting the European Union (DexEU), were created unto which the powers of the Foreign and Commonwealth Office were partitioned. Boris Johnson, the Secretary of State for Foreign and Commonwealth Affairs, Liam Fox, Secretary of State for International Trade, and David Davis, Secretary of State for Exiting the European Union share the grounds and the 115 rooms of the FCO because they are also sharing what were formerly the united powers of the Foreign & Commonwealth Office (FCO). These bureaucrats could be labelled clear winners of Brexit in the UK central government. Equipped with an unknown but likely handsome budget, they have been asked by the Prime Minister to shape the political future of Britain.

The rational, fact-based impact assessment and analysis provided in this book, and the broken promises of the Leave campaign (apart from leaving itself), make one wonder if anybody else besides the three Brexiteers and their departments benefit from leaving the EU. Organisations and people can take either of two approaches, the traditional British stoicism of "*Keep calm and carry on*" or a pro-active stance summed up in a motto like "*Surf the Brexit-wave or get drowned*". The real winners of Brexit are not the general public, which faces economic uncertainty, inflation and tax increases, but the following groups:

(1) *Transformation Programme Advisors* (Mergers & Acquisitions): Uncertainty swirls around Britain's leaves the EU. As the announcements since the referendum from financial services show, many UK-based businesses that rely on access to the Single Market, or want access, plan to set up European subsidiaries. What is underreported in the press is that, even if the UK government touts advantageous deals for certain industry sectors, why to wait and take the risk? By setting up an EU-based entity and taking full advantage of existing trade agreements that

the EU has forged with countries around the world, they are likely to do better than the trade deals that the UK now must forge. The authors predict an ongoing exodus of UK companies to the EU. This does not mean they are all deserting the country, but they *will* move certain operations to the EU. They will also explore strategic and tax efficiencies. Business organisations are more agile and creative than bureaucracies, especially when somebody tries to cut off their lifeline.

The uncertainty of the future relationship between the UK and EU, and the opportunity to set-up branches or move headquarters to the EU requires advisors with experience. These advisors will help to set up the most lucrative company structures, identify cost saving opportunities, and will provide support to opening a new entity in the EU.

(2) *Legal advisors*: Lawyers can support businesses in incorporating new entities, advise on contract law, and help with settling-in. Global law firms with offices in every major city can provide cross-border advice. Since the EU Referendum, all major law firms have started offering Brexit advice, and if a hard Brexit takes place, they will help find loopholes so that companies still can get access to the Single Market.

(3) *Accountants and tax advisors*: Like lawyers, accountants assist business organisations to set up legal entities domiciled in the European Union. They will bring along tax advisors to set up tax-efficient structures – meaning there will be an ongoing loss of tax revenue and even tighter budgets for the UK government. Countries like Luxembourg will be likely winners, as by placing branches of business entities there, corporations are able to cut taxes from their expenses. The financial sector accounts for 28% of the Luxembourg's GDP already, and employs more than 11% of its entire labour force, which is likely to get even bigger. The UK will not only be losing highly skilled professionals, but also millions in tax revenue.

(4) *Financial services advisors*: Financial services are especially hard hit by Brexit, as asset managers could lose current automatic *passporting* rights (effectively a single EU-wide banking licence) if Britain leaves the EU. An estimated €1 trillion of UCITS (Undertakings for Collective Investment in Transferable Securities) funds currently domiciled in the UK could be deprived of access to the European market unless their domicile is moved to the European Union. This would be particularly bad for the Edinburgh fund management industry and the City of London (New Financial, April 2016).

As the UK and European capital markets are tightly interconnected, to keep the benefits of the capital markets union (CMU) and access to the Single Market as a "third party", much EU regulation may have to be retained in UK law. The Alternative Investment Fund Managers Directive (AIFMD), the Capital Requirements Directive (CRD), the European Market Infrastructure Regulation (EMIR), the Undertakings for the Collective Investment in Transferable Securities

(UCITS), and the Markets in Financial Instruments Directive (Mifid) are some of the EU regulations that enable financial services to operate EU-wide. It is worrying that UK and EU regulatory regimes could diverge, leading to increased costs and potentially an increased risk to the UK's future access to the Single Market. To be on the safe side, and in order to retain their automatic access, banks in the UK may have to set up separately capitalised subsidiaries inside the EU, and investment banks may have to set up separate broker-dealers in the EU (New Financial, April 2016:3). Financial services advisors will benefit from these complex challenges that banks and insurance companies face. They will provide solutions and contingencies for financial services organisations to make the best of a costly exercise.

(5) *Information Technology and Infrastructure technologists*: Business organisations will look for smart solutions that cause as little disruption as possible. Moving an entire financial services operation to the EU could be quite expensive, so instead they may improvise technologies that will keep trading activities in London, while the trades are actually executed in the EU. Organisations may also employ IT specialists who can help them to identify cost-effective data centres in the EU, where they can run some of their business activities.

(6) *Traders*: Uncertainty leads to turmoil in stock exchanges, which also creates opportunities. Volatility traders and FX traders that trade with currencies look forward to a few bonfire nights when the UK leaves the EU. For the City boys, chaos is opportunity, and a crash of the pound, followed by recovery, will generate millions for those who understand how to operate on the stock market.

(7) *Regulatory and compliance consultants*: Highly regulated industries in particular, such as financial services, the pharmaceutical industry, and utilities need advice on how to adapt to possible changes in laws and regulations, while at the same time they need access to the Single Market. How to comply with laws and regulations from *both* the UK and the EU will be essential, as non-compliance with EU data protection laws, health and safety standards, banking regulations, and so on will deprive them of the opportunity to sell their services and goods to the EU. The costs of access (*i.e.*, tariffs *vs.* free access) will be subject to future negotiations; however, this is unrelated to the necessity of complying with EU regulations. Countries that are not in the EU, like Switzerland, Iceland and Norway, still have to implement EU laws and regulations in order to gain access the Single Market. Regulatory specialists with knowledge of EU laws and markets will be in demand.

(8) *Politicians and Regulators*: There is no question that Brexit will keep politicians "busy" for years to come. The whole exercise of sifting through EU law, having debates, making changes, then passing it through Parliament adds the same value as carrying coal to Newcastle. Pressure groups, unions, business associations, every type of stakeholder will try to get certain EU regulations embedded in UK

law changed. To do this, they will knock on the doors of Westminster politicians, who if true to form will start a lengthy and (at least for taxpayers) costly exercise of tweaking legislation. Some Brexiteers might start a *witch hunt* to change evil laws and regulations that are totally sensible, only because they are derived from the EU. This unnecessarily costly exercise could go on for years, adding more uncertainty.

Regulators like the UK Financial Conduct Authority could be buried under questions about European *passporting* or how to run business from a non-European Economic Area country. Utility regulators could see similar questions once their industries lose access to the Single Market. Equally, EU regulators will be requested to open new legal entities in EU countries. All this requires manpower, particularly as regulators are usually understaffed. For businesses it means extra costs and loss of time that otherwise could have been spent on developing their trade and the country's economy.

5.2 OUR VISION: BRITAIN IN 2026 – TEN YEARS AFTER BREXIT

In the in-out referendum the UK voted to leave the EU in order to "take back control". However, when actual negotiations started a year later, the UK realised it was about to embark on a journey without clear end-goals. In the 1970s, when Britain was in process of joining the EU, the country was dubbed "the sick man of Europe", a role previously played by the Ottoman Empire in the late 19th century. Industrial unrest intensified, growth was slow, and the question was asked how the country could be made more competitive. The hope was that joining the EEC in 1973 would boost the economy. Although a number of factors were in play, including Margaret Thatcher's drastic economic and social reforms, by the mid-1990s Britain clearly had managed to get back on track. Even a decade ago, London was considered to be overtaking New York as the world's financial centre (Buttonwood, 2017). Now, one year after Brexit, an inexorable feeling that the country is in decline is setting in.

The real causes of Britain's exit are gradually being revealed. It includes overstretched internationalisation, regional development disparities, low real wages, and overstated productivity. Instead of tackling these problems, the Government, tabloid press, even politicians are content to blame the EU for homemade economic failures. Additionally, the Brexit referendum was exploited by media and politicians to drive a wedge into British society. The result is a Britain on its way to isolation, facing new challenges of redefining its future international economic and trade position – and falling back into years of uncertainty for businesses, investors and consumers. Such an unstable economic environment risks that, since the last election in June 2017, a reinvigorated Labour Party could take over the government at the latest in the next scheduled elections on 5 May 2022. If Jeremy Corbyn comes to power even earlier, then the UK economy may be exposed to higher taxes on businesses in addition to nationalisation of utilities and other public services and an anti-Western foreign policy. In consequence, public spending would rise with taxes insufficient to cover the deficit spending. Credit institutions would downgrade the creditworthiness of the state. The closing of the accruing financial gap by attracting foreign investors would demand higher yields and may even result in a deficit increase. Businesses and entrepreneurs would avoid any further investments, and might even consider exiting the UK market. At a single blow, the UK could wake up as the sick man of Europe for a second time (Buttonwood, 2017).

Despite the tight poll result in June 2016, the UK population immediately noticed that the decision for Brexit required changes for themselves. According to a ComRes telephone-based survey in July 2016[74] (ComRes, 2016), about a thousand Britons stated the following:

- "More Britons (53%) think it is likely that the UK will no longer exist in ten years' time than think England can win a major football tournament (13%). Around a quarter of Britons (25%) think it is likely that the UK will be a member of the EU is ten years' time.
- Most Britons think that maintaining access to the single market should be the priority for the Government when negotiating the UK's withdrawal from the EU (66%), while just a third says this of restricting freedom of movement (31%).
- Half of British adults (52%) expect immigration to fall after the UK leaves the EU. Around one in three expect levels of immigration to remain about the same (36%).
- Half of the British public (47%) think the UK economy will be worse in two years' time, a third think it will be better (32%).
- Around three quarters of British adults (72%) say they do not trust leading politicians to do a good job of carrying out the will of the British people during the process of the UK's withdrawal from the EU, while half do not trust civil servants (50%)" (ComRes, 2016).

At this stage, the British Government is well on its way to fulfilling peoples' survey expectations. Once the Government clearly stated its intention of exiting the EU, Scotland and Northern Ireland began hankering for independence to avoid regional and national trade impacts – bedevilled now by a revival of the cross-border conflict between Northern Ireland and the Republic of Ireland, and by Britain's damaged relationship with Spain over Gibraltar. The United Kingdom risks falling apart to a popular revolt against the way they have been governed over the last three decades (Wellings, 2016).

---

74   ComRes interviewed 1,004 British adults aged 18 plus by telephone from 7th-10July 2016, website at http://www.comres.co.uk/polls/bbc-news-brexit-expectations-poll (accessed July 2017).

The most recent election result in June 2017 forced Conservatives to rethink pursuing a hard Brexit strategy. The Government's determination to leave the Customs Union makes it difficult to see a soft landing for the UK. The fact that four decades of shared history and about 20,000 EU rules have to be dealt with in the next two years of Brexit negotiations illustrates the complexity of precedent. Subsequent negotiation of a trade deal with the EU should take between seven and ten years – an amount of time that industry and investors are hardly prepared to give a tattered Government and country. This includes reaching an interim trade deal with the EU. Moreover, the major asymmetry of trade flows – where the UK exports 40% of its exports to the EU but the EU only receives 15% of its imports from the UK – will translate into a bargaining asymmetry. On top of that, during the negotiation period, continuing membership of the EU will disallow the UK to sign new trade deals with other countries; meaning that this will not materialise. The closing of new free trade agreements cannot be finalised until after the UK has left the EU (Baschuk *et al.*, 2017). Furthermore, promised trade deals with China, India and the Americas will probably not, even if they eventuate, be able to replace previous trade volumes with neighbouring countries, following the old economist's rule "twice the distance, half the trade" (Kelly, 2017). The dream of the UK transforming into a "Singapore on the Thames" in terms of corporate tax is not feasible due to being bound to the OECD guidelines curbing tax breaks. The Brexiteers might think they can ignore the OECD guidelines, but the consequences would very likely include retaliation by other OECD member states. Moreover, the EU's remaining 27 Member States and 34 national and regional Parliaments will not suffer such undermining competition (Doyle, 2017).

The free movement of EU citizens is a basic principle of the Single Market. EU negotiators are therefore interested in preserving the rights of the 3.3 million EU citizens resident in the UK, a pivotal negotiation point for reaching agreement. The UK will also have to accept the jurisdiction of the European courts for EU citizens' legitimate claims. It is highly uncertain whether EU citizens living in the UK are entitled to healthcare and pensions. The retail sector employs about 200,000 EU nationals who will be difficult to replace at once by UK nationals. For instance, the UK construction industry could lose more than 175,000 EU workers – or 8% of the sector's workforce, an acute shortage in the short to medium-term. Not only big infrastructure projects but also UK's £500 billion infrastructure pipeline might be delayed due to a shortage of construction professionals.

The British government should secure access to the Single Market or develop alternative plans to easily employ non-EU workers (Fletcher, 2017). The Government cannot implement a new immigration system till March 2019 at the earliest, even if they have to allow EU migrants into the country in the meantime. Interim and long-term employment rules have to be found for the 15% of academic staff at UK universities in order not to jeopardise the reputation of UK's universities. Less workforce migration will undermine the social and pension systems. According to a report by centre-left group Institute for Public Policy Research (IPPR) (Lawrence, 2016), the rapidly ageing population might open a funding gap for adult social care of up to £13 billion by 2030-31. On the other hand, the looming advent of high-functioning robotics is projected to obsolete two-thirds of current jobs and put at least 15 million people at risk of automation unemployment. This will cause a labour glut, not a shortage, and jobs will become insecure and get re-organised. The net result will be even more income for already high-income households, whose income is projected to rise 11 times faster than for low income households (Simpson, 2016). Thus, Brexit by restricting immigration will likely ease to some extent the challenge to labour market in the UK.

One year after Brexit, the British pound has indeed dropped, but the broader British economy has held up better than expected by those who predicted a hard fall. On the day of the ballot, the pound could be bought for about $1.50, but has slid since then to a 30-year low below $1.33, and traded as low as about $1.20 in January 2017, down 20% from pre-vote levels. By July 2017 the pound was trading for around $1.31, making imports more expansive for the economy. Analysts do not expect the pound to recover its lost ground in the future. The consumer price index jumped to 2.6% in June 2017, above the 2% target rate of the Bank of England, the Bank dares not raise interest rates lest it slows the economy. Difficult negotiations with the EU will not produce changes in the short-term. In contrast, the FTSE has increased by nearly 20% since the Brexit. As about 75% of revenue of the FTS 100 is generated outside the UK, listed companies benefit from the weak pound by translating their profits back into pounds. Still, the retail sector is suffering from sluggish consumer spending as wages shrink and prices for staples climb. The weak pound has increased prices for imported goods like cars, electronics and certain foods.

House prices are expected to come under pressure soon due to households' limited spending power. So far, UK employment has proved resilient under Brexit, with unemployment holding at 4.5% in May 2017 (Sjolin and Mozee, 2017). Bearing in mind that statistics lag behind reality and Brexit negotiations have just begun, the economic impact is likely to kick in noticeably in the next two years, when the negotiation results become more obvious. Finally, the lower pound will further cut consumer purchasing power and increase business supply chain operating costs. The real economy will show the symptoms in the next few quarters.

Given an unclear negotiating target for Brexit, there is a real risk that Britain will stumble out of the EU on March 29th, 2019 with no trade agreement with the EU. In such a scenario, the new post-Brexit era will burden the trade economy with costs such as tariffs and processing delays with EU customs. Some industry will prefer to leave the country. If the Brexiteer government implements its dream of cutting the company tax rate from 17% to 10%[75] or the income tax bracket from 40% to 25%, this may be fiscally unsustainable. Personal income tax cuts directly benefit only about 15% of taxpayers, and each percentage point cut in the top rate will cost British government about £1 billion if nothing else changes. In consequence, the government might have to cut public spending and public services. Such a hard landing for the UK could worsen the widening gap between rich and poor, fomenting radical ideologies and isolationism. To avoid a worst-case scenario, Britain must hatch a new economy policy that aligns trade liberalism and social security with economic framework rules to reinvent the British economy. This will require political vision and a regaining of the credibility of politicians for achieving governmental majorities.

The second round of Brexit negotiations in Brussels in July 2017 brought to light that the UK government's Brexit negotiations approach lacks any clear goals. The lack of enthusiasm for the European Free Trade Association (the Norwegian model) makes any projection of outcomes difficult. Especially problematic is a forecast of the outcome of new trade negotiations with the EU and the other 50 countries or groups of countries embedded in the framework rules of the WTO. Thus, it is almost impossible to qualify the outcome of Brexit for the British economy. It is obvious that rejection of the free movement of people entails at least to some extent an inhibition of the free movement of services, and that the EU will therefore not be disposed to make any special deals with the UK. The UK will have lost access to the EU *passporting* framework, which will severely hit the banks and financial services industry, which encompasses 5,500 companies or more. The narrow two-year negotiating window will have meant that the Government should have pursued clearer targets and a unified strategy for Brexit talks. The governmental departments should have worked faster and more flexibly, and addressed new challenges in a unified way. The development of a cross-departmental plan on Brexit implementation should have been brought forward to avoid post-Brexit surprises for the businesses and citizens of the UK (Syal, 2017).

If these post-Brexit scenarios are heeded, there is optimism that the relationship between the UK and the EU can be enhanced and taken to a new level, depending on a reasonable negotiating result. The two partners, even if they squabble over congeneric economic disparities such as economic power, currency, trade, investments, worker migration, *etc.*, may be goaded into *rapprochement* by their common economic and social

---

75   On the other hand, US Presidents Kennedy and Reagan have proved that cutting income and company tax rates can stimulate economic growth and encourage business start-ups and expansion in the US. After the Kennedy tax cut of 1964, the US economy enjoyed eight and a half years of growth above 5% annually, and after the Reagan tax cut of 1986, the economy grew by more than 4% annually for a decade. President Trump is attempting to duplicate this performance with company tax cuts, especially, with the objective of preventing companies moving abroad to better tax environments and if possible attracting companies back to the US which had already fled. (Kudlow and Domitrovic, 2016).

problems (McRae, 2017). Finally, global economic forces and technological progress require common solutions, but politicians lack a way to manage these future evolutions. It is time for change on both sides to prepare for these looming global challenges. Brexit could be the trigger to remodel the EU and its relations with its neighbours for European peace and welfare.

5.3 STONGER OR WEAKER: THE EUROPEAN UNION IN 2026

Brexit has initiated a new discussion about the purpose and pursuit of the EU's guiding idea – to establish economic prosperity and political stability within Europe. With the exit of the UK, the EU loses the world's fifth largest economy, a nuclear power, and a member of the UN Security Council. Perhaps worse, the leading critical and liberal voice in the EU is to disappear. The EU must now adapt to this and take on its new global role: it must shore up its diplomatic and military power to help shape the global governance architecture for peace and security. The idea of an EU army must be realised; a subvened build-up of a new military sector is essential for Europe to be taken seriously internationally. The retreat of the US from globalist leadership underlines the necessity of the EU taking on global responsibility to rebalance and retain economic and political power for Europe (Foster, 2017).

The risk certainly exists that Brexit could foster nationalism in Member States instead of the federalist instincts of the Commission and the Parliament. The EU as a whole has been making little progress towards a "super state" and centrifugal forces could even tear the Union apart. As a result, the closely integrated core group of Member States may be unable to reach consensus with the Member States who want a less binding EU without adoption of a policy of a differential-speed EU. Current and strong Eurosceptic movements in the Netherlands, France, Italy and Poland endanger the stability of the EU. A prevalent dissatisfaction with the EU for its failure to generate enough jobs and economic stability exposes Member States to not only radical nationalism but also external shocks. The resilience of the system is not a given nor is it yet manageable enough to prevent any further disintegration. The EU economy, for example, is still struggling to recover from the financial crisis which is undermining the Italian banking system and deepening the Greek debt crisis. The tsunami of migrants from Africa and the Middle East challenges the economies of the Member States and EU political solidarity and integrity. The zero (or negative) interest and quantitative easing policies of the European Central Bank (ECB) are not only showing scant improvement for the real economy, but they also abuse the public finances to support non-reform-minded Member States. Evidently, the Eurozone is still dependent on non-bank sources of finance such as alternative lending funds, to stabilise the European economy and help fund long-term investment and new startups. The independence of the ECB to preserve monetary soundness has been undercut by political interests involved in solving the Eurozone-crisis triggered by excessive indebtedness in Cyprus, Ireland, Greece *etc*. Due to these recent problems, the ECB has had to limit deflation risk and to avoid unbearable market shocks. Finally, the EU is confronted and must compete with neoliberal Anglo-Saxon capitalism, which is much less regulated and calls for international frameworks of financial regulation such as Basel IV.

Brexit will leave the EU with a budget contribution hole of about €10 billion, causing more tension for the Member States. On top of this, they must fear monetary support will be reduced for Member States that joined after 2004. A budget contribution rise for the strong EU economies will polarise national interests and lead to demands for an increase of decision-making power to reshape the EU. The transfer of EU funds ought to be correlated to attainment of type and degree of milestones in the *acquis* process, in particular for the new Member States. Member States' commitment to the European idea as well as their political will is the basis for stimulating investment-led growth. In fact, the European idea of peace and prosperity ought to be earned by Member States in order to qualify for fiscal transfers, which even ought to be periodically reviewed in the case of recalcitrant Member States like Hungary and Poland.

The role of the European institutions in mediating the power relations between Brussels and its members needs to be clarified. The diversity of EU Member States requires a stringent process of integration and asymmetric centralisation of Member States policies to drive the European idea forward and set priorities. The EU addressed these increasing tensions among Member States with Commission President Juncker's white paper setting out five scenarios for the future of the EU-27 by 2025 (EC, March 2017). This speculative paper makes one part of an endeavour to avoid a further levelling to the lowest common denominator of the EU consensus that could result in lost tempo for integration and whet the appetite more for financial transfers than for economic and political reforms of Member States' systems. The EU must recover the power to act lest by muddling through it fails to consolidate the EU's *telos* of peace and prosperity for Europe. Brexit has nudged the EU into a mood of gathering itself up, affording the opportunity to drive economic and financial policy in the teeth of the remaining euro-out countries. The Capital Market Union could be pushed further toward the realisation of its common regulatory regime. Chances are also available for a centralisation for the European energy markets (Bond *et al.*, 2016).

The EU must cross the Rubicon of leaving behind its negative image and the widespread perception of democratic deficits in its decision-making processes. As its governing bodies ought to have the same democratic legitimacy as national governments and parliaments, more processual transparency is called for as well as more publicity about its costs and benefits. In particular, the EU must address declining incomes due to globalisation and recraft its relevant policies. Winners and losers must be taken equally into account if the EU would achieve social peace and economic stability through free trade and open markets. The EU must set the wider economic framework, which includes market incentives combined with basic social security rights for EU citizens, and integrate them into market policies. The strict fiscal rules falling out of the financial crisis have exacerbated the division into booming and stagnating Member States. The neoliberal view must be supplemented with minimum social security programmes for all EU citizens under national governmental control, but funded by the Member States under EU mandate and regulation. The cost of austerity and structural reforms must be carefully distributed amongst the Member States, as there is no empirical evidence that reforms in the labour markets and in the production markets will boost economic growth (De Grauwe and Ji, 2016; IMF, 2015; De Grauwe, 2016). European funding programmes must support structural changes but also require fiscal policy reforms by Member States. However, only by setting the goal of a targeted "ordoliberal"[76] policy matrix will sustainable growth and a fair distribution that encourages winners and supports losers be achieved.

The centralisation of decisional competence in the EU institutions has met a hostile reception from France and Germany. There is a risk of trading-off of economic and social interests for financial interests, whilst leading EU member states like France and Italy suffer high unemployment and low growth, and are preoccupied with their mounting joint and several debt liabilities. The recent crisis of the EU – Eurozone , Ukraine, floods of refugees – have imposed on the Member States in the European Council a greater role both in setting the EU's strategic direction whilst managing its response to these challenges. The fact remains that the EU lacks a clear vision of its own future development and is ignoring one of its core problems – the crisis of the Eurozone. A decade after the financial crisis began, Eurozone financial institutions are still undercapitalised, governments are still adding to their debts, and the ECB is still pumping money into government and corporate bonds at a monthly volume of €60 billion to stabilise the capital markets. The Stability and Growth Pact is a set of EU-mandated rules requiring Member States to pursue sound public finances and coordinate their fiscal policies. This has been weakened and sometimes violated by the Eurozone countries, and the stipulated ban on monetisation of Member State debts is now routinely ignored. As the Member States grow economically weaker, their self-interest prompts them to convert the Eurozone into a sovereign condominium of joint and several liability – a bailout- or income-transfer union (whereby the solvent are forced to transfer their assets to the insolvent). Such an *ex post* transformation embodies France and Italy's bid, supported by the European insitutions, to deepen the Eurozone's liability solidarity and to widen the scope of the EU's economic policy competence, heedless that this undermines the stability of the euro itself. So long as candid discussion of a strategy for the Eurozone's future remains under interdict, the Eurozone will not be

---

76   Ordoliberalism is a sub-variety of social liberalism, whereby the State is called to intervene to suppress extreme forms of capitalism that could pervert uncontrolled market forces and incentives. This is supposed to produce the Pareto-optimal outcome for businesses and individuals. This concept is widely advocated by politicians in Continental countries such as Germany and France.

supported by all Member States and their citizens. Three basic strategies are available to deal with the Eurozone crisis (Becker and Fuest, 2016):

- *Strategy 1*: The EU "gears" the Monetary Union so that Member States are jointly liable for each other's debts and do transfer to the EU the competence to determine their several debt levels.
- *Strategy 2*: Member States conserve the right to incur debt and leeway to organise their economic policies. There is no liability solidarity for sovereign debt and clear rules for State insolvency are stipulated.
- *Strategy 3*: The euro is abolished and national currencies reintroduced, with all the risks for the European integration process that this entails.

Each strategy would need to be analysed for its impact on the current financial situation of each of the Members States to avoid any further financial crisis. But the result would be to make transparent the real workings of both the Eurozone and the EU, and could be addressed with the chance to develop a long-term Eurozone strategy acceptable to all Member States and to their citizens (Becker, Fuest, 2016).

The five scenarios for the EU-27 up to 2025 which were laid out above in Chapter Three (3.2.34 Institutions) are a sound basis for debate to avoid further policy standstill. The European Commission's discussion papers on the social dimension of Europe, the Monetary Union, the risks of globalisation, the future defence of Europe, and the EU's finances could also intensify the debate on the EU's direction. However, broad agreement does not suffice for taking essential steps if the functioning of the EU institutions is not universally respected. Member States need to materialise and commit resources to tackling the EU's problems and communicating the results to their citizens. As for Brexit negotiations, the EU must take a tough, clear position sending a message to prospective secessionists. Simply put, it is always easier to "run away" (without even a plan) than to invest time and resources to make it better. The EU ought to remember that ever since the UK joined the EU in 1973, it was often seen as a trouble-maker who did not subscribe to deeper integration and harmonisation. The current Brexit negotiation approach reveals that the British strategy remains the same; *i.e.*, to weaken the forces that aim to make Europe stronger. The UK demands a special deal with the EU, all the benefits of the Union without sharing the costs (De Grauwe, 2016), as the first negotiation rounds about free movement commence, as British politicians' statements toward settling their €100 billion EU bill indicate. It is proper that the EU takes a firm stance against a leaving Member State blithely wish-listing its relations with the Union. This will also signal to any other potentially exiting Member State that it will have to bear the costs and will be treated like any other non-Member State. This should boost the EU spirit and may even make the UK reconsider its hard-Brexit decision, including exit of the Single Market. By the end of this negotiation, new terms for future "divorces" will have been defined that should deter any more backsliding.

Brexit must be taken for Europe's chance to take its destiny into its own hands. Besides their current disagreements, the remaining 27 Member States must face their responsibility for security, welfare, and international leadership. The need to reform EU institutions and secure its borders is likelier to drive the EU more together than apart, because it stands for peace, freedom, democracy and welfare, which are worth standing up for. Economic problems and global challenges are too complex to be managed by any one Member State. It will be hard to realise unilateral action like a return to border patrols and protectionism. Technological innovations and productivity revolutions like digitalisation calls for development of a social and economic perspective if one would create a liveable environment for all EU citizens. To win its citizens' to support, the EU must have a long-term vision. Additionally, the EU must take a clear stance on its core values: defended borders, controlled immigration, pursued happiness, and religious charity. The EU must therefore restore confidence, trust and fellow feeling by explaining and integrating Member States and citizens into its multiannual work programmes. All media must be utilised to teach the population the benefits and costs of the EU. At the same time, the EU itself is sorely in need of scrutinising its efficiency, professionalism and administrative overhead for the sake of its citizens. The European Union is more than a public good that bundles national and collective interests to form a Single Market. It stands for freedom, rights, opportunities to develop for each citizen; diversity and solidarity based on European values. These are too many achievements to give up in exchange for perverse ideologies and superseded worldviews.

Betting is a hoary British tradition; the Brits will bet on anything – sports, the outcome of the British or American presidential election, whether it will snow on Christmas, or whether a movie star would win an Oscar. William Hill odds on the "Next country to leave the EU" (aside from the UK) stands until 31 December 2017 at 2/1 for Greece, followed by 5/2 for Italy, 6/1 for Sweden, 10/1 for France, 12/1 for Hungary, and 12/1 for Ireland. In the middle field was Germany at 40/1, Spain at 66/1, and at the other extreme were Latvia at 100/1 and Luxembourg at 150/1 (William Hill website). (Interestingly, William Hill's bet on what will happen when the UK next goes to the polls gave 11/10 for a Labour majority, 15/8 for no overall majority, and only 12/5 for a conservative majority.)

5.4 BUSINESS PREPARATION FOR BREXIT

In the aftermath of the Brexit referendum, there was great uncertainty about what Brexit would mean for businesses, trading partners in the EU, foreign workers in the UK, and British citizens abroad. The question that everyone has been asking was *What will Brexit look like?* The UK government has not been very transparent about its exit strategy and no detailed plan has been forthcoming. Instead, cabinet ministers have been contradicting each other in statements, adding to the confusion, and making it impossible for business to plan ahead in a meaningful way. Even after Article 50 was triggered and the EU-27 leaders published the negotiating guidelines, the staged-process approach still did not provide any real information about how the future of the UK outside the EU would look like in detail.

Theresa May has said, "The country voted to leave the European Union, and as prime minister I will make sure that we leave the European Union." Other than this, everything else has been left up in the air – the form of Brexit, timelines, possible transitional arrangements, and exceptions for certain industry sectors or foreign workers. What is business to do now that Article 50 has been triggered and negotiations with the European Union have started? How is business supposed to manage a process of fraught with high uncertainty or develop contingency plans?

The UK government's vision, the EU's negotiation strategy and timelines are all still known; detailed planning is difficult. However, we highly recommend for companies to get started right away setting up working groups, conducting initial assessments, and working out contingency plans for the scenario that the government decides on a strategy that compromises companies' profitability and prospects in the long term. It is crucial for businessmen to grasp what regulatory regimes having which qualities will impact them, and start up a direct or indirect dialogue (for example through business associations) with the Government to help them reshape the regulatory landscape. David Davis, Secretary of State for Exiting the European Union, told the Commons on the 5th September 2016 that the UK government is "determined to build a national consensus around our negotiating position [and we are] going to talk to as many organisations, companies and institutions as possible". Before the June 2017 election, this important point was widely ignored; however, the hung parliament has put the government under pressure to build consensus and find alliances that support their strategy. For larger organisations that have teams already in place dedicated to public affairs or European affairs, this will be nothing new. Smaller organisations and even individuals can use industry fora or associations to make their voices heard.[77]

Outlined below is the authors' suggested approach to engaging with Brexit at this early stage. It is important to take the initiative and a proactive role if you and your company are to manage the greatest uncertainty that the country has faced in a generation, instead of allowing that uncertainty to overtake your organisation.

1. **Mobilise cross-company Brexit working groups**

    At this point, while the Brexit path remains inchoate, companies should keep their spending low on external advisors and internal resources. However, they should

---

77   For further information, see Guido Reinke (2012) "Industry Governance and Regulatory Compliance: A Theoretical and Practical Guide to European ICT Policy" (GOLD RUSH Publishing).

set up their Brexit working groups (Brexit WGs) right away. Preliminary actions should include:

- Identify key individuals in the organisation who have good subject-matter knowledge in technical areas such as contract law, trade and sales, data governance, and employment law.
- Set up a simple governance structure that will allow these Brexit WGs to meet regularly, to monitor and discuss the latest developments, and to report to a Brexit Steering Committee (Brexit SteerCo) which should meet at least once every quarter.

2. **Pro-active information gathering and external networking**

Businesses need to make informed decisions and not decisions driven by political or personal ambition. Unlike full-time politicians, businesses do not follow a four-year evaluation cycle; they are under constant scrutiny. Customers, suppliers, employees and markets will test, sometimes brutally, whether your business strategy is sound, competitive, and meets their needs. For this reason, information on the following topics relating to Brexit needs to be collected:

- Identify business associates and external working groups that may be dealing with important topics concerning your business.
- Create an inventory of key events to be hosted by business associations, the government, law firms and other professional groups. Make sure that someone from your Brexit WG attends key events and reports back to the team.
- Information gathering and external networking must be carried on as essentials. Business associations, professional associations, law firms and business organisations are hosting events with thought leaders, regulatory experts and peers that debate Brexit topics in a pragmatic way.

3. **Conduct a business impact assessment, identify key regulations, and set up a risks register**

The Brexit WGs should not just "monitor the situation" and report back to the Brexit SteerCo, but proactively conduct a business impact assessment and a Brexit risk assessment. The key deliverables of the Brexit working groups are:

- Conduct a (high-level) business impact assessment, which should be updated on a regular basis. To help top management to understand the issues, the impact assessment should be presented in the form of a SWOT Analysis, which identifies the organisation's internal strengths and weaknesses, as well as its external opportunities and threats from Brexit.
- Compile and maintain a list of laws and regulations that, if changed, could impact how the organisation is able to operate.
- Update the domain of specific risks on a much more granular level than the risk registers within which many organisations already (think they) cover Brexit.

4. **Develop a Brexit position paper**

   Once the business impact assessment and risk register have been reviewed, we strongly recommend developing a position paper that articulates what a "good Brexit" would look like, and what would be unacceptable. This means that:

   - One important outcome of the working groups should be a *Brexit position paper*, which should outline the organisation's key profit centres. It should take a clear position on topics such as tax and tariffs, access to the Single Market, employment of foreign workers, and collaboration and trade with EU partners.

   - The position paper should be authorised by the SteerCo and top management, and categorised as pubic-unclassified, which would allow representatives of the organisation to present it at pubic events; share it with other organisation and associations; and even discuss it directly with government officials.

   - In the run-up to the referendum, the top management of many organisations did took no position and kept mum as if the outcome had no impact on them. Now it's time to articulate clearly where the organisation stands, or it will have to live with the decisions that public servants will make on their own.

5. **Understand the key stakeholders in the process and which channels to engage them through**

   It is important that the Brexit WGs understand the process and the stakeholders that will shape the organisation's future relationship with the EU. The actions required are:

   - Attain an overview of the UK and EU authorities and other stakeholders who will be involved in the negotiations. Indicative timelines should be added.

   - Identify the authorities and stakeholders with whom the business should establish contact.

   - Assess how best to establish contact (*e.g.* directly or through industry associations?).

6. **Influencing government corporately or through associations**

   - Develop a communications plan for engaging effectively with internal and external stakeholders. Brexit will be not a one-off event, but a lengthy process requiring a long-term campaign.

   - It is necessary to influence the government corporately or through business associations. Government officials do have only very limited knowledge about how different industrial sectors operate; how they interact with the EU and the rest of the world; and what a bad Brexit would look like. Ultimately, the government is responsible for guaranteeing a stable political environment in which business can flourish, in order to secure job creation and continuous tax revenue. If industry sectors can form a united voice, the government will have to listen or it knows it will compromise the future of the country.

7. **Stay positive, but be prepared with a contingency plan**
   - The Brexit WGs have to assess and evaluate alternatives as they emerge for their effect on single businesses as well as on the whole sector. The ongoingly updated, modified assessments provide informational grist for the Brexit WGs to project likely Brexit scenarios. The Brexit WGs must define short-, medium- and long-term actions that need approval by the SteerCo and top management. Reports issued by the WGs and that consider different stakeholder views will promote plans to cope with different Brexit scenarios. Furthermore, businesses are well advised to set up a contingency plan, including measures for adjustments and transition to a new business environment.

5.5 POSSIBLE BREXIT SCENARIOS

Although the May Government seems to assume a hard Brexit, there are actually options. For example, the EFTA states – Iceland, Liechtenstein, Norway and Switzerland – have their own special relationship with the EU. Norway and Switzerland were among the founding members of EFTA in 1960. Iceland joined in 1970, followed by Liechtenstein in 1991. Norway (from 1994), Iceland (from 1994) and Liechtenstein (from 1995) are parties to the European Economic Area (EEA), while Switzerland has signed a set of bilateral agreements with the EU (EFTA, 2017). Unlike the EFTA countries, which are all in the Schengen Area, the UK never signed up to the Schengen Agreement; thus, it already maintains internal border controls and its own visa policy. EFTA, therefore, though not EU Member States, are integrated on the same level as, if not higher than the UK. This is also evidenced by their immigration levels (from all countries of origin): Liechtenstein leads with 33.1%, followed by Switzerland with 28.9%, Norway with 13.8%, and Iceland with 10.7% (based on the 2015 UN report Trends in International Migrant Stock). This compares to just 11.3% immigrants from all sources out of the population of the UK. Leave campaigners who kept suggesting a "Swiss model" or "Norwegian model" either did not understand those arrangements or were hoping people would associate them with Swiss chocolate and the Alps.

The following table provides an overview of possible Brexit models.

Figure 16: Summary of Brexit Models

Model	Background	Schengen Agreement party?	Total immigration (2015)	Access to Single Market	Adoption of EU legislation	Contribut-ion to EU budget (2015)
UK (current)	Directly involved in EU policy-making with full voting rights.	No	11.3%	Full access	Full	Yes €18,209 m
Iceland	EEA and EFTA member	Yes	10.7%	Yes	Yes Indirect not direct	Yes (reduced)
Lichtenstein	EEA and EFTA member	Yes	33.1%	Yes	Yes Indirect not direct	Yes (reduced)
Norway	EEA and EFTA member. Vast majority of EU legislation is adopted. Exempt are fishery, agriculture, financial policy, and foreign policy. Norway has less influence over content of EU legislation than a member state and no formal voting power.	Yes	13.8%	Full access	Yes Indirect not direct	Yes (reduced)
Switzerland	EFTA member. Sector-specific bilateral agreements with the EU. Participation in EU energy market. Adoption of most EU regulations.	Yes	28.9%	Sector specific based on bilateral agreements	Partly Indirect in some areas	None Yes (reduced)
Andorra	Special microstate EU-relationship. Participates in EU Customs Union and its official currency is the euro. Special relationship with the EU and is treated as an EU member for trade in manufactured goods (no tariffs) and as a non-EU member for agricultural products.	In principle (no visa require-ments)	N/A	Partly Customs union with the EU	Partly (environ-ment, communi-cations, transport, taxation)	From 2017
Monaco	Participates in EU Customs Union. Close relationship with France and the EU; relations are based on a collection of agreements covering specific issues	In principle (no visa require-ments)	N/A	Customs union with the EU (European monetary union)	Partly (goods, excise duties and VAT)	None

Model	Background	Schengen Agreement party?	Total immigration (2015)	Access to Single Market	Adoption of EU legislation	Contribut-ion to EU budget (2015)
San Marino	Participates in EU Customs Union Close relationship with Italy and the EU; relations are based on a collection of agreements covering specific issues; negotiations ongoing of greater integration of San Marino into the EU	In principle (no visa require-ments)	N/A	Customs union with the EU (incl. agri-cultural products, (European monetary union)	Partly (sales tax, consum-ption tax)	None
Canada (Free trade agreement)	Comprehensive free trade agreement (CETA) with the EU allowing access to the internal market for goods, and less for services.	No	N/A	Partly	No	None
Turkey	Participates in EU Customs Union. No tariffs on industrial goods.	No	N/A	Partly Customs union with the EU	Partly	None
WTO	Defined tariffs will apply under the rules of the World Trade Organisation	No	N/A	No	No	None

Source: (Wikipedia, 2017; BBC, June 2016; Colson, 2016)

A study of these diverse agreements, arrangements and relationships with the EU gives some indication of a targetable Brexit model. The differences between these models determine the shape and impact of a new UK relationship with the EU. The negotiation of it links up to legal and political processes that may require a trade-off of prioritised aspects of models and establishment of specific agreements with the EU. A "pick and mix" menu of different models is one approach to reaching for the future of UK-EU relations (Hogan Lovells, 2016).

5.6 CONCLUSIONS: WHAT ARE THE LESSONS OF BREXIT

For more than 40 years British politics has been markedly more Eurosceptic than people on the Continent. Unlike on the Continent, the UK's national curriculum for schools utterly neglected education in European politics. The authors have reviewed the history and citizenship syllabuses, but found that no reference to the UK's relationship with Europe Union is any longer made, thus there is no requirement for pupils to study the EU at all at the primary and secondary school level (Telegraph, September 2016). As the outcome of the referendum has made clear, whole generations of British people still believe stereotypes such as that the EU is the extinction of British culture, whilst remaining ignorant of just the rudiments of how the EU institutions work. Even more worrying is that even MPs can't be counted on to master these rudiments, not even the requirements of the free movement of people, capital, services, and goods. Some of the old guard who preach tolerance and diversity in Britain don't apply the same values to collaboration and integration of common interests with Europe.

And then there is the British Empire, on which the sun never set. Unlike the EU, all these dominions, colonies, protectorates, mandates and other territories were able to be ruled by the British Empire, which in 1913 held sway over 412 million people, roughly the current population of the EU, or 23% of the world's population, inhabiting 24% of Earth's total land area. Today Britain is sovereign over only 14 territories outside the British Isles, which were renamed the British Overseas Territories in 2002. Most of the Empire has become independent whilst remaining in the Commonwealth of Nations, which has 53 member states forming a voluntary association of equal members. But the dream lives on, and EU-28 with a population of over 510 million, was always seen as uncontrollable competition. The memories have been kept alive by the most Excellent Order of the British Empire, which make knights of men and dames of women. Citizens of Commonwealth countries have been allowed to vote in UK national elections where EU citizens, even if living in the UK for 15 years, were not.

When a nation in this condition was called to an in-out EU Referendum, all this combined with the refugee crisis gave the upper hand to nationalistic and populist politicians. The referendum question was not anything like "*Yes, we can reform*" or "*Let's join hands make things better*", but rather "*Let's take* back *control*" and make the UK "great again". The world, however, has a nasty habit of moving on. It's global, complicated and controlled by big business and bilateral agreements between economic blocs. There are no colonies anymore, no tax havens (at least to create new ones would be a challenge under OECD and other frameworks) and no new worlds lie open to discovery. The world is a crowded place where ne'er-do-wells like politicians, lawyers, professionals, and powerful businesses have the last word. Fighting political and trade battles in a globalised world alone will not breed success; countries need strong alliances and partners with common values and interests in this utterly changed situation.

On June 23 "the British people decided" to leave the European Union. Did they really? EU citizens residing in the UK were not disenfranchised, even British citizens living in the EU (around 2.2 million) and overseas (around 5.5 million). Yet citizens of Commonwealth countries, most of which had no relationship to EU, were enfranchised. A bare question was put to just these people, but rules of participation seemed arbitrary and the consequences of exit, and how they should be managed, were not even addressed. The promises made were irrelevant, and at some point it felt like "Dick Whittington and His Cat" had been sold to the people as a true story. But the stubborn fact remains on the morning after that one can no more make a fortune off the rat-catching abilities of a cat than the streets outside the EU are paved with gold.

Clearly, democracy needs some kind of framework of sober orderliness. One might put every conceivable question to The People *via* referendum, but if the outcome has predictably, overwhelmingly negative consequences, or leads to political unrest, instability, constitutional crisis, or unnecessary polarisation of the populace, a referendum should at least be more solicitously managed. No one would put to a referendum a question like, "Shall the monarchy be abolished and the UK become a republic?" Or, "Shall capital punishment be reintroduced?", or "Shall all taxes be cut by 10%?", or "Shall the UK be dissolved into four nations: England, Wales, Scotland and North Ireland?". Who would let The People declare war and peace or ask in a referendum, "Shall Britain go to war with *evil country xyz?*". No MP would dare show the same enthusiasm for that as for Brexit if the question had been, "Shall the number of the members of the House of Commons be reduced from 650 to 325?". Those referenda ought not to be held the consequences of which one would not like to live with and is unprepared for.

What is the legacy and what will future generations remember about Brexit? If the disintegration of the "United" Kingdom continues and no compromise is forthcoming, Boris Johnson and Nigel Farage will be remembered not only for taking the country out of the EU, but also for precipitating the breakup of the more than 300-year-old Union between Scotland and England. The Act of Union 1707 might be dissolved soon after The European Communities Act 1972 c. 68 is repealed. Without doubt, this is one legacy no one really wants to be remembered for in years to come.

Scotland's taxpayers are not net beneficiaries of EU largesse either. They pay more than £1.4 billion towards the EU every year and receive only about £1.1 billion back through the Rebate and EU funding like Common Agricultural Policy subsidies. Also, based on figures released by the Institute for Fiscal Studies, the UK subsidies Scotland by around £900 million of tax revenues from the rest of the UK.

The following Sections summarise some of the conclusions to be drawn from the facts and figures presented in previous chapters of this book.

5.6.1 "The people have spoken", but not all people were asked

It's a legitimate question to ask why EU citizens who were registered residents, had lived for five years or more in the UK, and paid taxes were not allowed to vote? It could as legitimately be asked why residents from Commonwealth countries and the Republic of Ireland were eligible? Resident EU citizens had far more at stake than immigrants from the Commonwealth. For that matter, why were 16- and 17-year-olds disenfranchised in contrast to the Scottish Independence referendum, to say nothing of the 6.8 million British citizens living abroad? *Of course* there must be electoral rules, but let us not entertain sweeping statements like "the British people have spoken". Considering the narrow margin of the vote, it seems as if the decision could have been achieved by flipping a coin.

To sum it up, the point is not that the Scottish referendum eligibility rules are some kind of moral absolute; it is rather that no single truth or universal justice can subsist unless there is a single standard of comparability. So long as there is inconsistency between UK referenda concerning who is eligible to vote, the claim that "the people have spoken" is incoherent and not perfectly legitimate, especially given a situation where the referendum is won by a small margin and a significant number of campaign promises are cavalierly broken.

5.6.2 We want our country back: A shift in political powers

The slogan endlessly repeated by the Leave campaign was "We want our country back" and "Take back control". What these politicians failed to mention was *who* wants to take back control. Clearly it isn't the working class people in Liverpool, the academics in Oxford, the dockworkers and construction workers at the shipyard in Chatham, the people depending on tourism in York, or the public administrators in Lincoln. Democracy allows them to participate every four years in elections, participate in meetings with their local Councils, and if they are lucky, they are allowed to give their opinion in a referendum.

The real power lies with the money and media that can make or break (career) politicians in national parliaments and governments, and the public officials at regional and local level that the politicians appoint, guided by the invisible hand of the financial market. Brexit will lead to a power shift; but not from Brussels to The People, but from Brussels bureaucrats to other "usual suspects" in the UK – "civil servants", political bundlers, media moguls, big business players and high financiers in the City. After some initial chaos, a new power is emerging, and PM Cameron's negotiation triumphs and 43 years of European integration have been wiped out overnight.

Who is back in power became clear during the Tory Party conference in Birmingham in October 2016. For a few months the country saw who was in charge. PM May promised to "take Britain out of the European Union" at the Birmingham International Convention Centre, which was built in 1991 with £49.7 million in funding from the European Council towards its construction. The mood of Euroscepticism and patriotism was celebrated and applauded. The announcement that Article 50 would be executed by March and that Britain would become "a fully sovereign and independent country" pleased hard-line Eurosceptic conservatives if not UKIP politicians, as the Tory Party had succeeded in stealing UKIP's thunder. Nigel Farage, the figurehead of UKIP, gamely stated that he could not have said it better, but he must have been aware that the follow-on local and national elections saw a complete meltdown of UKIP's support as their voters deserted to the Tories instead.

In her keynote speech at the conference, May outlined her vision for Brexit. She described Brexit as "a turning point for our country, presenting a once-in-a-generation chance to change the direction of our nation for [the] good". She also said: "This

Government will not waver in its commitment to put the interests of the British people first." That specific promises were made to "British people", in particular to "give our NHS the £350m the EU takes every week" and "A vote for leave will be a vote to cut immigration" were not on the table any more (*The Guardian*, 27 June 2016).

5.6.3 Different views between Westminster and Brussels

Two different worldviews clash between Brussels and Westminster, both before and after the referendum. The European view is to unite, integrate and harmonise. Anybody who has ever had the good fortune to work in Brussels or Luxembourg – either for business or in political affairs – will affirm that working in this European-infused atmosphere is stimulating, and foments interest in other European cultures. This view requires compromise at all levels, learning from history and remembering post-War, divided Europe, which is a constant reminder that uncompromisingness leads to conflicts.

The Eurosceptic view is a self-absorbed, egocentric one, which often forgets that the United Kingdom consists of four nations (three with now-devolved governments) which have different interests just like EU Member States. European cross-fertilisation as one finds on the Continent, where diversity inspires new ideas for collaboration, is considered secondary and is even seen by many hardliners as undesirable. This is more the view of an islander looking out from Westminster over the channel at what is happening on the Continent. A view shared by many Westminster politicians is that the country needs to retake control to form "special partnerships" with the USA and Commonwealth countries rather than joining-in with its European neighbours. History is remembered in the UK much more in a heroic and positive way than on Continental Europe, and for many, the British Empire still lives on in their hearts and minds. High hopes that post-Brexit Britain can boost Commonwealth trade are nostalgic, and a relaunch of Empire 2.0 is another fairy tale spread by hardliner Brexiteers and even by some inside Whitehall (Olusoga, 19 March 2017). These views may explain why some British people find it difficult to "surrender" to the European idea of integration.

5.6.4 The British Isles: Isolation *versus* immigration

At the Birmingham Tory Party conference, the PM announced that ministers will consider new tests to "ensure people coming here are filling gaps in the labour market, not taking jobs British people do". This means that the May Government is committed to violating the basic principles of the European project. Business demands access to cheaper qualified labour supplied in part by EU citizens, the Government is also failing to satisfy the demands of private business. The same logic applies to state-owned entities like the National Health Service, which also demands easy access to qualified nurses and other staff without having to pay more, so that even the interests of the public sector and the quality of their services may be compromised, at least in the short run. And do not forget that in the early 2010s one-third of doctors were immigrants (Economist, 2017).

International Trade Secretary and leading Brexiteer Liam Fox added to the anti-EU sentiment, saying that immigrants who "consume" Britain's wealth are not welcome in the country. This xenophobia runs consistently through the Leave campaign, and now finds itself in the mainstream of Westminster politics. Previously these views were associated with UKIP and political parties of the far left and right, but now it is a widely accepted view, notwithstanding that the facts herein tell a different tale.

On the other side of the debate, it is also true that the widespread assumption is mistaken that mere growth of the gross domestic product (or company profits for that matter) will benefit the average person. The merits of both governments and businesses are inaptly judged by raw growth numbers, as this predicts gross tax revenue for governments and gross profits for businesses. But this tells nothing about *per capita* income and therefore personal wealth. The latter might even fall, or inflation might depress *per capita* income. Thus, the net personal wealth of the citizenry of a country is quite independent of immigration and its effect on raw growth statistics, and the proper standard of well-being should be average personal income not GDP.

5.6.5 Brexit: A gigantic transformation programme

Democracy typically entails engagement with stakeholders at all levels of civic society. At least one would expect that major players such as the First Minister of Scotland, the Mayor of London, mayors from cities in North England, and delegates of corporations that employ hundreds of thousands should be involved in the bargaining. When the Brexit negotiations began to be planned, there was no template of who should be part of the inner circle and decide the future of EU citizens living in the UK. Until the snap election in June 2017 there was little evidence (specific actions, not just words) that the Government was engaging with all these stakeholders. One year after the referendum, PM May's statement that she would not give a "running commentary on Brexit negotiations" exacerbated the "huge uncertainty" over Brexit. Conflicting signals and mixed messages might leak out from time to time, undermining confidence and predictability. Corporations may lose patience and investors just decide to walk away. Ex-PM Cameron's apocalyptic warning that leaving the EU is a "leap in dark" may be fulfilled. And then there is the uncertainty that Brexit might prove a "No Deal". With a multi-billion pound so-called Brexit Bill (*a.k.a* Brexit Divorce Bill) still to be agreed, Brexit Secretary David Davis has admitted that a no-deal leaving definitely could happen (Curtis, 5 August 2017). The fateful words in the Conservative manifesto that "No Deal is better than a bad deal" is still on the table. It rings true on an emotional level, but it still lacks a clear definition of what "bad" means, even if the outcome does depend on the effort the UK team puts into preparing, forming clear positions, their technical understanding how the EU operates and willingness to compromise. Many would note that little evidence shows any of this in place yet. Expecting a good result while the UK position remains unclear and tensions roil the UK government is unrealistic. It almost seems like the Government are preparing the country for an "utterly disastrous" outcome that could cost the economy between 2.6% and 5.5% of GDP, or between £50 billion and £100 billion, by 2020 (Chu, 28 May 2017).

5.6.6 Money flows in both directions

Voters who never questioned the claims made by the campaigns received the impression that funds only flowed from Westminster to Brussels. The fact is that Brussels is a mighty centrifuge redistributing funds from richer countries to poorer countries and sub-national regions. The authors have presented data in the various chapters above about financial affairs; how much the UK has been contributing to the EU budget; and how much the UK is receiving from the EU.

5.6.7 A constitutional crisis: Turmoil and the cost of Brexit

The same grievances Eurospectics bring against the EU could with equal justice be turned on Westminster. Due in part to the first-past-the-post electoral rule, Westminster is said to incur a notorious democratic deficit. And PM May was never elected by the people outside of her constituency when she inherited her office after the referendum. The Brexit plans (if any) seem not to have been shared with her own MPs, not to mention the British people, for the first year after the referendum. What kind of democracy is this?

Ex-Chancellor of the Exchequer George Osborne warned that leaving the EU would hit the economy hard and force tax increases. Many independent institutes also warned of the consequences. It is only to be expected, then, that if things go sour, the Government will have to increase taxes and cut benefits – all with the justification that the British people knew of the consequences but against all odds decided to regain their sovereignty through a difficult process that requires sacrifice. That way, nobody can blame the bad process, bad negotiations, or the self-interest of the Westminster elite.

The EU has become like a dinosaur. Reaching consensus amongst 28 (soon 27) Member States is much harder than amongst the EU-15, the halcyon days that ended with East Enlargement in 2004. After living on Earth for about 165 million years, the dinosaurs went extinct at the end of the Cretaceous Period 65 million years ago. The EU will go extinct – maybe not overnight as some Eurosceptic politicians predict, but a slow death over many years – unless it reforms. But this is only possible by listening to European citizens. After all, everybody loves a dinosaur! Even Walt Disney saw commercial and educational value in producing the movie "Living with the dinosaurs". So it's worth making the European institutions fitter for survival as well as more likeable.

5.6.8 The Third Force: The markets

Theresa May sees herself as a leader who "provides strong leadership" to execute the "will of the people", but without inquiring too deeply into what the people want or entertaining any prospect of letting them decide in another referendum if they really like the eventual Brexit deal. A large-scale transformation programme like Brexit calls for stakeholder engagement and consensus.

Brexit is going to be decided by three factors other than the May Government nevertheless. The first force is the British people. As evidenced in Chapter Two, if the Scottish Independence referendum rules had been applied to Brexit, it could easily have altered the outcome. There was no united voice, but young *versus* old, cities *versus* countryside, establishment *versus* the protest vote. The £142.4 million estimated cost of conducting the referendum could have been saved by flipping a coin (*Daily Express*, 23 April 2016).

The second force is the European Union and its Member States. The outcome of the EU Referendum caused chaos, and in order to prevent this the Member States made commitments to Cameron to sweeten the UK's membership, so long as this would not lead them to deviate from the four principles. Cameron's success in negotiating a special status for the UK just 6 months before the referendum was brilliant, but Brexiteers and the media both totally ignored the extent of his victory or even ridiculed him for it.

The third force is the markets. The markets are generally defined as the sum total of what happens when buyers meet sellers. The financial markets, manufacturers and exporters of products, and the service industry will decide the success of Brexit … or lead to its collapse. If the economy contracts, the pound depreciates, and people lose their jobs over the next 2-3 years, Brexit will have been a disaster. Regardless of the outcome of the referendum, nobody voted to be poorer. On 7 October a flash crash caused a 7% drop of the pound Sterling in Asia. Once Article 50 was triggered and months of uncertainty were started, with rumours and leakage of information emerged, and the volatility of the pound on the forex markets increased. If panic kicks in, if corporations employing thousands of people decide to move headquarters, if shareholders and pensioners start to lose their savings, and inflation increases, it may lead to social unrest and calls for new election and/ or referendum, and anything is possible. It is a huge gamble, and most economists and businesses are worried. The third force is the most powerful. The old saw is true, that the markets decide, not politicians.

5.6.9 Benefits of immigration

Denunciations of the economic impact of immigrants was voiced at the Conservative Party conference in Birmingham in October 2016. Home Secretary Amber Rudd suggested that foreigners are "taking jobs British people could do", and the International Trade Secretary, Liam Fox, said some immigrants "come to the country and consume the wealth of the country without ever having created anything". Theresa May herself said in her closing speech that some Britons have been pushed out of work due to low-paid immigrants.

As detailed in previous sections of this book, there is consistent research indicating that Brexit and a lack of EU migrants could lead to disastrous labour shortages. The UK has already seen skill shortages in the health sector, where there are more than 20,000 vacancies for nurses, engineering, IT, carer work, seasonal agriculture, and accountancy. UK firms have reported difficulty filling vacancies and retaining existing staff. The government would need to craft an immigration policy better than what already exists lest the vulnerability of British businesses to losing key employees will abound (MacLeod and Roberts, 13 June 2017; IPPR report, 29 March 2017) A Deloitte study found out that 47% of high-skilled EU citizens employed in the UK are considering leaving the UK within the next five years. There are regional and sectoral variances in the perceptions of workers; for example, in the Northern Powerhouse region 21% are considering leaving, compared to 59% in London (Deloitte, April 2017).

The UK is seeking free trade deals with the EU which would allow extensive trade in both goods and services. Most trade deals the EU has with foreign states include provisions on immigration, and the Institute for Public Policy Research (IPPR) suggest six options for a UK-EU agreement on migration:

- Option 1: temporary controls on free movement: The government would temporarily introduce limits on free movement for particular sectors or regions during periods of high EU inflows.
- Option 2: free movement for those with a job offer: Free movement would continue as before for workers, students, family members and the self-sufficient, but jobseekers would no longer have the right to reside in the UK.
- Option 3: free movement for certain flows: Free movement between the UK and the EU would continue for particular workers – for instance, certain professions and workers in particular sectors – as well as non-active groups.
- Option 4: points-based system: EU nationals seeking the right to work in the UK would need to meet the requirements of a points-based system. Points could be allocated on the basis of criteria such as highest qualification level, age and language ability.
- Option 5: 'preferential' system for EU nationals: EU nationals coming to the UK to work would face a more relaxed version of the rules non-EU nationals currently face.
- Option 6: controls on EU labour migration; free movement for others: The UK would be at liberty to set its own rules for EU workers and the self-employed – in practice most likely applying the same system that currently operates for non-EU nationals – but would agree to facilitate continued free movement, as far as is feasible, for students, family members, and the self-sufficient.
(IPPR, 28 April 2017)

Concluding on immigration, the government needs to be more creative than bringing immigration from the EU to a standstill. The Australian-style points-system for immigration has been scrapped, and there are still more immigrants from non-EU countries than from EU countries; whilst EU nationals are the workforce group contributing the most to the economic productivity of the country and its taxable income.

5.6.10 What next: "God save the Queen" *versus* "Ode to Joy"

The authors of this book have a "can-do" attitude, and enjoy the freedoms that Europe offers. Coming of age at a time when walls and barbed wire fences divided Europe, and Communist regimes did not allow their citizens to travel freely, the authors grew up believing that talented, hard-working people who contribute to the society ought to be allowed to live and work throughout a united Europe.

By putting up psychic walls between the British people and the European mainland, the Government do not only harm business, but also the freedom and development of their people. For future generations, it will be more difficult to study and work abroad, and the standards of education and competitiveness risk falling behind the rest of Europe.

The European Union needs reform, no doubt. Sixty years of success have made many Eurocrats complacent. Some live in a gilded bubble, with tax-free incomes much higher than the average, insulated from what average working class people think. The Union needs to listen to its citizens again, and needs to perceive wake-up calls like David Cameron's "special status", proposed months before the referendum, not as a threat but as a harbinger of the need for improvement and reform. In this sense, Brexit might be a good thing, if the European institutions begin to listen much more carefully in future and get serious about certain self-improvement.

This does not mean that Britain should have run away from its responsibility for reforms. To hold a seat at the table is a stronger position than deserting and watching others make the hard decisions. But then, maybe it's in the British genes, or to put it more politely, the English *heritage* to "rule and not be ruled". Westminster politicians are not the best negotiators and compromisers, as evidenced by the current state of the United Kingdom: – Scotland wants independence; Wales complains that its interests are ignored; Northern Ireland's devolved government collapsed in January 2017; and London has big concerns about the Government's Hard Brexit course. In principle it ought to be so much simpler to find consensus between four nations than 28 Member States.

5.7 FINAL REFLECTIONS

This book has covered much ground and the authors have worked tirelessly to sift through the available data and assess the latest developments. In general, we tried to be as objective as possible in our analyses. As both authors have lived for many years both in the UK and on the Continent, our views are balanced by life experience. Both of us are used to taking an analytical, fact-based approach to decision-making.

Firstly, on the empirical side the authors have looked back at history. Since the UK joined the EU on 1 January 1973, the relationship with the EU has sometimes been turbulent, and yet widespread public perception to the contrary notwithstanding, even Margaret Thatcher passionately favoured Britain's membership of the EU in the first in-out referendum on 6 June 1975. She was the one who saved Britain's membership again by securing an EU budget rebate for the UK in 1984, and she strongly defended the UK's place in Europe. The outcome of a badly managed, consultative-only second referendum on 23 June 2016 has led to a different fate. The process of leaving the EU officially started by triggering Article 50 on 29 March 2017, and the clock is now ticking with a formal end date on 20 March 2019. Whilst the EU-27 follow a "clinical" process, the UK government take a rather flexible approach where, apart from 12 abstract "high-level priorities", no specific policy objectives were set from the beginning of the process.

Secondly, the authors took a statistical numbers-crunching approach. At the end of the day, numbers don't lie. There were more than 160 polls prior the referendum indicating that Remain would win, but the result was 48.1% for Remain *vs.* 51.9% for Leave. That is true. And yet Scotland, Northern Ireland, London, and Gibraltar voted by large majorities to remain. 73% of the 18-24 year olds voted to remain (but 20% of this age group even did not register to vote and only an estimated 36% actually did vote). This raises questions about what the outcome of a second referendum to pass judgment on the leaving-terms might be like, or what the results in five years time might look like when this age group takes a more active role in politics. And then there is the question what might have happened if the 3.3 million EU citizens in the UK had been allowed to vote, along with the estimated 6.7 million British expatriates, actual British citizens who live abroad, a significant fraction of whom were disenfranchised for having resided outside the UK for more than 15 years. One can take a critical view of polls and economic reports; however, only a few of these authors reviewed indicated that the UK would be better off once it left the EU.

The authors also provided an overview of the benefits of EU citizenship as defined in Articles 18 to 25 of the Treaty on the Functioning of the European Union. Leaving the EU means losing 27 passports just to save an annual average membership fee of £130.03 per person. To understand why, despite all odds, a small majority voted Leave, the authors analysed the reasons why the Leave campaign won.

Thirdly, the authors analysed the impact on 35 policy areas covered by the *acquis Communautaire*. These include literally everything in one's personal and work life. Besides the four EU principles of free movement of goods, people, services and capital, it covers good governance and rules for an effective and transparent public sector, including public procurement procedures; sub-national regional policy; economic and monetary policy; justice, freedom and security; external relations; foreign security and defence policy; financial controls and budgetary provisions; and other topics. Policy impacts on business and work life include company and competition law; various industry specific regulations (*e.g.* financial services, information society and media, agriculture, fisheries); taxation; social policy and employment; and the Customs Union. The quality of life is covered by policies on food safety; science and research; education and culture; transport policy; energy; environment; consumer and health protection. The authors defined and analysed the Brexit impact on each of these policy domains. The May Government have not conducted such an assessment, and their approach seems to be reactive rather than pro-active. Having huge resources available, the question is why the Government have never published detailed positions and impact analyses for any of these 35 domains before Brexit negotiations started. There are only three conclusions that could be made: (1) politicians in general and the current Government in particular lack the skills to manage large transformational programmes; (2) they had little understanding of how the EU functions; and/or (3) they have chosen to take the British "Keep calm and carry on" approach, which copes with being unprepared, hoping that muddling through will be possible. Whatever the reason is, it was clear from the beginning that the EU-27 had their ducks in a row: they defined the process; took clear positions and drew red lines; are united, unlike the UK; and are driving the process.

Fourthly, the authors tried to illustrate how democracy works: whether and under what circumstances the referendum in particular is a proper democratic tool. They looked at results of elections in the UK and the US, where candidates and parties won without an absolute majority of votes. They also investigated how referenda are run and the recommendations of the Electoral Reform Society on improving the conduct of future referenda. They provided data evidencing that if the same rules had applied to the EU Referendum as to the Scottish Independence referendum (*i.e.* EU citizens and 16- to 17-year-olds had been eligible), Remain would have won.

Lastly, the authors provided an overview of how businesses can deal with the extreme uncertainty: they can (1) mobilise cross-company Brexit working groups; (2) pro-actively gather information and network externally; (3) conduct business impact assessments, identifying key regulations and creating a risk register; (4) develop Brexit position papers; (5) understand the key stakeholders involved in the process and the channels by which to engage them; (6) influence government individually and through associations; and (7) stay positive, but be prepared with a continuity plan. The authors also touched on possible Brexit scenarios and how the future may look.

By analysing the motives and implications of Brexit, this book has given insight into its hard facts and likely consequences. The authors have attempted to avoid taking sides for or against any stakeholder who was and still is involved in the process – from the Remain and Leave campaign, to the UK government, to its domestic opposition, to the EU-27 and the EU negotiating team. The authors employed an empirical and practical approach, and drew conclusions based on facts and figures mainly provided by surveys, secondary sources and the press.

Every author has beliefs and political views. The authors of this book have in the past voted for parties across most of the political spectrum, except for extremists who only aim to destroy but have no programme to create a better world. They believe Brexit is a form of destruction or at least an attempt to turn back time and turn one's back on Europe. Nothing promised by the Brexiteers – from the £350 million a week for the NHS to lower immigration – did or will materialise. The Leave campaign and Government have confirmed this already. The only change that is likely if the UK goes ahead with a hard Brexit is that "we" (meaning the Westminster politicians and Brexiteers) get control. By no means will it mean that the four nations of England, Scotland, Wales, and North Ireland and their people will benefit. The man on the street will have to pay for it with higher taxes and fewer social services, but will still have to pay Council taxes and parking fines. Finally, the British population is likely to suffer from higher consumer prices, a weaker British pound, and increased inflation.

The EU is far from perfect. But since the EU Referendum, the EU-27 have become more united than Great Britain. The UK, its politicians, even politicians within their own parties, and the people as a whole are polarised. Instead of spending billions on a process of leaving the EU and trying to rebuild trade and other relationships over many years, with uncertain results – (some counties have already to demanded easier access to the UK labour market as part of any trade deal), – the time, money and energy would have been better spent on reforming the EU and benefiting from the new trade agreements that the EU has lately signed just since the referendum with countries like Canada and Japan.

If politicians in Westminster tell the public that the UK is not leaving Europe, but only the European Union, it is because the UK never did sign up to "ever closer union". Europe is a geographical, cultural, historical, and social construct with common values but without frontiers, where businesses can offer their goods and services, and people can freely move, live and work. This is guaranteed by the European Union and its Treaties. The Brexiteers have decided not be part of Europe. They prefer to chase nostalgia and dream of turning back time instead shaping the future with their close neighbours who share their common values.

BIBLIOGRAPHY

Agreement between the Conservatives and Unionist Party and the Democratic Unionist Party to support for the government in parliament (26 June 2017).

Allen, Robert; Thorley, Marc (2016) "Brexit effect on EU retail finance and consumer protection legislation", Simons & Simons, August 2016, website at http://www.el-exica.com/-/media/files/articles/2016/comsumer%20products%20and%20retail%20finance/brexit%20effect%20on%20eu%20retail%20finance%20and%20consum-er%20protection%20legislation.pdf (accessed October 2017).

Allen & Overy (8 February 2016) "Brexit – legal consequences for commercial parties: Tax and the implication of Brexit", Specialist paper No. 8, website at http://www.allenovery.com/SiteCollectionDocuments/AO_05_Brexit_Specialist_paper_Tax.pdf (accessed October 2016).

Amaro, Silvia (27 March 2017) "Here's how important the UK is to the European Union", CNBC, website at http://www.cnbc.com/2017/03/27/european-union-uk-important-brexit.html (accessed July 2017).

Andor, László (16 June 2016) "The economic and social consequences of Brexit", IMK Insitut für Makroökonomie und Konjunkturforschung, York, Festival of Ideas, website at http://www.boeckler.de/pdf/v_2016_06_16_vortrag_andor.pdf (accessed November 2016).

Ariès, Quentin; de La Baume, Maïa (25 October 2016) "Brexit throws EU budget off course", Politico, website at http://www.politico.eu/article/brexit-throws-eu-budget-off-course-uk-jes-geier-europe/ (accessed March 2017).

Arnold, Martin; Parker, George; Barker, Alex (16 October 2016) "UK looks at paying billions into EU budget after Brexit", *Financial Times*, website at https://www.ft.com/content/a8ec5e90-938c-11e6-a1dc-bdf38d484582 (accessed March 2017).

Aubrey, Thomas; Reed, Alastair (October 2016) "Report: rebalancing the UK economy – A post-Brexit industrial strategy", Centre for Progressive Capitalism, website at http://progressive-capitalism.net/wp-content/uploads/2016/10/Rebalancing-the-UK-economy-my-final-online-version.pdf (accessed November 2016).

Baldock, David; Buckwell, Allan; Colsa-Perez, Alejandro; Farmer, Andrew; Nesbit, Martin;Pantzar, Mia (March 2016) "The potential policy and environmental consequences for the UK of a departure from the European Union ", Institute for European Environmental Policy, website at http://www.ieep.eu/assets/2000/IEEP_Brexit_2016. pdf (accessed December 2016).

Balzan, Juergen (27 June 2016) "27,000 Maltese can vote in Brexit referendum", Malta Today.

Bank of England (BoE) "Inflation Report, August 2017", News and Publications, 3 August 2017 (pdf), website at http://www.bankofengland.co.uk/publications/Pages/inflationreport/2017/aug.aspx (accessed August 2017).

Barbière, Cécile (18 June 2016) "Brexit will end EU investment in the UK", translated by Samuel White, website at http://www.euractiv.com/section/uk-europe/news/brexit-will-end-eu-investment-in-the-uk/ (November 2016).

Barker, Alex; Parker, George (12 October 2016) "UK faces Brexit divorce bill of up to €20bn", *Financial Times*, website at https://www.ft.com/content/3c1eb988-9081-11e6-a72e-b428cb934b78 (accessed October 2016).

Bartlett, Evan (22 July 2017) "Sterling drops to 'lowest ever level' against euro as Britons offered just 88 cents for £1" at website https://inews.co.uk/essentials/news/uk/sterling-drops-lowest-ever-level-euro-holidaymakers-receive-just (accessed July 2017).

Barnard, Catherine (2016) "Brexit and free movement", Trinity College Cambridge, website at http://www.biicl.org/documents/696_catherine_barnard_-brexit_and_free_ movement.pdf (accessed 21 August 2016).

Barrington, Robert (27 June 2016) "What does Brexit mean for the UK's fight against corruption?", Transparency International UK, website at http://www.transparency.org.uk/what-does-brexit-mean-for-the-uks-fight-against-corruption/ (accessed December 2016).

Baschuk, Bryce; Torsoli, Albertina; Miller, Hugo (12 April 2017) "EU won't back trade deal if Britain chooses 'Singapore-on-Thames'", Bloomberg, website at https://www. bloomberg.com/news/articles/2017-04-12/eu-won-t-back-trade-deal-if-u-k-chooses-singapore-on-thames (accessed July 2017).

Bastsaikhan, Uuriintuya; Feli, Justine (15 May 2017) "UK economic performance post-Brexit", Bruegel, website at https://www.theguardian.com/business/2017/jun/21/uk-budget-deficit-philip-hammond-ons-may (accessed August 2017).

BBC (1975) Cockerell Michael "EU referendum... lessons from 1975", documentary, BBC Newsnight, YouTube website at https://www.youtube.com/watch?v=qMGkB5xu3wE (accessed September 2016).

BBC (24 June 2016a) "EU referendum: The result in maps and charts", website at http:// www.bbc.com/news/uk-politics-36616028 (accessed July 2016).

BBC (24 June 2016b) "EU Referendum Results", website at http://www.bbc.com/news/ politics/eu_referendum/results (accessed July 2016).

BBC (24 June 2016c) "Eight reasons Leave won the UK's referendum on the EU", website at http://www.bbc.co.uk/news/uk-politics-eu-referendum-36574526 (accessed July 2016).

BBC (June 2016), "Five models for post-Brexit UK trade", 27 June 2016, website at http://www.bbc.com/news/uk-politics-eu-referendum-36639261 (accessed September 2017).

BBC (22 February 2016), "TITLE", website at http://www.bbc.co.uk/news/uk-politics-eu-referendum-35634239 (accessed July 2016).

BBC (25 July 2016a) "Brexit: Sturgeon sets out key Scottish interests that 'must be protected'", BBC website at http://www.bbc.com/news/uk-scotland-scotland-politics-36878081 (accessed July 2016).

BBC (4 January 2017) "Sir Ivan Rogers' letter to staff in full", website at http://www.bbc.co.uk/news/uk-politics-38503504 (accessed January 2017).

BBC (4 January 2017) "Sir Ivan Rogers' letter to staff in full", website at http://www.bbc.co.uk/news/uk-politics-38503504 (accessed January 2017).

BBC (22 February 2017 "EU referendum - The five key issues", explained by Norman Smith, video, website at http://www.bbc.co.uk/news/video_and_audio/features/uk-politics-eu-referendum-35632046/35632046 (accessed March 2017).

BBC (21 June 2017a) "Reaction to the Queen's Speech", BBC website at http://www.bbc.co.uk/news/live/uk-politics-40347339 (accessed June 2017).

BBC, 21 June 2017b "Queen's Speech: Brexit bills dominate government agenda", BBC website at http://www.bbc.co.uk/news/uk-politics-40345280 (accessed June 2017).

BBC (5 September 2017b) "Brexit Britain: What's the mood of the nation?", BBC website at http://www.bbc.co.uk/programmes/p046n65h (accessed September 2016).

BBC (21 June 2017) "Reaction to the Queen's Speech", BBC website at http://www.bbc.co.uk/news/live/uk-politics-40347339 (accessed June 2017) and BBC (21 June 2017) "Queen's Speech: Brexit bills dominate government agenda", BBC website at http://www.bbc.co.uk/news/uk-politics-40345280 (accessed June 2017).

BDO (4 April 2016) "Article: Brexit – the tax implications of leaving or remaining", website at https://www.bdo.co.uk/en-gb/insights/business-edge/business-edge-2016/brexit-the-tax-implications-of-leaving-or-remain (accessed October 2016).

Bean, Emma (27 March 2017) "Keir Starmer: Labour has six tests for Brexit – if they're not met we won't back the final deal in parliament", LabourList website at https://labourlist.org/2017/03/keir-starmer-labour-has-six-tests-for-brexit-if-theyre-not-met-we-wont-back-the-final-deal-in-parliament (accessed June 2017).

Becker, Johannes; Fuest, Clemens (13 December 2016) "Deutschlands Rolle in der EU – Planloser Hegemon", Frankfurter Allgemeine Zeitung, website at http://www.faz.net/aktuell/wirtschaft/eurokrise/deutschlands-rolle-in-der-eu-planloser-hegemon-14554184.html?printPagedArticle=true#pageIndex_2 (accessed December 2016).

Bennett, Asa; Kirkup, James (10 March 2017) "How much money does Britain currently pay the EU?", The Telegraph, website at http://www.telegraph.co.uk/news/0/how-much-do-we-spend-on-the-eu-and-what-else-could-it-pay-for/ (accessed July 2017).

Berry, Mike (June 2016) "Understanding the role of the mass media in the EU Referendum", in: EU Referendum Analysis 2016: Media, Voters and the Campaign, published by The Centre for the Study of Journalism, Culture and Community, report available at https://meandeurope.com/wp-content/uploads/EU-Referendum-Analysis-2016-Jackson-Thorsen-and-Wring-v2.pdf (accessed June 2017).

Best for Britain, website at https://bestforbritain.org/ (accessed May 2017).

Bilimoria, Karan (28 June 2016) "What if the will of the people is now for a second referendum on Brexit?", *The Guardian*.

Biondi, Filippo; Goncalves, Raposo, Inês (22 December 2016) "The impact of Brexit on Northern Ireland: a first look", Bruegel Blog Post, website at http://bruegel.org/2016/12/the-impact-of-brexit-on-northern-ireland-a-first-look/ (accessed January 2017).

Blumler, Jay (June 2016) "EEC/EU campaigning in long-term perspective", in: EU Referendum Analysis 2016: Media, Voters and the Campaign, published by The Centre for the Study of Journalism, Culture and Community, report available at https://meandeurope.com/wp-content/uploads/EU-Referendum-Analysis-2016-Jackson-Thorsen-and-Wring-v2.pdf (accessed 25 June 2017).

Boland, Vincent (15 January 2017) "Ireland: Brexit vote forces Dublin to seek new EU friends", *Financial Times*, website at https://www.ft.com/content/3d0fdb18-d97b-11e6-944b-e7eb37a6aa8e (accessed January 2017).

BMG Research (BMG) (22 June 2016) "Electoral Reform Society/BMG Poll: BBC named the most important source of referendum information", posted 22 June 2016 in Polling, website at http://www.bmgresearch.co.uk/bbc-important-referendum-information/ (accessed July 2017).

Blitz, James (3 July 2017) "Will Britain's fishermen be better off after Brexit?", *Financial Times*, website at https://www.ft.com/content/84f51c84-5fe2-11e7-91a7-502f7ee26895 (accessed August 2017).

Blitz, James and Houlder, Vanessa (9 October 2017) "White papers tackle challenges of 'no deal' Brexit", *Financial Times*.

Bond, Ian et al. (April 2016) "Europe after Brexit – Unleashed or undone?", Centre for European Reform, website at http://www.cer.eu/sites/default/files/pb_euafterBrexit_15april16.pdf (accessed July 2017).

Boffey, Daniel and Rankin, Jennifer (17 July 2017) "David Davis leaves Brussels after less than an hour of Brexit talks", *The Guardian*.

Breat, Will (1 September 2016) "The people have spoken. Or have they? Doing referendums differently after the EU vote", LSE blog website http://blogs.lse.ac.uk/brexit/2016/09/01/the-people-have-spoken-or-have-they-doing-referendums-differently-after-the-eu-vote/ (accessed September 2016).

Breat, Will (1 September 2016) "The people have spoken. Or have they? Doing referendums differently after the EU vote", LSE blog website http://blogs.lse.ac.uk/brexit/2016/09/01/the-people-have-spoken-or-have-they-doing-referendums-differently-after-the-eu-vote/ (accessed September 2016).

Breat, Will (September 2016) "It's good to talk: Doing referendums differently after the EU vote", Report for the Electoral Reform Society (http://www.electoral-reform.org.uk).

Bronstein, Michael et al. (30 March 2016) "How would a Brexit impact on employment law in the UK?", Dentons, website at http://www.lexology.com/library/detail.aspx?g=144b579a-6a46-448b-9383-9c0fcca6ddb0 (accessed November 2016).

Bruegel (2017) "The UK's Brexit bill: could EU assets partially offset liabilities?" at http://bruegel.org/2017/02/the-uks-brexit-bill-could-eu-assets-partially-offset-liabilities/ (accessed June 2017).

Burchard, von der Hans (17 February 2017) "Juncker predicts Brexit deal will take more than two years", Politico, website at http://www.politico.eu/article/juncker-predicts-brexit-deal-will-take-more-than-two-years/ (accessed June 2017).

Burke, John (8 July 2016) "How Brexit can affect the European economy", Investopedia, website at http://www.investopedia.com/articles/markets/070816/how-brexit-can-affect-european-economy-ms-db.asp (accessed November 2016).

Buttonwood (19 July 2017) "Britain: back to being the sick man of Europe?", The Economist, website at https://www.economist.com/blogs/buttonwood/2017/07/1970s-show (accessed July 2017).

Calatozzolo, Rita (March 2017) "The budgetary procedure", Fact Sheets on the European Union, website at http://www.europarl.europa.eu/atyourservice/en/displayFtu.html?ftuId=FTU_1.4.3.html (accessed April 2017).

Cambridge Dictionary (2017), website at https://dictionary.cambridge.org/dictionary/ (accessed November 2017).

Cameron, David (24 June 2016) "EU referendum outcome: PM statement", speech, UK Government website at https://www.gov.uk/government/speeches/ (accessed July 2016).

Campbell, Denis; Brindle, David; Butler, Patrick (14 June 2016) "What would Brexit mean for the NHS, social care and disabled people?", The Guardian, website at https://www.theguardian.com/society/2016/jun/14/brexit-nhs-health-social-care-disabled-people-eu-referendum (accessed November 2016).

Canton, Naomi (17 January 2017) "India sees Brexit as "an opportunity": Indian High Commissioner YK Sinha", website at http://asiahouse.org/india-sees-brexit-opportunity-indian-high-commissioner-yk-sinha/ (accessed July 2017).

Carrington, Damian (14 June 2016) "UK's out vote is a 'red alert' for the environment", The Guardian, website at https://www.theguardian.com/environment/damian-carrington-blog/2016/jun/24/uks-out-vote-is-a-red-alert-for-the-environment (accessed December 2016).

Carroll, Michelle (8 March 2016) "Brexit or no Brexit, free movement of capital across Europe is vital to Britain's success", website at http://www.cityam.com/236163/brexit-or-no-brexit-free-movement-of-capital-across-europe-is-vital-to-britains-success (accessed September 2016).

Castle, Stephen (25 December 2016) "E.U. Agency in Limbo as Hidden Costs of 'Brexit' Continue to Mount, The New York Times, website at https://www.nytimes.com/2016/12/25/world/europe/eu-medicines-agency-britain-brexit.html?_r=0 (accessed January 2017).

CBI, BDO (2015) "Stepping up – Fixing the funding ladder for medium-sized businesses", website at http://www.cbi.org.uk/news/incentivise-savers-to-boost-investment-for-mid-sized-firms/stepping-up-fixing-the-funding-ladder-for-medium-sized-businesses (accessed September 2016).

CBI (5 May 2016) "Government and business must work together to revitalise a modern industrial strategy", CBI Press Team, website at http://www.cbi.org.uk/news/government-and-business-must-work-together-to-revitalise-a-modern-industrial-strategy/ (accessed November 2016).

CBI, TUC (30 June 2016) "CBI and TUC publish joint statement on the impact of the EU referendum vote on workers and the economy", Trades Union Congress, website at https://www.tuc.org.uk/economic-issues/public-spending/labour-market/industrial-issues/cbi-and-tuc-publish-joint-statement (accessed November 2016).

Centre for Economic Policy Research (CEPR) (28 November 2013) "Trade and Investment -Balance of Competence Review", Project Report, p 58, website at https://www.gov.uk/government/uploads/system/uploads/attachment_data/file/271784/bis-14-512-trade-and-investment-balance-of-competence-review-project-report.pdf (accessed November 2016).

CEBR, Centre for Economics and Business Research (13 February 2012) "London's taxes prop up the rest of the UK", CEBR report, This is money website at http://www.thisismoney.co.uk/money/news/article-2100345/Londons-taxes-prop-rest-UK-One-pound-earned-capital-funds-rest-country.html (accessed September 2016).

Change.org (2016) "Declare London independent from the UK and apply to join the EU", website at https://www.change.org/p/sadiq-khan-declare-london-independent-from-the-uk-and-apply-to-join-the-eu (accessed May 2017).

Chrysostomou, Annette (19 June 2016) "So how many Brits are there in Cyprus?", CyprusMail, website at http://cyprus-mail.com/2016/06/19/many-brits-cyprus/ (accessed September 2016).

Chu, Ben (5 October 2016) "What do immigrants do for the UK economy? Nine charts Conservative ministers seem to be ignoring", The Independent, website at http://www.independent.co.uk/news/business/news/immigration-uk-economy-what-are-the-benefits-stats-theresa-may-amber-rudd-tory-conference-speeches-a7346121.html (accessed November 2016).

Chu, Ben (28 May 2017) "Theresa May's 'no deal is better than a bad deal' Brexit logic could end up destroying the British economy", Independent website at http://www.independent.co.uk/voices/brexit-theresa-may-tories-no-deal-better-bad-deal-brussels-destroy-british-economy-a7760026.html (accessed June 2017).

Cleary, Gottlieb (July 2016) "Industrial Strategy Post-Brexit: The UK's Power To Block Mergers On Public Interest Grounds", Alert Memorandum, website at https://www.clearygottlieb.com/~/media/cgsh/files/alert-memos/alert-memo-pdf-version-201676.pdf (accessed November 2016).

Cole, Neal (24 June 2016) "The psychology of Brexit – why emotions won over logic!", website at http://www.conversion-uplift.co.uk/psychology-behind-uk-leaving-eu/ (accessed 24 June 2016).

Cole, Neal (19 July 2016) "7 Marketing lessons from the Brexit campaigns", website at http://www.conversion-uplift.co.uk/marketing-lessons-from-brexit-campaigns/ (accessed 25. June 2017).

Colson, Thomas (27 November 2016) "Boris Johnson's new advisor could be Britain's hope for avoiding a 'Hard Brexit'", *Business Insider*, website at http://www.businessinsider.de/boris-johnson-advisor-david-frost-whole-industries-could-be-destroyed-by-hard-brexit-article-50-2016-10?r=UK&IR=T (accessed September 2017).

ComRes (14 July 2016) "BBC News Brexit Expectations Poll", ComRes, website at http://www.comres.co.uk/polls/bbc-news-brexit-expectations-poll (accessed July 2017).

Connelly, Tony (30 January 2012) "The Fiscal Stability Treaty: what happens next?", RTE News, website at https://analysis.rte.ie/european/2012/01/30/the-fiscal-stability-treaty-what-happens-next/ (accessed November 2016).

Cook, James (18 June 2017) "A new poll shows the public is overwhelmingly opposed to 'Hard Brexit'", Business Insider UK website http://uk.businessinsider.com/survation-poll-shows-public-is-overwhelmingly-opposed-to-hard-brexit-2017-6 (accessed July 2017).

Copenhagen European Council (21-22 June 1993) "Presidency Conclusions: 7. Relations with the Countries of Central and Eastern Europe, A. The Associated Countries".

Council of the European Union (22 June 2017a) "Relocation of UK based agencies", website at http://www.consilium.europa.eu/en/policies/relocation-london-agencies-brexit/ (accessed in October 2017).

Cremades, Miguel Tell;Novak, Petr (January 2017) "Brexit and the European Union: General institutional and legal considerations", Committee on Constitutional Affairs – Directorate General for Internal Policies of the Union, website at http://www.europarl.europa.eu/RegData/etudes/STUD/2017/571404/IPOL_STU(2017)571404_EN.pdf (accessed May 2017).

Croft, Jane (28 April 2016) "Britons abroad refused right to vote in EU referendum ", *Financial Tines*.

Curtis, Jonathan (5 August 2017) "Theresa May ready to walk away from EU without a deal", Your Brexit website at http://yourbrexit.co.uk/news/breaking-theresa-may-ready-to-walk-away-from-eu-without-a-deal/ (accessed August 2017).

Daily Express (23 April 2016) "EU Referendum 2016: How much has the referendum cost?".

D'Arcy, Conan (26 September 2016 "Brexit and the audio-visual sector – facing up to life outside the single market", Global Counsel, website at https://www.global-counsel. co.uk/blog/brexit-and-audio-visual-sector-%E2%80%93-facing-life-outside-single-market (accessed November 2017).

Da Rold, Vittorio (15 September 2016) "Italy is second –largest user of EU's 'Juncker fund' after the UK", European View, website at http://www.italy24.ilsole24ore. com/art/business-and-economy/2016-09-14/juncker-plan-taking-stock-130103. php?uuid=ADfgRHKB (accessed November 2016).

Davies, Howard (29 February 2016) "Why the UK wants to stay out of the EU banking union", World Economic Forum, website at https://www.weforum.org/agenda/2016/02/why-the-uk-wants-to-stay-out-of-the-eu-banking-union (accessed October 2016).

Davies, Rob; Treanor, Jill (28 June 2016) "Vodafone among firms that may move HQs from post-Brexit UK, website at https://www.theguardian.com/business/2016/jun/28/firms-plan-investment-freeze-amid-brexit-fallout-cbi (accessed August 2016).

De Grauwe, Paul (September/ October 2016) "What Future for the EU after Brexit?", Intereconomics, Volume 52, Number 5, pp. 249-251, website at http://archive.intereconomics.eu/year/2016/5/what-future-for-the-eu-after-brexit/ (accessed July 2017).

De Grauwe, Paul; Ji, Y. (2016) "Crisis Management and Economic Growth in the Eurozone", in: F. Caselli, M. Centeno, J. Tavares (eds.): After the Crisis. Reform, Recovery, and Growth in Europe, Oxford 2016, Oxford University Press, pp. 46-72.

Delahunty, Louise (9 August 2016) "Brexit, risk mitigation & corporate crime", New law journal, website at https://www.newlawjournal.co.uk/blogs/201608/brexit-risk-mitigation-corporate-crime (accessed December 2016).

Deloitte "Power up: The UK workplace" (April 2017), Deloitte website at https://www2. deloitte.com/uk/en/pages/international-markets/articles/power-up.html   (accessed June 2017).

Dominiczak, Peter; Hughes, Laura (21 November 2016) "Theresa May to give Britain lowest corporation tax of world's top 20 economies", *The Telegraph*, website at http:// www.telegraph.co.uk/news/2016/11/21/theresa-may-to-offer-business-an-olive-branch-with-hint-of-futur/ (accessed November 2016).

Doyle, Dara; Champion, Marc (18 July 2016) "Brexit fallout affecting Ireland more than any other EU country", *The Independent*, website at http://www.independent.co.uk/news/business/news/brexit-fallout-affecting-ireland-more-than-any-other-eu-country-eu-referendum-a7142781.html (accessed January 2017).

Department for Exiting the European Union (30 March 2017) "Legislating for the united Kingdom's withdrawal from the European Union", Cm9446, Presented to Parliament by the Secretary of State for Existing the European Union by Command of her Majesty.

Department for Exiting the European Union and The Rt Hon David Davis (2 February 2017) "The United Kingdom's exit from and new partnership with the European Union White Paper", HM Government.

Department for Exiting the European Union and The Rt Hon David Davis (2 February 2017) "The United Kingdom's exit from and new partnership with the European Union White Paper ", HM Government.

Department for Exiting the European Union (30 March 2017) "Legislating for the united Kingdom's withdrawal from the European Union", Cm9446, Presented to Parliament by the Secretary of State for Existing the European Union by Command of her Majesty.

Dilnot, Andrew (21 April 2016), "Letter from the UK Statistics Authority", available online at https://www.statisticsauthority.gov.uk/wp-content/uploads/2016/04/Letter-from-Sir-Andrew-Dilnot-to-Norman-Lamb-MP-210416.pdf (accessed November 2016).

Dilnot, Andrew (21 April 2016) "Letter of Sir Andrew Dilnot CBE", UK Statistics Authority.

Doyle, Dara (20 January 2017) "UK can't be Singapore-on-Thames after Brexit, Noonan says", Bloomberg, website at https://www.bloomberg.com/news/articles/2017-01-20/u-k-can-t-be-singapore-on-thames-after-brexit-noonan-says-iy5rlsde (accessed July 2017).

Dunford, Daniel and Kirk, Ashley (27 June 2016) "How right or wrong were the polls about the EU referendum?", *The Telegraph*, website at http://www.telegraph.co.uk/news/2016/06/24/eu-referendum-how-right-or-wrong-were-the-polls (accessed August 2016).

Economic and Financial Affairs (EFA) "European Economic Forecast – Spring 2017", Institutional Paper 53, 11 May 2017, website at https://ec.europa.eu/info/publications/economy-finance/european-economic-forecast-spring-2017_en (accessed August 2017).

Economist (13 July 2017) "If Britain became "Singapore-on-Thames – The British economy if the country crashes out of the European Union", The Economist, website at https://www.economist.com/news/world-if/21724909-idea-british-economic-policy-after-hardest-brexits-british-economy-if (accessed July 2017).

EFTA (2017), Information about the EFTA Member States: Iceland, Liechtenstein, Norway and Switzerland, website at http://www.efta.int/about-efta/the-efta-states (accessed August 2016).

Electoral Commission (24 Jun 2016) "Official result of the EU Referendum is declared by Electoral Commission in Manchester", website at https://www.electoralcommission.

org.uk/i-am-a/journalist/electoral-commission-media-centre/news-releases-referendums/official-result-of-the-eu-referendum-is-declared-by-electoral-commission-in-manchester (accessed July 2016).

Electoral Commission (2016b) "EU referendum results [by region]", website at http://www.electoralcommission.org.uk/find-information-by-subject/elections-and-referendums/past-elections-and-referendums/eu-referendum/electorate-and-count-information (accessed July 2017).

The Electoral Commission (September 2016a) "Report on the 23 June 2016 referendum on the UK's membership of the European Union" (United Kingdom).

The Electoral Reform Society (September 2016b) "Doing referendums differently", website at https://www.electoral-reform.org.uk/doing-referendums-differently/#sthash.ml8QMBkt.dpuf (accessed September 2016).

Electoral Commissions (2017) "Who is eligible to vote at a UK general election?", website at http://www.electoralcommission.org.uk/faq/voting-and-registration/who-is-eligible-to-vote-at-a-uk-general-election (accessed August 2017).

Electoral Commission (October 2013) "Referendum on the United Kingdom's membership of the European Union", Advice of the Electoral Commission on the referendum question included in the European Union (Referendum) Bill.

Elkes, Neil (Month 2014) "Birmingham City Council jobs bombshell as 6,000 more staff face the axe", Birmingham Mail website at http://www.birminghammail.co.uk/news/midlands-news/birmingham-city-council-jobs-bombshell-7781977 (accessed July 2017).

Elliot, Matthew (2016) "Change, or go – How Britain would gain influence and prosper outside an unreformed EU, Business for Britain, website at https://forbritain.org/cog-wholebook.pdf (accessed November 2016).

Elsy, Dick (4 July 2016) "Industry needs post-Brexit assurances from government", The Engineer, website at https://www.theengineer.co.uk/industry-needs-post-brexit-assurances-from-government/ (accessed November 2016).

Emmott, Mike (10 August 2015) "The impact of 'Brexit' on employment law", CIPD Community blog, website at http://www.cipd.co.uk/community/blogs/b/policy_at_work/archive/2015/08/10/the-impact-of-brexit-on-employment-law (accessed November 2016).

Energy Community (2015) "Energy Community Facts in Brief", Energy Community Secretariat, website at https://www.energy-community.org/portal/page/portal/ENC_HOME/DOCS/4218380/370C282CF2600DF8E053C92FA8C0EC6A.pdf (accessed October 2016).

Energy and Environment Sub-Committee (13 July 2016) "The potential implications of Brexit on energy and climate change policy", House of Lords, Revised transcript of evidence taken before the select committee on the European Union, website at http://data.parliament.uk/writtenevidence/committeeevidence.svc/evidencedocument/eu-energy-and-environment-subcommittee/he-potential-implications-of-Brexit-on-energy-and-climate-change-policy/written/35153.pdf (accessed October 2016).

Energy and Environment Sub-Committee (7 September 2016) "Subject: Brexit: Fisheries", UK Parliament Meeting, taped broadcast, website at http://parliamentlive.tv/Event/Index/976c3d5d-80bc-424e-a81c-9a2a3532f2e0 (accessed October 2016).

Erkelens, Catherine; Briggs, Paul; Phippard, Simon; Boström, Tim; Bell, Jim (7 July 2016) "How will Brexit affect the airline industry from a regulatory perspective?, Bird & Bird, News Centre, website at https://www.twobirds.com/en/news/articles/2016/uk/how-will-brexit-affect-the-airline-industry-from-a-regulatory-perspective#consumer%20 protection (accessed December 2016).

EU ABC.com, website at http://en.euabc.com/word/12 (accessed July 2017).

Euroactiv (14 November 2016) "Study: Brexit throws GBP 65 billion of investment into doubt", website at http://www.euractiv.com/section/uk-europe/news/study-brexit-throws-65bn-of-investment-into-doubt/ (accessed November 2016).

Europa Chapters of the Acquis website at http://ec.europa.eu/enlargement/policy/conditions-membership/chapters-of-the-acquis/index_en.htm (accessed August 2016).

Europa website "EU expenditure and revenue 2014-2020" at http://ec.europa.eu/budget/figures/interactive/index_en.cfm (November 2016).

Europa Education and Training (October 2017) "Initiatives", website at http://ec.europa.eu/education/initiatives_en (accessed October 2017).

European Banking Authority (12 October 2017a) "EBA provides guidance to authorities and institutions on Brexit relocations", EBA website at http://www.eba.europa.eu/-/eba-provides-guidance-to-authorities-and-institutions-on-brexit-relocations (accessed October 2017).

European Banking Authority (12 October 2017b) "Opinion of the European Banking Authority on issues related to the departure of the United Kingdom from the European Union", EBA/Op/2017/12, http://www.eba.europa.eu/documents/10180/1756362/EBA+Opinion+on+Brexit+Issues+%28EBA-Op-2017-12%29.pdf (accessed October 2017).

European Central Bank (ECB) "European Union – EU institutions and other bodies", website at https://europa.eu/european-union/about-eu/institutions-bodies/european-central-bank_en (accessed March 2017).

European Commission (EC) (January 2015) "2015 Management Plan – Employment, Social Affairs and Inclusion", website at http://ec.europa.eu/info/sites/info/files/mangement-plan-2015-dg-empl_july2015_en.pdf (accessed October 2016).

European Commission (29 June 2015) "EU-Singapore Free Trade Agreement. Authentic text as of May 2015", Trade website at http://trade.ec.europa.eu/doclib/press/index.cfm?id=961 (accessed March 2017).

European Commission (EC) (16 July 2015) "Budget: Financial report 2015 – Foreword", Kristalina Georgieva, Vice-President for Budget and Human Resources, website at http://ec.europa.eu/budget/financialreport/2015/foreword/index_en.html (accessed June 2017).

European Commission (24 July 2015) "2015 Management Plan – Health & Foody Safety – Directorate-General", Ref. Ares(2015)3117203, website at http://ec.europa.eu/info/sites/

info/files/management-plan-2015-dg-sante_july2015_en.pdf (accessed 25 September 2016).

European Commission (EC) (30 October 2015) "Completing the Economic and Monetary Union", Factsheets on economic and monetary union, The Juncker Commission: One year on, 30 October 2015, website at http://ec.europa.eu/priorities/publications/completing-economic-and-monetary-union-one-year_en (accessed October 2015).

European Commission (23 March 2016) "Strategic Plan 2016-2020 – DG Environment", website at http://ec.europa.eu/atwork/synthesis/amp/doc/env_sp_2016-2020_en.pdf (accessed December 2016).

European Commission (EC) (13 June 2016) "Financial Services – General Policy", website at http://ec.europa.eu/finance/general-policy/index_en.htm (accessed September 2016).

European Commission (EC) (July 2016) "The Economic Outlook after the UK Referendum: A First Assessment for the Euro Area and the EU", Institutional Paper 032, ISSN 2443-8014 (online) (Luxembourg: Publications Office of the European Union).

European Commission (EC) (August 2016) "EC Growth – The European Single Market", website at https://ec.europa.eu/growth/single-market_en (accessed August 2016).

European Commission (EC) (8 November 2016) "The Investment Plan for Europe", The Investment Plan: two years on, website at https://ec.europa.eu/priorities/sites/beta-political/files/2-years-on-investment-plan_en_1.pdf (accessed November 2016).

European Commission (EC) (11 November 2016) "DG Growth – Internal market, industry, Entrepreneurship and SMEs: About us", website at http://ec.europa.eu/growth/about-us (accessed November 2016).

European Commission (EC) (3 December 2016) "Fundamental Rights", website at http://ec.europa.eu/justice/fundamental-rights/index_en.htm (accessed December 2016).

European Commission (EC) (1 December 2016) "EU Budget 2017", Fact Sheet, website at http://ec.europa.eu/budget/library/biblio/documents/2017/budget-adoption-factsheet-2017_en.pdf (accessed June 2017).

European Commission (EC) (1 December 2016) "EU budget 2017 approved", website at http://ec.europa.eu/budget/news/article_en.cfm?id=201612011726 (accessed December 2016).

European Commission (EC) (2016) "Financial Report 2015", EU, website at http://ec.europa.eu/budget/financialreport/2015/lib/financial_report_2015_en.pdf (accessed 6 November 2017).

European Commission (EC) (16 February 2017) "Budget", European Commission DG Budget, website at http://ec.europa.eu/budget/index_en.cfm (accessed February 2017).

European Commission (17 February 2017) "Comprehensive Economic and Trade Agreement", European Commission Trade website at http://ec.europa.eu/trade/policy/in-focus/ceta/ (accessed March 2017).

European Commission (EC) (1 March 2017) "White paper on the future of Europe", EC COM(2017)2025, website at https://ec.europa.eu/commission/sites/beta-political/files/white_paper_on_the_future_of_europe_en.pdf (accessed April 2017).

European Commission (EC) (April 2017) "Reflection Paper on the future of EU finances – Facts and figures", EC Budget, website at https://ec.europa.eu/commission/sites/beta-political/files/future-eu-finances-facts-and-figures-factsheet_en.pdf (accessed July 2017).

European Commission (12 June 2017) "Essential Principles on Citizens' Rights", Task Force for the Preparation and Conduct of the Negotiations with the United Kingdom under Article 50 TEU, Position paper.

European Commission (19 June 2017) "Terms of Reference for the Article 50 TEU negotiations".

European Commission (EC) (5 July 2017) "Taxation and Customs Union: Welcome and mission statement", website at https://ec.europa.eu/taxation_customs/about/welcome-mission-statement_en (accessed 5 July 2017).

European Commission (19 June 2017) "Terms of Reference for the Article 50 TEU negotiations", website at https://ec.europa.eu/commission/sites/beta-political/files/eu-uk-art-50-terms-reference_agreed_amends_en.pdf (accessed July 2017).

European Commission (8 July 2017) EU-Japan Free Trade Agreement" at European Commission Trade website http://ec.europa.eu/trade/policy/in-focus/eu-japan-free-trade-agreement/ (accessed August 2017).

European Commission (EC) (2017) "Financial Report 2016", EU, website at http://ec.europa.eu/budget/library/biblio/publications/2017/financial-report_en.pdf (accessed 6 November 2017).

European Commission – Mobility and Transport (2017) "International aviation: United States", website at https://ec.europa.eu/transport/modes/air/international_aviation/country_index/united_states_en (accessed September 2017).

European Commission, DG Justice "EU citizenship" website at http://ec.europa.eu/justice/citizen/ (accessed August 2016).

European Commission, Task Force for the Preparation and Conduct of the Negotiations with the United Kingdom under Article 50 TEU (12 June 2017), Position paper on "Essential Principles on Citizens' Rights".

European Commission, TF50 (2017)19 – Commission to EU 27 (8 December 2017) "Joint report from the negotiators of the European Union and the United Kingdom Government on progress during phase 1 of negotiations under Article 50 TEU on the United Kingdom's orderly withdrawal from the European Union", Task Force for the Preparation and Conduct of the Negotiations with the United Kingdom under Article 50 TEU and the UK, presented jointly by the negotiators of the European Union and the United Kingdom Government.

European Commission, TF50 (2017)20 – Commission to EU 27 (8 December 2017) "Citizens' rights", Task Force for the Preparation and Conduct of the Negotiations with the United Kingdom under Article 50 TEU and the UK, the joint technical note attached expresses the detailed consensus of the UK and EU positions.

European Commission "EU-Singapore Free Trade Agreement", European Commission Trade website at http://trade.ec.europa.eu/doclib/press/index.cfm?id=961 (accessed June 2017).

European Commission "Comprehensive Economic and Trade Agreement" at European Commission Trade website at http://ec.europa.eu/trade/policy/in-focus/ceta/ (accessed June 2017).

European Commission "The EU in 2016", website at http://publications.europa.eu/webpub/com/general-report-2016/en/ (accessed June 2017).

European Commission – European structural and investment funds, website at https://ec.europa.eu/info/funding-tenders/european-structural-and-investment-funds_en (accessed October 2017).

European Council (2017) "EU restrictive measures in response to the crisis in Ukraine", European Council Policies, website at http://www.consilium.europa.eu/en/policies/sanctions/ukraine-crisis/ (accessed February 2017).

European Council (29 March 2017) "European Council (Art. 50) guidelines following the United Kingdom's notification under Article 50 TEU", website at http://www.consilium.europa.eu/en/press/press-releases/2017/04/29/euco-brexit-guidelines/ (accessed May 2017).

European Council (31 March 2017) "Draft guidelines following the United Kingdom's notification under Article 50 TEU", XT 21001/17.

European Council (29 April 2017) "Guidelines following the United Kingdom's notification under Article 50 TEU", BXT10, CO EUR 5, CONCL 2.

European Council (22 June 2017) "Procedure leading up to a decision on the relocation of the European Medicines Agency and the European Banking Authority in the context of the UK's withdrawal from the Union".

European Council (22 June 2017) "Decision on the procedure for relocation of EU agencies currently located in the UK", Press Release 405/17.

European Council (22 June 2017) "Procedure leading up to a decision on the relocation of the European Medicines Agency and the European Banking Authority in the context of the UK's withdrawal from the Union, 22/06/2017".

European Court of Auditors (ECA) (2017), "European Union – EU institutions and other bodies", website at https://europa.eu/european-union/about-eu/institutions-bodies/european-court-auditors_en (accessed April 2017).

European Court of justice (ECJ) "European Union – EU institutions and other bodies", website at https://europa.eu/european-union/about-eu/institutions-bodies/court-justice_en (accessed April 2017).

European External Action Services (15 December 2016) "Implementation Plan on Security and Defence", Fact Sheet, website at https://eeas.europa.eu/sites/eeas/files/2016-12_-_factsheet_-_implementation_plan_on_security_and_defence.pdf (accessed February 2017).

European External Action Service (EEAS) (2017) "About the European External Actions Services, website at https://eeas.europa.eu/headquarters/headquarters-homepage/82/about-the-european-external-action-service-eeas_en (accessed February 2017).

European Medicines Agency (EMA) (2016) "Coordination Group for Mutual Recognition and Decentralised Procedures - Human (CMDh)", website at http://www.ema.europa.eu/ema/index.jsp?curl=pages/about_us/general/general_content_000310.jsp&mid=WC0b01ac05800986a3 (accessed January 2017).

European Parliament (EP) (2017) "The EU's external relations", Fact Sheets on the European Union, website at http://www.europarl.europa.eu/atyourservice/en/displayFtu.html?ftuId=theme6.html (accessed January 2017).

European Union (EU) (2017) "Foreign & Security Policy", Topics of the European Union, website at https://europa.eu/european-union/topics/foreign-security-policy_en (accessed February 2017).

European Union EU administration - staff, languages and location website at https://europa.eu/european-union/about-eu/figures/administration_en#languages (accessed July 2017).

European Union (EU) (5 November 2017) "EU institutions and other bodies", European Union, website at https://europa.eu/european-union/about-eu/institutions-bodies_en#eu_institutions_in_brief (accessed October 2017).

Eurostat (2017) "Labour Market", website at http://ec.europa.eu/eurostat/web/labour-market/earnings/database (accessed April 2017).

Eversheds (2016) "Making sense of Brexit: What will it mean to leave the EU?", brochure.

Excell, Jon (8 November 2016) "Last week's poll: Have your say on the Nissan deal", The Engineer, website at https://www.theengineer.co.uk/this-weeks-poll-have-your-say-on-the-nissan-deal/ (accessed November 2016).

ExEdUK (June 2016) "Supporting International education in the UK".

EY Item Club (July 2016) "EY ITEM Club Summer Forecast: The world post Brexit", website at http://www.ey.com/UK/en/Issues/Business-environment/Financial-markets-and-economy/ITEM---Forecast-headlines-and-projections (accessed July 2016).

Faleg, Giovanni (26 July 2016) "The Implications of Brexit for the EU'S Common Security and Defence Policy", CEPS, website at https://www.ceps.eu/publications/implications-brexit-eu%E2%80%99s-common-security-and-defence-policy (accessed February 2017).

Falola, Anthony (9 December 2011) "European Union leaders agree to forge new fiscal pact: Britain the only holdout", The Washington Post, website at https://analysis.rte.

ie/european/2012/01/30/the-fiscal-stability-treaty-what-happens-next/ (accessed October 2016).

FAZ, Frankfurter Allgemeine Zeitung (1 May 2017) "Das desaströse Brexit-Dinner", website at http://www.faz.net/aktuell/brexit/juncker-bei-may-das-desastroese-brexit-dinner-14993605.html?GEPC=s3 (accessed May 2017).

FAZ, Frankfurter Allgemeine Zeitung (3 May 2017) "The Disastrous Brexit Dinner", Website at http://www.faz.net/aktuell/politik/theresa-may-jean-claude-juncker-and-the-disastrous-brexit-dinner-14998803.html (accessed April 2017).

Fenton, Siobhan (17 October 2016) "Brexit will have a 'devasting' impact on Ireland, Martin McGuinness warns", *The Independent*, website at http://www.independent.co.uk/news/uk/politics/brexit-ireland-economy-impact-devastating-martin-mcguinness-a7364961.html (accessed January 2017).

Financial Times (4 September 2016) "Brexit is 'huge opportunity', Davis to tell MPs".

Fingar, Courtney (03 March 2016) "Is Brexit a threat to foreign direct investment?", website at http://www.ft.com/cms/s/3/6df1db7a-e159-11e5-8d9b-e88a2a889797.html?siteedition=intl#axzz4JkNeaJuj (accessed September 2016).

Fletcher, Nick (15 March 2017) "Single market exit: UK construction 'could lose 175,000 EU workers'", *The Guardian*, website at https://www.theguardian.com/business/2017/mar/15/single-market-exit-brexit-uk-construction-sector-lose-175000-eu-workers (accessed July 2017).

Forbes (21 March 2017) "Where The Wealthiest Live: Cities With The Most Billionaires", Forbes Billionaires website at https://www.forbes.com/sites/ryansalchert/2017/03/21/where-the-wealthiest-live-cities-with-the-most-billionaires (accessed May 2017).

Foster, Peter (28 March 2017) "What will happen to the EU after Brexit?", *The Telegraph*, 28.03, website at http://www.telegraph.co.uk/news/0/will-happen-eu-brexit/ (accessed July 2017).

Foster, Peter (14 June 2016) "EU deal: What David Cameron asked for... and what he actually got", *The Telegraph*, website at http://www.telegraph.co.uk/news/2016/05/19/eu-deal-what-david-cameron-asked-for-and-what-he-actually-got (access July 2017).

Foster, Peter; Kirkup, James (14 June 2016, 24 February 2017)"What will Brexit mean for British trade?", *The Telegraph*, website at http://www.telegraph.co.uk/news/0/what-would-brexit-mean-for-british-trade/ (accessed August 2017).

FPH, Faculty of Public Health (24 June 2016) "We need to ensure the best aspirations of the Leave campaign are delivered and the worst predictions of the Remain campaign are avoided", UK Faculty of Public Health, website at http://www.fph.org.uk/'we_need_to_ensure_the_best_aspirations_of_the_leave_campaign_are_delivered_and_the_worst_predictions_of_the_remain_campaign_are_avoided' (accessed January 2017).

Fry, William (27 June 2016) "Brexit and your business, Financial services generally: Top 5 issues", website at http://www.lexology.com/library/detail.aspx?g=f2fdf636-1837-47fa-b390-0633938e0fdc (accessed on September 2016).

Full Fact (4 July 2016) "EU debate: does Brussels employ fewer bureaucrats than Derbyshire?" website at https://fullfact.org/europe/eu-debate-does-brussels-employ-fewer-bureaucrats-derbyshire/ (accessed July 2017).

Full Fact UK (3 April 2017) "Everything you might want to know about the UK's trade with the EU", website at https://fullfact.org/europe/uk-eu-trade/ (accessed in August 2017).

Gay, Jean-Jacques (December 2016) "Budgetary Control", Fact Sheets on the European Union, website at http://www.europarl.europa.eu/atyourservice/en/displayFtu.html?ftuId=FTU_1.5.5.html (accessed February 2017).

Gifford, Chris (June 2016) "Brexit: the destruction of a collective good", in: EU Referendum Analysis 2016: Media, Voters and the Campaign, published by The Centre for the Study of Journalism, Culture and Community, report available at https://meandeurope.com/wp-content/uploads/EU-Referendum-Analysis-2016-Jackson-Thorsen-and-Wring-v2.pdf (accessed June 2017).

Global Future (May 2017) "Building Globally Successful Societies: The case for immigration", website at: http://ourglobalfuture.com (accessed June 2017).

Gotev, Georgi (12 January 2017) "Kalfin: Brexit is an opportunity for the future EU budget", EURACTIV, website at http://www.euractiv.com/section/euro-finance/interview/kalfin-brexit-is-an-opportunity-for-the-future-eu-budget/ (accessed March 2017).

Governing The State and Localities (2017) "States With Most Government Employees: Totals and Per Capita Rates", website at http://www.governing.com/gov-data/public-workforce-salaries/states-most-government-workers-public-employees-by-job-type.html (accessed July 2017).

Gov.uk (11 September 2013) "National curriculum in England: citizenship programmes of study" website at https://www.gov.uk/government/publications/national-curriculum-in-england-citizenship-programmes-of-study (accessed November 2016).

Gov.uk "UK visa sponsorship for employers" Gov.uk website at https://www.gov.uk/uk-visa-sponsorship-employers/immigration-skills-charge (accessed June 2017).

Grabbe, Heather; Lehne, Stefan (8 September 2016) "How to build a more flexible EU after Brexit", Carnegie Europe, website at http://carnegieeurope.eu/2016/09/08/how-to-build-more-flexible-eu-after-brexit-pub-64507 (accessed February 2017).

Grant, Charles (2016), "The Brexit negotiations: the UK government will have incentives to compromise", Centre of European Reform, website at http://blogs.lse.ac.uk/brexit/2016/08/04/the-brexit-negotiations-the-uk-government-will-have-incentives-to-compromise/ (accessed October 2017).

Harris, Kathleen (9 November 2016) "'Brexit' and its Potential Effects on Economic Crime", Arnold & Porter Advisory, website at http://www.arnoldporter.com/en/perspectives/publications/2016/11/brexit-and-its-potential-effects-on-economic (accessed November 2016).

Harvey, Fiona (28 June 2016) "British fishermen warned Brexit will not mean greater catches", *The Guardian*, website at https://www.theguardian.com/environment/2016/jun/28/british-fishermen-warned-brexit-will-not-mean-greater-catches (accessed November 2016).

Hern, Alex (24 June 2016) "British tech firms eye relocation after Brexit vote", website at https://www.theguardian.com/technology/2016/jun/24/british-tech-firms-eye-relocation-after-brexit-vote (accessed August 2016).

Heyes, Jason (9 March 2016) "Why Brexit would be a disaster for your employment rights", *The Independent*, website at http://www.independent.co.uk/news/uk/eu-brexit-uk-referendum-leave-employment-rights-disaster-explained-a6921126.html (accessed November 2016).

Heywood, Debbie (June 2016) "Brexit – the potential impact on the UK's legal system", Taylor Wessing LLP, website at https://united-kingdom.taylorwessing.com/download/article-brexit-uk-legal-system.html (accessed November 2016).

Higher Education Statistics Agency (HESA) (12 January 2017) "Higher education student enrolments and qualifications obtained at higher education providers in the United Kingdom 2015/16", website at https://www.hesa.ac.uk/news/12-01-2017/sfr242-student-enrolments-and-qualifications (accessed October 2017).

HM Government (June 2017) "The United Kingdom's exit from the European Union: safeguarding the position of EU citizens living in the UK and UK nationals living in the EU", Cm9464.

HM Treasury (4 March 2015a) "Issue briefing: starting tax rate for savings interest", website at https://www.gov.uk/government/publications/issue-briefing-starting-tax-rate-for-savings-interest/issue-briefing-starting-tax-rate-for-savings-interest (accessed December 2016).

HM Treasury (December 2015) "European Union Finances 2015: Statement on the 2015 EU Budget and measures to counter fraud and financial mismanagement".

HM Treasury (2016b) "Tax and tax credit rates and thresholds for 2015-16" website at https://www.gov.uk/government/publications/tax-and-tax-credit-rates-and-thresholds-for-2015-16/tax-and-tax-credit-rates-and-thresholds-for-2015-16 (accessed December 2016).

HM Treasury (13 September 2016) "How public spending was calculated in your tax summary", website at https://www.gov.uk/government/publications/how-public-spending-was-calculated-in-your-tax-summary/how-public-spending-was-calculated-in-your-tax-summary (accessed August 2017).

HM Treasury (15 December 2016) "Guidance: Annual tax summary" website http://www.gov.uk/annual-tax-summary (accessed August 2017).

HM Treasury (October 2017) "Customs Bill: legislating for the UK's future customs, VAT and excise regimes", Cm 9502.

Hogan Lovells (19 July 2016) "Impact of Brexit on Debt Capital Markets – Capital Markets Union, Hogan Lovells (pdf), website at https://www.hoganlovells.com/en/

events/impact-of-brexit-on-debt-capital-markets-capital-markets-union   (accessed September 2016).

Hogan Lovells (2016) "Possible models for the UK/EU relationship", July 2016, website   http://www.hoganlovellsbrexit.com/_uploads/downloads/11075_CM_BREXIT-UKEU_INFO_E.pdf (accessed 09 September 2017).

Honnefelder, Stephanie (May 2016) "Competition Policy", website at http://www.europarl.europa.eu/atyourservice/en/displayFtu.html?ftuId=FTU_3.2.1.html (accessed September 2016).

House of Commons, Westminster Hall (5 September 2016), Video on parliament TV website at http://parliamentlive.tv/Event/Index/cb2f33f6-f9fe-463e-a6d5-40eca4b614c0# (accessed September 2016).

House of Lords (13 December 2016) "Brexit: the options for trade", European Union Committee, 5th Report of Session 2016-17, website at https://www.publications.parliament.uk/pa/ld201617/ldselect/ldeucom/72/72.pdf (accessed July 2017).

House of Lords (17 December 2016), "Brexit: fisheries", European Union Committee, 8th Report of Session 2016-17, Parliament website at https://www.publications.parliament.uk/pa/ld201617/ldselect/ldeucom/78/78.pdf (accessed August 2017).

House of Lords (4 March 2017) "Brexit and the EU budget", House of Lords, European Committee, 15th Report of Session 2016-17, March 4, 2017, website at https://www.publications.parliament.uk/pa/ld201617/ldselect/ldeucom/125/125.pdf   (accessed March 2017).

House of Lords website (16 March 2017) "House of Lords: Largest Votes Recorded"), website   http://researchbriefings.parliament.uk/ResearchBriefing/Summary/LIF-2017-0023 (accessed March 2017).

Hüffel, Clemens; Plasser, Fritz; Ecker, Dietmar (2015) "Österreich und die EU", 1x1 der Politik, (Holzhausen Verlag: Vienna).

Hüttl, Pia; Schoenmaker, Dirk (4 February 2016) "Should the 'out' join the European banking union?", publication by Bruegel, website at: http://bruegel.org/2016/02/should-the-outs-join-the-european-banking-union/ (accessed October 2016).

Imbert, Florence Bouyala (September 2016) "Trade regimes applicable to developing countries", Fact Sheets on the European Union, website at http://www.europarl.europa.eu/atyourservice/en/displayFtu.html?ftuId=FTU_6.2.3.html (accessed January 2017).

Inman, Phillip; Monaghan, Angela (21 June 2017) "UK budget deficit to increase this year amid living standards squeeze", *The Guardian*, website at https://www.theguardian.com/business/2017/jun/21/uk-budget-deficit-philip-hammond-ons-may (accessed August 2017).

Institute for European Environmental Policy (IEEP) (March 2016) "The potential policy and environmental consequences for the UK of a departure from the European Union", website https://ieep.eu/archive_uploads/2000/IEEP_Brexit_2016.pdf (accessed October 2017).

Institute for Fiscal Studies (April 2016) "The budget of the European Union: a guide", IFS Briefing Note BN181.

International Monetary Fund (IMF) (19 July 2016) "Global Economic Outlook Report", website at http://www.imf.org/en/News/Articles/2016/07/18/18/11/NA07192016-IMF-Cuts-Global-Growth-Forecasts-on-Brexit-Warns-of-Risks-to-Outlook (accessed July 2016).

International Monetary Fund (IMF) (2015) "World Economic Outlook", 2015.

International Monetary Fund (IMF) (July 2017) "World Economic Outlook Update", website at https://www.imf.org/en/Publications/WEO/Issues/2017/07/07/world-economic-outlook-update-july-2017 (accessed August 2017).

IPPR, Institute for Public Policy Research (29 March 2017) "Lack of EU migrant packers, food workers and cleaners could result in post-Brexit labour shortages", report, IPPR website at https://www.ippr.org/news-and-media/press-releases/lack-of-eu-migrant-packers-food-workers-and-cleaners-could-result-in-post-brexit-labour-shortages (accessed July 2017).

IPPR, Institute for Public Policy Research (28 April 2017) "Striking the right deal: UK–EU migration and the Brexit negotiations", IPPR website at https://www.ippr.org/research/publications/striking-the-right-deal#the-negotiations (accessed July 2017).

IPPR (July 2017) "Striking the right deal: UK–EU migration and the Brexit negotiations", website at https://www.ippr.org/research/topics/society-migration/ (accessed September 2017).

ITV Report (2 June 2016) "EU Referendum: How would a Brexit affect food?", ITV Report, website at http://www.itv.com/news/2016-06-02/eu-referendum-how-would-a-brexit-affect-food/ (accessed September 2016).

James, William (1 August 2016) "PM May resurrects industrial policy as Britain prepares for Brexit", Reuters Market News, website at http://www.reuters.com/article/britain-eu-industry-idUSL8N1AI537 (accessed November 2016).

Jefferson, Rodney (24 January 2017) "Scotland get closer to independence vote with Brexit ruling", Bloomberg Politics, website at https://www.bloomberg.com/politics/articles/2017-01-24/scotland-edges-closer-to-independence-vote-after-brexit-ruling (accessed November 2017).

Johnson, Boris (15 September 2017) "My vision for a bold, thriving Britain enabled by Brexit", *The Telegraph*, website at http://www.telegraph.co.uk/news/2017/09/15/boris-johnson-vision-bold-thriving-britain-enabled-brexit (accessed September 2017).

Johnston, Ian (27 May 2016) "Will Brexit help or damage the environment?", *The Independent*, website at http://www.independent.co.uk/environment/brexit-eu-referendum-what-will-happen-to-the-environment-damage-or-help-a7050911.html (accessed December 2016).

Johnston, Ian (27 June 2016) "Brexit loophole? MPs must still vote in order for Britain to leave the EU, say top lawyers", *The Independent*, website at http://www.independent.

co.uk/news/uk/politics/brexit-loophole-eu-referendum-mps-law-legal-legislation-constitution-a7105181.html (accessed May 2017).

Kelly, Matt (23 June 2017) "Brexit 2027: This is the UK 10 years on", The New European, website at http://www.theneweuropean.co.uk/top-stories/brexit-2027-this-is-the-uk-10-years-on-1-5075042 (accessed July 2017).

Ketteley, Joanna; Rudd, Michael (24 June 2016) "Brexit: Environmental law implications", Bird & Bird Brexit series, website at http://www.twobirds.com/en/news/articles/2016/uk/brexit-environmental-law-implications (accessed December 2016).

Khan, Sadiq, Mayor of London (22 September 2016) "Sadiq Khan to tell Pres of the European Parliament that London is Open", London Assembly website at https://www.london.gov.uk/press-releases/mayoral/sadiq-khan-to-meet-martin-schulz (accessed October 2016).

Kolassa, Doris (May 2016) "Fact sheet on the European Union – Free movement of capital", website at http://www.europarl.europa.eu/atyourservice/en/displayFtu.html?ftuId=FTU_3.1.6.html (accessed September 2016).

Kraatz, Susanne (October 2016) "Social and employment policy: general principles", Fact sheets on the European Union, website at http://www.europarl.europa.eu/atyourservice/en/displayFtu.html?ftuId=FTU_5.10.1.html (accessed November 2016).

Kudlow, Lawrence and Brian Domitrovic Time (2016) ""website at http://time.com/4511870/john-f-kennedy-and-ronald-reagan-tax-policy (accessed August 2017).

Kuper, Simon (26 January 2017) "Trump, Brexit and the age of broken promises", *Financial Times* (accessed May 2017).

Langfitt, Frank (8 November 2016) "Trump compares his campaign to Brexit. What do Britons think", Parallels – Many stories, one world.

Laubscher, Hendrik (3 May 2017) "The Impact of Brexit on UK Ecommerce", ecommerce platforms, website at https://ecommerce-platforms.com/articles/impact-brexit-uk-ecommerce (accessed November 2017).

Lawrence, Matthew (29 December 2016) "New IPPR report shows an accelerating wave of economic, social and technological change will reshape 2020s Britain", The Institute for Public Policy Research (IPPR), (accessed July 2017).

Lawyers for Britain (2017) "Brexit and the International Trade", Lawyers for Britain, website at http://www.lawyersforbritain.org/int-trade.shtml (accessed January 2017).

Lebrecht, Andy (2 November 2016) "Better deal for UK fishermen will be hard to catch", In Facts website at https://infacts.org/better-deal-uk-fishermen-will-hard-catch/ (accessed August 2017).

Leonard, Mark (24 June 2016) "Brexit: The foreign policy implications", European Council on Foreign Relations, website at http://www.ecfr.eu/article/commentary_brexit_the_foreign_policy_implications_7053 (accessed April 2017).

LGiU Local Government Facts and Figures, website at http://www.lgiu.org.uk/local-government-facts-and-figures/#how-many-councils-are-there (accessed September 2017).

Lock, Alex (24 June 2016) "What Brexit mean for UK employment law?", Lexology, website at http://www.lexology.com/library/detail.aspx?g=c8594589-147b-435e-81ee-13ed9c7c9fdb (accessed November 2016).

Lords Select Committee, UK Parliament website at https://www.parliament.uk/business/committees/committees-a-z/lords-select/eu-select-committee-/inquiries/parliament-2017/scrutiny-of-brexit-negotiations/brexit-negotiations/ (accessed July 2017).

Maciejewski, Mariusz; Hayer, Sarabjeet (September 2016a) "Consumer policy: principles and instruments", Fact Sheets on the European Union, website at http://www.europarl.europa.eu/atyourservice/en/displayFtu.html?ftuId=FTU_5.5.1.html (accessed December 2016).

Maciejewski, Mariusz; Hayer, Sarabjeet (September 2016b) "Consumer protection measures", Fact Sheets on the European Union, website at http://www.europarl.europa.eu/atyourservice/en/displayFtu.html?ftuId=FTU_5.5.2.html (accessed December 2016).

Maciejewski, Mariusz; Pengelly, Kendra (2016) "Fact sheets on the European Union - Freedom of establishment and freedom to provide services", website at http://www.europarl.europa.eu/atyourservice/en/displayFtu.html?ftuId=FTU_3.1.4.html (accessed August 2016).

MacLeod, Andrew; Roberts, Liz (13 June 2017) "We are going to face a massive employment crisis after Brexit", *The Independent*, website at http://www.independent.co.uk/voices/brexit-employment-eu-workers-small-businesses-recruitment-crisis-a7838711.html (accessed July 2017).

Magnus, Marcel (September 2016) "Banking Union", Fact Sheets on the European Union, website at http://www.europarl.europa.eu/atyourservice/en/displayFtu.html?ftuId=FTU_4.2.4.html (October 2016).

Marr, Andrew (6 November 2016), *Andrew Marr Show* on BBC, politics debate.

McKernan, Bethan (2016) "A journalist shared a story about Boris Johnson that completely undermines his authority on the EU", https://www.indy100.com/article/a-journalist-has-shared-a-story-about-boris-johnson-that-completely-undermines-his-authority-on-the-eu--bkoHJPBuVZ (accessed June 2017).

Marti Dominguez, Carmen-Paz (June 2016) "The Common fisheries Policy: origins and development", Fact Sheets on the European Union, website at http://www.europarl.europa.eu/atyourservice/en/displayFtu.html?ftuId=FTU_5.3.1.html (accessed November 2016).

Matthews, Rupert (2016) "Brexit & the EU's Common Fisheries Policy ", Better of out – No to the European Union, Yes to the Wilder World, website at http://www.betteroffout.net/wp-content/uploads/2016/01/A5-1-Designed-v1-booklet-Fisheries-Campaign_Layout-1.pdf (accessed October 2016).

May, Theresa (11 Juley 2016) "We can make Britain a country that works for everyone", Conservatives Press, website at http://press.conservatives.com/post/147947450370/we-can-make-britain-a-country-that-works-for (accessed November 2016).

McBride, James (17 January 2017) "The Debate Over Brexit", Council on Foreign Relations, website at http://www.cfr.org/united-kingdom/debate-over-brexit/p37747 (accessed January 2017).

McGough, Louise; Piazza, Gabriele (7 July 2016) "10 years of tax: London is an international city, and we want to remain at the heart of Europe", Centre for Cities.

McRae, Hamish (29 March 2017) "This is what the UK and the EU's relationship will look like in ten years' time", *The Independent*, website at http://www.independent.co.uk/voices/article-50-brexit-eu-what-happens-next-in-10-years-time-a7656671.html (accessed July 2017).

McTague, Tom (22 November 2016) "EU set for 'dirty Brexit'", Politico, website at http://www.politico.eu/article/eu-set-for-dirty-brexit-theresa-may-european-council/ (accessed March 2017).

Mellar, Balzas (May 2016) "Energy policy: general principles", Fact Sheets on the European Union, website at http://www.europarl.europa.eu/aboutparliament/en/displayF-tu.html?ftuId=FTU_5.7.1.html (accessed October 2016).

Merrick, Rob (11 January 2017) "UK employers would have to pay a £1,000-a-year fee per EU skilled worker after Brexit under new government plans", *The Independent*, website at http://www.independent.co.uk/news/uk/politics/brexit-latest-news-uk-employ-ers-pay-1000-per-eu-skilled-worker-european-immigration-skills-levy-a7521626.html (accessed March 2017).

Meyer, Christoph (June 2016) "Why facts did mater in the campaign", in: EU Referendum Analysis 2016: Media, Voters and the Campaign, published by The Centre for the Study of Journalism, Culture and Community, report available at https://mean-deurope.com/wp-content/uploads/EU-Referendum-Analysis-2016-Jackson-Thorsen-and-Wring-v2.pdf (accessed June 2017).

MHRA (27 June 2016) "Medicines and Healthcare products Regulatory Agency statement on the outcome of the EU referendum", website at https://www.gov.uk/govern-ment/news/medicines-and-healthcare-products-regulatory-agency-statement-on-the-outcome-of-the-eu-referendum (accessed January 2017).

Michail, Niamh (28 June 2016) "What are Britain's post-Brexit options and how will it impact industry?", Brexit Briefings: Interview, Food navigator, website at http://www.foodnavigator.com/Policy/What-are-Britain-s-post-Brexit-options-and-how-will-it-impact-industry (accessed September 2016).

Migration Watch UK (2016a) "Votes for Commonwealth Citizens", Immigration System & Policy: MW 315, website at https://www.migrationwatchuk.org/briefing-pa-per/11.29 (accessed August 2017).

Migration Watch UK (2016b) "The British in Europe – and Vice Versa", European Union: MW 354, website at http://www.migrationwatchuk.org/briefing-paper/354 (accessed September 2016).

Migration Watch UK (2016c) "Population by Country of Birth" website https://www.mi-grationwatchuk.org/statistics-population-country-birth (accessed September 2016).

Migration Watch, website at https://www.migrationwatchuk.org/statistics-net-migration-statistics (accessed June 2017).

Miller, Vaughne (26 April 2011) "The EU's Acquis Communautaire", SN/IA/5944, House of Commons Library, Section International Affairs and Defence Section.

Miller, Vaughne (26 August 2016) "Brexit: impact across policy areas", House of Commons, Briefing Paper Number 07213, website at: http://researchbriefings.files.parliament.uk/documents/CBP-7213/CBP-7213.pdf (accessed October 2016).

Minford, Patrick (15 March 2016) "Brexit will boost our economy and cut the cost of BMWs and even brie", The SUN, website at https://www.thesun.co.uk/archives/politics/1086319/brexit-will-boost-our-economy-and-cut-the-cost-of-bmws-and-even-brie/ (accessed August 2106).

Milt, Kristiina (September 2016) "Judicial cooperation in criminal matters", Fact Sheets on the European Union, website at http://www.europarl.europa.eu/atyourservice/en/displayFtu.html?ftuId=FTU_5.12.6.html (accessed November 2016).

Mody, Ashoka (10 October 2016) "Don't believe what you've read: the plummeting pound sterling is good news for Britain", *The Independent*, website at http://www.independent.co.uk/news/business/news/why-the-plummeting-pound-sterling-is-good-news-for-britain-a7353846.html (accessed October 2016).

Morel, Philippe; Teschner, Charles; Martin, Duncan; Rhode, Will; Bohn, Andreas (2016) "Global Capital Markets 2016: The Value Migration (Part 2) – Assessing the Impact of Brexit", White Paper, Boston Consulting Group Inc.

Moret, Erica (23 March 2016) "What would Brexit mean for EU sanctions policy?, European Council on Foreign Relations, Commentary, website at http://www.ecfr.eu/article/commentary_what_would_brexit_mean_for_eu_sanctions_policy6046 (accessed February 2017).

Morris, Jenny (25 September 2016) "What might a Brexit mean for food control?", TiF-SiP The institute of Food Safety Integrity & Protection, website at https://www.city.ac.uk/__data/assets/pdf_file/0007/301588/6-Jenny-Morris-Implications-of-Brexit.pdf (accessed September 2016).

Morrison, Natalie (14 September 2016) "Ireland calls for "fully Brexit-proofed" budget with thousands of food jobs at stake", Trends Brexit, Food Navigator, website at http://www.foodnavigator.com/Trends/Brexit/Ireland-calls-for-fully-Brexit-proofed-budget-with-thousands-of-food-jobs-at-stake (accessed September 2016).

Moshinsky, Ben (19 July 2016) "Leaving London: Confidential Brexit briefing shows where Deutsche Bank thinks other banks will go", Business Insider, website at http://www.businessinsider.de/confidential-deutsche-bank-briefing-where-banks-post-brexit-2016-7?r=UK&IR=T (accessed on September 2016).

Moussis, Nicholas (2011) "Access to European Union: law, economics, policies", 19th updated edition, Rixensart.

Murkens, Jo; Trotter, Sarah (25 February held on 25th February 2016, LSE European Institute, website at http://www.lse.ac.uk/europeanInstitute/LSE-Commission/Hearing-6---The-implications-of-Brexit-for-fundamental-rights-protection-in-the-UK.pdf (accessed December 2016).

Mulholland, Hélène (22 June 2019) "Tories unveil group of controversial new allies in European parliament", *The Guardian*, website at http://www.theguardian.com/politics/2009/jun/22/conservatives-new-eu-group July 2016).

NCA (23 June 2015) "National Strategic Assessment of Serious and Organised Crime 2015", National Crime Agency (UK), website at http://www.nationalcrimeagency.gov.uk/publications/560-national-strategic-assessment-of-serious-and-organised-crime-2015/file (accessed December 2016).

NCA (9 September 2016) "National Strategic Assessment of Serious and organised Crime 2016", National Crime Agency (UK), website at http://www.nationalcrimeagency.gov.uk/publications/731-national-strategic-assessment-of-serious-and-organised-crime-2016/file (accessed December 2016).

New Financial - Rethink capital markets (April 2016) "The potential impact of Brexit on European Capital Markets: A qualitative survey on market participation".

NHS Confederation (29 June 2016) "The UK voted to leave the EU: what now for the NHS?, Elisabetta Zanon, website at http://www.nhsconfed.org/blog/2016/06/brexit-what-now-for-the-nhs (accessed January 2017).

Noonan, Laura (15 July 2016) "European banks face €30bn-€40bn capital bill after Brexit", *Financial Times*, website at https://www.ft.com/content/61ef4104-49c9-11e6-8d68-72e9211e86ab (accessed on September 2016).

Norton Rose Fulbright (June 2016) "Impact of Brexit on the energy sector", publication, website at http://www.nortonrosefulbright.com/knowledge/publications/136979/impact-of-brexit-on-the-energy-sector (accessed October 2016).

Novak, Petr (December 2016) "Intergovernmental decision-making procedures", Fact Sheets on the European Union, website at http://www.europarl.europa.eu/atyourservice/en/displayFtu.html?ftuId=FTU_1.4.2.html (accessed April 2017).

O'Carroll, Lisa (12 April 2017) "Catastrophe looms at ports after Brexit, shipping industry warns", *The Guardian*, website at https://www.theguardian.com/politics/2017/apr/12/catastrophe-looms-at-ports-after-brexit-shipping-industry-warns (accessed May 2017).

OCCRP (8 July 2016) "Analysis: Brexit, UK upheaval threatens anti-corruption efforts", Organized Crime and Corruption Reporting Project, website at https://www.occrp.org/en/daily/5452-analysis-brexit-uk-upheaval-threatens-anti-corruption-efforts (accessed March 2016).

OECD, EU (2016) "Health at a Glance: Europe 2016 – State of Health in the EU Cycle", OECD Publishing, Paris, website at http://dx.doi.org/10.1787/9789264265592-en (accessed December 2016).

Office of National Statistics (2015) "Annual Survey of Hours and Earnings: 2015 Provisional Results", interactive website at http://www.neighbourhood.statistics.gov.uk/HTMLDocs/dvc126/index.html (accessed September 2016).

Office of National Statistics, Pink Book 2015 (2015), "Table 9.9: UK official transactions with institutions of the EU", excel spreadsheet, website at http://www.ons.gov.uk/file?uri=/economy/nationalaccounts/balanceofpayments/compendium/unitedkingdombalanceofpaymentsthepinkbook/2015-10-30/unitedkingdombalanceofpaymentsthepinkbook/pinkbook2015chapter9_tcm77-422053.xls (accessed December 2016).

Office for National Statistics (July 2016) "UK trade: July 2016", website at https://www.ons.gov.uk/economy/nationalaccounts/balanceofpayments/bulletins/uktrade/july2016#main-figures-for-july-2016 (accessed August 2017).

Office for National Statistics (July 2017) "UK Labour Market: September 2016", ONS UK Labour Market website at https://www.ons.gov.uk/employmentandlabourmarket/peopleinwork/employmentandemployeetypes/bulletins/uklabourmarket/July2017 (accessed in August 2017).

Ohliger, Tina (2016) "Environment policy: general principles and basic framework", Fact Sheets on the European Union, website at http://www.europarl.europa.eu/atyourservice/en/displayFtu.html?ftuId=FTU_5.4.1.html (accessed December 2016).

Oliver, Tim (2016) "Brexit: What happens next?, LSE IDEAS Strategic Update 16.2, website at http://www.lse.ac.uk/IDEAS/publications/reports/pdf/LSE-IDEAS-Brexit-What-Next.pdf (accessed August 2016).

Olusoga, David (19 March 2017) "Empire 2.0 is dangerous nostalgia for something that never existed", *The Guardian*, website at https://www.theguardian.com/commentisfree/2017/mar/19/empire-20-is-dangerous-nostalgia-for-something-that-never-existed (accessed June2017).

Oxera (June 2016) "Brexit: implications for competition enforcement in the UK", Oxera Consulting LLP, website at http://www.oxera.com/Latest-Thinking/Agenda/2016/Brexit-implications-for-competition-enforcement-in.aspx (accessed September 2016).

Oxera and O&O (May 2016) "The impact of crossborder access to audiovisual content on EU consumers", website at http://baseorg.uk/policy/ (accessed November 2017).

Parliament UK (15 September 2016) "What are the human rights implications of Brexit", Joint Select Committee, website at https://www.parliament.uk/business/committees/committees-a-z/joint-select/human-rights-committee/news-parliament-2015/brexit-human-rights-launch-16-17/ (accessed November 2016).

Patel. Oliver; Reh, Christian (2016) "Brexit: The Consequences for the EU's Political System", UCL Constitution Unit Briefing Paper, website at https://www.ucl.ac.uk/constitution-unit/research/europe/briefing-papers/Briefing-paper-2 (accessed April 2017).

Paternoster, Dario (May 2016) "General tax policy", Fact Sheets on the European Union, website at http://www.europarl.europa.eu/atyourservice/en/displayFtu.html?ftuId=FTU_5.11.1.html (accessed October 2016).

Pathak, Neelesh (24 June 2016) "Impact of Brexit on Payment Systems in EU & UK", website at https://www.linkedin.com/pulse/impact-brexit-payment-systems-eu-uk-neelesh-pathak (accessed September 2016).

Paton, Graeme (07 Feb 2013) "European Union slashed from the National Curriculum", *The Telegraph*, website at http://www.telegraph.co.uk/education/educationnews/9856220/European-Union-slashed-from-the-National-Curriculum.html (accessed November 2016).

Peers, Steve (12 June 2016) "EU Referendum Briefing 2: How could Brexit affect young people?", website at http://eulawanalysis.blogspot.co.at/2016/06/eu-referendum-briefing-2-how-could.html (accessed August 2016).

Peterson Institute for International Economics (19 Juley 2017) "Posen discusses the damage of Brexit to the British economy", video at https://piie.com/newsroom/short-videos/posen-discusses-damage-brexit-british-economy (accessed at September 2017).

Petropoulos, Georgios (6 July 2016) "Brexit and competition policy in Europe", Blog post by Bruegel, website at http://bruegel.org/2016/07/brexit-and-competition-policy-in-europe/ (accessed September 2016).

Philippe, Denis (15 July 2016) "The judicial impact of the Brexit", Publicaties-News, website at http://www.philippelaw.eu/Front/c3-760/Actualites.aspx?News=438 (accessed November 2016).

Press Association (2016) "How MPs intend to vote", SnapAP website at http://snappa.press.net/#!/assets/8fdf9aa2-2072-3deb-a5b5-1746633e319e?feedId=mps (accessed July 2017).

Preston, Peter (26 June 2016) "The people have spoken on Brexit. But did the media tell them the truth?", *The Guardian*, website at https://www.theguardian.com/media/2016/jun/26/people-spoken-brexit-did-media-tell-the-truth-eu-referendum (accessed July 2017).

Price Waterhouse Coopers (PwC July) "UK Economic Outlook – Prospects for the UK economy and housing market after Brexit", July 2017 (pdf), website at https://www.pwc.co.uk/services/economics-policy/insights/uk-economic-outlook.html (accessed August 2017).

Prochaska, Elizabeth (22 June 2016) "A vote to leave is a vote to needlessly destroy our legal system", *The Guardian*, website at https://www.theguardian.com/commentisfree/2016/jun/22/vote-leave-destroy-legal-system-take-back-control-brexit (accessed December 2016).

QBE European Operations (April 2016) "What Brexit means for business", QBE, website at http://www.qbeeurope.com/documents/research/What%20Brexit%20means%20for%20business.pdf (accessed August 2016).

Raczova, Orsolya (20 February 2017) "The impact of Brexit on British security and defence", Global Risk Insights, website at http://globalriskinsights.com/2017/02/impact-brexit-british-security-defence/ (accessed February 2017).

Ramet, Valerie (September 2016) "A general survey of development policy", Fact Sheets on the European Union, website at http://www.europarl.europa.eu/atyourservice/en/displayFtu.html?ftuId=FTU_6.3.1.html (accessed January 2017).

Rankin, Jennifer (22 June 2016) "Europol chief says Brexit would harm UK crime-fighting", *The Guardian*, website at https://www.theguardian.com/politics/2016/jun/22/europol-chief-says-brexit-would-harm-uk-crime-fighting (accessed December 2016).

Rawlinson, Kevin (27 March 2017) "Immigration levels will sometimes rise after Brexit, says David Davis" *The Guardian*, website at https://www.theguardian.com/politics/2017/mar/27/immigration-levels-will-sometimes-rise-after-brexit-says-david-davis (accessed Match 2017).

Reinke, Guido (2012) "Industry Governance and Regulatory Compliance: A Theoretical and Practical Guide to European ICT Policy" (GOLD RUSH Publishing, London).

Reinke, Guido (July 2015) "The Regulatory Compliance Matrix: Regulation of Financial services, Information and Communications Technology, and Generally Related Matters" (GOLD RUSH Publishing, London).

Rhodes, Chris (14 October 2016) "Industrial Strategy", House of Commons Library, Briefing Paper Number 07682, website at http://researchbriefings.parliament.uk/ResearchBriefing/Summary/CBP-7682 (accessed November 2016).

Roberts, Dan (2 July 2017) "New customs union with EU after Brexit is still option, analysts say", *The Guardian*, website at https://www.theguardian.com/politics/2017/jul/02/new-customs-union-with-eu-after-brexit-is-still-an-option-analysts-say (accessed July 2017).

Ruparel, Raoul (28 July 2016) "Open Europe, Post Brexit, leaving the customs union is a no-brainer", website at http://openeurope.org.uk/today/blog/post-brexit-leaving-customs-union-no-brainer/ (accessed October 2016).

Russel Group (29 March 2017) "Article 50 – open letter", website at http://russellgroup.ac.uk/news/article-50-open-letter/ (accessed October 2017).

Sánchez-Barrueco, María-Luisa (3 February 2017a) "Sketching the budgetary implications of Brexit", The UK in a changing Europe, 3 February 2017, website at http://ukandeu.ac.uk/sketching-the-budgetary-implications-of-brexit/ (accessed October 2017).

Sánchez-Barrueco, María-Luisa (2 February 2017b) "The Brexit budgetary debates II: the budgetary consequences of no agreement", EUFINACCO: Financial Accountability in the EU, website at https://eufinacco.wordpress.com/2017/02/02/the-brexit-budgetary-debates-ii-the-budgetary-consequences-of-no-agreement/ (accessed October 2017).

Scherer, Peter; Söhnchen, Markus (December 2016) "Auswirkungen des Brexit auf M&A-Verträge", M&A Review.

Schoenmaker, Dirk (September 2016) "Written evidence for The House of Lords EU Sub-Committee on Financial Affairs chaired by Baroness Falkner of Margravine on the future of Financial Services in the UK following the vote to leave the European Union" (Bruegel: Brussels).

Schoenmaker, Dirk (30 June 2016) "Lost passports: a guide to the Brexit fallout for the City of London", Blogpost (Bruegel: Brussels).

Schonard, Martina (December 2016) "Supranational decision-making procedures", Fact Sheets on the European Union, website at http://www.europarl.europa.eu/atyourservice/en/displayFtu.html?ftuId=FTU_1.4.1.html (accessed April 2017).

Shearman & Sterling (21 March 2016) "Brexit: Options for and Impact of the Possible Alternatives to EU Membership", Client Publication.

Shearman & Sterlin (5 August 2016) "Brexit: Free Movement of Persons", Client Publication Financial Institutions Advisory & Financial Regulatory, website at http://www.shearman.com/~/media/Files/NewsInsights/Publications/2016/08/Brexit-Free-Movement-of-Persons-FIAFR-080516.pdf (accessed September 2016).

Simpson, Fiona (29 December 2016) "Britain faces '10-year economic shock' after Brexit vote", Evening Standard, website at http://www.standard.co.uk/news/politics/britain-faces-10year-economic-shock-after-brexit-vote-a3429246.html (accessed July 2017).

Sjolin, Sara; Mozee, Carla (24 June 2017) "A year after Brexit vote, the pound has suffered, but U.K. employment healthy-in charts", MarketWatch, website at http://www.marketwatch.com/story/brexits-impact-on-markets-and-the-uk-one-year-after-the-vote-in-charts-2017-06-23 (accessed July 2017).

Sky Data tweet (25 June 2016) "% who got through our final #EUref poll turnout filter by age group" at https://twitter.com/SkyData/status/746700869656256512 (accessed August 2017).

Smit, Harry (March 2017) "Weighing up Future Food Security in the UK: The Impact of the Brexit on Food and Agribusiness in Europe and Beyond", Rabobank.

Solana, Javier; Blockmans; Steven (6 December 2016) "EU defence plan is 'no game-changer'", euobserver, website at https://euobserver.com/opinion/136315 (accessed February 2017).

Sosa-Iudicissa, Marcelo; Tejedor del Real, Purificacion (October 2016) "Public health", Fact Sheets on the European Union, website at http://www.europarl.europa.eu/atyourservice/en/displayFtu.html?ftuId=FTU_5.5.3.html (accessed December 2016).

Staniforth, Jesse (4 August 2016) "Brexit's Impact on Food Industry", Food Quality & Safety, website at http://www.foodqualityandsafety.com/article/brexits-impact-food-industry/?singlepage=1 (accessed September 2016).

Stone, Jon (8 December 2017) "Brexit: Theresa May agrees to pay £39bn divorce bill to the EU", The Independent, website at http://www.independent.co.uk/news/uk/politics/brexit-divorce-bill-financial-settlement-39-billion-theresa-may-juncker-agreement-northern-ireland-a8099076.html (accessed December 2017).

Sweney, Mark (21 October 2015) "UK media plurality threatened by dominant group of large firms", *The Guardian*.

Sweney, Mark (19 June 2012) "Ofcom backs regular plurality reviews for powerful media firms", *The Guardian*.

Swinford, Steven (27 August 2016) "Theresa May will trigger Brexit negotiations without Commons vote", *The Telegraph*, website at http://www.telegraph.co.uk/news/2016/08/26/theresa-may-will-trigger-brexit-negotiations-without-commons-vot/ (accessed June 2017).

Syal, Rajeev (13 July 2017) "Brexit plans could fall apart 'like a chocolate orange', says auditor general", *The Guardian*, website at https://www.theguardian.com/politics/2017/jul/13/brexit-plans-fall-apart-chocolate-orange-auditor-general (accessed July 2017).

Taylor, Cliff (16 October 2016) "The harder the Brexit, the worse it is for Ireland", The Irish Times, website at http://www.irishtimes.com/business/economy/the-harder-the-brexit-the-worse-it-is-for-ireland-1.2829838 (accessed January 2017).

Taylor Wessing (11 July 2016) "UK consumer law in the wake of the EU Referendum", Legal Insights, website at https://united-kingdom.taylorwessing.com/en/insights/uk-consumer-law-in-the-wake-of-the-eu-referendum (accessed January 2017).

Terlow, Gemma (3 September 2017) "Low skills and poor infrastructure blamed for UK productivity gap", *Financial Times*.

TEU (Consolidated Version of the Treaty on the functioning of the European Union) (26 October 2012), Official Journal of the European Union C 326/49.

The Chartered Institute of Building (CIOB) (2015)"CIOB Perspectives: An Analysis on Migration in the Construction Sector".

The EU Framework Programme for Research and Innovation, website at http://ec.europa.eu/programmes/horizon2020/en/what-horizon-2020 (accessed October 2017).

The Guardian, 9 April 1975, "Case for staying in – by Mrs Thatcher", p8.

The Guardian (27 November 2015) "Britons among least knowledgeable about European Union", Website at https://www.theguardian.com/news/datablog/2015/nov/27/brits-least-knowledgeable-european-union-basic-questions (accessed June 2017).

(27June 2016) "The leave campaign made three key promises – are they keeping them?", Guardian website at https://www.theguardian.com/politics/2016/jun/27/eu-referendum-reality-check-leave-campaign-promises (accessed July 2016).

The Guardian (11 November 2016) "Hard Brexit will cost Treasury up to GBP66bn a year, ministers are told", Press Association, leakage papers, website at https://www.theguardian.com/politics/2016/oct/11/hard-brexit-treasury-66bn-eu-single-market (accessed October 2016).

The Guardian (17 January 2017) "Key points from May's Brexit speech: what have we learned?", website at https://www.theguardian.com/politics/2017/jan/17/key-points-from-mays-what-have-we-learned (accessed June 2017).

The Guardian (27 February 2017) "The Guardian view on the Trump-May meeting: they are playing with fire", Theresa May Opinion, website at https://www.theguardian.com/commentisfree/2017/jan/27/the-guardian-view-on-the-trump-may-meeting-they-are-playing-with-fire (accessed February 2017).

The Irish Times (21 September 2016) "UK deficit leaves Hammond few options for Brexit budget boost", The Irish Times, website at http://www.irishtimes.com/business/economy/uk-deficit-leaves-hammond-few-options-for-brexit-budget-boost-1.2799464 (accessed March 2017).

The Independent (3 July 2017) "Brexit: Remain would win if new EU referendum vote were held tomorrow, poll finds", website at http://www.independent.co.uk/news/uk/politics/brexit-latest-remain-win-new-eu-exit-vote-survation-poll-a7820286.html (August 2017).

The Royal Society Science Policy Centre (December 2015) "UK research and the European Union – The role of the EU in funding UK research", website at https://royalsociety.org/~/media/policy/projects/eu-uk-funding/uk-membership-of-eu.pdf (accessed November 2016).

The Telegraph (28 April 2016) "700,000 expats will not be able to vote in EU referendum", website at http://www.telegraph.co.uk/news/2016/04/28/david-cameron-and-former-union-boss-warn-brexit-would-be-a-disas/ (accessed October 2016).

The Telegraph (9 November 2017) "I am determined to give our country the best possible Brexit", interview with Theresa May.

The UK in a Changing Britain (18 November 2015) "Votes at 16: What effect would it have?", website http://ukandeu.ac.uk/votes-at-16-what-effect-would-it-have (accessed September 2016).

Toor, Amar (24 June 2016) "UK scientists face an uncertain future after Brexit", The Verge, website at http://www.theverge.com/2016/6/24/12023230/brexit-impact-science-research-uk-eu-funding-collaboration (accessed November 2016).

Trade Union Congress (25 February 2016) "UK employment rights and the EU – Assessment of the impact of membership of the European Union on employment rights in the UK", website at https://www.tuc.org.uk/international-issues/europe/employment-and-social-policy/eu-referendum/tuc-report-outlines-workers%E2%80%99 (accessed February 2016).

Troszczyńska-van Genderen, Wanda; Legrand, Jérôme (December 2016) "Foreign policy: aims, instruments and achievements", Fact Sheets on the European Union, website at http://www.europarl.europa.eu/atyourservice/en/displayFtu.html?ftuId=FTU_6.1.1.html (accessed February 2017).

UK Co-coordinating Body, CAP Payments Search, website at http://cap-payments.defra. gov.uk/ (accessed August 2017).

UK Government (26 June 2017) "Agreement between the Conservatives and Unionist Party and the Democratic Unionist Party to support for the government in parliament".

UN (2015) "UN report Trends in International Migrant Stock", Population Division – International Migration, website at http://www.un.org/en/development/desa/population/ migration/data/index.shtml (accessed July 2017).

Union of International Associations (UIA) (8 July 2017) "EU Customs Union", Open Yearbook, website at https://www.uia.org/s/or/en/1100045669 (accessed July 2017).

United Nations, Department of Economic and Social affairs, Population Division (2015), website at http://www.un.org/en/development/desa/population/migration/data/estimates2/estimates15.shtml (accessed May 2017).

UK Parliament Petitions (5 September 2016) "EU Referendum Rules triggering a 2nd EU Referendum" https://petition.parliament.uk/petitions/131215 (accessed September 2016).

UK Parliament (2016) "Parliamentary scrutiny on Brexit - Summary of conclusions and recommendations", UK Parliament website at https://www.publications.parliament. uk/pa/ld201617/ldselect/ldeucom/50/5013.htm (accessed October 2016).

Verbeken, Dirk (November 2016) "Economic and Monetary Union", Fact Sheets on the European Union, website at http://www.europarl.europa.eu/atyourservice/en/displayFtu.html?ftuId=theme4.html (accessed November 2016).

Viilup, Elina (September 2016) "The European Union and its trade partners", Facts on the European Union, website at http://www.europarl.europa.eu/atyourservice/en/displayFtu.html?ftuId=FTU_6.2.1.html (accessed January 2017).

Ward, Benjamin (11 July 2016a) "What Brexit Means for Human Rights", published in: politics.co.uk, website at https://www.hrw.org/news/2016/07/11/what-brexit-means-human-rights (accessed November 2016).

Ward, Benjamin (5 September 2016b) "Britain's Brexit Hate Crime Problem", Human Rights Watch, website at https://www.hrw.org/news/2016/09/05/britains-brexit-hate-crime-problem (accessed November 2016).

Watts, Joe; Fenton, Siobhan (24 January 2017) "Brexit ruling: Supreme Court judges defy Government and empower Parliament", *The Independent*, website at http://www.independent.co.uk/news/uk/politics/brexit-supreme-court-ruling-judges-defy-theresa-may-and-hand-power-to-parliament-a7542406.html (accessed July 2017).

Weilandt, Ragnar (4 August 2016) "Brexit's trifling impact on EU external affairs", Europe's World, website at http://europesworld.org/2016/08/04/brexits-trifling-impact-eu-external-affairs/ (accessed January 2017).

Welfare, Richard; Klinger, Thorsten (2016) "Brexit - What could it mean for the Retail and Consumer Goods Industry?", Hogan Lovells, website at http://www.lexology.

com/library/detail.aspx?g=64111dfc-6aa4-450b-8c04-4ea1e8f34d96 (accessed August 2016).

Wellings, Ben (24 June 2016) "First, the Brexit: Now the United Kingdom is falling apart", The Globe and Mail, 24 June 2016, website at https://beta.theglobeandmail.com/opinion/after-the-brexit-will-the-united-kingdom-fall-apart/article30605937/?ref=http://www.theglobeandmail.com& (accessed July 2017).

What UK Thinks (July 2017) "EU Referendum Poll of Polls" (results from 168 polls), What UK thinks website http://whatukthinks.org/eu/opinion-polls/poll-of-polls/ and http://whatukthinks.org/eu/questions/should-the-united-kingdom-remain-a-member-of-the-eu-or-leave-the-eu/ (accessed at July 2017).

Whish, Richard (2016) "Brexit and EU Competition Policy" in Oxford Journals Law & Social Sciences Jnl of Euro Competition Law & Practice, Volume 7, Issue 5, Pp. 297-298.

Wikipedia "Referendums related to European Union", website at https://en.wikipedia.org/wiki/Referendums_related_to_the_European_Union (accessed June 2017).

William Hill website at http://sports.williamhill.com/bet/en-gb/betting/e/9537370/Next%2bCountry%2bTo%2bLeave%2bEU%2b%2528without%2bUnited%2bKingdom%2529.html (October 2017).

Wintour, Patrick (4 September 2016) "Japan's Message to the United Kingdom and the European Union", The Guardian, website at http://www.theguardian.com/politics/2016/sep/04/britain-japanese-brexit-letter-eu (accessed October 2016).

Woods, Ben (11 January 2017) "Brexit: warning of 232,000 finance sector job losses", The Scotsman, website at http://www.scotsman.com/business/companies/financial/brexit-warning-of-232-000-finance-sector-job-losses-1-4336009 (accessed June 2017).

Wyman, Oliver (October 2017) "The Impact of the UK's exit from the EU on the UK-based financial services sector".

YouGov UK (29 March 2017), "Attitudes to Brexit: Everything we know so far", website at https://yougov.co.uk/news/2017/03/29/attitudes-brexit-everything-we-know-so-far/ (accessed April 2017).

Your Europe (August 2017) Tendering rules and procedures website at http://europa.eu/youreurope/business/public-tenders/rules-procedures/index_en.htm (accessed August 2017).

Your Europe Public (September 2017) contracts website at http://europa.eu/youreurope/business/public-tenders/rules-procedures/index_en.htm#Thresholds-EU-rules (accessed September 2017).

Your Europe – Tendering (2017) "Tendering rules and procedures" website at http://europa.eu/youreurope/business/public-tenders/rules-procedures/index_en.htm (accessed September 2017).

Zeffman, Henry (14 October 2017) "Splendid isolation or lunacy? What hard Brexit means", The Times.

27623607R00208

Printed in Great Britain
by Amazon